The Great Armies of Antiquity

The Great Armies of Antiquity

Richard A. Gabriel

PRAEGER

Westport, Connecticut
London

Library of Congress Cataloging-in-Publication Data

Gabriel, Richard A.
    The great armies of antiquity / Richard A. Gabriel.
      p. cm.
    Includes bibliographical references and index.
    ISBN 0–275–97809–5 (alk. paper)
    1. Armies—History—To 1500. 2. Military art and science—History—To
    500. 3. Military history, Ancient. I. Title.
    U29.G2333   2002
    355'.0093—dc21   2002025301

British Library Cataloguing in Publication Data is available.

Library of Congress Catalog Card Number: 2002025301
ISBN: 0–275–97809–5

First published in 2002

Praeger Publishers, 88 Post Road West, Westport, CT 06881
An imprint of Greenwood Publishing Group, Inc.
www.praeger.com

Printed in the United States of America

The paper used in this book complies with the
Permanent Paper Standard issued by the National
Information Standards Organization (Z39.48–1984).

10 9 8 7 6 5 4 3 2 1

To Uncle John and Aunt Eileen
with love and respect

and for

James and Rosemarie
in gratitude for Suzi

Contents

Illustrations

FIGURES

TABLES

MAPS

Foreword

W hy did the author write this book? What does it offer the
reader? What can one learn from it? These are legitimate questions to ask of any book. In the case of *The Great Armies of
Antiquity*, by Richard A. Gabriel, the subject matter raises additional
questions. What does one obtain from a study of ancient armies? Has
not the world changed so radically since the time of the ancient Assyrians, Greeks, or Romans that their experiences have been overcome by
events? Has not the enormous change in technology negated the utility
of studying military organizations armed with spears and bows? The
implication of this line of reasoning is that ancient history is not an
appropriate subject for serious scholarship except, perhaps, in the limited
world of archeologists and classicists. History in general and military
history in particular labors under the constant burden of perceived irrel-
evance. Historians often bemoan the fact that the common man does not
take his craft seriously, demanding instead demonstrable modern utility.
Better to face the issue head-on than to ignore it. What, then, makes the
study of ancient armies important, and how is it useful in the modern
world?

One might begin by citing Santayana's aphorism about those who do
not learn from history being doomed to repeat it. Or, one might offer
Richard Neustadt's and Ernest May's not quite so familiar but more
compelling thesis from *Thinking in Time* that everything has a history

and knowing that history makes understanding and solving any problem easier. Beginning one's study with the ancients, therefore, provides a deeper understanding of the modern historical context. However, both these responses are inadequate since in most cases one does not have to retreat to the ancient world to discover the roots of modern problems. There is nonetheless a simple and compelling reason for the seeker of modern relevancy to explore ancient history: All history consists of elements of change and continuity—some things are the way they were previously and some things are different. Modern society is no exception and reflects the past—even the ancient past—even as it simultaneously appears new and different. Emphasizing the elements of continuity in human history gives ancient history human relevance and meaning. If one believes that human behavior, especially group behavior, follows predictable patterns that change slowly over time in response to environmental or cultural stimuli, it makes sense to begin any study with the simplest society available. For example, if one is interested in the role of political, social, religious, cultural, or technological innovation or institutions in societal development, it is often useful to begin one's investigations in a period where those phenomena might be observable without the complicating factors introduced by a more complex and integrated world. The frequent scarcity of ancient sources sometimes hampers such investigations, but competent scholars can usually reach reliable conclusions with the material at hand. The comparatively simple nature of the society or institution being examined often makes up for the difficulty. So it is that the fact that much of human behavior has not changed since ancient times makes the study of ancient history important.

This same logic applies to the question of why one studies ancient wars and armies. The most basic features of war have changed little since the time of Sargon the Great or Ramses II. Technological progress, of course, has produced changes in the manner in which war is waged, but the basic nature of warfare has remained remarkably constant. Tanks may have replaced chariots and laser-guided bombs replaced catapults on the battlefield, but the ultimate questions of victory and defeat are still decided not by technology but by the participant who first recognizes that he has been beaten. In this respect the simplicity of ancient technology and the institutions employing it is a bonus to the scholar. It is much easier to analyze warfare when opponents can see one another, maneuver in the single dimension of ground combat, and fight it out face-to-face than it is to analyze a conflict like the one recently conducted in Kosovo where aircraft at high altitude dropped bombs with pinpoint accuracy on unseen targets that were powerless to respond. Nevertheless, these two types of war are very much alike in their basic nature. It has become fashionable to criticize Clausewitz for developing a philosophy of war based on the post-Westphalian nation-state, particularly as it appeared in Europe during the Napoleonic era. Critics often conclude that Clausewitz's work is inapplicable both to the pre-Treaty of Westphalia period and to the modern world where the nation-state is challenged by other socio-political institutions for supremacy in the area of political decision making. The argument is unconvincing. Clausewitz's basic concepts of war—violence, friction, fog, political context, and so on—remain as useful today and in the ancient world as they were in Clausewitz's time. Although war is characterized by violence, chance, and uncertainty, it remains one of the most important means available to political leaders to address the problems of state and national interests. So, too, in the ancient world. The problems of national defense policy and strategy confronting the pharaohs are not significantly different from those facing modern nation-states, and their solutions equally reflect the goals and interests of the state, the actual or perceived threat to those goals or interests, and the resources available to counter those threats to achieve its interests. In short, exactly the challenge confronting modern leaders.

If one accepts the study of ancient warfare as a useful endeavor, then why examine all the organizational details inevitably involved in the study of ancient armies? Why not concentrate on the battles themselves or, perhaps, the leaders? These would seem to provide the most immediately applicable lessons of strategy, tactics, and effective leadership. From the author's perspective, of course, one should indeed examine these two subjects first, and Gabriel's two previous volumes, *The Great Battles of Antiquity*, and his more recent, *The Great Captains of Antiquity*, certainly provide the opportunity to do so. There are legitimate reasons, however, to examine ancient military institutions in their own right. First, it never fails to amaze a careful student how "modern" the ancient military systems were in many respects. Organizations exist to solve problems and to coordinate activities, and it should surprise no one that ancient soldiers often faced some of the same problems that confront modern soldiers, and that both developed organizations to address them. To go to war one needs to recruit, train, and equip soldiers and leaders; to organize them into efficient and manageable units; to determine where, when, and how they should be employed; to move them to the selected place of employment; to sustain them once deployed; to employ them to the utmost advantage; to re-deploy them if necessary for refitting or reconstitution. The list implies the additional organizational functions (not strictly necessary for war fighting) of keeping records and conducting other administrative activities. All societies in all ages have faced these problems. Their solutions may be unique and reflect influences peculiar to their times, but both the process and organizational product always offer something to the modern analyst.

For example, skeptics often point to changed technology as a primary reason to ignore ancient warfare and armies. The root issue is how organizations adapt to changes in technology. What causes armies to adopt new technology, especially radically different technology? Closely related is the question of what new weapons or technologies do armies adopt and what do they ignore? The decision to adopt new technology is just the first of the important decisions that arise. How is the new technology integrated with existing technology (now called legacy systems)? How is the new technology used? Does the basic doctrine and, perhaps, even culture of an army change as it adopts new technology? Is there a process to manage all this or is it done by trial and error? Of course, no society will face the problem of integrating the chariot into its military system, although the sight of U.S. special forces soldiers in Afghanistan armed with laser target designators riding into battle on horseback suggests the need for caution in such predictions. Integrating new technology into military organizations still requires the same kind of thinking and problem solving that the ancients had to use. They, too, had to develop or copy the technology, and the warfighting doctrine to support it, construct the organization to fight it, and evolve the tactics for its efficient employment in war. The solutions to each of those problems influenced other aspects of the military equation that often facilitated and/or limited the employment of the new military instrument. A brief examination of a high-tech weapons system of the ancient world, the chariot, illustrates the point.

Why adopt the new technology of the chariot? In the case of the ancient Egyptians, the answer was that the Hyksos had chariots and the Egyptians could not drive the foreigners out of Lower Egypt without them. In other societies the chariot seems to have evolved from a status vehicle for the king to a practical instrument of war based as much on the prestige of riding into battle as any real military advantage it might have offered. Once the chariot came into common use, it became the symbol of a modern army. Thus, there was pressure to field chariots just to retain the prestige and reputation of possessing a first-rate fighting force. It is often believed that most modern nations develop and deploy new technology precisely to counter genuine threats just as the ancient Egyptians did. But modern states also adopt technology as a prestige or status symbol. Consider the Latin American armies that purchase the latest versions of tanks and jet aircraft when there is no demonstrable threat to justify the expense. When there exist genuine threats, nations naturally seek the most effective military technology. But the element of prestige still plays a role in some technology acquisition. This is precisely the case with regard to the desire of minor states to possess nuclear weapons. Why, for example, did South Africa develop nuclear weapons if not for reasons of national prestige?

The case of the chariot also illustrates different doctrinal approaches to both the design and the use of new technology. Like the modern tank, the chariot was a carefully balanced compromise between speed, firepower, and armored protection. Small, light, two-horse chariots like the Egyptian model had great speed and maneuverability but possessed less firepower and shock due to its light construction and two-man crew, only one of whom could fire the bow. The alternative design in the armies of the Levant offered a larger and more solid vehicle (in some cases with four wheels) that required up to four horses to pull it. It carried a crew of three or four. These chariots sacrificed speed for better protection, firepower, and shock potential. Obviously, one would not adopt the same warfighting doctrine for these different chariots. The Egyptians used their chariots much like light cavalry of later days. They provided front and flank protection for marching armies and excelled in pursuit. During battle, the Egyptian chariots sought the enemy flanks and rear and engaged them with long-range archery fire. The tactical doctrine of heavier chariot forces was closer to that of modern mechanized infantry mixed with a large dose of medieval heavy cavalry tactics. They were of little utility except in battle where they closed with the enemy using the momentum of vehicle and horses for its shock value.

Once in contact, the crew dismounted to fight as infantry. As the modern U.S. Army transforms itself for the future, it is attempting to develop an armored vehicle that is lethal, survivable, and sufficiently light weight to be strategically transportable. The history of the chariot suggests two considerations for the leaders of that transformation to keep in mind. First is the iron rule of technological trade-offs. Developing a light-weight, lethal, survivable, and agile tank has always been the goal. The problem is that those characteristics are so intertwined that emphasizing one inevitably results in decreased performance in others. Just as the Hittites had to add horses when they increased the crew size of their chariots, an engine powerful enough to propel a well-armored, lethal tank will necessarily increase vehicle weight. Next is the problem of doctrine. How does one fight these light-weight, agile, lethal, survivable tanks? The ancients had different tactics for chariots with different capabilities.

The doctrinal application of future tanks will also reflect their capabilities. The United States is pursuing technology to address a strategic mobility problem rather than to perform essential tactical missions. Consequently, the employment doctrine for the new technology is not yet established. The temptation will surely be to use the new vehicle in much the same way as traditional tanks and will likely result in a less than optimal solution to the evolution of an effective warfighting doctrine. The ultimate doctrine will almost certainly contain some aspects of existing armor doctrine, but, conversely, slavish adherence to existing doctrine will doom the new technology to failure.

How does an army integrate new technology with its existing technology? In the case of chariots, perhaps the best illustration is the example of the integration of existing chariots with the new technology of cavalry. The gradual displacement of chariots occurred as cavalry increased in capability and proved its worth on the battlefield. The chariot did not disappear completely or even quickly, and there was always a period of overlap and at times a resurgence in the popularity of the older technology leading to its occasional re-use. Using the example of today's transformation of the U.S. Army, the plan calls for deployment of interim brigades where new technology can be tested and exercised before the eventual fielding of objective brigades containing the advanced technology. The legacy force will coexist with both the interim and objective brigades until the concept is proven. Over time, both the legacy force and the interim brigades will be phased out. These are modern terms for the process the Assyrians used to transform their force from an infantry-chariot army through an infantry-chariot-cavalry army to an infantry-cavalry army.

Beyond questions of technology as a reason for studying the ancient world is the issue of the relationship between a society and its military. How do societies influence military organizations and how do military organizations reflect the possibilities or limits of their societies? A social, cultural, political, religious, and economic relationship exists in every society that influences the size, composition, and use of its military institutions. For example, the question of drafted versus volunteer service is as much cultural as political or economic, and is often completely divorced from considerations of threats to the national interest. No answer is fixed but changes as the environment changes. The Roman army began as an organization of free citizens exercising their civic duty by serving in times of need. It evolved into an army of professional citizens serving the state, an army of professional citizens and foreigners serving their commanders, and eventually into an army of non-citizen foreigners that was virtually a mercenary establishment. One can point to some specific causes for that evolution, perhaps the increased frequency and length of wars that made a short-service militia of citizens impractical, but the overall relationship between political, social, cultural, religious, and economic factors that caused all the changes was far too complex for comprehensive analysis. Yet, those relationships are exactly the sort of modern issues we need to understand in order to analyze contemporary society and the great issues of military policy. We may never encounter as clear and uncomplicated a relationship as that between the Mongol culture and its military or as overtly militaristic a society as the Spartans, but each may provide insight into elements of modern cultures, societies, and armies.

A final issue is, Why define the ancient world as broadly as the author does? Conventionally, the ancient world ends with the fall of the western Roman Empire or at least sometime during the late Roman period. Gabriel goes on to talk about cultures and armies a thousand years after that date. Purists may grumble, but actually this is a major strength of his work. The most interesting and important aspect of this book and its predecessors is their broad scope both geographically and temporally. *The Great Armies of Antiquity* discusses armies from east Asia to the British Isles and most of the territory in between. Temporally it spans almost 5,000 years of history from 3500 B.C.E. to 1453 C.E., from the early Bronze Age to European feudalism. It is a brave and rare author who tackles such a broad and diverse range of subjects. The specialist in a particular period may be unsatisfied with some detail of the presentation, but that should not overshadow the commendable and successful effort to synthesize a vast amount of historical material into a comprehensive, integrated, and readable whole. The historical discipline needs more books like this, particularly at a time when we often seem to be falling into the academic pit of excruciating detail about what privates thought about some minor skirmish of the Civil War or the step-by-step advance of a rifle company across Europe in World War II. Both are interesting to our overall understanding of their respective wars. But no matter how well the tales are told or how compelling the heroism depicted, the events themselves remain mere historical trivia. They are insignificant pieces of a much larger and more important whole. Worse, in most cases they represent a return to the drum and trumpet school of military history that the profession has tried to deemphasize since the 1960s. Richard Gabriel is one of the few authors writing about the ancient period who synthesizes major trends over sweeping cross-cultural and cross-temporal periods. He deserves credit for his efforts and his book deserves serious attention.

—J. Boone Bartholomees, Jr., Ph.D.

Preface

The Great Armies of Antiquity is the last volume in a project that began more than a decade ago when I was professor of Military History and Politics at the United States Army War College, where I introduced the systematic study of ancient military history to the curriculum. In attempting to select books that provided the student with a comprehensive overview of the field that were, at the same time, sufficiently detailed to permit the student an encounter with the rich literature that renders the study of ancient history so useful and interesting, I discovered that selections were few. Specialization, the curse of academic life in the modern era, had worked against the recent production of general, yet sufficiently detailed, works on the subject. What acceptable texts there were were usually more than fifty years old and tended, like Delbruck's work, to offer detail at the expense of overall comprehension or, like Liddell-Hart's, were often short and incomplete. To deal with this difficulty I wrote *The Great Battles of Antiquity: A Strategic and Tactical Guide to the Great Battles that Shaped the Development of War*, a detailed study of eighteen battles in the ancient period that I deemed to be the most significant for my students to learn about the development of war in the ancient world.

The book worked well enough, but was met with the immediate criticism that it offered too few insights into the personalities of the great captains whose actions in war and politics shaped so much of the development of the ancient world. To meet this criticism, I wrote *The Great Captains of Antiquity*. Modeled on Liddell-Hart's work of the 1920s, *Great Captains*, my book offered a study of the personalities and leadership of six "great captains"—Thutmose III of Egypt, Sargon II of Assyria, Philip II of Macedon, Hannibal, Scipio Africanus, and Augustus Caesar—whose actions influenced much of the history of the ancient world. This, too, worked well enough (although by now I was retired from my faculty posting and writing from afar) or so I am told by those using the book in my old class in ancient history which, I am pleased to report, still survives in the War College curriculum.

As I continued my work even in retirement, it came to me that the field also lacked a sufficiently comprehensive treatment of another important aspect of ancient military history, namely the instruments of social violence that had in fact served so much to forge the ancient cultures into what they were, the ancient armies themselves. It was the attempt to fill this need that led me to write the third and last volume in the series, *The Great Armies of Antiquity*. For whatever shortcomings may remain in these three volumes, it is nevertheless of some value that students and teachers of ancient military history (few though they may be!) have available to them a teaching and research tool for approaching the field in a systematic and, one hopes, somewhat complete manner.

The approach that I have taken in *The Great Armies of Antiquity* is the same as that used in the first two volumes and encompasses four elements. First, an analysis of the organizational structure and weapons of each of the nineteen armies studied is offered. Second, since armies are first and foremost societal institutions more than technical devices (this despite the protests of generals through the ages to the contrary!), the societal culture that produced each army is analyzed with a view to revealing the degree to which cultural values and imperatives shaped the form and application of military force. Third, the tactical doctrines and specific operational capabilities of each army are analyzed with a view toward explaining how certain technical limitations (the absence or presence of iron, for example) and societal/cultural imperatives (the social structure of the horse-borne Germanic tribes ensured the dominance of cavalry on the battlefield for a thousand years) affected the operational capabilities of ancient armies. Finally, I have striven throughout the analysis of each army to make cross-cultural and cross-historical connections to ground the analysis in the larger historical context that was the ancient world. Given that my students and colleagues found this approach of some value in the earlier volumes, it is my hope that it offers similar value in the present one.

The last volume ends where the first one began, with the affirmation that there is much to be gained from the study of ancient military history that is directly relevant to those in the modern age whom we entrust with the responsibility of protecting the nation through the design and implementation of national defense policy. One may, of course, quibble with the value of studying this or that battle, field commander, or army, but overall, the value of studying history to expand the context within which the decision maker must act, is surely beyond any reasonable debate. For soldiers, citizens, and policymakers to remain ignorant of what has gone before in the history of warfare is almost to guarantee that the egregious errors of the past will be repeated, if only in analogous form, by the generals and politicians of the present day. *The Great Armies of Antiquity* and the previous companion volumes are one old teacher's attempt to prevent this.

1

War in the Ancient World
2500 B.C.E.–1453 C.E.

The invention and spread of agriculture coupled with the domestication of animals in the fifth millennium set the stage for the emergence of the first large-scale, complex urban societies. These societies appeared almost simultaneously around 4000 B.C.E. in both Egypt and Mesopotamia. Within five hundred years stone tools and weapons gave way to copper and then to bronze, and with bronze manufacture came a revolution in warfare.

While this period saw the development of many new weapons, it is incorrect to conclude that new weapons themselves were responsible for the great increase in the scale of warfare that characterized this period of human history. Improved weaponry, by itself, would have produced only a limited increase in the scale of warfare unless accompanied by new types of social structures capable of sustaining large armies and providing them with the impetus to fight on a heretofore unknown scale. The military revolution of the Bronze Age occurred more in the development of truly complex societies than in weapons technology.

What made the birth of warfare on a modern scale possible was the emergence of social orders characterized by fully articulated social structures that provided stability and legitimacy to new social roles and behaviors. The scale of these fourth-millennium urban societies was a result of an efficient agricultural ability to produce adequate food resources that could sustain large populations. It is no accident that the two earliest examples of these societies, Egypt and Sumer, were states where large-scale agricultural production was first achieved. But it was the revolution in social structures that rested upon the new economic base that was most important to the emergence of war.

These early societies produced the first examples of state-governing institutions, initially as centralized chiefdoms and later as monarchies. These new governmental structures gave a degree of stability and permanence to the centralized direction of social resources on a large scale. Chiefdoms supported by organized but still small armed forces forged the scattered elements of the protosocieties into true social orders. At the same time centralization demanded the creation of an administrative structure capable of directing social activity and resources toward communal goals. It was these new types of social organizations that permitted Narmer of Egypt, for example, to create a truly national irrigation system for the 700-mile-long Nile in 3200 B.C.E. By 2700 B.C.E. similar administrative structures were present throughout the city-states of Mesopotamia.

The development of central state institutions and a supporting administrative apparatus inevitably gave form and stability to military structures. The result was the expansion and stabilization of the formerly loose and unstable warrior castes that first emerged in the tribal societies of the fifth millennium. By 2700 B.C.E. in Sumer, and earlier in Egypt, there was a fully articulated military structure organized along modern lines. The standing army emerged for the first time as a permanent part of the social structure and was endowed with strong claims to social legitimacy. It has been with us ever since.

As important as these developments were, they could not have worked as they did unless there had been a profound change in the psychological basis of people's social relationships with the larger community. The aggregation of large numbers of people into complex social orders also required that those living within them refocus their allegiances away from the extended family, clan, and tribe toward a larger social entity, the state. This psychological change was facilitated by the rise of religious castes that gave meaning to the individual's life beyond a parochial context. Organized belief systems were integrated into the social order and given institutional expression through public rituals that linked religious worship to political and military objectives that had become national in scope. Thus, the Egyptian pharaoh became divine, and the military achievements of great leaders were perceived as divinely ordained. In this manner the terrible propulsive power of religion was placed at the service of the state and its armies.

It is important to remember that the period from 4000 to 2000 B.C.E. was a truly seminal period in the development of the institution and instrumentalities of war. When this period began, people had not yet invented cities or any of the other social structures required to support communal life on a large scale. Agriculture, which became the basis for the nation state during this period, was still in its infancy and could not yet provide a food supply adequate to sustain populations of even moderate size. Psychologically, people had not yet learned to attach meaning to any social group larger than the extended family, clan, or tribe. The important force of religion had not yet been given specific social focus and institutional expression to the extent where it could become a powerful psychological engine to drive the spirit of conquest and empire. There were only the embryonic beginnings of a warrior caste still only loosely embedded in a tribal social structure, a structure that lacked both the physical and psychological requirements to produce war on any scale. Military technology and organization were primitive, and the professionalization of armies had not yet begun. In any meaningful sense warfare had not yet been embedded in the social structure as a legitimate and permanent function of government.

The 2,000 years following the dawn of the fourth millennium changed all this. As a mechanism of cultural development, the conduct of war became a legitimate social function supported by an extensive institutional infrastructure, and it became an indispensable function of human social order. This period saw the emergence of the whole range of social, political, economic, psychological, and military technologies that made the conduct of war a characteristic element of human social existence. In less than 2,000 years, man went from a condition in which organized social violence was relatively rare and often ritualistic to one in which death and destruction were achieved on a modern scale. In this period warfare assumed truly modern proportions in terms of the size of the armies involved, the administrative mechanisms required to sustain them, the development of weapons, the frequency of occurrence, and the scope of destruction achievable by military force. The ancient world had given birth to a level of warfare that would have been instantly recognizable in all its elements by a soldier of the present day. This book is about the armies that emerged and developed during this period, 2500 B.C.E. to 1453 C.E. As terribly destructive as these armies were, there is no doubting their importance as instruments of history, for it was the armies of the ancient world that often provided the means through which the emperors, tyrants, and demi-gods of the period shaped the history of the world. Without them, that history would have been very different indeed.

To study the armies of the ancient world, then, is to attempt to comprehend human history itself, together with one of mankind's most fascinating social inventions, war.

The historical period addressed by this study is both long and complex. Encompassing as it does the period from 2500 B.C.E. to 1453 C.E., the study of war within it ranges from the end of the Bronze Age, through the Iron Age, to the period of the Dark Ages, and the Age of European Feudalism. While the organization and conduct of war *within* each period manifested a high degree of consistency of application, the conduct and organization of war *between* periods is often diverse. Thus, as the Bronze Age was ending, man had succeeded in inventing and institutionalizing the conduct of war into truly complex societies. By the Iron Age, the increase in social complexity and organization produced an era in which warfare reached levels of application that were virtually modern. Following the collapse of Rome, however, the decline in levels of social organization brought with it a steep decline in the quality of warfare. As the social orders of the Dark Ages plunged to almost Bronze Age levels, so, too, did their ability to produce armies capable of sophisticated operations. The highly organized and sophisticated armies of Rome were replaced with tribal armies whose conduct of military operations can be described as little more than squalid butchery. By the eighth century, however, the West was once again beginning to rediscover the secrets of societal organization and control as feudalism became the dominant form of social organization. While the armies of this period were more sophisticated than the armies of the Dark Ages, they were only marginally so. When the ancient world finally met its demise at the siege of Constantinople in 1453 C.E., armies had still not achieved the level of organization and sophistication evident in the Iron Age.

The period from 1500 B.C.E. to 100 C.E. was one in which there occurred a genuine revolution in most aspects of people's social existence and organization. It was a period also characterized by a revolution in the manner of conducting warfare. The Iron Age was marked by almost constant war, a time in which states of all sizes came into existence only to be extinguished by the rise of still larger empires which, in their turn, were destroyed by military force. During this time humankind refined the social structures that were essential to the functioning of genuinely large and complex social orders and, in doing so, brought into existence a new and more destructive form of warfare. The Iron Age also saw the practice of war firmly rooted in man's societies and experience and, perhaps more importantly, in his psychology. This age produced the prototype of every weapon of war that was developed for the next 3,000 years.[1] Only with the introduction of gunpowder weapons would a new age of weapons and warfare begin. It was during the Iron Age that a military revolution began that eventually produced the age of modern war.

One of the more important stimuli for this military revolution was the discovery and use of iron, first employed as a technology of war by the Hittites.[2] Iron's importance as a technology of war rested in the fact that unlike bronze, which required the use of relatively rare tin to manufacture—a fact that had limited the spread of bronze weapons manufacture—iron was commonly and widely available almost everywhere.[3] The plentiful supply of this new strategic material made it possible for states to produce enormous quantities of reliable weapons cheaply. No longer was it only the major powers that could afford enough weapons to equip a large military force. Now almost any state could do it. The result was a weapons explosion that dramatically increased the frequency, scope, and scale of warfare.

The armies of this period were the first to practice conscription on a regular basis. While the Sumerian and Egyptian armies had used conscription much earlier, the scale and regularity with which conscription was used by Iron Age armies dwarfed this experience. The Iron Age gave birth to the standing national army. The emergence of the standing national army increased the professionalization of military establishments. A constant flow of conscripts required a permanent cadre of professionals to train, lead, and integrate conscript units. While conscripts could be easily used to fill out garrison forces within an empire, only under the tutelage of professionals could their fighting ability and loyalty be achieved. Ultimately, of course, only the fighting ability and political loyalty of the professionals could be relied upon by the national governments. The Assyrians and Persians always retained a large corps of professionals as the centerpiece of their military establishments and ensured that loyal professionals remained in control of key logistics and supply functions of the various national and conscript units under imperial command.[4]

The military revolution made itself felt in a number of key areas of military development, all of which had the cumulative effect of changing the nature, scope, and scale of war. Among the more important military developments of this period were changes in the size of armies, logistics, transport, strategic and tactical mobility, siegecraft, artillery, staff organization, military training, and weaponry. In almost every one of these military capabilities the armies of the Iron Age reached a level of development that was not surpassed until the Age of Napoleon. In still others, it required the invention of the mechanical weapons and powered machines to surpass the level of ability demonstrated by the ancients.

SIZE OF ARMIES

While the size of the armies in the late Bronze Age were quite large by comparison to those at the beginning of the period, they were minuscule by comparison to armies that fought in the Iron Age. The Persians, for example, routinely deployed field armies that were *ten times larger* than anything seen in the Bronze Age. Some examples of the size of these armies are instructive. The Egyptian army in the time of Ramses II (1300 B.C.E.) is estimated to have had over 100,000 men.[5] This force was largely comprised of conscripts, most of whom garrisoned strong points throughout the empire and carried out public works projects. The actual field army was organized into divisions of 5,000 men and could be deployed individually or as a combined force of several divisions.[6] The Assyrian army of the eighth century B.C. was comprised of between 150,000 and 200,000 men and was the largest standing military force that the Middle East had witnessed to this time.[7] An Assyrian field army numbered approximately 50,000 men with various mixes of infantry, chariots, and cavalry.[8] In modern terms an Assyrian field army was equal in size to five modern heavy American divisions or almost eight Soviet field divisions. When arrayed for battle the army took up an area of 2,500 yards across and 100 yards deep. The Assyrian army was also the first army to be entirely equipped with iron weapons.[9]

Even the Assyrian army, as great as its size, was easily dwarfed by the Persian armies that appeared 300 years later. Darius' army in the Scythian campaign numbered 200,000, and the force deployed by Xerxes against the Greeks numbered 300,000 men and 60,000 horsemen.[10] Even at the end of the empire, the Persians could deploy very large forces. In 331 B.C.E., just before Alexander destroyed the Persian empire at Arbela, Darius III fielded a force of 300,000 men, 40,000 cavalry, 250 chariots, and 50 elephants.[11] Philip of Macedon could field a combat army of 32,000 men, and the army of Alexander sometimes exceeded 60,000 men. The Roman military forces which, at the end of the empire, totaled 350,000 men, could routinely field armies of 40,000. The one exception to the ability of Iron Age armies to deploy large numbers was the armies of classical Greece. Being products of small city-states, classical armies were usually small even by Bronze Age standards.[12] The growth in the size of armies of the Iron Age was almost exponential when compared to earlier armies. Sustained by larger populations, cheap and plentiful weapons, the need to govern larger land areas of imperial dimension, and the evolving ability to exercise command and control over larger military establishments, the armies of this period were larger than anything the world had seen to this point. After the fall of Rome, tribal forces were often just as large. But the low level of organizational structure of these armies hardly qualifies them as armies as such. By feudal times, with the exception of the Mongols, armies became generally smaller, but still retained the decentralized organizational structure which, more than size, limited their ability to conduct truly sophisticated warfare.

LOGISTICS AND TRANSPORT

As the size of armies and the scale of battles increased, ancient armies had to master the task of logistically supporting these armies in the field. The need to support armies in the field for months, sometimes years, was a function of the rise of the imperium. Armies now had to conduct combat operations over far wider areas for longer periods than ever before. Changes in the composition of military forces also added to the logistics burden. The development of the chariot required repair depots and special mobile repair battalions to ensure that the machines remained functional on the march.[13] The Assyrian invention of cavalry brought into existence a special branch of the logistics train to ensure that the army could secure, breed, train, and deploy large numbers of horses to support these new forces. This special branch, the *musarkisus*, was able to obtain and process 3,000 horses a month.[14] Advances in siegecraft required an army to transport siege towers and engines, and artillery, first introduced by the Greeks but brought to perfection under the Romans, added yet another requirement to transport catapults and shot. The need to manufacture, issue, and repair the new iron weapons in unprecedented numbers required yet more innovations in logistics. Among the more important requirements of the logistics trains of ancient armies was the need to supply large numbers of men and animals with food and water. Of all the achievements of the ancient armies, those in the area of logistics often remain the most unappreciated by modern military planners.

During the Bronze Age the standard mechanism of transport was the donkey (Egypt) or the solid-wheeled cart drawn by the onager (Sumer). Ramses II revolutionized Egyptian logistics by introducing the ox-drawn cart, which quickly became the standard mode of military logistical transport for almost a thousand years.[15] Xenophon recorded that the normal pack load for a single ox-drawn cart in Greek armies was twenty-five talents, or approximately 1,450 pounds.[16] Studies by the British War Office in World War I noted that a mule could carry upward of 300 pounds, and the camel slightly less.[17] The Persians used teams of oxen to haul their large wooden siege and mobile towers. Xenophon noted that sixteen oxen were required to pull the tower, which weighed approximately 13,920 pounds.[18]

While the ox cart allowed armies to move heavier loads, it slowed their rate of movement to a crawl. It is important to remember that there were few packed roads and none of the paved roads introduced later by the Romans. The animal collar had not been invented yet, so that harnesses pressed on the windpipes of the baggage animals and increased the rate of physical exhaustion. Under the best of conditions an ox cart could travel two miles an hour for five hours before the animals became exhausted.[19]

As the armies grew in size, the logistical burden threatened to reduce drastically their rate of movement and their ability to maneuver at all. The introduction by the Assyrians of the horse allowed a slight increase in logistics capacity, as did their innovation of using the camel as a military beast of burden. Five horses could carry the load of a single ox cart, but could move the load at four miles an hour for eight hours.[20] Equally important, the horse could move easily over all types of terrain, and five horses required only half the forage required to feed a team of two oxen.[21] It was the Persian army that introduced a major innovation in logistics. While the Egyptians sometimes used small coastal vessels to supply their armies, the Persians were the first to introduce a large-scale navy used primarily in support of ground operations.[22] By the time of Alexander the logistics trains of ancient armies had matured to a point where they could regularly supply large armies for longer periods. However, the problem of speed and flexibility of movement over rough terrain remained.

Philip of Macedon increased the rate of movement of his armies by forbidding the practice of taking wives and camp followers along with the army.[23] He eliminated the ox cart from the logistics train and replaced it with a mix of horses and mules. By requiring the soldier to carry his own equipment, Alexander created the lightest, most mobile, and fastest army the world had ever seen. Alexander's army could routinely move at thirteen miles a day, and separate cavalry units covered twice that distance.[24] These same reforms introduced in the Roman army by Marius in 99 B.C.E. produced the same results.

STRATEGIC MOBILITY

A tremendous increase in strategic mobility resulted from the ability of Iron Age armies to deploy larger and larger armies and to sustain them logistically in the field. Strategic mobility can be defined as the ability of a military force to project power over a given area. After the fall of Rome, only the armies of the Mongols and Islam could match the strategic mobility of these earlier armies. The typical range of a Bronze Age army was approximately 350 miles by 150 miles. The earliest armies of Sumer conducted military operations over a range of 250 by 125 miles.[25] Egyptian armies of the same period projected force over a 600 by 200 mile area.[26] By the Iron Age, strategic range had increased enormously.

The Egyptian army of 1400 to 1250 B.C.E. had a strategic range of 1,250 by 200 miles or more than twice the range of the earlier period. Assyria conducted military operations over 1,250 miles by 300 miles, five times the range of the Sumerian armies. The armies of Persia, Alexander, and Rome (and later the Mongol and Islamic armies) attained strategic ranges typical of present-day armies. The Persian army, for example, conducted operations from the Iaxartes and Indus Rivers to Thrace, Cyrene, and Thebes, a strategic range of 2,500 by 1,000 miles. Alexander's armies ranged from the Hellespont to the Caspian Sea to the Persian Gulf, a range of 2,600 by 1,000 miles.[27] The range of Roman armies was 3,800 miles by 1,500 miles. On average, the armies of the late Iron Age had a strategic range that was nine times greater than the range of the armies in the Bronze Age.

The increased mobility of some of these armies was also a function of the military road. Early imperial states had the advantage of interior lines and regular travel over regular routes, a practice that packed down and widened dirt trails into usable, good-weather roads. Regular routes of travel made the use of military maps a regular practice for the first time. The Persian empire was tied together by a system of royal roads that facilitated military control and communication with the provinces at the empire's rim. A system of regular bridges over streams and other terrain obstacles, more than the surface of the road itself, greatly increased rates of movement. The most amazing system of military roads was the Roman road network, which crisscrossed the entire empire. As Rome established her hegemony over the Western world, she connected the entire empire with a network of military roads. The Romans constructed over 250,000 miles of roads, including 50,000 miles of paved, permanent roadways, most of which still exist.[28] The effect on the mobility of Roman armies was amazing. On dry, unpaved roads a Roman legion (6,000 men) could move no more than eight miles a day.[29] In wet weather, movement was almost impossible at any speed. On paved roads, however, a legion could move twenty to thirty miles a day in all kinds of weather. The Roman military road network not only increased strategic range and mobility, but revolutionized logistics and transport as well.

TACTICAL FLEXIBILITY

The armies of this period also made revolutionary advances in tactical mobility and proficiency, which had important effects on the conduct of war. Tactical mobility can be defined as the ability of small combat units to perform sophisticated tactical maneuvers to increase the combat power of these units, thereby increasing the overall combat power of the army as a whole. Even seemingly small innovations had considerable impact. The Assyrian invention of the leather jackboot is an excellent example. The lack of adequate footgear was a major factor in limiting the tactical mobility of early ancient combat units. The Assyrians were the first to improve the military footgear of the ancient soldier. The Assyrian soldier wore a knee-high, leather jackboot with thick leather soles complete with hobbed nails to improve traction. The boot had thin plates of iron sewn into the front to provide shin protection.[30] The high boot provided excellent ankle support for troops who fought regularly in rough terrain, and served as excellent protection in cold weather, rain, and snow. The boot kept foot injuries to a minimum, especially in an army with large contingents of horses and other pack animals. The Assyrian boot was a major factor in the ability to develop an all-weather combat capability for the Assyrian army. Within a short time of the Assyrian innovation, military boots of various designs became standard equipment for all the later armies of the period.

The growth in small-unit tactical ability was also evident in the ability of armies to develop an all-weather capability for ground combat. The Assyrians regularly fought in the summer and winter months and even carried out siege operations during the winter.[31] They also fought well in marshlands. Placed aboard light reed boats, tactical units became waterborne marines who used fire arrows and torches to burn out the enemy hiding among the bushes and reeds.[32] The ability to mount military operations in all kinds of weather and terrain quickly became a major characteristic of all later Iron Age armies.

The regular use of tactical combat engineering units provided yet another increase in the combat power of field units. Assyrian engineers built the first portable military pontoon bridges from palm wood planks and reeds.[33] At times they used inflated animal skin bags to float men and equipment over rivers.[34] The large cavalry contingents of the Persian armies required that their combat engineers become skilled at the construction of bridges with vertical sides so that horses could cross steep ravines without fear driving them to bolt. Military engineering skills reached their height in the ancient world under the Romans, including the ability to construct a fortified camp every night while on the march. The regular presence of combat engineering crews within field armies, itself a major military innovation, greatly increased the capabilities of tactical combat units.

Among the most difficult tasks of any commander, ancient or modern, is the ability to control his tactical combat units once committed to battle. For the most part, armies tried to control units by introducing semaphore flag signals and sounds from drums and trumpets. Alexander made good use of a corps of staff riders who could ride to combat units and pass instructions, an innovation copied by Napoleon. The Romans used a combination of these techniques, as the Mongols did later, but improved on them by having a special signaler within each cohort. The Greeks seem to have been the first to introduce the use of the signalling mirror to pass orders.[35] A Roman innovation was to stress small unit tactical proficiency in training, making the soldier able to respond instantly to formation and other commands given by his unit leader. The earliest armies were essentially infantry forces, with little in the way of tactical capability. While the early Egyptian armies organized their infantry by the types of weapon it carried, this did little to increase tactical flexibility. The result was packed infantry formations that could hardly move once arrayed for battle. When rival infantry formations clashed and one side broke, the victor had no opportunity to pursue and increase the kill rate. This situation changed completely with the Egyptian adoption of the chariot.

The Egyptian chariot, a much improved version over the old Sumerian, Hyksos, and Cananite machines, introduced a radically new tactical capability to the battlefield: mobility. The chariot added a new dimension to the traditional use of shock tactics and, when equipped with archers armed with the composite bow, provided the world's first mobile firing platform. It was the only weapon that could participate in all phases of the battle with equal effectiveness.[36] Its archer crews could engage the enemy at long range. Upon closing, the crews switched to the javelin and the axe and attacked as infantry. Once the enemy was scattered, the chariot could be used to mount a truly lethal pursuit. In addition, the chariot could be used to inflict surprise, a tactic that had never been possible with densely packed infantry formations. The chariot also permitted another major tactical innovation, the use of mobile reserves that could be committed at a propitious moment to turn a flank or exploit a breakthrough. It was the high-tech fighting machine of its day.

The tactical flexibility of the Assyrian army relied on providing a mix of units acting in concert. The firepower of their archer companies was increased by as much as forty percent by introducing an innovation in the shoulder quiver that allowed the arrows to be brought within easy reach of the bowman.[37] The Assyrian chariot was a larger and heavy vehicle pulled by three horses, and carried a crew of four. The Assyrian chariot's tactical role was to maximize the use of shock. The idea was to attack enemy infantry from as many directions as possible and deliver maximum shock. Once engaged, the crews dismounted and fought as infantry. The Assyrians were the first to introduce the use of mounted infantry, and their use of the chariot strongly parallels the use of armored personnel carriers in modern armies.

The scope of Assyrian military action required it to fight in all types of terrain, a condition to which the heavy chariot was not suited. A major Assyrian revolution in battlefield capability was the invention of cavalry. Assyrian cavalrymen used the saddle girth, crupper, and breast strap to stabilize the rider, and the horse was controlled by leg and heel pressure of the boot. (The spur and stirrup had not been invented yet.) These innovations made possible the first use of mounted archers, the famed "hurricanes on horseback" mentioned in the Old Testament. The ability of the horse to traverse uneven terrain made the cavalry especially lethal in the pursuit. This same capability made cavalry forces highly flexible and valuable for reconnaissance in force, providing flank security, and inflicting tactical surprise. The Persians expanded the role of cavalry in their fighting formations. By the time of Cyrus, the Persian army's ratio of cavalry to infantry was 20 percent cavalry to 80 percent infantry.[38] It was the largest cavalry force in the world.

Throughout the classical period, the primary killing arm of Greek armies had been heavy infantry. Philip's reforms had created the Macedonian phalanx, which, if anything, was even heavier and less capable of complex battlefield maneuver than the old phalanx. Alexander's tactical contribution was to use his heavy infantry in an entirely new manner while reducing its role as the primary killing arm. Alexander used his heavy infantry to anchor the center of the line and to act as a platform for the maneuver of his primary striking arm, the heavy cavalry armed with the javelin. He coupled this new tactical idea with another, the oblique formation. The infantry was not deployed as the foremost frontal point of the line but held back obliquely in the center while the heavy cavalry deployed in the strength on the right, connected to the infantry by a hinge of elite cavalry. The idea was to engage the enemy on the flank and force him to turn toward the attack. Alexander was the first of the ancient commanders to use cavalry as the primary combat arm of an army and bequeathed the lesson to future armies that cavalry is always to be used in concert with infantry. When both Wellington and Ney forgot this lesson at Waterloo, the result was a disaster for both British and French cavalry forces.

The tactical proficiency of ancient armies went through several phases. First was the primacy of infantry; then the Egyptian use of the chariot introduced the new element of mobility to the battlefield. The Assyrians found a new role for the chariot, mounted infantry, but relied more heavily upon cavalry to provide mobility and flexibility. The great reliance upon cavalry by the Persians led to the neglect of heavy infantry, and Alexander's use of ponderous infantry formations as a platform of maneuver signaled the emergence of cavalry as the primary striking force of ancient armies. In each phase of tactical development, the role of infantry as the main maneuver and killing force on the battlefield declined. How surprising, then, that the next major army to appear on the ancient battlefield found its primary strength in the role of its heavy infantry formations.

The spine of the Roman army was its heavy infantry formations. Unlike infantry of the past, the Roman maniples and, later, cohorts were more maneuverable than any infantry formations the world had seen to that point. They also far surpassed the killing power of earlier infantry formations to an almost exponential degree. The secret of the Roman killing machine was that the Roman soldier was the first soldier to fight within a combat formation while at the same time remaining somewhat independent of its movement as a unit. He was also the first soldier to rely primarily upon the sword, the *gladius*, instead of the spear.[39] The Roman gladius was responsible for more death on the battlefield than any other weapon until the invention of the firearm.[40]

The old phalanxes of the past were virtually immobile as a result of their density. The Roman innovation was to build in spaces between soldiers and units, thereby greatly increasing tactical flexibility and mobility. Each soldier could move freely over five square yards of ground *within the unit*, seeking and destroying individual targets. Each line of infantry was separated from the next by an interval of approximately 100 yards. This *quincunx* or checkerboard arrangement provided maximum flexibility for each maniple and allowed it to deliver or meet an attack from any direction while delivering maximum killing power.

Tactical flexibility was increased by the relationship between the lines of infantry. If, after the first line engaged, it was unable to break the enemy formation or grew tired, it could retire upon command in good order through the gaps left in the second line. The second line then moved to the front and continued the attack. This maneuver could be repeated several times, with the effect that the Roman front line was always comprised of rested fighting men. The ability to maneuver tactically through one's own lines offered yet another tactical innovation. The inability of earlier infantry formations to replace men in the front ranks often turned the defeat of the front rank into a rout of the whole unit. No army until the time of Rome had learned how to break contact and conduct a tactical retreat in good order. The ability of individual lines to pass to the rear, withdrawing through the gaps, allowed the Romans to master the art of disengagement and tactical withdrawal.

The resurgence of infantry as the primary tactical killing arm inevitably reduced the role of cavalry to a secondary one. Roman infantry ruled supreme in the ancient world until its fatal defeat at the battle of Adrianople (378 C.E.). The defeat of Roman infantry at the hands of barbarian cavalry shook the tactical thinking of the ancient world. Followed as it was by years of invasion by tribal armies that generally used loose, tribal cavalry armies, the empire in the West eventually collapsed and with it went the primacy of infantry. The death of disciplined infantry forces was a natural consequence of the social organization of the new tribal states of Europe. Infantry decayed and the primacy of cavalry became complete. The battle of Hastings in 1066 C.E. settled the question for hundreds of years.

During the Middle Ages the armored knight became the prototype of the successful warrior, and infantry all but disappeared. The Islamic and the Mongol threats to Europe reinforced that idea that infantry was no longer an effective fighting arm. Tactics of any sort declined greatly, so much so that most battles of this period could be described as little more than semiorganized brawls. Although the Swiss had shown at Paupen (1339 C.E.) that disciplined infantry could deal effectively with cavalry, and Crecy (1346 C.E.) demonstrated their vulnerability to the new long-range weapon—the long bow—cavalry remained supreme.[41] The supremacy of infantry and tactical flexibility did not begin to appear again until the invention of the musket. By that time, the armies of the ancient world were long dead.

SIEGECRAFT

Siegecraft came into existence in an attempt to deal with one of the most powerful defensive systems produced by the Iron Age, the fortified city. The first fortified city to appear in the Middle East was at Jericho, although it is by no means clear that the walls of this city were originally built for military reasons.[42] By the Bronze Age, however, there was unambiguous evidence of fortifications built exclusively for military purposes. Within two hundred years, fortification of urban areas had become commonplace.

Fortified cities placed field armies at great risk. Safe behind the city's walls, defending armies could provision themselves for long periods, while attacking armies were forced to live off the land until hunger, thirst, or disease ravaged them. Worse, no army bent on conquest could force a strategic decision as long as the defender refused to give battle. A conquering army that tried to bypass fortified strong points placed itself at risk of surprise attack from the rear at a time of the enemy's choosing. Even in ancient times, then, the success of a conquering army depended upon its ability to overcome fortified strong points and cities if it was to achieve its strategic and tactical objectives.

Not surprisingly, the military engineers of ancient armies invented the techniques of siegecraft, one of the most sophisticated expressions of the military art. One of the earliest inventions to overcome fortifications was the battering ram, which dates from at least 2500 B.C.E.[43] The ability to secure large spear blades to long beams allowed engineers to pry stones loose from the walls until a breach was achieved. The Hittites used the technique of building an earthen ramp at a low spot in the wall and then rolling larger, covered battering rams into place. The Assyrians built wooden siege towers taller than the defensive walls and used archers to provide cover fire for the battering ram crews working below. The Assyrians also perfected the use of the scaling ladder to mount soldiers with axes and levers who dislodged the stones in the wall at midpoint. Longer ladders were used to insert combat forces over the walls. To an army on the march, fortifications had to be overcome quickly to preserve the offensive.

The development of siegecraft continued during the reigns of Philip and Alexander. Philip realized that the new Macedonian army would remain a force fit for obtaining only limited objectives if it were not provided with the capability to rapidly reduce cities. Alexander's far-flung victories would have been impossible without this capability. Philip introduced the use of siegecraft into his army, copying many of the techniques first used by the Assyrians and passed to him by the Persians. Both Philip's and Alexander's armies made regular use of siege towers, battering rams, fire arrows, and the *testudo*.[44]

The Roman ability to reduce fortifications was probably the best in the ancient world, but it relied primarily upon organization and application rather than on engineering innovation. For the most part Roman siege engines were significantly improved versions of the old Greek and Persian machines. The Romans raised the art of circumvallation and countervallation to new heights. Mostly, it was Roman determination and discipline, Roman *gravitas*, that proved more effective than machinery. Once the Romans were committed to a siege, the results were almost inevitable no matter how long it took.

ARTILLERY

It was Philip of Macedon who first organized a special group of artillery engineers within his army to design and build catapults. Philip gave Greek science and engineering an opportunity to contribute to the art of war, and by the time of Demetrios I (305 B.C.E.), known more commonly by his nickname "Poliocetes" (the Besieger), Greek inventiveness in military engineering was probably the best in the world.[45]

The most important contribution of Greek military engineering of this period was the invention of artillery, the earliest of which took the form of catapults and torsion-fired missiles. The earliest example dates from the fourth century B.C.E., and was called a *gastraphetes*, literally, "belly shooter."[46] Later, weapons fired by torsion bars powered by horsehair and ox tendon (the Greeks called this material *neuron*,) springs could fire arrows, stones, and pots of burning pitch along a parabolic arc. Some of these machines were quite large and mounted on wheels to improve mobility. One of these machines, the *palintonon*, could fire an eight-pound stone over 300 yards, a range greater than that of some Napoleonic cannon.[47] All these weapons were designed for use by Philip in siege warfare. But it was Alexander who used them in a completely new way—as covering artillery—and gave birth to a new branch of the combat arms.

Roman advances in design, mobility, and firepower of artillery produced the largest, longest-ranged, and most rapid-firing artillery pieces of the ancient world. Roman catapults were much larger than the old Greek models and were powered by torsion devices and springs made of sinew kept supple when stored in special canisters of oil. Josephus recorded in his account of the siege of Jerusalem that the largest of these artillery pieces, the onager, could hurl a 100-pound stone over 400 yards.[48] Vegetius later noted that each legion had ten of these machines, one for each cohort.[49] Caesar required that each legion carry thirty smaller versions of these artillery pieces, giving the legion a mobile, organic artillery capability. Smaller machines fired iron-tipped bolts. Designed much like the later crossbow but mounted on small platforms or legs, these machines required a two-man crew and could be used as rapid-fire field guns against enemy formations. They fired twenty-six inch bolts over a range of almost 300 yards. These machines could fire three to four bolts a minute and were used to lay down a barrage of fire against enemy troop concentrations.[50] They were the world's first rapid-fire field artillery guns.

The emergence of siegecraft and artillery as basic implements of ancient armies represented a major innovation in warfare. Without the ability to reduce cities and strongpoints in hostile territory, no army could hope to force a strategic decision with any rapidity. The very idea of empire would have been unthinkable. After the collapse of Rome, artillery and siegecraft generally fell into decline as much of the required technical knowledge was lost. The art remained in practice in Byzantium which, through military contact, passed it to the armies of Islam. In Asia, the Mongols became adept at using Chinese techniques of siegecraft and artillery. Although siegecraft and artillery represented the birth of a major new idea in the technology of war, it was an idea that came to full fruition only with the introduction of gunpowder.

STAFF ORGANIZATION

The emergence of large, complex armies brought into existence the specialized staffs required to make them work. The invention of the military staff may be compared in importance with the rise of the administrative mechanisms of the state that appeared at the same time. In the modern age we are so accustomed to various forms of social organization and bureaucracy that we are prone to forget how important a social invention administrative mechanisms were. Without them it would have been impossible for the states of the period to generate the high levels of social and economic complexity that they did, and it would have been impossible to produce large and sophisticated armies.

The first military staffs emerged in Egypt during the period of the Old Kingdom (2686–2160 B.C.E.). While the complete structure is unknown, through an analysis of titles there is ample evidence of sophisticated staff organization. The organizational principle, then as now, was probably based on function. A clearer command and staff structure emerged during the Middle Kingdom (2040–1786 B.C.E.), when titles for general officers in charge of logistics, recruits, frontier fortresses, and shock troops were found.[51] For the first time there was evidence of a military intelligence service.[52] Surprisingly, there is clear evidence of the first use of the commander's conference for staff planning on the battlefield.[53]

The citizen armies of classical Greece were essentially part-time affairs, and there does not appear to have been any permanent staff organization except for Sparta, itself a military society. Yet, this period may have produced the first written treatises on tactics and strategy.[54] Earlier evidence reveals the existence of cuneiform manuals for military physicians in Assyria, a datum that could imply that the Assyrians may also have written and used military textbooks to train their officers. The armies of Philip and Alexander, while more structurally articulated in staff organization than the armies of classical Greece, do not appear to have reached the level of sophistication of earlier armies. The structures of these armies were essentially extensions of the personalities of their respective commanders, and did not survive long enough to acquire institutional foundations of their own.

The height of military staff development was achieved by the Romans. So effective was the Roman staff organization that more than any other army, it still serves as a model for modern armies. Each senior officer had a small administrative staff responsible for paperwork, and the Roman army generated considerable numbers of files. Each soldier had an administrative file that contained his full history, awards, physical examinations, training records, leave status, retirement bank accounts, and pay records. Legion and army staff records included sections dealing with intelligence, supply, medical care, pay, engineers, artillery, siegers, training, and veterinary affairs.[55] The degree of sophistication and organization evident in the army of Rome was not achieved again until, at least, the armies of the American Civil War.

COMBAT TRAINING

As armies became more complex, the need to train the soldier in more skills increased. The first evidence of military training is found in ancient Egypt. A surviving scrap of papyrus warns the soldier against military life because of its rigors and the propensity of commanders to use beatings and other physical punishments.[56] A description of military training among the Persians was produced by Strabo, who noted that Cyrus introduced universal military training among the Persians. Training was vigorous and included physical conditioning, instruction in the bow and javelin, and horsemanship. Recruits were also trained to forage for their food, prepare meals in the field, and make and repair weapons.[57] The first code of military ethics, the code of the Persian army, taught the recruit to "ride well, shoot straight, and tell the truth."

The training regimen of the classical Greeks was directed more at physical conditioning than at the development of specific military skills. This focus was logical in light of the fact that the phalanx tactics of the day required more stamina and bravery than skill to implement. The Roman mix of equipment and special military skills required special training, which, in turn, required an intelligent soldier. The legions screened applicants for military service and selected only the best physical specimens. Equally important was the selection of men who could read, write, and perform some mathematical calculations.[58] The most intelligent soldiers were trained in the special skills needed by the army. The Roman army trained its own medical personnel and surgeons, and operated its own hospitals. As a professional army, the legions ran their own specialized training programs in everything from military engineering to artillery gun repair. The complexity of war, as in modern times, made the mental skills of the soldier at least as important as his physical skills. In 105 B.C.E., the Roman army adopted the training methods heretofore used by professional athletes in the gladiatorial school.[59] It was also common practice to ship units to special exercise areas to build up skill proficiency prior to embarking upon campaign.[60]

When taken together, all the elements discussed above made possible a military revolution that increased the capabilities of armies to levels that gave birth to war on a modern scale. The increased size and complexity of these armies resulted in an increase in the size of battles and the accompanying destruction. These battles often involved numbers of men that were not usually exceeded in battles of the modern period until Waterloo and Gettysburg. The increased destructive power of these armies permitted the destruction of whole cities on almost a routine basis. The destruction of some cities of the period was as complete as if they had been struck by a nuclear attack. In some instances whole cultures were destroyed and disappeared, never to emerge again.[61]

But what distinguishes modern warfare from primitive warfare is more than the level of military capability and destructive power. The key defining quality of modern war is strategic endurance, and this quality is a function of the total integration of social, economic, and political resources of the state in support of military operations. For much of the early ancient period, armies could often force a strategic decision with a single battle. As the states of the period grew in complexity, their ability to remain at war increased exponentially. Because armies could now draw upon the total mobilized resources of their states to support military operations, a single battle no longer decided their fate. The staying power or strategic endurance of some of the ancient armies increased to a level at least equal to that of the armies of World War I.

WEAPONS TECHNOLOGY

The advent of metals technology did not greatly affect the weaponry of warfare. The most significant impact was its contribution not to offensive weapons, but to defensive systems. The development of protective body and head armor had a tremendous impact on warfare and tactics, and the development of new metal weapons represented an attempt to thwart the effectiveness of defensive armor. Metals technology, early on, did permit the introduction of two important new weapons, the penetrating socket axe and the sickle sword, whose effectiveness depended directly upon the ability to cast metal into required shapes. Neither weapon revolutionized warfare on any significant scale. Indeed, the most important and revolutionary weapons of the metals age, the composite bow and the chariot, did not depend upon metals technology at all.

The Bronze Age is normally dated as encompassing 4000 to 1200 B.C.E., at which date the Iron Age is generally held to have begun. Even when metals technology had found its way into most states of the Middle East, say by 2600 B.C.E., its military use was dictated by factors other than the technology itself. In Mesopotamia, where warfare among rival city-states was constant, metal weapons assumed an immediate importance. Frequent war accelerated the rate of weapons development and accounted for the large number of weapons innovations introduced by the Mesopotamian states of this period. In other states, most notably Egypt, metals technology had far less impact on weapons technology, and the rate of innovation was slow. Technological progress in bronze weapons was slowed further by the rarity and expense of tin needed to fashion bronze. The supply was never adequate for large-scale weapons manufacture, and the cost of production remained high. The wide availability of iron, first used as a technology of war by the Hittites around 1200 B.C.E., and its ease of extraction marked the first true revolution in metal weapons by bringing them within easy reach of even small states. Metals technology from the beginning did provide the ability to fashion an effective body armor. Once body armor was introduced, weapons development is most properly seen as an attempt to overcome the effectiveness of armor, a task that was never truly mastered. Thus, the basic weapons revolution of the age of metals was in defensive systems.

ARMOR AND HELMETS

The first recorded instance of body armor is found on the Stele of Vultures in ancient Sumer, which shows Eannatum's soldiers wearing leather cloaks on which are sewn spined metal disks.[62] The disks do not appear to be arranged in any order, and we do not know if the disks were made of copper or bronze. By 2100 B.C.E. the victory stele of Naram Sin appears to show plate armor, and it is likely that plate armor had been in wide use for a few hundred years. Plate armor was constructed of thin bronze plates sewn to a leather shirt or jerkin. The plates themselves were two millimeters thick and had slightly raised spines to allow them to hang correctly.[63] This type of armor became standard protection for the Egyptian soldier of the New Kingdom (1600–1000 B.C.E.). The rise of the iron army of Assyria saw the introduction of a new and more effective form of body armor called lamellar armor. Assyrian armor was comprised of a shirt constructed of laminated layers of leather sewn or glued together. To the outer surface of this coat were attached fitted iron plates, each plate joined to the next at the edge with no overlap and held in place by stitching or gluing. A conservative estimate of the weight of this armor is thirty pounds.[64]

By the time of classical Greece and ancient Rome (600 B.C.E.), armor had changed considerably. Instead of laminated leather and iron plates, the Greeks and early Romans introduced the cast bell muscular cuirass made of bronze. This form of armor bears no connection to earlier developments in Assyria, Sumer, or Egypt and represents a totally new type of armor. The cuirass weighed about twenty-five pounds, was hot and uncomfortable, and slowed movement.[65] By the third century B.C.E., the bell cuirass had given way in Greece to the linen cuirass. Constructed of strips of linen glued and sewn together in lamellar fashion, it was cheaper, more flexible, and lighter than the bronze cuirass.[66]

The third century B.C.E. saw the introduction of iron chain mail, probably invented by the Celts.[67] A shirt of mail weighed about thirty pounds, but was much easier to make in quantity than cast bronze armor. The Romans adopted the chain mail armor for their own troops, and the mail shirt remained the basic armor of the Roman infantryman until the first half of the first century B.C.E. By the first century C.E. the Roman army was equipped with laminated leather armor that provided sufficient protection against the tribal armies that they encountered most. Perhaps the ultimate body armor appeared at the same time, the *lorica segmentata*. It was constructed of plates of thin sheet steel riveted to leather plates held together by straps and a series of buckles and locks. At twenty pounds it was considerably lighter than the traditional chain mail.[68] Figure 1.1 provides examples of each of the different types of armor discussed above.

The earliest evidence for the helmet is found in Sumer at the Death Pits of Ur dating from 2500 B.C.E. Similar helmets appear on the Stele of Vultures. The Sumerian helmet was made of a cap of hammered copper approximately two to three millimeters thick fitted over a leather cap. It remains unclear why the Sumerians did not use bronze for their helmets. Once the helmet made its appearance, it became standard military equipment, at least until the seventeenth century C.E. In Assyria the helmet was constructed of iron and shaped to an acute point so as to reduce its area and increase its ability to deflect arrows and blows. The Assyrian helmet, like all helmets of the period, required an inner cap of leather or wool, which helped absorb impact and dissipate heat. The helmet chin strap was introduced by the Sea Peoples to Egypt early in the New Dynasty. Greek helmets were constructed of bronze and had cheek and face plates. Roman helmets also came to have face plates. Face plates were never a major feature of helmets in the Middle East, probably because they made the head too hot. The Romans were the first to mass-produce bronze helmets, casting them in state arms factories.

The body armor and helmet of the ancient soldier afforded him good protection against the weapons of the day. Table 1.1 provides data on empirical tests with replicas of ancient weapons and data on the amount of impact energy that can be produced through muscle power for a range of weapons. Also provided is the amount of impact energy relevant to the size of the striking surface required to penetrate standard bronze and iron armor of the period. The data suggest that the helmet and body armor of the ancient soldier provided excellent protection except against the penetrating axe.

The advent of gunpowder is commonly thought to have made body armor obsolete. Yet, it was two hundred years after the introduction of gunpowder that the musket was sufficiently powerful to pierce the plate armor of the Renaissance knight. The result was that armies completely abandoned the search for personal protection for the soldier, and body armor and the helmet disappeared from the battlefield. This was a tragic mistake. The fact is that the body armor and shield of the ancient armies would have provided excellent protection against firearms well past the

Figure 1.1
The Development of Body Armor

SUMER (2500 B.C.)

EGYPT (1700 B.C.)

ASSYRIA (900 B.C.)

GREECE (400 B.C.)

CELTIC CHAIN MAIL (200 B.C.)

ROME (100 A.D.)

Table 1.1
Energy Required to Penetrate Bronze and Iron Armor

Weapon	Energy Produced	Energy Required	
		Bronze	Iron
Gladius (hacking)	101 fpds.	151 fpds.	251 fpds.
Penetrating Axe	77 fpds.	66 fpds.	110 fpds.
Sickle Sword	77 fpds.	245 fpds.	408 fpds.
Spear (overhand)	71 fpds.	137 fpds.	228 fpds.
Cutting Axe	70 fpds.	189 fpds.	314 fpds.
Eye Axe	70 fpds.	85 fpds.	141 fpds.
Javelin	67 fpds.	99 fpds.	165 fpds.
Arrow	47 fpds.	76 fpds.	126 fpds.
Gladius (thrust)	21 fpds.	182 fpds.	302 fpds.
Spear (underhand)	14 fpds.	137 fpds.	228 fpds.

Note: Energy required is a function of the impact area on the weapon and the area made by the wound. The larger the wound and impact area, the greater force or work required to penetrate. It requires less than two foot-pounds of work to penetrate the viscera of the human body if the force is concentrated in one square inch.

age of Napoleon. When the dispersion of field formations, inaccuracy of the firearms, and rates of fire are factored in, the ancient soldier would have been safer on the battlefields of the eighteenth century than he was on his own. No army wore helmets from the sixteenth century to the nineteenth century, even though this period saw the birth of artillery and the exploding shell, both of which produced shrapnel at alarming rates. Infantrymen of the Crimean War, the Civil War, the Franco-Prussian War, and the Russo-Japanese War, and even in the early days of World War I, went into battle with no protective headgear while a storm of steel crashed around them.

WEAPONS OF WAR

The primary short-range weapons of the ancient soldier were the mace, axe, sickle-sword, spear, and sword. The oldest of these weapons was the mace, the most commonly used close-range weapon of war from 4000 to 2500 B.C.E. In the Egyptian Old Kingdom the mace was such an important weapon that it was the symbol of pharaonic authority. The introduction of the helmet in Sumer was sufficient to drive the mace from the battlefield in that, as modern analysis shows, it could not be wielded with sufficient force to fracture the skull of a helmeted soldier.[69]

The data also demonstrate that in most cases, the helmet provided sufficient protection to prevent being rendered unconscious by a blow to
the head. While the mace disappeared from Sumerian portrayals of war
before 2500 B.C.E., it remained the major weapon of the Egyptians until
the Hyksos invasions of the seventeenth century B.C.E. While the Sumerians had the helmet early on, the Egyptians did not use it until after
the Hyksos invasions. Interestingly, at the same time that the mace disappeared from Egyptian monuments as the symbol of pharaonic authority, it was replaced by the *kopesh* or sickle-sword.[70]

The primary weapon of ancient armies for close-order combat was the
spear. The dominance of the spear for more than 3,000 years shaped the
tactical deployment of armies more than any other weapon. If men were
to fight effectively, they had to fight in groups. If soldiers armed with
the spear were to fight effectively in groups, they had to arrange themselves in close-order formation, thereby giving rise to the infantry phalanx. The first recorded instance of a phalanx formation appears in Sumer
in 2500 B.C.E.[71] The unwieldy nature of the spear in meeting an attack
from any direction except the front also required that men fight in closely
packed formations if they were to protect themselves from assault from
the flanks. Thus, the spear produced the phalanx, and the closely packed
infantry phalanx remained the basic infantry formation until the first
century B.C.E., when the Romans replaced it with the open, staggered
checkerboard formation for which the legion was famous. By then the
Romans had abandoned the spear as the basic weapon of the infantry
and replaced it with the sword.

When arrayed in phalanx formation, ancient infantry could not wield
the spear very effectively against an armored enemy. Two soldiers facing
each other within contesting phalanx formations would have a difficult
time delivering a fatal blow. In the first instance the shield offered excellent protection, and the soldier had to be constantly aware that a blow
to the shield might result in his spear being stuck fast, a condition that
left him defenseless to a counterthrust. Second, the spear could be used
effectively only when held overhand at a downward angle. But this attack
position reduced the target area that could be hit. The soldier could use
the spear in an underhand position, which provided a good opportunity
to strike the opponent in the legs, but the trade-off was reduced thrusting
power and greater exposure of his own chest area. Finally, if his opponent was equipped with helmet, body armor, and neck guard, the chances
of landing a fatal blow to any area except the face were very remote.
Unless the soldier was fortunate enough to land a blow directly to the

face, under the chin, or in the space between the neck collar and chest armor, the spear was not likely to be an especially lethal weapon in phalanx combat, at least as long as one's opponent stood his ground.

Among the most effective close-order weapons was the axe, the evolution of which over 1,500 years of warfare provides an excellent example of the search for a new weapon to deal with the advances in protective body and head armor. The availability of bronze blades greatly increased the penetrating power over the older stone or copper blades; however, ancient armorers encountered the problem of how to securely affix the blade to the shaft. The Sumerians solved the problem by inventing the first bronze-cast socket and blade in one piece; they invented the socket axe. They also hit upon the innovation of making the axe slightly heavier and narrowing the blade so as to reduce its impact area, thereby increasing its penetrating ability. The result was the socketed penetrating axe, one of the most devastating close-combat weapons of the ancient period. For 2,000 years it remained the only close-combat weapon that could defeat protective body and head armor.

Among the more interesting short-range weapons of the ancient soldier was the sickle-sword. Introduced by the Sumerians around 2500 B.C.E., this weapon derived originally from the axe and not the sword.[72] The sickle-sword could be cast in one piece, blade and handle together, thus giving the weapon greater reliability and striking power. As with the common axe, however, its large impact area and wound-producing circumference made it a poor penetrating weapon against body armor. While in Sumer the sickle-sword quickly gave way to the penetrating axe, in Egypt it remained a major weapon for centuries thereafter. For a thousand years the Egyptians used the sickle-sword effectively against unarmored enemies, and it superseded the mace as a symbol of kingly authority. When the Bible speaks of someone's being "smoted by the edge of the sword," the reference is to the sickle-sword.

The sword was never a major weapon of ancient armies until the second century B.C.E., when the *gladius* became the standard weapon of the Roman legions. The old problem of reliably affixing the blade to the handle and the success of the penetrating axe probably reduced interest in developing the sword. More importantly, the preeminence of the spear used in dense formations strongly worked against the development of the sword. Dense infantry formations were not well suited to swordplay in that they afforded little room for the individual infantryman to maneuver. As long as the phalanx remained the basic infantry formation of the ancient armies, the sword remained a secondary weapon.

All armies after the seventeenth century B.C.E. carried the sword, but in none was it a major weapon of close combat; rather, it was used when the soldier's primary weapons, the spear and axe, were lost or broken. For the sword to emerge as a major infantry weapon required a change in battle formations from the densely packed phalanx to a looser formation, with built-in spaces between men to allow the soldier the room to wield his sword against individual targets. A looser formation, however, required a higher degree of discipline and training than the pre-Roman armies were able to produce. The Roman army in the second century B.C.E. produced the first open infantry formations of the ancient world. With the change in tactics, Rome abandoned the spear and produced the first soldier whose primary weapon was the sword. In the hands of the highly trained Roman legionnaire, the sword became the most deadly of all weapons used by ancient armies, and it killed more soldiers than any other weapon in history until the invention of the gun.[73]

The close-combat weapons of ancient armies—with few exceptions—never truly succeeded in overcoming the defensive armor of the soldier, at least not in a technical sense. Yet, armies fought battles, weapons were brought to bear, and men died. Given the operational characteristics of these weapons, its seems clear that the combatants who suffered the most casualties were those that remained behind the advances of the defensive armor of the day. The classic case was Egypt. From at least 3000 to 1700 B.C.E., the Egyptian army fought armies much like itself, armies whose only personal protection was the shield. Under these circumstances any of the close-range weapons of the second millennium would have wrought devastating kill rates. Warfare in Sumer, however, was a far different matter. Here the common culture of the area, its relatively short distances, and its constant opportunity for war ensured that any technological advance in weapons capabilities would rapidly spread to the armies of the other city-states. The parties to any combat would always be fairly evenly matched, and death rates would be low as the effect of defensive systems offset the killing power of the offense.

In cases in which an army equipped with efficient weapons and body armor fought an army without this equipment, the result was horrendous slaughter. When the Hyksos invaded Egypt, for example, they confronted an army with no helmets, body armor, or penetrating axes. The Egyptians were protected only by the wooden shield and had only simple and compound bows. The Hyksos, by contrast, possessed all the weapons of the Sumerian tradition, including the horse-drawn chariot. The result was a slaughter of the first magnitude.

The primary long-range weapons of the ancient armies were the bow and the sling. The bow was probably between 6,000 and 10,000 years old by the dawn of the Bronze Age, and it may well have been man's first attempt to construct a composite tool. It certainly was man's first successful effort to concentrate energy.[74] The bow underwent three stages of development, beginning with the simple bow, followed by the compound bow, and culminating in the composite bow. The bow remained a primary weapon of war in the Middle East, Asia, and Europe until the collapse of Rome. Among the European armies of the tenth and eleventh centuries the bow gave way to the crossbow, although the bow was still used in significant numbers at the battle of Hastings in 1066 C.E. The Mongol invasions reacquainted European armies with the composite bow, but the armies of the Middle Ages seem never to have produced the composite bow for military use. Instead, the simple long bow made its appearance with devastating effect at the battle of Crecy, and sealed the fate of the composite bow for military use by European armies. In the Middle East and Asia, however, the composite bow remained a powerful and common implement of war. The range, rate of fire, and penetrating power of the composite bow easily outperformed the rifle, at least until Napoleonic times and, perhaps, even later.

The first evidence of the composite bow appears on the victory stele of Naram Sin (2254–2218 B.C.E.), the grandson of Sargon the Great. The composite bow was a mixed military blessing. It could easily outrange the simple and compound bow and deliver long-range fire on the enemy, but unless the target was unarmored or wore armor less than two millimeters thick, the composite bow would not penetrate the body armor of the day. The composite bow produced greater power from a shorter draw, but this advantage was partially offset by the strength required to draw it at all. It was smaller, however, and could be more easily carried, a quality that made it useful to horse archers. Yet, the composite bow was difficult to manufacture with any degree of consistency, and its composition made it very susceptible to moisture, which rendered it useless.

Once introduced, the composite bow spread to other armies over a period of 500 years. It appeared in the armies of Palestine around 1800 B.C.E. and was introduced to Egypt by the Hyksos a century or so later. Its killing ability was enhanced by the Egyptian innovation of placing the archer in a chariot, combining for the first time a powerful weapon with increased battlefield mobility. The Assyrians also used the bow on the chariot, but, more importantly, were the first to use the horseborne archer, further increasing mobility and killing power. The armies of the Persian empire centered their force on the horseborne archer but failed to develop heavy infantry to support him.

To the classical Greeks the bow was an immoral weapon whose ability to kill indiscriminately at a distance ran contrary to the Greek ethos of war and individual heroism.[75] This belief, combined with their reliance upon heavy infantry, led the Greeks to generally neglect the bow's development and use. The Romans, too, were aware of the bow, but generally did not develop its potential in any significant way. The Roman reliance upon flexible heavy infantry formations and close-order combat precluded the use of the bow as a major weapon.

The most common use of the bow in ancient armies was as a weapon of indirect fire support of infantry on the battlefield or in siege operations. Large groups of archers positioned behind the main bodies of the contesting armies fired in salvo to rain down a hail of arrows upon the enemy. In terms of a modern analogy, ancient armies used archers as close-fire support. Combatants during this period usually formed up about 100 yards apart. As long as the enemy remained in place, archery fire could be brought to bear. However, once the armies began to close with one another, the angle between the archers and the enemy formation became so acute as to make firing in salvo very difficult. At the same time, the target area shrank as the angle decreased, reducing the probability of a hit. Whatever else archers were, they were by no means a decisive factor in the outcome of a battle.

It is interesting to compare archery accuracy rates with those of the standard muzzle-loading musket of the eighteenth century. Compared with archery fire in ancient armies, the rifle fire of eighteenth-century armies was largely ineffective.[76] Whereas an archer could place all of his arrows within a fifty-foot target area at 250 yards, the musketeer would be fortunate to place 16 percent of his rounds within the enemy formation. In terms of actual hits, the musketeer could hit his target slightly less than once in 200 attempts, while the ancient archer could easily hit an individual target within the formation 22 percent of the time.[77] In purely statistical terms, then, the ancient soldier was at forty-four times greater risk of being struck by an arrow than the eighteenth-century soldier was of being hit by a bullet!

To determine how effective archery fire at long range was in producing casualties, it is noted that the chance of hitting the target at all was 22 percent.[78] Given the exposed area of the armored soldier, the chances of an arrow's striking the target in an unprotected place were approximately one in ten.[79] Thus, approximately one in every ten rounds fired could cause either death or wounding. Ancient archery fire was about twenty times as effective in causing death and injury as was eighteenth-century musket fire. This rate of casualty production is greater than can be achieved by modern artillery. While the statistics are interesting, it must be said that such high casualty rates usually did not occur.

And the reason was the shield. A wooden, hide-covered shield measuring two by four feet was sufficient to protect the entire exposed target area of the soldier from arrow fire.[80] If the soldier was armored, the combination of armor and shield reduced the probability of an arrow strike to a vulnerable area to almost zero, rendering arrows fired in salvo almost totally ineffective in generating casualties within an infantry formation. Unless a lucky shot struck an inattentive or poorly trained soldier, the infantry formations of ancient armies had little to fear from archery fire. Of course, the same was not true of the soldiers of the eighteenth and nineteenth centuries, who took the field without helmets, body armor, or shield. It was not, therefore, the inherent lethality of the firearm that produced so many casualties but the failure to develop and utilize body armor.

Although archery fire may not have been very effective against massed infantry, it was effective against chariots and cavalry. Both chariots and cavalry had to form in mass, and when in range, they provided excellent targets. The two-horse chariot teams provided a great deal of target area. A single arrow striking a horse effectively removed the charioteer or the cavalryman from the battle. Once a chariot or cavalry charge began, if the infantry stood its ground and gave the archers sufficient time to fire, a hail of arrows into the charge could cause havoc as wounded horses fell to the ground, spilled their riders, and caused machines to crash into one another. The bow, therefore, was a weapon to be feared among charioteers and cavalry, and encouraged the charioteer and cavalryman to become bowmen themselves.

Next to the bow and the spear, the sling ranks among the oldest weapons of war.[81] The sling could fire a variety of lead and clay shot varying in weight from one to ten ounces and in size from a small plum to a tennis ball.[82] Heavier shot could be lobbed into enemy formations at distances up to 200 yards; smaller shot could be fired along an almost flat trajectory up to seventy-five yards. Short-range shot was often plum-shaped and made of lead, and was designed to increase the penetrating capability of the projectile. Xenophon noted that plum shot inflicted horrible wounds, and the wide head and tapered tail allowed the tissue of the wound to close behind the missile and make extraction from the body very difficult. Vegetius noted that the Roman standard for a combat-qualified slinger was his ability to hit a man-sized target at 600 feet, a feat he suggested could be accomplished with regularity.[83]

As a combat weapon, however, the sling was far less effective than Vegetius's comments would suggest. In the first place, the sling required a high degree of training and experience to hit a target at any range, a fact that encouraged armies to hire professional slingers as auxiliaries rather than develop their own. To be effective, slinger units had to be employed in mass, which increased their own vulnerability to sling and archery counterfire. Such formations had no means of defending themselves from close attack by infantry, chariots, or cavalry. For the most part slinger formations were usually quite small in relation to the other combat arms and were used mostly as skirmishers at the beginning of the battle.

The weapons examined remained the basic weaponry of armies right through to the introduction of the firearm. After the collapse of Rome a number of military innovations were introduced. Among the most important were the horseshoe and the stirrup. The latter was particularly important insofar as it made cavalry charges more stable by making the rider more secure, a development that allowed the javelin to metamorphose into the lance. Other weapons, such as the morningstar, the halberd, and the crossbow, were but variations on old themes. It was at least three centuries after its introduction that the modern cannon could outrange the Roman catapult, and even then it fired a projectile only one tenth as heavy. In retrospect, it was not weaponry per se that made an army lethal in the conduct of its operation. Far more important was the tactical manner in which these weapons were employed by various commanders.

BATTLE DEATH

The weapons of the ancient armies could be deadly when wielded by a competent soldier. Yet, the destructive power of any weapon depended very much on the nature of the battle in which it was used. In modern times we are unaccustomed to witnessing wars in which the combat killing power of an army is significantly different from that of its adversary. In the ancient world, this rough approximation of combat power between two contesting armies existed only occasionally. This pattern of superior armies fighting inferior ones was already evident in the second millennium B.C.E.

The Hyksos armies, for example, made short work of the Egyptian because of superior military technology and tactics. Once the Egyptians caught on, however, they forged an empire based on military force, and for almost 400 years they never fought an enemy equivalent to themselves in any significant military respect. The armies of Alexander enjoyed a significant tactical advantage against the Persians in almost every battle. Although the Persians always had the strength of numbers, Alexander's cavalry, infantry, weapons, logistics, and tactical maneuvers were always better. After the destruction of the Greeks in 197 B.C.E., the Roman armies rarely fought an enemy that was militarily their equal. In only a few instances can one find examples of equivalent armies fighting one another. Certainly the legions of Rome that clashed during the civil war are an example. Ancient Sumer was another; here, for almost 2,000 years, the armies of the Sumerian city-states were evenly matched and made war a constant feature of Sumerian civilization. Like the classical Greeks, whose armies were almost always equally matched, the Sumerians fought wars for generations with no single state being able to gain a strategic advantage for very long before it was challenged anew, often by the same enemy.

In determining the level of risk faced by the ancient soldier in battle, we must keep in mind that risk levels varied greatly depending upon the army in which one fought and at what point in history one saw combat. It is common to assume that battles involving masses of men engaged in close combat were horrifically bloody; in fact, they were rarely so, at least as long as the units remained engaged. Most of the power of the packed phalanx could not be brought to bear on the actual fighting. When front lines came together, only the second rank could move into the spaces of the first line and engage the enemy. Thus, no more than two of the eight or ten ranks could actually engage in killing. If the infantry was armed with the spear, the ability to maneuver one's weapons against the enemy in the press was considerably reduced. The result was likely to be great fear among the few ranks locked in battle, but with little successful killing. Once the Romans deployed the open infantry formation, this state of affairs changed considerably. Now individual swordsmen could cut their way deeply into the enemy formations with devastating results.

As long as the men within the phalanx held their ground and remained together, it was difficult even for cavalry to be decisive. Cavalry charges were inherently unstable until the invention of the stirrup and lance, and horses do not throw themselves against a packed wall of humanity, especially if the spears of the formation were raised against them. The real killer on the ancient battlefield was fear.[84] Sometimes the actions of a single soldier were sufficient to set off a panic in an entire unit. Once the integrity of the formation began to erode, the soldier was at very great risk of death or injury.

Table 1.2
Combat Death Rates of Ancient Armies

Date/BC	Battle	Adversaries		# Troops		# Killed		% Defeated
		Victor	Defeated	Victor	Defeated	Victor	Defeated	KIA
2250	•••	King of Akkad	Ur	5,400	13,500	•••	8,040	59.5%
334	Granicus	Alexander	Memnon	36,000	40,000	125	10,000	25.0%
333	Issus	Alexander	Darius III	36,000	150,000	200	50,000	33.0%
331	Arbela	Alexander	Darius III	40,000	340,000	300	100,000	29.4%
237	Mactaris	Hamilcar Barcas	Mercenaries	10,000	25,000	•••	6,000	24.0%
218	Trebia	Hannibal	Sempronius	50,000	40,000	few	20-30,000	50.0%
216	Cannae	Hannibal	Varro	50,000	80,000	5,500	70,000	87.5%
202	Zama	Scipio Africanus	Hannibal	50,000	50,000	2,000	20,000	40.0%
197	Cynoscephalae	Flamininus	Philip V	20,000	23,000	700	8,000	34.7%
168	Pydna	Aemilius Paullus	Perseus	30,000	44,000	•••	20,000	45.4%
102	Aix	Marius	The Teutons	40,000	100,000	300	90,000	90.0%
86	Chaeronea	Sulla	Archelaus	30,000	110,000	14	100,000	90.9%
48	Pharsalus	Caesar	Pompey	22,000	45,000	300	15,000	33.0%
45	Munda	Caesar	Pompey	48,000	80,000	1,000	33,000	41.2%

Commonly a phalanx would suddenly shatter and take flight as the once cohesive fighting formation became a mob of frightened, isolated individuals trying to escape. Soldiers fled in all directions and often cast away their weapons, shields, and armor as they sought to escape. For much of the early period this technique worked, as armies had scant means to engage in lethal pursuit. The chariot, and then the spear and archer cavalry of the Assyrians, changed this situation. Fleeing soldiers became easy targets, and the pursuit, once a rare event, developed into the primary means for destroying a defeated army. The chariots and cavalry would ride through and around the fleeing mob and take up positions to herd it back together where the victors could spend all day killing them. Unless the commander of the victorious army halted the slaughter to take prisoners to be sold or used as slaves, often an entire army would be mercilessly slain—not a single soldier would be left alive.

Table 1.2 presents data for fourteen battles that occurred between 2250 and 45 B.C.E. The data presented include battles of the armies of Sumer, Persia, classical and imperial Greece, tribal engagements, and Roman armies over a range of two thousand years, thus allowing for an accounting of changing and more lethal technology as it affected casualty rates. The information as to the size of the forces has been extracted from accounts of battles as they appear in classical literature.[85] There is no way to verify the accuracy of these numbers, as both Delbruck and Engels have noted.[86]

The data in Table 1.2 suggest that, on average, the percentage of dead killed in action (KIA) suffered by a defeated army was 37.7 percent of its total force. Death rates for victorious armies, however, average only 5.5 percent. The great disparity in kill rates suggests strongly that most of the killing occurred after one side or the other broke formation and could be hunted down and slain with comparative ease. Approximately 35.4 percent of the defeated army could expect to suffer wounds serious enough so that they would be abandoned on the battlefield. When these figures are added to the number of dead, no fewer than 73 percent, seven of every ten men who took the field, could expect to be killed or wounded before the day was finished.[87] There is no certain way to measure the number of wounded suffered by the victor. When it is recalled, however, that most casualties suffered by the vanquished occurred after the formations broke, a situation that presented no risk to the victors inflicting death and wounding, then a wound rate of around 5 to 6 percent for the victor does not appear too high.

If the battles presented in Table 1.2 are analyzed in terms of those that saw a tactically and technologically superior army defeat an inferior army, it is clear that these factors made a considerable difference in kill and wound rates. Six battles meet these conditions: Issus, Arbela, Granicus, Cynoscephalae, Pydna, and Aix-en-Provence. In these battles the tactically and technologically superior force killed, on average, 42.6 percent of the inferior force, inflicting 5 percent more casualties than expected. At the same time, the victors in these battles suffered far fewer casualties themselves. Under normal conditions a victorious army could expect to lose 5 or 6 percent of its force in battle. Tactically and technologically superior armies, on average, suffered only 2.4 percent of their forces killed in action, a force multiplier of more than 100 percent.

BATTLE WOUNDS

The nature of close combat in ancient battles suggests that, except in the pursuit, the chances of suffering a wound were greater than being killed. It is interesting to speculate as to the type and nature of wounds most commonly suffered by soldiers of this period. The *Iliad* provides the oldest account of battle wounds suffered during this time. Frolich's analysis, although a century old, provides some basic data on battle wounds of the ancient Greek period.[88] Of the 147 wounds recorded by Homer, 114 or 77.7 percent resulted in fatalities. This compares with a wound mortality rate of 20 percent during the Crimean War and 13.3 percent in the Civil War, considerably below the wound mortality rate of ancient armies.[89] Not surprisingly, the areas of greatest lethality were the head and chest, areas that still account for most battle wound fatalities in the modern era. Frolich notes that of the thirty-one wounds to the head recorded by Homer, all were fatal.[90] This compares to the Crimean War where 73.9 percent of head wounds resulted in fatalities, and to the Civil War, in which 71.7 percent of head wounds caused death.[91]

Frolich's analysis notes that arrows accounted for less than 10 percent of the wounds suffered by the soldiers of the *Iliad*. The mortality rate, 42 percent, is the lowest for all the weapons examined. Arrows from a composite bow would not penetrate body armor to sufficient depth unless they struck a seam. Statistically, the most likely place for an arrow wound was in the extremities and the neck. Wounds to the arms and legs, which provided much greater target area, would have been much more common, and Frolich notes that 16 percent of the total wounds in the *Iliad* were to the upper and lower extremities. These wounds would have caused fatal shock or bleeding only if the arrow struck an artery, a comparatively rare event.

Blood loss and shock probably killed most men on the ancient battlefield. Until the time of the Roman military medical service, the art of tying off a major artery to stop bleeding was unknown. Even in World War II, in which ligature was widely practiced, 59 percent of the soldiers who underwent ligature and survived required the amputation of the limb.[92] Amputation was not practiced until introduced by the Romans, and it is unlikely that it was much help. In the Civil War the overall mortality rate produced by surgical amputation averaged 40 percent and, in the early days of the war, was as high as 83 percent.[93]

Not surprisingly, the most lethal weapon of the ancient Greeks was the spear, responsible for 106 of the 147 wounds recorded by Homer. As our earlier description allows, it was not easy to land a fatal blow with the spear. The most likely wounds caused by the spear were slashing cuts that, while not initially fatal, were debilitating enough to provide one's opponent with the opportunity to strike a fatal blow. As noted earlier, the sword was not a primary weapon of any of the ancient armies until Rome. The fact that only 15 percent of wounds described in the *Iliad* were taken by swordpoint suggest the propensity of the ancients to use this weapon only when their primary weapons were lost or broken.

Probably the most common wound suffered by the ancient soldier was a broken bone. The fact that ancient Egyptian and Sumerian medical texts discuss the treatment of broken bones extensively indicates that military physicians were quite familiar with them. The first evidence for a splint applied to a broken bone appears on mummies in ancient Egypt. One reason that broken bones were common is precisely because they were so easy to inflict. With the exception of the skull, there is very little difference in the amount of force required to fracture any of the bones in the human body. Even the thicker bones of the upper leg require only marginally more force to fracture than do the thinner bones of the forearm. On average, 67.7 foot-pounds of impact energy will produce a fracture to any bone except the skull.[94] Any of the ancient weapons could easily cause a fracture.

The data extracted from the *Iliad* and presented by Frolich provide the only glimpse into the wound profile suffered by the ancient soldier. The data have value only insofar as they provide a primitive baseline of measurement since it is clear that the frequency and type of wounds must have varied considerably in light of the weapons, armor, and battle tactics employed by an army in a specific battle. Of course, little of the analysis applies to armies that broke in combat and tried to flee. They would have been defenseless before almost any type of attack with any weapon by the pursuing force.

INFECTION

It is an intriguing comment on the nature of warfare to note that the threat to the ancient soldier of dying from an infected wound in the period under study here was no greater than that faced by any soldier until at least the early days of World War I. The wounded soldier of ancient times was at risk of battle wound infection from three major microbiological threats: tetanus, gas gangrene, and septicemia. By far the most common infection was tetanus. Tetanus is caused by an anaerobic bacterium named *Clostridium tetani*, which enters the body through deep breaks in the skin and viscera. The tetanus bacterium is endemic to soil and is found mainly in the richly manured soil typical of the agricultural societies of the ancient world. It is common where sanitation is poor and where human waste is present, and domestic animals also contribute to its presence. Any soldier whose wound was contaminated with soil was at risk of infection. Since there was no way of preventing tetanus infection until the introduction of immunization in World War I, it is likely that the rates of tetanus infection in ancient armies were equivalent to those found in armies of the pre-World War I era. If rates of tetanus infection are computed for the Peninsula War, Crimean War, Civil War, Franco-Prussian War, and the early days of World War I, the average rate of infection is 5.6 percent, with a mortality rate of 80 percent.[95] In neither ancient nor modern times was there a means for treating the infection once it began.

Gas gangrene presented the wounded of ancient armies with a second risk of infection. Gas gangrene is caused by six species of bacteria generically named *Clostridium perfingens*, and like tetanus, it is anaerobic and found in common soil. Until the middle years of World War I, the average incidence of gangrene infection among wounded soldiers was 5 percent. We may safely assume that the mortality rate among ancient armies was 100 percent.[96] If caught in time, the threat of death could be reduced by amputation, but amputation was an art not practiced by ancient military physicians.

Septicemia or blood poisoning also represented a threat to the wounded soldier, although somewhat less so. Blood poisoning is caused when a common body bacterium, *Staphylococcus bacteri*, enters the bloodstream through a puncture wound and is allowed to spread to the normally sterile blood. The rate of such wounds is approximately 1.7 percent.[97] Septicemia was usually fatal until very modern times, when the introduction of antibiotics made it possible to combat a blood infection.

If the data on wound mortality and infection are combined, it is possible to construct a crude statistical profile of the causes of wound mortality among the wounded of ancient armies. Of 100 soldiers wounded in action, 13.8 percent would die of shock and bleeding within two to six hours of being wounded. Another 6 percent would likely contract tetanus infections, and 80 percent of them would die within three to six days. Another 5 percent would see their wounds become gangrenous, and 80 to 100 percent would die within a week. A septicemic infection from arterial or venous wounds would be contracted by two percent of the wounded, and almost all of these would die within ten days. On average, then, one in four soldiers would die of wounds from these causes.

DISEASE

In ancient armies, as in all armies until the Russo-Japanese War of 1905, far more soldiers met their death as a result of disease than at the hands of enemy weapons.[98] Disease outbreaks in ancient armies were most likely to occur when large numbers of men were assembled for long periods out of garrison, where normal, if primitive, sanitary facilities were not available. Aside from the Egyptian armies and the armies of

Rome, which routinely took great care in the field to construct and segregate sanitation facilities from the food and water supplies, most armies took no precautions at all. After the collapse of Rome, much of the knowledge regarding sanitation was lost, with the consequence that armies of the Dark and Middle Ages were routinely decimated by disease.

Military operations also reduced the resistance of the soldier to disease insofar as armies in the field usually provided inadequate nutrition to sustain the body's ability to ward off disease. Armies on the march probably had less chance of epidemic since they moved away from infection sites. This certainly seems to have been true of the Mongol armies, which suffered recordable outbreaks of disease only after they became an occupying force in urban areas. The most likely place for a devastating outbreak of disease was in siege operations, in which large numbers of men lived in close proximity to one another amid sanitary and nutritional conditions that were generally poor.

Although Roman physicians hinted strongly at what we now call the germ theory of contagion, most descriptions of disease in the ancient world are not sufficiently precise to allow their identification with certainty. Modern medical writers, for example, cannot determine exactly if the great plague described by Thucydides, which killed a quarter of the Athenian army in the Peloponnesian War, was in fact caused by typhus. And while the description of the Antonine plague, which decimated the population of Rome in the second century, suggests an outbreak of smallpox, diagnosticians cannot be certain. Some diseases, such as cholera and bubonic plague, have relatively recent origins and can be safely omitted from the list of diseases that afflicted ancient armies. Others, like dysentery, typhus, typhoid, and smallpox, can be asserted with some confidence to have been common problems.

Probably the most common disease of ancient armies was dysentery. Commonly called "campaign fever," it is probably the most common form of disease among soldiers throughout history. The first description of the disease appears in the Ebers papyrus around 1550 B.C.E.[99] Dysentery is accurately described in the writings of Hippocrates, and Roman medical texts outline detailed hygienic practices for preventing its outbreak. Dysentery afflicted the armies of the Middle Ages and accounted for more deaths during the Crusades than were caused by Saracen arrows. It has been called the "most dangerous and pervasive disease in human history."[100] While some variants of the disease have a mortality rate as high as 50 percent, the usual rate does not exceed 5 percent.[101] The major impact of the disease on military operations, however, is that for periods of two to three weeks, the infection immobilizes large numbers of men who cannot be used as combat assets. Even marginal care requires the use of additional men to look after the sick and further reduces the combat force.

Typhoid fever is caused by the bacterium *Salmonella typhi*, which lives in the human digestive tract and is transported by human feces. Floods often cause an outbreak of this disease because of contamination of water supplies, and it is probable that the Egyptian and Assyrian armies, both products of societies familiar with floods, were aware of this disease. Typhoid can also be spread very rapidly by the common housefly. Drawn to exposed feces, the fly transmits the disease to the human food supply. An army caught in the midst of a typhoid outbreak would be rendered useless as a combat force. The mortality rate of 10 to 13 percent was very high indeed, but even for those who recovered, the disease required four weeks of serious pain and delirium fever to run its course.[102]

Some ideas as to how debilitating an outbreak of typhoid could be to an army can be surmised from examining statistics from epidemics in armies of the modern era. In the Napoleonic wars, 270 of every 1,000 men who succumbed to disease did so from typhoid.[103] In the Crimean War typhoid was a more common cause of death than enemy fire. During the Boer War the British lost 13,000 men to typhoid while an additional 64,000 were invalided home; by contrast, only 8,000 men were lost to hostile fire.[104] During the Spanish-American War, 90 percent of new units shipped to Cuba suffered outbreaks of varying severity, and 20 percent of the entire American combat force actually contracted the disease.[105] Most probably in ancient times, especially in southern Europe and the Middle East, the disease was epidemic rather than endemic.

Typhus is among the most common and deadly of the diseases associated with armies throughout history. It is caused by an organism midway between a bacterium and a virus that lives in the blood of various animals including, but not limited to, rats. It is transmitted by a number of insect vectors, but the most common is the human body louse, *Pediculus humanus*, living in the clothes and hair of an infected individual. Typhus is a disease of crowded humanity, and it occurs most commonly in conditions in which large numbers of people are required to live close to one another. It is found commonly in jails, on ships, in armies, and in overcrowded housing conditions.

The mortality rate of typhus is generally between 10 and 40 percent, but the disease has been known to kill entire armies.[106] In Napoleon's winter campaign in Russia, the disease decimated the French army. In the single town of Vilna, Napoleon abandoned 30,000 typhus cases; almost all the patients died.[107] While medical writers do not agree, the preponderance of opinion is that the great plague that struck the Athenian army during the Peloponnesian War was probably due to typhus.

Smallpox outbreaks were probably fairly common in the ancient world, although medical information does not make this statement certain. The earliest provable case of the disease occurred in 1160 B.C.E., when Pharaoh Ramses V died of the disease.[108] Ancient accounts suggest that smallpox was among the most feared of ancient diseases because of its tendency to blind, cripple, and severely scar the victim. It is also likely that many ancient accounts of outbreaks of leprosy were really epidemics of smallpox. The great Antonine plague, which decimated Rome in the second century, was probably caused by smallpox brought by legions returning from the eastern provinces.[109]

The retirement records of the Roman army allow a partial glimpse into the threat that general disease played in the life of the ancient soldier. In the Roman legions of the first century C.E., 50 percent of the soldiers who began service at age eighteen would still be alive at age forty-two to collect retirement. If the previous analysis is correct, approximately 6 percent of the soldiers would have died in battle, and another 8 to 10 percent would die as a result of wounds received in combat. Thus approximately 35 percent of the soldiers died either from accidents or disease during their tour of service. Disease was an important factor in the life of the soldier, and a far greater threat than enemy weapons.

INJURIES

An army in the field suffers considerable manpower loss through injury. In World War I the manpower loss for Allied armies on the western front was almost 6,000 men a month from such injuries as accidents, falls, accidental wounds, frostbite, trenchfoot, and heatstroke. An army on the march can expect to lose a considerable percentage of its combat force to injuries in the act of moving to the battlefield. Moving an army of 10,000 men is no easy task, and the march took a heavy toll on the health and safety of the soldier. Ancient armies moved in column for the same reason eighteenth-century armies moved in column: there were no roads, and the column formation was the best device for maintaining organizational integrity of the army.

The air breathed by the men in the center of the formation was putrid. The dust choked their nostrils, eyes became irritated, and lungs became congested. In only a single day nosebleeds, eye irritation, and respiratory problems would cause injury of such severity that men would begin to drop out of the formations to be left behind. In hot or cold climates the rate of injury increased.

Nutrition was a major problem. Modern armies estimate that an average soldier carrying a moderate load for eight hours of walking requires 3,402 calories and 70 grams of protein a day.[110] The stress and effort of combat field operations increases the amount of food required to keep the soldier healthy and functioning. In desert or semiarid climates, climates with high temperature and low humidity, the soldier requires a minimum of nine quarts of water per day. These nutritional requirements are minimums and will keep the soldier functioning for the first few days. If nutritional requirements are kept at this level over a march of ten days, most of the column would be unable to function at all, even if they suffered no additional health conditions or injuries. As Engels' analysis of the military diet of the ancient soldier demonstrates, his diet was not nutritionally sufficient for sustained military operations.[111]

Under these poor nutritional conditions the ancient soldier carried a load that averaged sixty pounds. The more mobile an army became by reducing its reliance on its baggage train, the greater the load that had to be carried by the individual soldier. The Roman army was probably the lightest field force among the ancient armies, and its soldiers carried approximately fifty-five pounds.[112] Alexander's soldiers carried slightly more, about sixty pounds.[113] Under these conditions it is not difficult to imagine a considerable portion of the army melting away on the march.

An army on the march was always vulnerable to heat stroke. Carrying sixty pounds amid conditions of high temperature and low humidity, aggravated by dust and putrid air, can cause a soldier to succumb to heat exhaustion. Sunburn was also a major problem. Soldiers could protect themselves from sunburn by applying palm or olive oil, but there is no record of these supplies being used in this manner before the time of Rome. In one account, Aelius Gallus, the Roman governor of Egypt in 24 B.C.E., led his army into Arabia. Almost the entire army, at least one legion, died of heatstroke and thirst. Many of the survivors of the ordeal suffered permanent damage and had to be mustered out of service.[114]

A general idea of the loss rates that were experienced by armies in the field can be approximated from the results of a navy/marine experiment conducted at Twenty-Nine Palms desert training area in 1984.[115] Although the troops in the exercise were given the best nutrition, clothing, and shelter, more than sufficient water, frequent rest periods, and precise instructions on how to conserve body energy, even under these ideal conditions 110 men had to be hospitalized for heat exhaustion over a fifteen-day period. Another 53 suffered debilitating headaches induced by heat, 31 were hospitalized for severe body cramps and nausea, 46 suffered nosebleeds from the dust, and another 46 were hospitalized for eye irritations even though they had been issued protective goggles.[116] In all, 286 men were lost to heat-related illness alone even though the exercise involved only foot and vehicle maneuvers and required no sustained marching.

Ancient armies suffered many of the injuries that plague modern armies, injuries including accidents, falls, contusions, cuts, bruises, sprains, and broken bones, all of which can make a soldier become a casualty. In the Twenty-Nine Palms study, 1,101 men suffered some injury serious enough to require attention at the battalion aid station or evacuation farther to the rear.[117] Among the most common injuries were blisters, lacerations, and abrasions; 228 men suffered these injuries. Another 169 suffered some general trauma serious enough to take them out of the field. Another 152 soldiers had irritations of the nose and throat. The generous category of "other" injuries listed 377 requiring medical treatment. Armies are accident-prone, and these accidents take a significant toll in combat manpower.[118] In the Twenty-Nine Palms experiment, no less than 17 percent of the total force required medical treatment or hospitalization for general injuries sustained on the exercise after only fifteen days.[119]

Ancient armies also fought in cold climates. The Assyrian incursions into Armenia and Kurdistan required fighting in snow, rain, and freezing temperatures. Roman armies fought in Germany, the Alps, eastern Europe, and the mountains of Spain, all of which have climates that challenged the survivability of modern soldiers in World War II. Xenophon recorded in the *Anabasis* that he almost lost his entire army in the mountains of Turkey when they slept unprotected and awoke to a snowstorm.[120] Sometimes cold weather wrought tremendous casualties. Alexander crossed the Hindu Kush with 100,000 men to arrive on the other side thirteen days later with only 64,000, a loss rate of 36 percent. Hannibal managed to cross the Alps, but at terrible cost. His army of 38,000 infantry and 8,000 cavalry lost 18,000 infantry and 2,000 cavalry by the time he reached Italy. Studies of cold casualties in World War II demonstrated that under modern conditions, only 15 percent of soldiers injured by cold could be returned to service, a statistic suggesting that most cold injuries then and now were serious indeed.[121]

An ancient army on the march was a medical disaster. At the minimum an army of 10,000 could expect to lose 400 men to heatstroke or exhaustion. And 1,700 men would be lost to routine injuries on the way to the battlefield. As the army moved, its general resistance to disease declined. The soldiers were subjected to chronic discomfort. As they marched in column, the dust choked their lungs, dried out their sinuses, and produced chronic coughing, blinding headaches, and severe nosebleeds. Blisters from the leather thongs on the sandals or from ill-fitting boots must have been endemic. In hot or cold climates, many of the soldiers would die of heat or cold. Others would be so afflicted that their health would be damaged for all time. Then, as now, warfare tended to be quite dangerous to the soldier's health.

The purpose of the foregoing pages is to provide a general overview of the operational capabilities of ancient armies during the period 2200 B.C.E. to 1453 C.E. and the general conditions under which soldiers of those armies had to fight. To be sure not all capabilities or conditions described here applied equally or simultaneously to any army within each historical period nor, indeed, for any given battle. As general descriptors of ancient armies and warfare for the period, however, they remain sufficiently valid to provide a larger context within which the analysis of the ancient armies contained within this book may be more easily understood.

NOTES

1. Yigael Yadin, *The Art of Warfare in Biblical Lands in Light of Archaeology*, 2 vols. (New York: McGraw-Hill, 1963), vol. 1, 36–40.

2. *Encyclopedia Britannica*, 15th ed., s.v. "Mettalurgy."

3. *Encyclopedia Britannica*, 15th ed., s.v. "Bronze Age."

4. Yaha Zoka, *The Imperial Iranian Army from Cyrus to Pahlavi* (Teheran: Ministry of Culture and Arts Press, 1970), 12–13.

5. The strength of the Egyptian army is based on an extrapolation of population figures provided by Robert J. Wenke, *Patterns of Prehistory: Mankind's First Three Million Years* (New York: Oxford University Press, 1980), 486.

6. Arther Ferrill, *The Origins of War* (London: Thames and Hudson, 1985), 58.

7. Ibid., 70.

8. T.N. Dupuy, *The Evolution of Weapons and Warfare* (New York: Bobbs-Merrill, 1980), 10.

9. Ibid.

10. These figures are taken from Plato's account of the war and are considerably less than those offered by Herodotus, who places the size of the Persian army at 2,641,640 men.

11. Data extracted from the chart on comparative battle strengths in Robert Laffont, *The Ancient Art of Warfare*, 2 vols. (New York: Time-Life Books, 1966), 38–39.

12. The small size of classical Greek armies is testified to by Thucydides, who recorded that at the beginning of the Peloponnesian wars in 431 B.C., Athens could field only 13,000 hoplites, 16,000 older garrison soldiers, 1,200 mounted men, and 1,600 archers. But even these small numbers represented a supreme military effort for Athens in time of crisis. Thucydides noted that after the military situation had stabilized a decade later, Athens could muster only 1,300 hoplites and 1,000 horsemen. See Thucydides, bk. 2:13 (Pericles).

13. Yadin, vol. 1, 89.

14. Ferrill, 72.

15. R.O. Faulkner, "Egyptian Military Organization," *Journal of Egyptian Archaeology* 39 (1953): 32–47.

16. Xenophon, *Cyropaedia*, bk. 6, 50–55.

17. These data are reported in S.L.A. Marshall, *The Soldier's Load and the Mobility of a Nation* (Quantico, Va.: Marine Corps Association, 1950), 22–25.

18. The calculation of the tower's weight is based upon Xenophon's statement that the number of talents normally carried by an ox was twenty-five. *Webster's New Universal Unabridged Dictionary*, 2d ed., notes that the weight of a talent in the ancient world varied widely by time and place. However, in no instance did the talent equal less than fifty-eight pounds. It is this minimum weight that was used as the basis for the calculations presented here.

19. *"Animal Management"* (London: British Army Veterinary Department, 1908), 299.

20. Donald W. Engels, *Alexander the Great and the Logistics of the Macedonian Army* (Berkeley: University of California Press, 1978), 15.

21. Ibid.

22. Zoka, 90–96 on the Persian imperial navy.

23. Richard A. Gabriel, *The Culture of War* (Westport, Conn.: Greenwood Press, 1990), 96–99.

24. Engels, table 7, 153.

25. Laffont, vol. 1, chart 3, 46.

26. Ibid.

27. Ibid.

28. Michael Grant, *History of Rome* (New York: Charles Scribner, 1978), 264.

29. "The Roman Empire and Military Airlift," *Wall Street Journal*, 9 December 1988, A7.

30. On the subject of boots see Laffont, vol. 1, 45. See also Georges Conteneau, *Everyday Life in Babylon and Assyria* (London: Edward Arnold, 1954), 44.

31. W.F. Saggs, "Assyrian Warfare in the Sargonid Period," *Iraq* 25 (Autumn 1963): 145–46.

32. Yadin, 303.

33. Conteneau, 46.

34. Richard A. Gabriel and Karen S. Metz, *From Sumer to Rome: The*

Military Capabilities of Ancient Armies (New York: Greenwood Press, 1991), 23.

35. Harris Gary Hudson, "The Shield Signal at Marathon," *American Historical Review* 42 (1936–1937): 443–59.

36. Gabriel, *The Culture of War*, 95.

37. The estimate of increased rates of fire was provided by several professional archers. While the innovation in quiver design undoubtedly provided some rate of increase, the exact rate of increase suggested here must be regarded as highly tentative.

38. Zoka, 19.

39. Robert L. O'Connell, "The Roman Killing Machine," *Quarterly Journal of Military History* 1 (Autumn 1988): 37–38.

40. Ibid.

41. The Swiss won at Paupen by the reinvention of the Macedonian phalanx complete with long sarissa-like spears. The striking power of the Swiss phalanx was increased, however, by the presence of halberdsmen wielding double-bladed and hooked axes.

42. James Mellaart, *The Neolithic of the Near East* (New York: Charles Scribner, 1975), 50–58.

43. Yadin, vol. 1, 55, 147.

44. A good account of Greek siege machinery can be found in J.K. Anderson, "Wars and Military Science: Greece," in Michael Grant and Rachael Kitzinger, eds., *Civilization of the Ancient Mediterranean* (New York: Charles Scribner, 1988), vol. 1, 679–89.

45. Dupuy, 29.

46. Ibid., 30.

47. Ibid.

48. Josephus, bk. 5:6, 3.

49. Vegetius, ii, 25.

50. Dupuy, 30.

51. Faulkner, 39; The definitive work on military titles and rank in the Egyptian army is Alan Richard Schulman, *Military Rank, Title, and Organization in the Egyptian New Kingdom* (Berlin: Bruno Hessling Verlag, 1964).

52. Faulkner, 39.

53. Gabriel, *The Culture of War*, 125.

54. Hans Delbruck, *History of the Art of War*. 4 vols. (Westport, Conn.: Greenwood Press, 1975), vol. 1, 159–63.

55. For the Roman staff organization, see Peter Connolly, *Greece and Rome at War* (Englewood Cliffs, N.J.: Prentice-Hall, 1981), 223. See also Dupuy, 98–101.

56. Guido Majno, *The Healing Hand* (Cambridge, Mass.: Harvard University Press, 1975), 84.

57. See Strabo, *The Geography of Strabo*, trans. Horace Leonard Jones (London: Loeb Classical Library, 1917–1932), book 15: 18–19.

58. The ability to read, write, and do calculations was a requirement for the promotion of Roman centurions.

59. G.R. Watson, *The Roman Soldiers: Aspects of Greek and Roman Military Life* (Ithaca, N.Y.: Cornell University Press, 1969), 56. Marius was impressed by the army of Rutilius, who first used gladiatorial methods to train his troops. Marius adopted these methods for the entire army.

60. Roy Davies, *Service in the Roman Army* (New York: Columbia University Press, 1989), chap. 4 on military training.

61. The total destruction of the Assyrian civilization is one example.

62. Yadin, vol. 1, 135.

63. Ibid., 197.

64. The estimate as to weight was provided by Karl Netsch, blacksmith, based on the area covered by iron armor two millimeters thick.

65. Connolly, 58.

66. Ibid.

67. Ibid., 230.

68. Ibid., 231.

69. Gabriel and Metz, 57.

70. Yadin, vol. 1, 41.

71. O'Connell, 34–35.

72. Ibid., 45.

73. Ibid., 38.

74. Yadin, vol. 6.

75. Gabriel, *The Culture of War*.

76. Christoper Duffy, *The Military Experience of the Age of Reason* (New York: Atheneum, 1988), 207–09 for an analysis of the accuracy rates of the early musket.

77. Gabriel and Metz, 71.

78. Ibid.

79. Ibid.

80. Ibid.

81. The definitive work on the sling is Manfred Korfmann, "The Sling as a Weapon," *Scientific American* 229, no. 4 (October 1973): 34–42.

82. Ibid.

83. Watson, 60.

84. For a history of psychiatric breakdown in battle see Richard A. Gabriel, *No More Heroes: Madness and Psychiatry in War* (New York: Hill and Wang, 1987).

85. The data presented here are taken from Laffont, 101.

86. For a serious analysis of the problem of determining the size of ancient armies see Delbruck and Engels, cited earlier.

87. Gabriel and Metz, 87.

88. H. Frolich, *Die Militarmedicin Homers* (Stuttgart 1879), 56–60.

89. Peter A. Aldea and William Shaw, "The Evolution of the Surgical Man-

agement of Severe Lower Extremity Trauma," *Clinics in Plastic Surgery* 13, no. 4 (October 1986), 561.

90. Frolich, 58–60.

91. E. Stephen Gurdjian, "The Treatment of Penetrating Wounds of the Brain Sustained in Warfare: A Historical Review," *Journal of Neurosurgery* 39 (February 1974), 165.

92. Aldea and Shaw, 565–66.

93. Ibid., 558.

94. H.M. Frost, *Orthopaedic Biomechanics* (Springfield, Ill.: Charles C. Thomas, 1973), 198.

95. Gabriel and Metz, 97.

96. Aldea and Shaw, 561.

97. Ibid., 568.

98. Robert E. McGrew, *Encyclopedia of Medical History* (New York: McGraw-Hill, 1985), 103.

99. Ibid., 104.

100. Ibid., 103.

101. Engels, 123–26.

102. Ibid., 348.

103. Ibid., 349.

104. Ibid.

105. Ibid.

106. Ibid.

107. Ibid., 352.

108. Ibid., 313.

109. Ibid.

110. Engels, 123–26.

111. Ibid.

112. Marshall, 26–27.

113. Ibid.

114. S. Jarcho, "A Roman Experience with Heat Stroke in 24 B.C.," *Bulletin of the New York Academy of Medicine* 43, no. 8 (August 1967): 767–68.

115. Morris Kerstein and Roger Hubbard, "Heat Related Problems in the Desert: The Environment Can Be the Enemy," *Military Medicine* 149 (December 1984), 650–56.

116. Ibid., 653.

117. Ibid., 654.

118. Ibid.

119. Ibid.

120. Alan Steinman, "Adverse Effects of Heat and Cold on Military Operations," *Military Medicine* 152 (August 1987): 389.

121. P. Byron Vaughn, "Local Cold Injury: Menace to Military Operations," *Military Medicine* 145 (May 1980): 306.

2

The World's First Armies, Sumer and Akkad
3500–2200 B.C.E.

Modern Iraq is the site of ancient Sumer and Akkad, two city-states that produced the most sophisticated armies of the Bronze Age. The Greeks called the area Mesopotamia, literally, "the land between the two rivers," a reference to the Tigris and Euphrates valley. In the Bible, the area is called *Shumer*, the original Sumerian word for the southern part of Iraq, the site of Sumer itself with its capital at the city of Ur. If the river is followed northward from Sumer for about 200 miles, the site of ancient Akkad can be found. From here, in 2300 B.C.E., Sargon the Great launched a campaign of military conquest that united all of Mesopotamia and gave the world its first military dictatorship.

Sumerian civilization is among the oldest urban civilizations on the planet. It was here that man's first attempts at writing emerged to produce ancient cuneiform, a form of writing that began as a means of commercial record-keeping written as wedged strokes on clay tablets. It was in ancient Sumer that the first detailed records of military campaigns appeared, written on clay or carved in stone. No society of the Bronze Age was more advanced in the design and application of military technique than was Sumer, a legacy it sustained for 2,000 years before bequeathing it to the rest of the Near East.

The evidence suggests that humans first settled Lower Mesopotamia in the Neolithic period, and perhaps even earlier. By 5000 B.C.E. the

Sumerians had certainly arrived in the area.[1] The cities of Sumer, first evident in 4000 B.C.E., provide the world's first examples of genuine urban centers of considerable size and complexity. In these early cities, specifically in Eridu and Urak, humans first showed evidence of the high degree of cooperative effort necessary to make urban life possible.[2] Both cities reflected this cooperation in the dikes, walls, irrigation canals, and temples—especially the giant ziggurats, which date from the fourth millennium. An efficient agricultural system made it possible to free large numbers of people from the land, and the cities of ancient Sumer produced social structures comprised largely of freemen who met in concert to govern themselves. Even the great warrior hero, Gilgamesh, had to acquire the permission of the council to wage his wars.[3] These early Sumerian cities were characterized by a high degree of social and economic diversity, which gave rise to artisans, merchants, priests, bureaucrats, road and temple architects, and professional soldiers.[4]

Ancient Sumerian civilization consisted of a mixture of ethnic people, much like the present-day United States. Yet, all of the fourteen city-states of the area shared essentially the same culture. For the most part all Sumerian states had the same political institutions, economic practices, religious beliefs and rituals, gods, legends, administrative language, and general way of life.[5] Not surprisingly they also developed the same military forms. So culturally consistent was Sumerian civilization that when it was conquered by Sargon of Akkad, a Semitic prince from the north, he was not regarded as a foreigner.

A period of great interest for the military historian seeking to trace the evolution of ancient armies is the period from 3000 to 2334 B.C.E., the date that Sargon the Great united all of Sumer into a single state and changed its governmental and military organization. This earlier period was marked by almost constant warfare among the major city-states. For the most part these wars arose from boundary disputes over arable land and water rights, but a number of these states also fought wars against foreign enemies. Among the more common foreign adversaries of the southern Sumerian city-states were the Elamites, the peoples of northern Iran. The conflict between the Sumerians and Elamites probably had its roots in the Neolithic period, when rival clans struggled for control of arable fields. But the first *recorded* instance of war between these two peoples appeared in 2700 B.C.E. when Mebaragesi, the first king on the Sumerian King List, undertook a war against the Elamites and "carried away as spoil the weapons of Elam."[6] This first "Iran-Iraq War" was fought in the same area of modern Basra and the salt marshes that witnessed the recent conflict of 1980–1988.

The almost constant waging of war among the Sumerian city-states for 2,000 years spurred the continuous development of military technology and technique far beyond any similar development found elsewhere in the Near East at this time. The first Sumerian war for which there is detailed evidence occurred between the states of Lagash and Umma in 2525 B.C.E.[7] In this conflict Eannatum of Lagash defeated the king of Umma. The importance of this war to the military historian lies in a commemorative stele that Eannatum erected to celebrate his victory. This stele is called the *Stele of Vultures* for its portrayal of birds of prey and lions tearing at the flesh of the corpses of the dead as they lay on the desert plain. The stele represents the first important pictorial portrayal of war in the Sumerian period.

Written Sumerian records of the battle tell of how Eannatum "hurled the great net [the army] upon them and heaped up piles of their bodies in the plain. . . . The survivors turned to Eannatum, they prostrated themselves, for life they wept."[8] The *Stele of Vultures* portrays the king of Lagash leading an infantry phalanx of armored, helmeted warriors armed with spears, as they trample their enemies underfoot. The king, with a socket-axe in hand, rides a chariot drawn by four *onagers* (wild asses). In a lower panel of the stele Eannatum holds a sickle-sword. The information provided by the stele is priceless and allows us to make some reasonable assumptions about the nature of warfare during this period.[9]

The stele seems to indicate that Sumerian troops fought in phalanx formation organized six files deep with an eight-man front, a formation somewhat similar to that used in Archaic Greece.[10] The Sumerians used both the decimal and sexigesimal system based on multiples of six (they were the first to divide an hour into sixty minutes!) and most probably the organization of the army was based on multiples of 6, 60, 120, etc. The texts of Shurrupak indicate units of 600 "going into battle." Fighting in phalanx requires discipline and training, permitting the conclusion that the soldiers portrayed on the stele were probably professionals. Another indication is the presence of titles associated with military command. Even in times of peace, temple estate employees were organized into groups commanded or supervised by *ugula* (commanders), and *nu.banda* (captains). The Sumerians seemed to have kept the same organization used for corvee labor for use in the military. The word for both laborers and soldiers was *erin*, a word that originally meant yoke or neckstock, perhaps implying the nature of such service! Other explicitly military titles were *shub.lugal* or "king's retainer" and *aga.ush*, which literally means "follower." The *aga.ush* were really *erin* who regularly served as soldiers rather than as laborers in fullfilling their obligations as royal or

temple tenants. Military units were of regular size and were designated by the rank of their commander with a numerical suffix indicating size. Thus *ugala.nam10* meant a unit of ten run by a commander. The typical Neolithic army of men brought together to meet a temporary crisis, as found in Egypt throughout the Old Dynasty period, had been clearly superseded in Sumer by the professional standing army. We know from another source, the Tablets of Shuruppak (2600 B.C.E.), that even at this early date the kings of the city-states provided for the maintenance of 600 to 700 soldiers on a full-time basis. The provision of the military equipment for these soldiers, probably a permanent body guard, was a royal expense.[11] Gone was the practice of each warrior fashioning his own equipment. Soldiers of the king received monthly rations of food and oil as wages from the temple and palace granaries. Important officials also serving as generals in time of war received grants of land and temple estates. The *Stele of Vultures* seems to provide evidence of the world's first standing professional army.

The first historical evidence of soldiers wearing helmets is also provided on the stele. From the bodies of soldiers found in the Death Pits of Ur dating from 2500 B.C.E. we know that these helmets were made of copper and were probably worn with a leather cap underneath.[12] Since bronze manufacturing technology was already known in Sumer at this time, the use of copper to make helmets remains a mystery. Nonetheless, the appearance of the helmet marks the first defensive response to the killing power of an important offensive weapons, the mace. The mace was among man's oldest weapons (at least 6000 B.C.E. at Catal Huyuk) and was, no doubt, the direct descendant of the club. It was an extremely effective weapon against a soldier with no protection for his head. So important was the mace in Sumer and elsewhere that in Egypt it remained the symbol of pharaonic authority until 1700 B.C.E.[13] This development made sense in Egypt, whose armies fought only enemies with no armor or helmets. But in Sumer the presence of a well-crafted helmet indicates a major development in military technology so effective that it drove the mace from the battlefield.

The first representation of the military application of the wheel is depicted on the stele that shows Eannatum riding in a chariot. Interestingly, the Sumerians also invented the wheeled cart, which became the standard vehicle of logistical transport in the Near East until the time of Alexander the Great. The Sumerian invention of the chariot has to be ranked among the major military innovations in history, although its true exploitation as a genuine vehicle of war had to await the Mitanni. The Sumerian chariot was usually a four-wheeled vehicle—although there

are examples of the two-wheeled variety in other records—carried a crew of two, and required four *onagers* to pull it. In truth, however, the Sumerian "chariot" is more accurately called a battle-car since it lacked many of the refinements that later made it an effective fighting vechicle. Sumerians also used "straddle-cars," a cabless platform pulled by *onagers* on which the driver maintained his balance by straddling the car. It is likely that Sumerian chariots of this period were used mainly by high-ranking members of the royal household. A text from Shurrupak notes that the "chief mason of Kish" was having his battle-car repaired in Shurrupak's palace workshop. Another text indicates that the ruler of the state of Umma had an elite unit comprised of sixty vehicles. This is the only evidence we have of the number of battle-cars that could be mustered by one state. But even if each state could field only sixty such vehicles, a powerful ruler such as Lugalzagesi, who controlled all southern Sumer could, by drawing upon his vassal states, field more than 600 battle-cars in a major engagement. The Sumerians can also be credited with inventing the rein ring for use with the chariot to provide the driver some control over the *onagers*.[14] Even so, at this early stage of its development the chariot probably would not have been a major offensive weapon because of its size, weight, and instability. The placement of the axle in the middle or front of the carrying platform made the vehicle heavy and unstable at speed. In all likelihood it was not produced for war in quantity, and its use was limited to high-ranking nobles in the king's household. Later, however, in the hands of the Mitanni, Hyksos, Hittites, Egyptians, and Assyrians it became the primary vehicle of war of the late Bronze and early Iron Age armies.

Sumerian charioteers were armed with javelins and axes, and the absence of the bow in early Sumerian warfare suggests that the chariot was used to deliver shock to opposing infantry formations. In this role the chariot was used as transport for mounted heavy infantry. Still, the Sumerian chariot remained the prototype for Near Eastern armies for almost a thousand years. In the eighteenth century B.C.E. various Mesopotamian states introduced the horse-drawn chariot, a development that greatly increased its military capability. At the same time the appearance of the bit improved maneuverability and control of the animal teams at higher speeds. Over time, the drivers, shield bearers, archers, and spearmen borne into battle by chariots became the elite fighting corps of the ancient world.

The lower palette of the *Stele of Vultures* shows the king holding a sickle-sword, the weapon that became the primary infantry weapon of the Egyptian and biblical armies at a much later date. The version that

appears on the stele was much shorter than the version that evolved later and appears very much akin to an agricultural sickle, which could well have provided the prototype for this weapon. The sickle-sword appears on two other independent renderings of the period, suggesting strongly that it was the Sumerians who invented this important weapon sometime around 2500 B.C.E.

The stele also shows Eannatum's soldiers wearing what appear to be armored cloaks. Each soldier's cloak is secured around the neck and was probably made of cloth or, more probably, thin leather. At various places on the cloak were sewn metal disks with raised centers or spines like the boss on a shield. It is not possible to determine if these disks are made from copper or bronze, but a spined plate of bronze was certainly within the capacity of Sumerian metals technology. Although somewhat primitive in application, the cloak on the stele is the first representation of body armor in history, and whether the disks were made of copper or bronze, they would have afforded good protection against a spear thrust.

Other surviving archaeological sources show additional portrayals of important military innovations appearing for the first time in ancient Sumer. The king of Ur, for example, appears on a carved conch plate armed with a socket axe. The development of the bronze socket axe remains one of Sumer's major military innovations, one that conferred a very significant military advantage on its soldiers.[15] Ancient axe makers had great difficulty in affixing the blade to the shaft with sufficient strength to allow it to remain attached when striking a heavy blow. The use of the cast bronze axe socket, which slipped over the end of the shaft and was affixed with rivets, permitted a much stronger attachment of the blade to the shaft. It is likely that the need for a stronger axe arose in response to the development of some type of body armor that made the cutting axe less effective. In addition, the portrayals of Sumerian axes by 2500 B.C.E. clearly show a change in design. The most significant change was a narrowing of the blade itself to reduce the impact area and bring the blade to more of a point so as to concentrate the force of the blow. This development marks the appearance of the penetrating axe, whose narrow blade and strong socket made it capable of piercing bronze plate armor. The result was the introduction of one of the most devastating weapons of the ancient world, a weapon that remained in use for 2,000 years.

The military technology of the ancient world did not develop in a vacuum. There were, after all, no research and development establishments to invent and test new weapons. In the ancient world military technology arose in response to a perceived practical need arising from battlefield experience. In other countries, such as Egypt for example, that were sealed off from major enemies by geography and culture, there was little need to develop new military technologies. In these countries warfare remained static precisely because there was no outside stimulus to change it or because war itself was not as frequent an occurrence as it was among the Sumerian city-states. Under these conditions the weapons of Egypt remained technologically far behind those in Sumer simply because they were adequate to the military task at hand. There was neither need nor stimulus to develop body armor, helmets, or penetrating axe when one's adversaries did not possess them and when one's own weaponry killed and wounded at a perfectly acceptable rate.

But sophisticated weaponry and tactics require some form of larger social organization and impetus to give them shape and direction. We know very little about the military organization of Sumer in the third millennium B.C.E. We can judge from the Tablets of Shuruppak that the typical Sumerian city-state of this period comprised about 1,800 square miles in area, including its lands and fields. This area could sustain a population of between 30,000 to 35,000 people. The Tablets record a force of between 600 to 700 soldiers serving as the king's bodyguard, the corps of a professional army.[16] But a population of this size could easily support an army of regular and reserve forces of between 4 and 5 thousand men at full mobilization. It is highly likely that some form of military conscription existed, at least during times of emergency, since there was a common practice of using corvee labor to maintain the dikes and build the temples. Perhaps like the Egyptians of the second millennium, this force was also subject to conscripted military service.

Yet the military confrontations of the time may not have required very large armies. Conscript troops would not usually be capable of the training and discipline required of an infantry phalanx fighting in formation. If conscript troops were used, they were likely to have been armed with some other weapon like the simple bow. An adult of average intelligence could be trained to fire this weapon with some effect in a few days. Such marginally trained bowmen could have been trained to fire volleys of arrows from a distance while leaving the close combat to the professionals. There is, however, no surviving evidence to suggest that the Sumerians used the simple bow in their military formations.[17]

One fact contributing strongly to the possibility of some sort of military organization at this early date was that by 2400 B.C.E. the Sumerian kings had largely abandoned their religious functions to the permanent priesthoods while increasing their civic functions greatly.[18] The Sumerian king was, for example, no longer the high priest of the city as he had been from Neolithic times. Moreover, it simply is not reasonable to expect that a people who could organize themselves to tame the Tigris and Euphrates with an elaborate system of dikes, canals, and dams and who could sustain a sophisticated system of irrigation agriculture would, at the same time, have left simply to chance the organization of their military arm, among the most important civic functions of the king. More likely is that the absence of evidence is not the equivalent of the evidence of absence. There is no reasonable way in which ancient Sumer city-states could have waged so much war and developed their military technology without a high degree of military structure to accomplish both.

The period following Eannatum's death was characterized by more war, a situation that led to a relatively even development of weapons technology throughout the city-states of Sumer. Two hundred years after Eannatum's death, King Lugalzagasi of Umma succeeded in establishing his influence over all Sumer, although there is no evidence that he introduced any significant changes. Twenty-four years later the empire of Lugalzagasi was destroyed by the armies of a Semitic prince from the northern city of Akkad, Sargon the Great. Sargon bequeathed to the world the first prototype of the military dictatorship.[19] By force of arms Sargon conquered all of the Sumerian city-states, the entire Tigris-Euphrates valley, and brought into being an empire that stretched from the Taurus Mountains to the Persian Gulf and, perhaps, even to the Mediterranean. He reunited both halves of Mesopotamia for the first time since 4000 B.C.E.[20]

As with most early Sumerian kings, we know little about Sargon the Great. Cuneiform records indicate, however, that he introduced a new concept of royal government by centralizing royal authority in a single monarch. For the first time Akkadian became the language of official inscriptions, a language passed to the rest of the Near East where it remained the *lingua franca* of diplomacy for almost 2,000 years. Sargon consolidated his rule of the Sumerian city states by replacing their rulers with his own governors, or *shakkanakum*, who were usually members of his own clan. In his fifty-year reign Sargon fought no fewer than thirty-four wars.[21] One account suggests that his army numbered 5,400 men, soldiers called *gurush* in Akkadian. If that account is correct, Sargon's army would have been the largest standing army of the period by far.[22] Stationed at his palace at Akkad, these men were professionals "who ate bread before the king." Yet, an army of this size is not as outrageous as it may seem. Unlike leaders of the previous wars between the rival city-states, Sargon created a truly national empire with a large resource base upon which to draw, and which would have required a much larger force than usual to sustain. In this sense Sargon faced the same problem as Alexander was to face. Like Alexander, once the city-states were brought to heel, Sargon would have required them to place some of their military forces at his disposal for wars against the rest. As noted earlier, each of the fourteen major city-states of Sumer could have sustained an army of between four and five thousand men with maximum effort, with professionals accounting for about one fifth that number. Yet another source of manpower for Sargon's army was the armies of the conquered non-Sumerian provinces. It was common practice right up to the Greek classical period to enlist the soldiers of conquered states into the imperial armies of the time. The armies of imperial Egypt, Assyria, and Persia all had large contingents of former enemies in their ranks.

That Sargon's army would have been comprised of professionals seems obvious in light of the almost constant state of war that characterized his reign. As in Sumer, military units appear to have been organized on the sexagesimal system. Sargon's army was comprised of nine batallions of 600 men each, each commanded by a *gir.nita* or colonel. Other ranks of officer included the *pa.pa/sha khattim*, literally "he of two staffs of office," a title which indicated that this officer commanded two or more units of sixty. Below this rank were the *nu.banda* and *ugala*, ranks unchanged since Sumerian times. Even if they had begun as conscripts, within a short time Sargon's soldiers would have become battle-experienced veterans. Equipping an army of this size would have required a high degree of military organization to run the weapons and logistics functions, to say nothing of routine administration that was characteristic of a people who could write and routinely kept prodigious records. But we know nothing definitive about these arrangements.

An Akkadian innovation introduced by Sargon was the *niskum*, a class of soldiers probably equivalent to the old *aga-ush lugai* or "royal soldiers." The *niskum* held plots of land by favor of the king and received allotments of fish and salt every three months. The idea, of course, was to create a corps of loyal semiprofessionals much along the later model of Republican Rome. Thutmose I of Egypt, too, introduced this system as a way of producing a caste of families who held their land as long as they continued to provide a son for the officer corps. The Akkadian system worked to provide significant numbers of loyal trained soldiers who could be used in war or to surpress local revolts. Along with the professionals, militia, and these royal soldiers, the army of Sargon contained light troops or skirmishers called *nim*-soldiers. *Nim* literally means "flies," a name that suggests the employment of these troops in spread formation accompanied by rapid movement.

During the Sargon period the Sumerians/Akkadians contributed yet another major innovation in weaponry, the composite bow. The introduction of this lethal and revolutionary weapon may have occurred during the reign of Naram Sin (2254–2218 B.C.E.), Sargon's grandson. Like his grandfather, Naram Sin fought continuous wars of conquest against foreign enemies. His victory over Lullubi is commemorated in a rock sculpture that shows Naram Sin armed with a composite bow. This sculpture marks the first appearance of the composite bow in history, and strongly suggests that it was of Sumerian/Akkadian origin.[23] The fact that the bow appears in the hand of the warrior king himself suggests that it was a major weapon of the time, even though there is no surviving evidence that the Sumerian army had previously used even the simple bow.

The composite bow was a major military innovation. While the simple bow could kill at ranges from 50 to 100 yards, it would not penetrate even simple leather armor at these ranges. The composite bow, with a pull of at least twice that of the simple bow, could easily penetrate leather armor and, perhaps, even the early prototypes of bronze armor that were emerging at this time. In the hands of even untrained peasant conscripts, the composite bow could bring the enemy under a hail of arrows from twice the distance of the simple bow. So important was this weapon that it became a basic implement of war of all armies of the Near East for the next 1,500 years.

In another development, the use of battle-cars seems to have declined considerably during the Akkadian period. Any number of reasons suggests themselves. Such vehicles were very expensive. In Sumer, a powerful king could commandere the cars of his vassals, which they maintained at their expense. But with the centralization of political authority under Sargon, these vassals disappeared, making the cost of these cars a royal expense. The professionalization of the army resulted in an infantry-heavy force which, under most circumstances, would have required few battle cars beyond those needed to transport the king and his generals. Finally, the Akkadian kings fought wars far from home in the mountains of Elam or against the Guti further north. These were lightly armed, highly mobile enemies fighting in mountains and heavily wooded glens. The chariot had come into being to fight wars between rival city-states on relatively even terrain. Their use in rough terrain at considerable distances from home probably revealed the battle-car's obvious deficiencies under these conditions, leading to a decline in its military usefulness. Still, they seem to have remained in use by couriers and messengers, at least within the imperial borders where they traveled regular routes known as "chariot roads."

The armies of Sumer and Akkad, the world's first armies for which we have any evidence, quickly developed into the most advanced military structures of the early Bronze Age. No army of the same period in history could match them in weaponry or military effectiveness. The civilization of Sumer produced no fewer than six major new weapons and defensive systems, all of which set the standard for other armies of the Bronze and Iron ages. For 2,000 years after Sumer was dust, its weapons continued to be employed by all the major armies of the Near East.

NOTES

1. For an excellent account of the settlement of Sumer see Hans Nissen, *The Early History of the Ancient Near East* (Chicago: University of Chicago Press, 1988), chaps. 2,3.

2. Georges Roux, *Ancient Iraq* (New York: Penguin, 1986), 457.

3. *Encyclopedia Britannica*, 15th ed., s.v. "Sumerian Civilization."

4. Robert L. O'Connell, *Of Arms and Men* (New York: Oxford University Press, 1989), 35.

5. *Encyclopedia Britannica*, 15th ed., s.v. "Sumerian Civilization."

6. Roux, 86.

7. Ibid., 135.

8. O'Connell, 35.

9. Roux, 137.

10. Yigael Yadin, *The Art of Warfare in Biblical Lands in Light of Archaeological Discovery* (New York: McGraw-Hill, 1963), vol. 1, 135–36.

11. O'Connell, 36–37.

12. Roux, 129.

13. Yadin, 49.

14. Ibid., 41. See also Marshall B. Davidson, *Lost Worlds* (New York: American Heritage, 1962), 131.

15. Ibid., 131.

16. Ibid., 137.

17. Roux, 129.

18. O'Connell, 38–39.

19. Roux, 133.

20. Gwynne Dyer, *War* (New York: Crown, 1985), 97.

21. Roux, 140.

22. O'Connell, 38.

23. Dyer, 21.

3

The Armies of the Pharaohs
3200–1000 B.C.E.

Human settlement in Egypt began very early. Climate and geographical conditions were highly favorable to the rapid development of a large-scale agricultural society. The 678-mile long Nile deposits tons of fertile silt during the annual floods along a broad swath of land ending in a huge fertile delta in the north. The soil is rich, and even simple stone tools could produce enough food to support as many as 450 people per square mile.[1] Estimates suggest that as early as 3000 B.C.E. Egypt had a population of almost 1 million.[2] It is interesting that the ease of cultivation made slavery unnecessary in Egypt. Unlike the less fertile states of Mesopotamia, where slavery was used as a means of freeing manpower from the land for war and other tasks, in Egypt the population was comprised largely of tenant farmers and craftsmen.

Egyptian society of 4000 B.C.E. was formed around provincelike entities that the Greeks later called *nomos* ruled by individual *nomarchs* or chiefs. Over time, these nomarchs assembled in loose feudal arrangements into two clusters of kingdoms, Upper and Lower Egypt. In 3200 B.C.E. the king of Upper Egypt, known variously to history as Narmer, Menses, or, probably most correctly, Hor-Aha (the Fighting Hawk), unified the two kingdoms by force into a single Egyptian state.[3] Hor-Aha established the first national irrigation control system and founded the first national Egyptian capital at Memphis. Thus began the reign of the pharaohs of the first dynastic period, which lasted for 700 years.

The kings that followed from 3100 to 2686 B.C.E. expanded the Egyptian state. Successful campaigns were launched against the Nubians to the south and the Libyans to the west. Expeditions were undertaken in the Sinai, and trade was established with the states north of Lebanon and Jordan. During this period a state bureaucracy was brought into existence, writing was introduced as a tool of centralized administration, and political institutions were transformed from a chiefdom into a theocratic state led by a divine pharaoh supported by religious, administrative, and military castes.

The period from 2686 to 2160 B.C.E. was the period of the Old Kingdom, and it was during this time that a definable military organization first emerged. The military organization of this period was shaped by two factors. First, Egypt was protected by formidable natural barriers to her east and west in the form of great deserts. The peoples of these areas, the Sand Peoples of Palestine and the Libyans to the west, were largely nomadic and represented more of a military nuisance than a real threat. Nubia to the south presented a real threat of invasion, but the fortresses and strong points built in 2200 B.C.E. along with the natural barriers presented by the Nile's depth and rapids contained the threat relatively well. To the north the Mediterranean itself presented a barrier to invasion, for shipbuilding had not yet reached the point where ships could be used to transport large numbers of troops across an open sea with any degree of safety. For a period of more than a thousand years Egypt was under no significant military threat from outside her borders. Second, Egypt's political order was fragmented. Although united in a single kingdom, the local nomarchs remained sufficiently powerful to obstruct pharaonic power. The nomarchs maintained their own military forces and often exercised control over strategic trade routes. The situation was not unlike that of feudal Europe, where the high king was dependent upon his ability to control local barons. These two factors combined to shape the structure of the Old Kingdom armies.

The impetus for the army came from the need of the central rulers to defend the state and deal with periodic revolts of the nomarchs. Pharaoh's army probably consisted of a small but regular standing force of several thousand troops organized much in the manner of household guards. Egypt introduced conscription during this time, levying one man in a hundred to service each year. The best of the conscripts went to the regular army, which probably did most of the training of conscripts as well. It was during this period that the first military titles appeared. There were titles of rank indicating "general of recruits" that carried with them the rank of general officer. The standing army was augmented by Nubian auxiliaries in the pay of the king.[4] The great bulk of the army was militia units organized under the command of the local nomarchs. These barons were required to make levies of men available to the pharaoh during times of emergency. In normal times, however, the troops were trained and kept at the local level. The political relationship between the king and the local rulers largely determined if and how many troops could be made available for dealing with national problems. A third element of the army was the large body of conscript troops levied under the system of national conscription that did not go to regular military units. These conscripts received some degree of military training and may have been primarily used to garrison the frontier forts and furnish labor for public works projects. It is unknown how long the term of service for conscript soldiers was, but apparently they remained in service with local militia units for some time after their period of national service was completed.

The structure of the army of the Old Kingdom is unknown, but it is clear that some distinctions were made between regular officer appointments and others. There appear a number of military titles, including those of specialists in desert travel and in frontier and desert warfare, garrison troops, frontier troops, quartermaster officers, and scribes, who seem to have functioned as senior noncommissioned officers.[5] There are also titles that refer to "overseers of arsenals," "overseers of desert blockhouses and royal fortresses," and caravan leaders.[6] The size of the combined army remains a mystery. Weni, a commander in the army of the Sixth Dynasty (2345 B.C.E.) recorded that his army was "many tens of thousands" strong.[7] A string of twenty mud-brick fortresses was built in approximately 2200 B.C.E. to guard the southern approaches to Egypt. Each required up to 3,000 men to garrison. This would suggest an army of at least 60,000 in the frontier force alone.[8] With Egypt's population approaching two million at this time, these force levels could easily have been achieved.

The Egyptian armies of the Middle Kingdom (2040–1786 B.C.E.) became more evidently structurally articulated as Egypt struggled through periods of anarchy and the weakening of centralized authority, leading eventually to its invasion and occupation by the Hyksos in 1720 B.C.E. This period saw a constant tug and pull between the pharaohs and the nomarchs, who still controlled their feudal armies, although the obligation to provide levies to the crown became clearer. The pharaohs retained their standing armies, supported by conscription, and still employed Nubian auxiliaries. A clearer command structure emerged, with the pharaoh acting as field commander on major campaigns and with general officers in charge of safeguarding the frontiers and managing logistics. There were clearer distinctions among junior officer ranks and titles.[9] Titles emerged for such ranks as commanders of shock troops, recruits, instructors, and commanders of retainers, the latter being personal guards of the king. The title of assault troop commander appears for the first time. Progression in junior rank seems to have been to move from command of seven men to a company of sixty men to a command of 100 men.[10]

Expectedly, the administrative mechanisms of the army became more complex with the proliferation of various titles. For the first time there was evidence of a military intelligence service, reflected in the title "Master of the Secrets of the King in the Army."[11] The army seems to have organized troops on the basis of experience and age, as the army of Republican Rome did later. Names appear for units of company and regiment, although the size of these units is not known. Terms for bowmen, garrison troops, police patrols, district officers, and military judges make their appearance. On balance the army of the Middle Kingdom appears more clearly articulated as to its structure than was its predecessor. Still, it is difficult to determine to what extent this difference may be a function of the survivability of records and other evidence rather than anything else.

By 1790 B.C.E. the centralized government of Egypt began to lose ground to the rebellious nomarchs, and the army proved insufficient to bring them to heel. Taking advantage of the disarray, the Hyksos invaded Egypt and established themselves for more than a century as the rulers of Upper Egypt. The name Hyksos is probably a Greek rendering of the Egyptian term *hik-khase*, meaning "chiefdom of a foreign hill country." In the Egyptian idiom this term meant bedouin sheikh.[12] The origins of the Hyksos remain obscure, but it may be that they were the seminomadic peoples of what is now Palestine and Jordan. Of Semitic origin, these peoples were wandering tribes and far below the cultural, economic, and military level of the Egyptians. The Egyptians called them "asiatics," a general term of contempt reserved by the Egyptians for nomadic desert peoples.

One of the more intriguing military mysteries of the Hyksos is, How was it possible for such a people to conquer an advanced culture like the Egyptians? The answer lies in their employment of very sophisticated military technology, technology unknown in Egypt at the time. The Egyptian army of the seventeenth century B.C.E. was an infantry force organized by function into units of bowmen, spearmen, and axemen. By contrast the Hyksos army was an army of mobility and firepower. The centerpiece of the Hyksos force was the horse-drawn chariot, but they also used the composite bow, sword, and penetrating axe. In addition

Hyksos soldiers were equipped with helmets and body armor and carried quivers for their arrows.[13] These weapons conveyed a decisive military advantage, and the Hyksos made short work of the Egyptian army.

Among the more interesting questions concerning the Hyksos is how these people of Palestine who, until that time, had shown no particular form of political or military organization, could have suddenly marshalled their resources on such a scale as to bring down the Egyptian state. In addition, one is at a loss to explain the appearance of the world's most advanced military technology among these relatively unsophisticated people. A possible answer may lie in the fact that the weapons of the Hyksos were the weapons of Sumer and Akkad. One possibility is that this was a time when Mesopotamian clans may have left Sumer because of the civil strife caused by the collapse of the Akkadian empire and foreign invasion. The *Bible* records the movement of one such clan, Abraham and his family, traveling from Ur to Palestine during this time. Any Mesopotamian clan on the move would have armed its young men with the weapons with which it was familiar, that is, the weapons of Mesopotamia. Once settled in Palestine, these clans may have passed the Akkadian military technology on to the local residents, who used it to conquer Egypt.

The Egyptian soldier confronting the Hyksos must have been terrified by these new weapons. While the Egyptians were forced to anchor their positions with exposed infantry formations, they could be killed from a considerable distance by the composite bow, which exceeded the range of their own bows by at least 200 yards. Egyptian formations were immobile while the Hyksos could mount horse-drawn chariot charges from all directions. The psychological impact of the horse on the Egyptian soldiers must have been significant for the horse was unknown in Egypt, so the soldiers had never seen one. The blade axe of the Egyptian soldier was no match for the killing power of the penetrating axe, and without body armor the sickle sword must have taken a heavy toll in close combat. In 1720 B.C.E. the Hyksos established their capital at Avaris (modern Tanis), and in 1674 they captured Memphis. For the next hundred years or so the Hyksos held control of most of Upper Egypt while Lower Egypt remained largely in the hands of the Theban princes.[14]

Over time the Theban princes rebuilt their military strength until, after a series of short but bloody clashes, Ahmose I (1570–1546 B.C.E.) drove the asiatics from Avaris and once again unified the country. Under Amenhotep I (1546–1526 B.C.E.) Egypt began the process of establishing a great empire. Amenhotep pushed Egypt's borders beyond those of the Old Kingdom and established an Egyptian presence in Asia. Thutmose

I (1525–1512 B.C.E.), one of Amenhotep's generals, pacified the south, and his successor, Thutmose II (1512–1504 B.C.E.), consolidated Egyptian power in Palestine to the Syrian border. His successor, Thutmose III (1504–1450 B.C.E.), became Egypt's greatest warrior pharaoh and established the empire far into Asia, exacting tribute from Babylon, Assyria, and the Hittites. In the process Thutmose III created a first-rate professional army through which Egypt reached its pinnacle as a military power.

The wars of liberation and expansion under the Thutmosids brought about profound changes in Egyptian society. For the first time there came into being a truly professional military caste. Military families were given grants of land to hold for as long as they provided a son for the officer corps.[15] The army rid itself of the local militias, reorganized its structure, and became a genuine national force based in conscription. The local militias continued in existence, but the nomachs were reduced in power and lost the ability to withhold military levies from the king. Thutmose III completely revamped Egyptian weapons and tactics. He adopted all the major weapons of the Hyksos—the chariot, composite bow, penetrating axe, sickle-sword, helmets, and armor—and made great improvements in both the physical design of the chariot and the tactical doctrines that governed its use on the battlefield. Thutmose mounted his newly composite bow-equipped archers on chariots and produced the most important military revolution in ground warfare yet seen in Egypt.

The national army was raised by conscription, with the levy being one man in ten instead of the traditional one man in a hundred.[16] The army was centrally trained by professional officers and noncommissioned officers (NCOs). The pharaoh himself stood as commander-in-chief and personally led his troops in battle. The vizier served as minister of war, and there was an army council that served as a general staff. The field army was organized into divisions, each of which was a complete combined-arms corps, including infantry and chariots. These divisions contained approximately 6,500 men, including logistics and support personnel, and each was named after one of the principle gods of Egypt. Later Ramses II organized Egypt and the empire into thirty-four military districts to facilitate conscription, training, and the supply of the army.[17] The administrative structure was also improved, and there were professional schools to train and test officers and scribes in the military arts.

The two major combat arms of the Egyptian army were chariotry and infantry. The chariot corps was organized into squadrons of twenty-five, each commanded by a "charioteer of the residence," equal to a modern company commander. Larger units of 50 and 150 vehicles could be rapidly assembled and employed in concert with other forces.[18] It was common practice to assemble units whose size depended on the nature of the mission and terrain, an example of the modern practice of "tailoring" a unit to specific function. The chariot corps was supported logistically by staffs who recruited and trained horses and by craftsmen whose task it was to repair the machines while the army was in the field. Egyptian divisions also had mobile chariot repair battalions to ensure the operability of the vehicles when the army was on the march. The fact that pharaoh was often portrayed as leading a chariot charge suggests that the chariot forces were the elite striking arm of the field force.

It is wonderfully paradoxical in an age of bronze that the most innovative and destructive weapons of war at this time—the chariot and the composite bow—were made of wood. The Hyksos invasion introduced the chariot to Egypt and by the fifteenth century B.C.E. the Egyptians had modified the vehicle into the finest fighting vehicle in the ancient world. The Egyptian chariot was constructed of a light wooden frame covered by stretched fabric or hide to reduce weight. Two men could easily carry the vehicle over streams and rough terrain. The platform supporting the rider and archer were made of stretched leather thongs covered with hide and fashioned in the shape of a "D." The cab was 1 meter wide, ¾ meter high, and ½ meter deep. Two horses, usually stallions, pulled the vehicle held by a central yoke pole and outer races guided by reins. The Egyptians were the first to move the axle to the far rear of the carrying platform, a development that increased the speed, stability, and maneuverability of the vehicle.[19] Belly bars and leg straps helped steady the riders at high speed. Bow, arrow and spear quivers, and axe were attached to each side for easy access during battle.[20] These weapons suggest that the chariot acquired new tactical functions under the Egyptians. It could now be used to engage the enemy with arrows at long range while closing to deliver shock in massed formations. Once the enemy was engaged at short range, the axes and javelins were brought to bear. After the enemy force was shattered, the chariot could be used in lethal pursuit to kill, primarily with the bow.[21] The Egyptian chariot combined the innovative dimensions of shock, lethality, and mobility, making the weapon the only one in ancient armies that could participate in all phases of the battle with equal killing power.

Egyptian infantry was organized into 50-man platoons commanded by a "leader of fifty." A *Sa*, or company, contained 250 men, five platoons, plus a commander, quartermaster, and scribe, and was identified by the type of weapon it carried. Units were further identified as being comprised of recruits, trained men, or elite shock troops. The next unit in

Figure 3.1
Idealized Egyptian Division of the New Kingdom

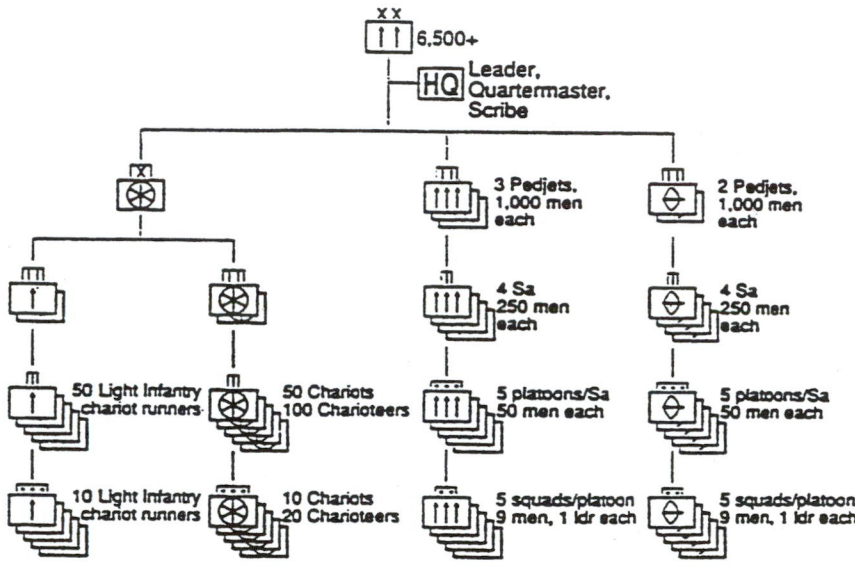

the chain of command was the regiment commanded by a "standard bearer," although we are not certain of the size of this unit. Above regiment was the *Pedjet* or brigade comprised of 1,000 men commanded by a "captain of a troop." This rank was also given to a fortress commander and may have been a general officer rank. A typical Egyptian field division was organized into five *Pedjets*, three heavy infantry brigades, and two archer brigades. The addition of 500 chariots organic to the field division brought the Egyptian division to approximately 5,500 fighting men, with a supporting force of almost a thousand men—technicians, carpenters, quartermasters, scribes, logisticians, intelligence officers, etc.—for a total of 6,500 men. To place the logistical burden of the chariot corps in perspective, one need only consider that 500 chariots require 1,000 horses with 250 in reserve. Mixing hay and grain in equal proportions, 12,500 pounds of fodder was required to feed the animals for a single day! The division was commanded by a royal prince or important retainer, but it is likely that the day-to-day command and operations of the division were in the hands of a senior general called the "lieutenant commander of the army," a system analogous to that used by the German Army between 1860 and 1918. The general structure of an Egyptian division is portrayed in Figure 3.1.[22]

Egyptian infantry regiments were organized into axemen, archers, clubmen, and spearmen. The latter carried shields and six-foot long spears. Their task was to protect against and disrupt hostile charges aimed at the chariot units. Infantry was the true arm of decision in Egyptian tactical thinking, and usually fought in formations five-men deep, with a ten-man front in a fifty-man platoon. These units could quickly form marching columns ten-men wide, providing a degree of flexibility in infantry employment. The roughest and most disciplined of the infantry were the *nakhtu-aa*, or "the strong-arm boys," tough, disciplined shock-troops armed with the bull-hide shield, the *dja* or short spear, the *kopesh*, literally "goat's leg" or sickle sword, the cast bronze penetrating axe, and the *taagsu* or dagger.[23] The division contained special elite infantry units as well. The *kenyt-nesu* or King's Braves appear to have been the Egyptian equivalent of the U.S. Army Rangers, elite special operations units of heavy infantry used especially for overcoming difficult positions. Thutmose III sent these units through the breaches in the walls at Kadesh. Like modern special operations forces, the Braves were comprised of ordinary soldiers who had distinguished themselves in battle. Hardened infantry veterans all, entry was by merit only. Egyptian light infantry was comprised mostly of mobile archer units called *megau*, literally "shooters."[24] Egyptian archers and charioteers carried the same bow, an instrument of Hyksos design constructed of a central wood core with thin strips of horn and leather laminated upon it. The bow was 1.3 meters long, and when drawn to the ear could send a reed shaft fletched arrow with bronze cast arrowhead through an ingot of copper three fingers thick. The bow was powered by a string of twisted gut and was a truly formidable weapon in the hands of a trained soldier.[25] Both archers and spearmen wore textile armor and bronze helmets. Elite infantry and charioteers wore body armor fashioned of thin (2mm) bronze plates sewn in overlapping patterns on a leather jerkin.[26]

The tactics of the Egyptian army were very well developed and supported by strong logistical functions. Ramses II introduced the ox-cart as the basic form of logistical transport of the Egyptian army at the battle of Kadesh in 1296 B.C.E. The use of the ox-cart spread quickly to the other armies of the Near East and remained the basic military logistics vehicle until Philip II replaced it with the horse a thousand years later.[27] Tactical expertise was increased by the presence of a professionally trained officer corps accustomed to maneuvering various types of large units. The Egyptians, by careful and integrated use of field intelligence gathered through patrolling and special collection units (spies, scouts, translators, interrogators, etc.) similar to those found in modern armies, were adept at moving large armies over considerable distances across hostile terrain without being detected. Thutmose III at Megiddo moved an army of more than 20,000 men 300 miles and arrived outside his objective without being detected. In his war against the Mitanni he transported hundreds of raft-like landing craft by wagons over 300 miles to cross the Euphrates and surprise his enemy. Egyptians also used counterintelligence and deception to gain maximum surprise. Prior to the final formulation of battle plans, the Egyptians routinely used the commander's conference, in which senior officers were urged to criticize the plan and give frank advice. The results of these practices were sound battle plans, that permitted Thutmose III to conduct seventeen major campaigns and win them all.

On the battlefield Egyptian forces usually deployed chariot units to act as a screen for infantry and to cover their maneuver during a movement to contact. Engaging the enemy with the long-range composite bow, the chariot archers began killing at a distance as they closed with the enemy. Archer units deployed ahead of the infantry, firing on the enemy as it moved to contact. Once the enemy was close, the archer units retired through the infantry ranks or to the flanks and continued to fire into the main body of enemy formations. The infantry now closed at a dead run to maximize shock, and a general melee resulted. Chariot units engaged the enemy at any exposed point, often dismounting and fighting as infantry once in contact. If the enemy gave ground, chariots in reserve could be committed to exploit the weakness. The mobility of the chariot allowed the use of highly mobile reserves, which could be committed at a propitious moment to turn a flank or exploit a breakthrough. It was a military capability that had never before existed in military history. If the enemy broke and a rout began, the chariot archers could engage in rapid pursuit with devastating effectiveness. If tactical surprise had been achieved, as at Megiddo, chariot units could engage an enemy not yet fully deployed for battle. If something went wrong, as with the battle plan of Ramses II at Kadesh, chariots could be used to rescue a desperate situation.

The Egyptian army lacked only cavalry formations, an innovation that would be introduced 600 years later by the Assyrian army. The failure of the Egyptians to develop cavalry remains curious in light of their knowledge of the horse gained through the Hyksos occupation. It is probable that the horse of that time was simply too small and weak to carry the weight of an armored soldier for very long. In addition, as extensive as the Egyptian empire was, it never included areas of wide grasslands around the Aral Sea, which produced the stronger horses of the later period in sufficient numbers to develop a cavalry force. With the single exception of cavalry, however, the armies of the pharaohs of the Egyptian imperial era were in every respect modern armies capable of conducting military operations in a modern manner and on a modern scale, including the ability to mount seaborne invasions and to use naval forces in conjunction with ground forces for supply and logistics. In its day, the army of imperial Egypt was the largest, best equipped, and most successful fighting force in the world.

NOTES

1. Yigael Yadin, *The Art of Warfare in Biblical Lands in Light of Archaeological Discovery* (New York: McGraw-Hill, 1963), vol. 1, 150–51.

2. Ibid., vol. 2, 313–28.

3. Robert J. Wenke, *Patterns of Prehistory: Man's First Three Million Years* (New York: Oxford University Press, 1980), 468.

4. Leonard Cottrell, *The Warrior Pharaohs* (New York: Dutton, 1969), 51.

5. Ibid., 18–19.

6. The definitive work on military titles in the army of ancient Egypt is by Alan Richard Schulman, *Military Rank, Title, and Organization in the Egyptian New Kingdom* (Berlin: Bruno Hessling Verlag, 1964).

7. Ibid.

8. Ibid.

9. Cottrell, 51.

10. R.O. Faulkner, "Egyptian Military Organization," *Journal of Egyptian Archaeology* 39 (1953): 39. This article remains the best work on the organizational structure of the Egyptian army even at this late date.

11. Ibid.

12. Ibid.

13. Cottrell, 55–56.

14. *The Cambridge Ancient History* (Cambridge: Cambridge University Press, 1973), vol. 2, part 1, 57.

15. Cottrell, 55–56.

16. *Encyclopedia Britannica*, 15th ed., s.v. "History of Egyptian Civilization."

17. See Schulman.

18. Ibid.

19. Yadin, vol. 1, 87–89, for a discussion of the design of the Egyptian chariot.

20. Richard A. Gabriel, *Great Captains of Antiquity* (Westport, Conn.: Greenwood Press, 2000), 28.

21. Richard A. Gabriel and Karen S. Metz, *From Sumer to Rome: The Military Capabilities of Ancient Armies* (New York: Greenwood Press, 1991), 77.

22. Richard A. Gabriel and Donald W. Boose, Jr., *The Great Battles of An-*

tiquity: A Strategic and Tactical Guide to Great Battles That Shaped the Development of War (Westport, Conn.: Greenwood Press, 1994), 49 for Figure 1.

23. Gabriel, *Great Captains of Antiquity*, 26.
24. Ibid., 27.
25. Ibid.
26. Ibid.
27. Faulkner, 41–47.

4

The Hittites and Iron Weapons
1450–1180 B.C.E.

The great empires of the ancient world rarely engaged in war for glory. Their highly literate and organized sociopolitical orders were as sophisticated in designing and executing national defense policy as are the states of the modern world. The notion that wars are fought for personal glory is a much newer idea, beginning with the classical Greeks among whom individuals proved their personal courage on the battlefield. War for glory reemerged during the European Middle Ages, when states were little more than tribal fiefdoms led by warrior clan kings for whom bravery in battle solidified their hold on their clans. In the present age, glory in war is sustained by the need to create and maintain patriotic fervor in modern states whose armies require the broad support of civilian populations to be effective instruments of national policy. War and diplomacy were serious enterprises in the ancient world and the Hittites were among its most serious practitioners.

The Hittites were a polyglot people who occupied the Anatolian peninsula from approximately 1900 to 1000 B.C.E. The origins of this rugged people skilled in mountain warfare remain obscure, but the evidence suggests that their settlement in Anatolia began with the tribal migrations of peoples whose origins lay in the area that stretches from the lower Danube along the north shore of the Black Sea to the northern foothills of the Caucases mountains. The date of migration is uncertain, but may have been as early as 2500 B.C.E. By 1900 B.C.E., however, there is clear evidence of the beginning of a separate society that can be classified as Hittite.[1] By this time there was a clearly defined Hittite governmental structure whose form and linguistic terminology suggest the conclusion that the Hittite state was the creation of an exclusive caste superimposed upon an indigenous population known as Hatti.[2] The Hittite society developed gradually emerging around 1500 B.C.E. into an imperial state with a new governmental structure and military structure that lasted until circa 1100 B.C.E. when, like the other states of Syria, Lebanon, and the Upper Euphrates, it was destroyed by the invasion of the Sea Peoples. Only Egypt survived these invasions when Ramses III defeated the armies of the Sea Peoples in a great land and sea battle on the banks of the Nile.

Archaeological evidence suggests that early Hittite society was essentially a feudal order based on land ownership, fiefdoms, and tenant holdings, and was governed nationally by a council of powerful families in support of a "great king." The king's family and kinsmen, called the Great Family, held the highest offices of the state. Their offices and titles included such positions as chief of the bodyguard, chief of the courtiers, chief of the wine-pourers, chief of the treasurers, chief of the overseers of 1,000, and father of the house.[3] These titles are, of course, formal positions within the palace establishment and convey positions of privilege more than actual functions. However, concurrent with these positions went positions of high military command, the officer corps and general staff of the core professional army. Originally such military and governmental positions had been reserved for the king's blood kin. But as the Hittites expanded their authority over the entire Anatolian peninsula and acquired territories in Syria and the Upper Euphrates, these appointments were made increasingly on the basis of proven competence to men bound by oaths of fealty to the king rather than blood ties. Gradually a governing aristocracy emerged, with its capital at Hattusas in northeast Anatolia.

Social organization remained feudal, however, and centered upon the fiefholder. The average citizen was mostly free of social controls, but could be called to annual corvee labor. Two classes of fiefholders were evident: the liegeman and the "man of the weapon," with the former being the more stable social position. The "man of the weapon" received his land from his lord or king on specific conditions of military service. Interestingly, this did not free him from the additional levy of civilian corvee labor. The soldier's family retained no title to the land in the event of the soldier's death. Instead, the land reverted to the king, who might bestow it upon another family—even a foreign captive—who then became a "man of the weapon."[4] It is not clear if such "weapon men" were true professionals or only semiprofessional militia, but the latter seems more likely.

As noted earlier, the Hittites were a foreign people who imposed themselves on the native peoples of Anatolia by force of arms and maintained themselves in the same manner. This meant that there was a constant tension between the central governing authority and powerful local vassals who often could not be controlled from the center. One result was a constant squabbling and frequent civil war over succession to the throne, involving assassinations, domestic revolts, and other political machinations—sometimes stimulated by Egypt and the Mitanni, Hatti's chief rivals in Syria and the northern Euphrates territories—to keep Hatti weak and penned up behind the mountains. These periods of domestic political instability exposed the country to the predations of its powerful neighbors and tribal incursions, which in turn provoked the rise of powerful kings to restore domestic peace and recover Hatti's lost provinces. This dynamic of ebb and flow produced a country that was only rarely unified and then only for relatively short periods. To the end, it remained a feudal society whose army was comprised of a core of loyal troops of the high king augmented by feudal armies contributed by vassals and foreign client states.[5] Map 4.1 portrays the domestic and foreign threats to the Hittite homeland during the imperial period.[6] The result was a national security problem not dissimilar to those of Germany and Russia in the eighteenth and nineteenth centuries. When weak, Hatti was subject to invasion and civil insurrection. When strong, it continually pressed outward against its neighbors in a search for security and revenge. This cyclical process continued throughout the country's history, brought to an end only by the final invasion of the Sea Peoples in 1180 B.C.E., who destroyed the state.

A significant dimension of these elements affecting Hittite national security was the constant threat they posed to the country's ability to provide itself with sufficient raw materials with which to manufacture weapons of war. From earliest times (circa 2000 B.C.E.), Anatolia had been the source of copper and silver exploited by early Assyrian merchants. With the arrival of the Hittites, these mines continued to produce these valuable metals. By the imperial period, however, there is evidence that these mines were becoming exhausted. Other sources of copper were available at Ergani Maden, but the route to them ran through the land of the Mitanni, Hatti's prime antagonist in Syria. When the Kaska peoples invaded and settled permanently along the Black Sea coast, Hatti's primary source of tin in Bohemia was cut off and never recovered. Tin

Map 4.1
Strategic Threats to the Hittite Homeland

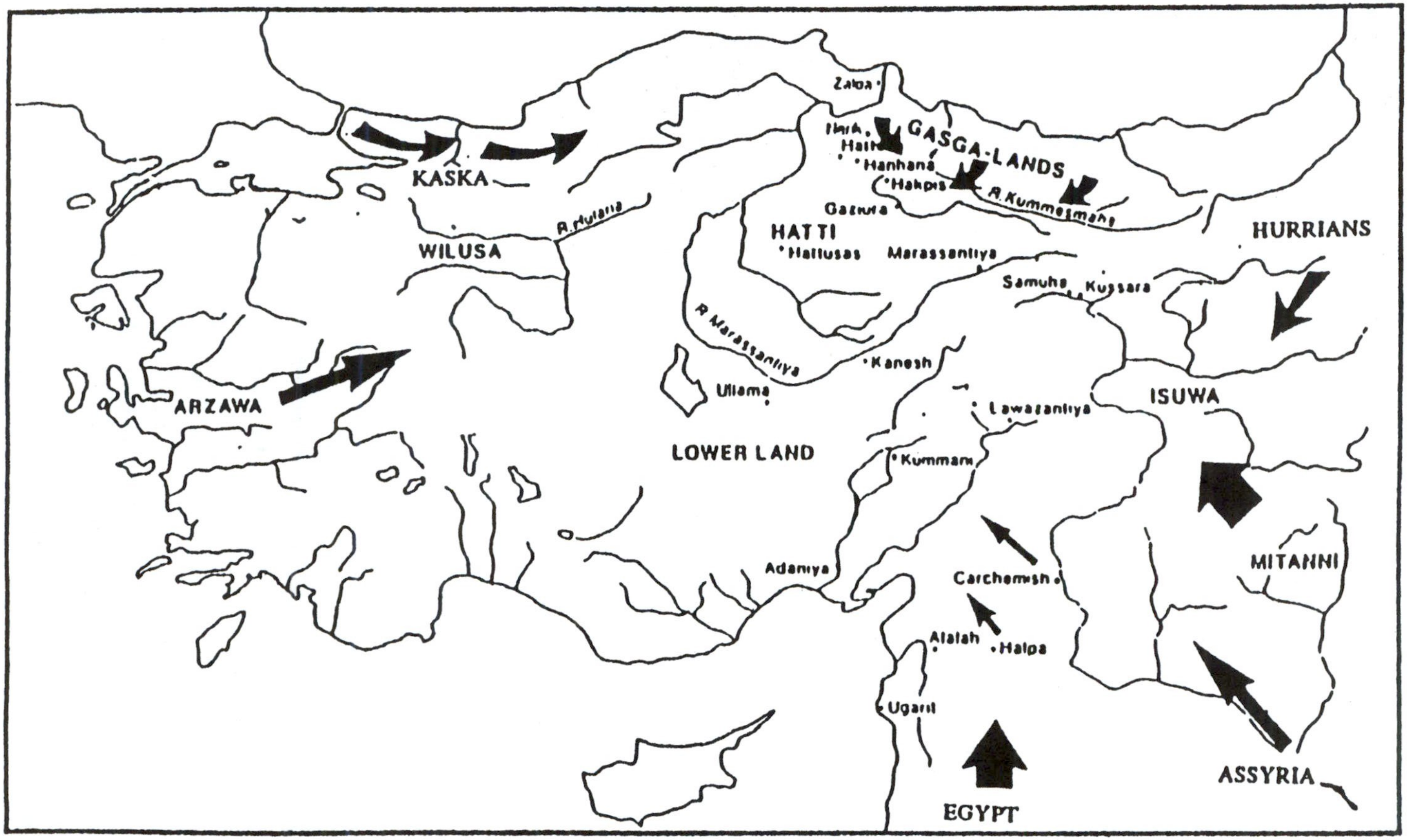

was available in Egypt and Assyria, its primary rivals in Syria and the Euphrates region. Without sufficient supplies of tin and copper, Hatti faced a threat to its ability to produce bronze weapons. This has led some to suggest that the Hittites were the first to exploit their enormous deposits of iron ore to manufacture and equip their army with iron weapons, thus giving birth to the Iron Age.

Were the Hittites the first army in the world to use iron weapons? The evidence is very much mixed. There is little doubt that the peoples of the Anatolian peninsula, probably from the beginning of the second millennium, discovered how to smelt iron, an activity that, in Hatti anyway, seems to have been carried on by skilled peasants during the winter when they could not work the land.[7] The ability to work iron into a useful shape, however, seems to have been confined to a small number of craftsmen, far too small to produce iron weapons on the scale required by the Hittite army. The evidence from archaeology is equally thin, with only a few examples of iron objects of any kind—pins, cups, small statues of gods and animals—that can be traced to the Hittite period with any certainty. In diplomatic texts there is mention of iron swords and dagger blades, but these seem to have been royal gifts to other kings rather than common instruments of war. No storehouses full of iron weapons, like those in Assyria from a later period, have been found nor are any mentioned in Hittite texts. Finally, the size of the Hittite army itself, as distinguished from the coalitions of units provided by vassal states that fought, for example, at Kadesh, seems to have been relatively small, perhaps not exceeding 6,000 men.[8] Hatti had enormous quantities of silver with which she could purchase sufficient supplies of tin and copper. During the imperial period Assyria was a vassal of the Mitanni, who would only have been delighted to supply the Mitanni's main enemy, Hatti, with the precious tin to make bronze. At the same time Hatti seems to have turned to Cyprus, the richest copper mines in the ancient world, for copper. No doubt some iron weapons were produced in small numbers and their use in war was probably restricted to high ranking officers and other nobility. Iron weapons may in fact have been invented by the Hittites, but there is no hard evidence that the Hittite army ever became an "iron army" to any significant degree.

Our best information regarding the Hittite army during the imperial period is derived from an examination of the Egyptian reliefs depicting the famous battle of Kadesh between Ramses II and Muwatallish, king of the Hittites in 1275 B.C.E., which Ramses II caused to be inscribed at Karnak. Hittite sources include their own monuments and the portrayal of the Hittite infantryman at the King's Gate at Hattusas (modern Boghazkoy) the Hittite capital. Although the Hittite army that fought at Kadesh was quite large, numbering between 17,000 and 20,000 men, an important fact about the Hittite army is that it was generally smaller than the armies of the other major states of the period. The army mustered at Kadesh was the largest military force ever assembled by the Hittite kings.[9] The unusual size is explainable by the fact that two successive Hittite kings had been successful in uniting the various vassals of the country and in concluding a number of mutual assistance treaties with the city-states of Syria, who now took the field on the side of the Hatti to weaken the Egyptian influence over them. The Hittite order of battle was dutifully recorded by the Egyptians in their reliefs. Of the 3,500 Hittite chariots, only about 1,500 belonged to the primary Hittite rulers, with only 500 attributed to Muwatallish's army.[10] Similarly, less than 25 percent of the infantry came from Muwatallish's army and other Hittite kings. The rest was provided by allies.[11] Egypt, by contrast, fielded between 25,000 and 30,000 men, but this was by no means a maximum effort by the Egyptians. In absolute terms, Egypt could easily put triple that number of men in the field if required by national emergency. Assyria, too, although somewhat later, could deploy 50,000-man field armies on a regular basis. Only the Mitanni of the other great powers deployed forces comparable in size to the Hittite armies and they, too, relied heavily upon allied contingents for maximum national efforts.

The Hittite army was organized around the decimal system common to the armies of the Near East at this time. Infantry, chariots, and archers all shared the same organizational structure, with squads of ten, companies of ten squads, and battalions of ten companies. Infantry deployed for battle in companies ten-men wide and ten-deep, with heavier battalions standing with 100-man fronts and ten-men deep. The heart of Hittite infantry was the massive phalanx formation of spearmen augmented by archers and light infantry. Although occasionally the Hittites seem to have used messengers mounted on horseback, there was no cavalry in the Hittite army of the imperial period. Special units of light infantry armed with bows—the *"troops of Sutu"*—were used for maneuvers requiring swift movement, perhaps ambush and reconnaissance. The baggage trains as portrayed in the Egyptian reliefs show the usual heavy wooden four-wheeled carts drawn by bullocks common to the area at this time. The organizational structure of the Hittite army is portrayed in Figure 4.1.[12]

Hittite infantry was somewhat more flexible in armament, equipment, and tactical deployment than Egyptian infantry. The Hittites had developed their infantry in the rough, mountainous, and wooded terrain of

Figure 4.1
Organizational Structure of the Hittite Army at Kadesh

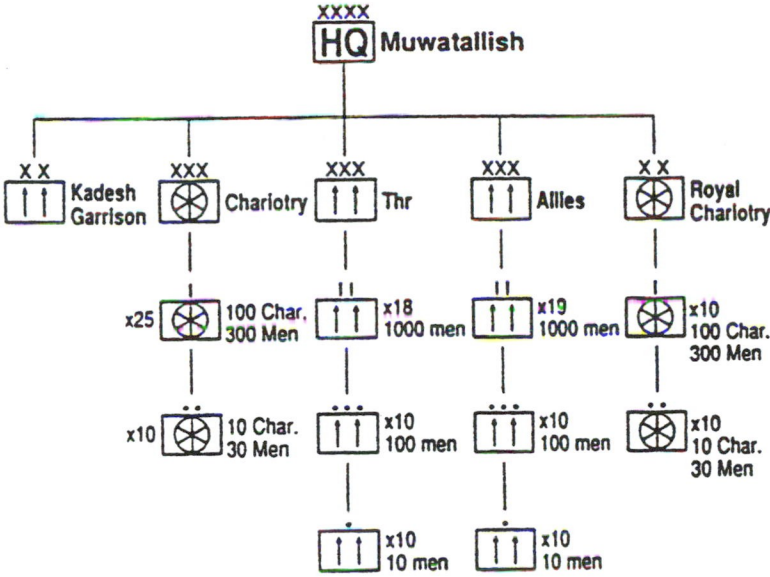

Anatolia, where the rugged ground placed a decided premium upon infantry that could be used in a variety of ways. Hittite commanders commonly changed the mix of infantry weaponry, clothing, and armor depending upon the nature of the terrain and the type of battle that the infantry was expected to fight. In mountain fighting Hittite infantry was equipped with sickle-sword, dagger, battleaxe, but no spear, a mix of weapons suited primarily to close combat. Mountain infantry were issued bronze helmets with ear pieces, cheek guards, a plume, and a hinged neck piece that protected the back of the neck, good boots, and leather or scale armor. A specially designed shield in the form of a figure-eight was also used. The narrow waist of the shield made it lighter while still affording good full-length body protection. The narrow waist also improved the ability of the soldier to see his adversary and provided the Hittite soldier with greater room to wield his sword or dagger when in close order battle. Later, the Hittites adopted the small round shield introduced by the Sea Peoples, a piece of equipment specifically designed for close combat.[13]

The infantry weapons and equipment described above were changed whenever Hittite infantry was required to fight in open terrain or in static defense. Muwatallish's infantry at Kadesh, for example, is portrayed in the Egyptian reliefs as wearing white robes and deployed in defense of the city walls. In open terrain the infantry's primary weapon was the long stabbing spear, and the fighting formation was the packed heavy phalanx. Archers deployed in company units armed with the long-range composite bow. One might surmise that Hittite infantry units, when deployed in open terrain, may have been somewhat more maneuverable than most infantry of the period. The core of the Hittite army, as we have seen, was comprised of skilled professional warriors augmented by "men of the weapon," whose skills surely reached the level of at least semiprofessional status. Training or suppressing revolts within the hostile terrain of Anatolia itself, a common occurrence for Hittite kings, likely placed a premium on stealth, rapid movement, movement at night, and quick deployment from line of march to fighting formation to avoid ambush. These abilities are the characteristics of a professional army or at least an army of semiprofessional soldiers perhaps similar in experience and ability to the feudal military classes of Europe during the Middle Ages.

The chariot probably made its appearance in the Hittite army sometime near the end of the Old Kingdom, or about the sixteenth century B.C.E. The evidence for its use before then is sparse, a single text noting the presence of eighty chariots in a single battle. The Hittites almost certainly acquired the battle chariot from the Mitanni. The archives of Boghazkoy provide us with the famous training manual of one Kikkuli of the land of the Mitannni, an expert in the training and breeding of horses, who came to the land of the Hittites and taught them how to breed and use horses in war.[14] It is unlikely that the Hittites would have employed this Mitannnian horse trainer if they were already knowledgeable about horses and the chariot. By the time of Suppiluliumas (circa 1375 B.C.E.) the chariot had become the most important arm of the Hittite army, its arm of decision.

The Hittite chariot was very different from the Egyptian vehicle of the same period, a result of the differences in tactical doctrine. The Egyptian army's arm of decision was its infantry, deployed in solid phalanx. The role of chariotry was to deliver shock, firepower, speed, mobility, and lethal pursuit. To accomplish these missions required a light vehicle, with its axle in the rear making it stable at speed and in turns. The Egyptian chariot carried a two-man crew, a driver, and an archer armed with the composite bow. Quivers of three-foot long javelins designed to be thrown were strapped to each side. With the driver also carrying a shield to provide protection for the archer, the Egyptian chariot was essentially a mobile firing platform.

By contrast, the Hittite tactical doctrine made its chariots the primary arm of decision, with the infantry playing a secondary role often as a platform of maneuver. The role of the Hittite chariot was to close rapidly with enemy infantry, delivering maximum shock to their formations in open terrain using the sheer weight of the vehicle to shatter them.[15] To accomplish this, the Hittite chariot was heavier—made mostly of wood— with strong six-spoked wheels, and its axle positioned in the center of the carrying platform. This arrangement made the vehicle much slower and less stable than the Egyptian chariot, but made it possible for the Hittite chariot to carry a crew of three. The crew was armed with the six-foot stabbing spear, designed not to be thrown but to be used as a lance while mounted and an infantry weapon when dismounted and engaged in close combat. The composite bow was occasionally carried aboard as well, but it never supplanted the stabbing spear as the primary weapon of the charioteer. Only one of the crew, the spearman, wore armor, usually metal scale, while the driver and the shield bearer were unarmored or, more probably, wore only upper body armor but no helmets. The shield bearer carried a smaller version of the figure-eight infantry shield, which allowed him to move it quickly to intercept enemy arrows or spear thrusts. The Hittites used their chariots as mounted heavy infantry, and they were the key to the success of the Hittite army fighting in open terrain.

One can more easily understand the role of Hittite chariotry by remembering that the Hittite art of war developed in the inhospitable terrain of the Anatolian plateau, which afforded few open plains where chariots could maneuver rapidly or over wide areas. The terrain of Anatolia presented a different tactical problem from that afforded by the open plains and deserts of Egypt or Syria. The rugged mountains, forests, glens, and defiles of the Hittite homeland offered great opportunity for a hidden army to strike an unsuspecting enemy. Under these conditions of short distances to combat closure, even a heavy machine could move fast enough to inflict sudden and decisive shock.[16] Whereas the open terrain of Egypt and Syria encouraged a tactical emphasis on speed of movement over expanses of open ground, the Hittite experience emphasized tactical surprise above all. It was typical of Hittite tactics to attempt to catch the enemy on the march and ambush him with a sudden rush of infantry-carrying chariots and to be upon him before he could deploy to meet the attack. At Kadesh, Muwatallish employed this tactic brilliantly and almost destroyed the Egyptian army.

From the time of Thutmose III, the Hittites played a critical role in the power politics of the Near East, first becoming the primary threat to the Mitanni, then to the Egyptians, and finally the blocking force to Assyrian expansion in the eleventh century B.C.E. until its destruction as an imperial state at the hands of the Sea Peoples around 1180 B.C.E. Egyptian records tell how in the reign of Ramses III "the foreign countries made a conspiracy in their lands . . . no land could stand before their aims."[17] All the states of Syria were overwhelmed by the invasion. Clay tablets found at Ugarit tell the story of the Hittite king, Suppiluliumas II, defeating the Sea Peoples in a naval battle near Cyprus. But within a few decades Assyrian records tell of an encounter between the Assyrian king Tiglathpileser I and hordes of Kaska and Mushki peoples far to the east, around the upper Tigris. If, as is believed, the Mushki are the Mysians who, according to Greek legend, had crossed from Greece into Macedonia about this time, the time of the Trojan War, then perhaps what happened to the Hittites was that they were overwhelmed by a coalition of their old foes, the Kaska, in alliance with the vigorous Sea Peoples who invaded and ravaged most of the Near East at this time. Only Egypt, its army ready and brave in war, avoided destruction.

NOTES

1. O.R. Gurney, *The Hittites* (London: Penguin Books, 1952), chap. 1.
2. Ibid., 55.
3. Ibid., 54.
4. Ibid., 84.
5. Richard A. Gabriel, "The Battle of Kadesh," *U.S. Army War College Ancient Battle Series* (Carlisle, Pa.: U.S. Army War College, 1991), 3.
6. Ibid.
7. Gurney, 67.
8. Mark Healy, *Qadesh: Clash of the Warrior Kings* (London: Osprey, 1993), 22 for the Hittite order of battle at Qadesh.
9. Gurney, 87.
10. Healy, 22.
11. Ibid.
12. Richard A. Gabriel, *Great Battles of Antiquity* (Westport, Conn.: Greenwood Press, 1994), 72.
13. The famous relief of a Hittite warrior that appears on the King's Gate of the Hittite capital is equipped in this manner.
14. Gurney, 86–87.
15. Healy, 24.
16. Gabriel, *U.S. Army War College Ancient Battle Series*, 13.
17. Gurney, 31.

5 _____

The Mitanni and the War Chariot

1480–1335 B.C.E.

T he people known to history as the Mitanni appeared upon the
stage of history for only a short time, perhaps less than two centuries, before disappearing forever. In that short period the Mitanni became a powerful nation around which swirled the great power
conflicts of the armies of the Near East from the fourteenth to the twelfth
centuries B.C.E. Egypt, Assyria, and the Hittites were all at one time or
another allies or enemies of the Mitanni, for her geographic position
astride the main trade, transportation, and communication routes of Anatolia, Mesopotamia, and Egypt forced her to play the role of balancer
among the great powers to preserve her own security. The Mitanni occupied the area of the northern Euphrates plain, the steppe between the
Euphrates and Tigris, an area the Assyrians called Hanigalbat, a term
that became synonymous for the Mitanni (Map 5.1). Its capital, Was-
hukkanni, lay at the head of the Khabur River. From here Mitanni power
spread eastward over the east Tigris region and Assyria, where she reduced the country to vassalage. All the Assyrian kings between 1500 to
1360 B.C.E. were vassals of the Mitanni,[1] and there is evidence of Mitannian military units stationed in Assyria at this time. To the north,
Mitanni power held sway in the ancient land of the Urartu, modern Armenia.[2] In the northwest the borders of Mitanni influence touched upon
Anatolia, the land of the powerful Hittites, and for more than two centuries constant tension and frequent wars marked the relations between

Map 5.1
The Mitanni and Her Neighbors, c. 1380 B.C.E.

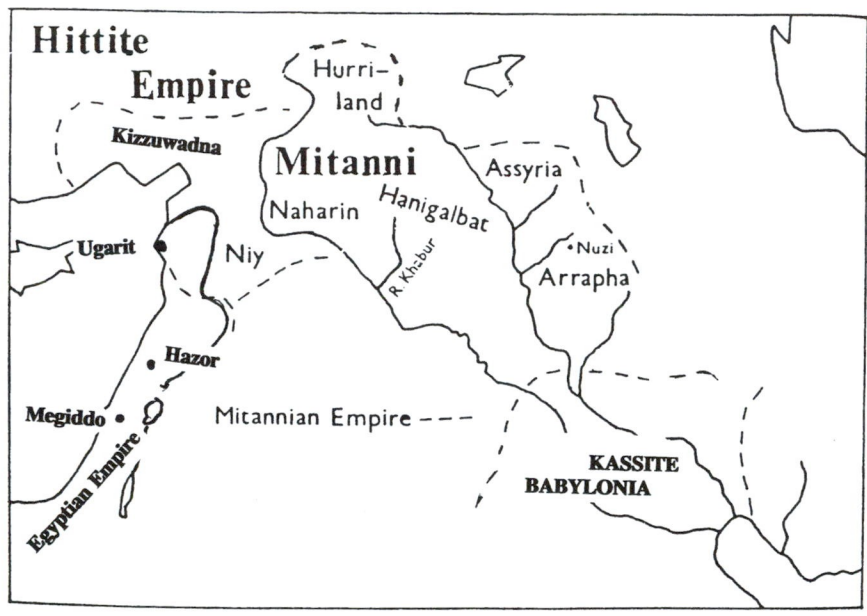

the two nations. Northern Syria to the west marked the point where Mitannian power rubbed against the northern frontiers of the Egyptian empire, where at one point Mitanni power ran to the Litani River and the city of Megiddo.[3] For more than two centuries northern Syria was the cockpit of great power politics, the place where the influence of three powerful states—the Hittites, Egypt, and the Mitanni—touched each other and rubbed each other raw. And the Mitanni were caught in the middle.

With few natural boundaries to protect her, with the routes to her sources of strategic metals and materials terminating in hostile territory, and surrounded by hostile powers, it is hardly surprising that, like their Hittite and Egyptian adversaries, the Mitanni became skilled at war. For two centuries the Mitanni kept Assyria under her heel, stationing troops throughout Assyria itself to guarantee its loyalty. Early on in the seventeenth century the Mitanni invaded the land of the Hittites and inflicted a major defeat. From that time forward the Mitanni consistently intervened in Hittite domestic politics, provoking civil wars among Hittite vassals and aiding foreign tribal peoples in their conflicts with Hittite rulers. The Mitanni forged alliances with powerful vassals along the borders of the Hittite homeland to keep Hittite power contained beyond the

Taurus range and the Cilician Gates by a ring of buffer states. In Syria proper Mitannian diplomacy aimed at establishing alliances with powerful city states like Ugarit and Carchemish, whose own rulers saw these alliances as a counterweight to Egyptian influence there. It was just such a Mitanni-inspired coalition that sought to block Egyptian influence at the battle of Megiddo. Thutmose III's policy of expanding Egyptian power to the Orontes succeeded in pushing the Mitannni back across the Litani, but over the next century a rough parity between Egyptian and Mitanni influence in Syria developed so that during the reigns of Thutmose IV and Amenhotep II, a mutual assistance treaty between the two nations was signed directed at containing Hittite ambitions in northern Syria. With the ascent of the religious fanatic Akhenaten to the Egyptian throne Egypt turned its attention elsewhere, with the result that Egypt proved a weak reed in upholding her military obligations under the treaty. With Egypt on the sidelines, the Hittites saw their chance to drive the Mitanni from Syria.

It was at this time that a vigorous king, Suppiluliumas I (1375–1335 B.C.E.), came to the Hittite throne determined to reduce the influence of the Mitanni and to establish a strong Hittite presence in Syria. For the first few years of his reign, Suppiluliumas was occupied with putting down local insurrections within Anatolia itself. Some of these rebellions were aided and abetted by the Mitanni, at least in the Hittite view. This done, the young king attempted a frontal assault by force of arms against the Mitanni, only to be pushed back. In a letter to the Egyptian pharaoh, Tushrata, the Mitannian king, tells of his great victory over the Hittites. In fact, however, historians now think that Suppiluliumas's attack was probably nothing but a reconnaissance in force designed to test the strength of the Mitanni's will to respond. Suppiluliumas spent the next two years forging an alliance with the important border state of Kizzuwadna in which the Cilician Gates, the most logical avenue of Hittite invasion into Syria, were located. This political turn of events did not go unnoticed by the Mitanni, who considered the alliance nothing less than a *causus belli*. Now that Suppiluliumas had the Mitanni's attention focused upon Syria, he struck at them from an entirely different direction.

Sometime shortly after 1370 B.C.E., Suppiluliumas launched a bold, sweeping attack into the Armenian highland, turned south, and descended upon the broad plains of Mesopotamia directly behind the Mitanni capital. Tushrata, his attention and much of his army focused on Syria, was taken completely by surprise and was forced to flee, abandoning the capital to Suppiluliumas. The Hittite king resisted the temptation to pursue turning west instead and crossing the Euphrates to gain access to northern Syria from behind. There he defeated the Syrian kings who were Mitanni vassals and took the important fortress towns of Carchemish and Aleppo. His back secure, Suppiluliumas turned his army south and marched along the Orontes River toward the mouth of the Bekka, where he destroyed Qatna. At Kadesh the crown prince attempted an ambush, but was defeated and deported to Anatolia. The expedition finally came to a halt in southern Lebanon after having brought Damascus to heel. Ever the brilliant strategist, Suppiluliumas recognized that any further movement south would likely provoke an Egyptian reaction.[4] In one bold stroke Suppiluliumas had reversed a century of Mitannian gains. The Mitanni were deprived of all their possessions west of the Euphrates and would never again threaten Hittite influence in Syria. The Syrian princelings acknowledged the shift in power and moved closer to the Hittites at Egyptian expense.

Over the next decade things went from bad to worse for the Mitanni. Although their power had been reduced in northern Syria, they remained a force to be reckoned with, and the Hittites and Assyrians began to maneuver to further reduce Mitannian influence. The Mitanni fell into a civil war among rival claimants to the throne. Tushrata had come to power by murdering his brother. Several members of the royal family, no doubt spurred on by the catastrophe Tushrata had brought about at the hands of the Hittites, called Tushrata's claim to the throne into question. His brother, Aratama, and some loyal vassals established a rival government in one of the larger fiefs, and Aratama declared himself King of the Hurri.[5] Not blind to the opportunity, the Hittites and Assyrians moved closer to the pretender as a way of weakening the Mitanni regime. In 1360 B.C.E. Tushrata was assassinated by his son, and the Assyrians, in alliance with the Alashe, moved against the Mitanni in the upper Tigris valley. History records that they "divided the land of the Mitanni between themselves."[6] And so it was that without having to fight a single battle, Ashur-uballit I of Assyria freed his country from Mitannian domination, which had lasted for almost two centuries. What was left of the Mitanni kingdom formed itself into a small state called Hanigalbat, from where it continued to play only a minor role in Near East politics until 1345 B.C.E. when the Assyrians moved north again, this time erasing all traces of the Mitanni kingdom. In that same year Suppiluliumas led a Hittite army into Syria in a demonstration of force to bring the city-states firmly into the Hittite orbit. When the great Hittite king died in 1345, all of Syria up to Damascus was in Hittite hands and the once powerful Mitanni kingdom had disappeared forever.

The origins of the Mitanni are uncertain but seem closely related to the history of the Hurrians, about whom we know only slightly more. The Hurrians are first mentioned in the Amarna texts and again in the Bible (*Genesis* 36: 20–30), where they are called *Horites*. The Hurrian language is neither Semitic nor Indo-European, but seems vaguely related to the Asianic group whose nearest relative is the language of the Urartu. It is likely, then, that the highlands of Armenia are the original homeland of the Hurrians.[7] The Hurrians appear to have been a people given to migration or clan travel, and there is evidence that colonies of Hurrians had been extant in various parts of Mesopotamia for millennia. There is, for example, sufficient evidence for a Hurrian element in ancient Sumer before 2000 B.C.E., and during the Akkadian period that followed there appears to have been a strong Hurrian community in the area of the Upper Tigris from which, we may reasonably surmise, they migrated into the Fertile Crescent proper.[8] By 1800 B.C.E. the Hurrians comprised a majority in the Syrian town of Alalah, between Aleppo and Antioch, and a century or so later they were a majority in northern Iraq itself. During this time they occupied the city of Gasur, changed its name to Nuzi, and adopted the language and customs of the former Semitic community there.[9] After 1600 B.C.E. the Hurrian element became dominant in northern Syria.

Hittite texts dating from the middle of the seventeenth century B.C.E. record a major attack on the Hittite homeland by a people called the Hurri, but the text suggests that they were not yet a unified people established in a single homeland but a confederation of peoples organized along clan lines. It is probably around this time that a warrior caste of Aryan (Indo-Iranian) dynasts came to impose themselves upon the Hurrian people and become a new aristocracy in command of war and government.[10] By 1550 B.C.E. Hittite texts reported that a major Hurrian-based kingdom known now as the Mitanni had come into being east of the Euphrates. Other smaller Hurrian states were extant in northern Syria at the same time. It is at this time that the Mitanni established their dominance over Assyria and became a major competitor to Hittite and Egyptian influence in Syria. This powerful Mitanni kingdom was called Hanigalbat by the Assyrians and Naharin (Two Rivers) by the Egyptians.

Just when and how the Hurrians were eclipsed or subsumed under the people who called themselves Mitanni is uncertain. The traditional idea that the Indo-Aryan Mitanni were equipped with the horse chariot, which permitted them a rapid conquest of the area is no longer given much credence, nor is the view that the Mitanni were an Indo-European people of the Russian steppe.[11] That the Mitanni were of Indo-Aryan origin seems probable, however, in light of the fact that several of their famous kings, including Tushrata and Mattiwaza, have names that are linguistically of Indo-Aryan origin. So, too, are the names of their gods. Wherever they came from, there is almost no dispute that by 1500 B.C.E. or so (and perhaps earlier) the Mitanni had imposed themselves as the new leaders of the Hurrian state. The name of the first Mitannian king, Paratarna, appears around 1480 B.C.E., by which time Mitannian influence is already evident as far south as Qatna and Ugarit.

What did the Mitanni bring to the Hurrian society that permitted them to rise to such heights of international power and prestige? Two answers suggest themselves. First, the Mitanni seem to have imposed themselves relatively peacefully and to have generally adopted the culture of the land into which they entered. Their main contribution seems to have been the introduction of a new form of political and social organization that was more effective at mobilizing and employing resources for war.[12] The pattern was a familiar one among Indo-Aryans, namely a strong king drawn from a "great family" tied by blood to his vassals, who acted as a kind of council of advisors. The system also permitted a council of elders and, perhaps, an assembly of free men (warriors) of the tribe who may have acted as advisors and whose consent may have been required for the king to undertake certain tasks.[13] The Mitanni system was not unlike that found earlier among the Hittites, whose origins, like those of the Mitanni, are obscure and involve superimposing a new caste upon the then extant Hatti society.

Second, the Mitanni may have been the first to truly exploit the possibility of the horse as an instrument of war, most particularly by using the horse with the spoked wheel-chariot as a primary combat vehicle. They did not, of course, introduce the horse to Mesopotamia, where it had been known from at least the Sumerian period. The Sumerians called the horse *anshe-kur-ra* or "the ass from foreign countries." During the Akkadian period it was known as *sisu* in Akkadian.[14] It is likely that it was the Hurrians who first used the horse as a draft animal for agricultural purposes, and may even have used the horse in this manner before the migrations. What is clear, however, is that the spoked-wheel war chariot made its first appearance among the Mitanni sometime soon after the Mitanni arrival in the Hurri land, or about circa 1600 B.C.E. Almost simultaneously the war chariot appears in Kassite Babylonia, among the Hittites, the Hyksos, and a short time later among the Egyptians. That the Mitanni claim to first-use of this weapon may be valid can be deduced from the Hittite texts of this time, which recount the story of Kikkuli of the Land of the Mitanni who was hired by the Hittite king to instruct his army in the breeding and use of horses.[15] Saggs (1984) suggests the evidence is sufficient to award the claim of first use, if not outright invention, to the Mitanni.[16] Whatever the case, the appearance of the war chariot as a major weapon of war in the Near East coincided closely with the arrival and emergence of the Mitanni as primary combatants in the former Hurri states. While neither the horse nor the chariot can be attributed to the Mitanni with certainty, it is true that the Mitanni were the inventors and first to use the chariot system, an innovation that changed the face of battle among the armies of the Near East for the next thousand years.

Most of the information concerning the military organization of the Mitanni is derived from two sources. The first and most detailed of these is the famous Nuzi archives. Nuzi was the capital of the province of Arrapha, situated on the eastern fringe of the Mitannian empire and strategically situated between Assyria and Kassite Babylonia. The second source of information is the renderings of Mitanni chariots and troops that appear on the sides of the war chariot of Thutmose IV of Egypt. The political structure of the Mitanni state, noted earlier as probably an innovation of the Mitanni superimposed upon the old Hurrian social order, seems as well to have been imposed upon Mitanni's vassal states, turning them, at least to some extent, into provinces whose governance and military administration were directed from the center. One result was a confusion of names when referring to the Mitanni state. Thus, in the Nuzi archives there are references to "man of the lands" of Hanigalbat, Arrapha, Mitanni, and Naharin, clearly implying that the Mitanni state was a confederacy of powerful subkings linked by fealty and kinship to a central "great king," or else that the Mitanni kingdom was comprised of a central kingdom and a confederacy of foreign vassal states.[17] Most likely the first alternative was obtained. Usually when different names for the Mitanni are found in ancient texts, they are used by different countries and may have been derived from the regions of the Mitanni empire with which the country had most frequent contact. So, for example, the Assyrians called the Mitanni Hanigalbat in their own language while the Kassites of lower Babylonia called them Arrapha. The Hittites called them Mitanni and the Egyptians Naharin. If we are correct in our assumptions, it is likely that the administrative structure of Arrapha described in the Nuzi texts was the same as that found in the other provinces/vassal states of the Mitanni empire.

The administrative structure of the Mitannian province belies a concern for war as well as for government. Each province was divided into districts called *halsu*, each of which possessed a fortified capital and armory. Other smaller towns (*alu*) throughout the district were also walled for defense. The province was administered for the king by a *halsuhlu* or *shakin mati*, a royal governor. Originally these governors would have been kin of the king. Later, however, they were probably replaced by men of competence tied to the king by an oath of fealty. The towns of the district were administered by a *hazannu* or "mayor." The countryside was divided into large estates (*dimati*) worked by tenants (*ashshabu*) and owned by a *bel dimtu* or lord. The warrior ethos of the Mitanni is reflected again in the fact that these estates were comprised of a few villages and a fortified manor house or keep for defense.[18] The mayor or *hazannu* appears to have had military duties as well and was responsible for the security of his district. Whether or not he also served as a field commander is unknown. It is clear, however, that cities, towns, and estates were required to raise militia forces while the larger cities and more strategic border towns were often garrisoned by professional troops of the royal army.

The centerpiece of the Mitanni army was the *nakhushshu* or warrior caste of military professionals bound by an oath of loyalty to the king to serve at his request. This oath was called the *isharu*, literally the "word of the man of arrows," or *ilku*. Soldiers were called *alik ilku* or "those who perform the *ilku* duty." The elite corps of the professional army were the chariot warriors known as *maryannu*. The term itself means "noble chariot warrior" and derives from the Indo-European word related to Sanskrit, *marya*, meaning "youth" or "hero." As one might expect in a country of fortified feudal fiefdoms, the elite chariot warriors held large estates, probably granted by the king in return for military service (not unlike the European feudal system of a later date), and some seem to have possessed a hereditary claim to these estates. There seems to have been more than one grade of *maryannu* status tied to military service, and one suspects that a system of subvassals pledged to the main lord by oaths of military service were sometimes referred to as *maryannu* as well. Over time the term itself seems to have been applied to both chariot and nonchariot warriors and professional and militia troops equally.

The organization of the army remains unclear. We are certain that the king possessed a bodyguard of chariotry known as *shepi sharri*, literally "the feet of the king," consisting of ten chariots. This bodyguard probably originally had its roots in the coterie of the tribal chief's best warriors, who accompanied him into battle. Later, however, it was probably comprised of the country's leading nobles and advisors rather than necessarily the best warriors. Much of the army was comprised of charioteers, known as *alik seri*, or "campaigners." There must also have been a central force of *maryannu* chariotry for we read of such units being sent to four towns to reinforce local garrisons. Infantry units, known as *shukuthlu*, comprised of both spearmen and archers equipped with swords, daggers, leather armor and helmets existed, but we know nothing of their organization or quality except that the *ashshabu* or tenant farmers were permitted to serve in their ranks.

Chariot units or *emanti* of five or ten vehicles were commanded by an officer called an *emanthuhlu*. These units could also be grouped into units based on multiples of six (the old Summerian/Assyrian system) commanded by a "chief *emantuhlu*" who was also responsible for supplying rations to his men. One of these is also described as commanding a garrison, so it is possible that the *emantuhlu* applied to commanders of infantry units as well. Other texts refer to officers called *rab*, with the decimal number of men under their command appearing next to the title. Thus *rab* (5), *rab* (10), *rab* (12), etc., refer to officers in command of units of these sizes. A confusing aspect of the Mitannian military organization is that it appears to have used no consistent numerical system as its base. Thus there are textual references to 3,000 *alik ilki* (perhaps combined units of chariots and archers), 536 charioteers, 82 archers, 55 bowmen, etc. There are references to "tablets of the left," and "brothers of the right," suggesting that the army had right and left wings, but such a conclusion is mostly speculation.[19] Further compounding the organizational problem is the fact that estates, towns, and cities may have been required to raise levies of militia troops at the request of the king. If the feudal period of later Europe is any guide, such numbers became meaningless in a practical sense in that the strength and organization of these militia units for battle were rarely recorded. That the Mitanni army was well-organized can be deduced from the fact that all armor, helmets, and other weapons were manufactured in royal arsenals as state industries and issued to the troops in a systematic manner. When military equipment was worn out or broken, it was turned in to be replaced at royal expense.[20]

With the chariot corps of the army of the Mitanni comprised mostly of nobility and being its arm of decision, it is not surprising that the Nuzi texts provide more information on this branch of the army than any other. The Mitannian chariot was constructed of light wood and hides. One text notes that twelve goatskins were required to cover a chariot frame and between nine and eleven sheepskins to cover the floor, suggesting, albeit roughly, that the Mitannian chariot was somewhat larger and heavier than the Egyptian variety but not as large as the Hittite chariot. Seals depict the Mitanni chariot with wheels of 4, 6, and 8 spokes, suggesting again that at least some Mitannian machines were quite heavy. It was regular practice to oil the spokes to prevent the wheels from warping.[21] A particularly interesting aspect of the Mitanni chariot was that some of them appear to have been armored with metal scales called *sariam*. One inventory mentions a unit of 100 chariots equipped with scale protection, and the depiction of the Mitanni chariots taken from the cab of Thutmose IV's war chariot shows them with armored cabs. A suit of Mitanni body armor consisting of 500 scales weighed approximately 35 pounds. Calculating the area of a Mitanni chariot cab to be almost twice the area required to outfit the human body in scale armor suggests that the armor added the considerable weight of 75–80 pounds to the chariot. It was another Mitanni practice to armor their chariot horses. Often this horse armor consisted of a textile coat of felt or hair about 3 centimeters thick, extending from the withers of the horse to the loins, that was called a *parashshamu*. Equally common was covering this textile coat with a leather, copper, or a bronze scale overcoat. Using the same formula as above, a coat of bronze horse armor would easily have weighed more than 100 pounds. Add to this that the Mitanni chariot warrior was usually equipped with a scale armor suit weighing approximately 35 pounds and a bronze helmet weighing another 12 or so pounds, and the load on the Mitanni chariot becomes considerable, far heavier than the Egyptian machine though not as heavy as the Hittite vehicle.

What this suggests is that the design of the Mitanni machine might have been somewhat of a compromise forced upon it by two factors: (1) the variable terrain in which the machine was required to operate, and (2) the multiple tactical roles it had to play depending upon the capabilities of the enemy chariots (Hittite or Egyptian) it had to engage. The Mitannian empire encompassed a land area of very different types of terrain. To the east where the Assyrian and Kassites had to be dealt with, the ground was flat, open, and grassy, conditions that placed a premium on speed and maneuverability. North and northwest, in Armenia and Annatolia, the terrain was mountainous and forested, conditions that favored the short distance attack from ambush. In northern Syria as well as further south in the Bekka and Lebanon, the terrain was mixed, requiring a machine that could serve either role depending upon circumstances. With each type of terrain came a different enemy whose own chariots reflected their respective tactical doctrines. The Hittite machine, for example, was very heavy, carried a crew of three spearmen, and was designed for short distance shock ambush. The need for the Mitanni chariot to fight in different types of terrain and to perform multiple tactical roles resulted in a machine both heavy and light enough to permit it to perform adequately in all types of terrain but probably not to excel in any one of them.

This, of course, may also have been the reason for the heavy armor worn by both Mitannian charioteers and their horses. This armament and the weapons carried aboard—two composite bows, two quivers of arrows, a shield, and a lance—suggest strongly that the tactical role of the Mitanni chariot was not to close and fight at close quarters as the Hittites did. Both the bow and lance were to be used either from afar, as in a movement to contact, or *en passant* if closely engaged. Firepower and shock, then, were the two tactical roles afforded by a moderately heavy chariot carrying a well-armored charioteer, both of which could be adequately employed against the heavy chariot of the Hittite used as a mounted infantry platform when fighting in uneven terrain. When fighting Egyptian chariots, the Mitanni machine gave their charioteers an equal capability in firepower since both Egyptians and Mitanni were armed with the same composite bow. The Egyptian machine would, of course, hold the advantage in speed and mobility, but the terrain in Syria did not offer many opportunities for battle on flat even plains. The heavier Mitanni vehicle with its far better protected charioteer would offer a greater advantage in delivering shock as well as increasing the survivability of the archer when engaged *en passant* at close range and employed in uneven terrain, where the Egyptian advantage in speed and maneuver could be neutralized by the ground itself. As with any weapon of war, the trick is to employ it properly. In the hands of an able field commander the Mitanni battle chariot afforded considerable advantages against different types of enemies provided one used the vehicle as it was designed to be used, that is, with proper consideration for the terrain upon which the battle was to be fought and the tactical objectives for which the machine was being employed. Some validity may be lent to the above analysis by noting that of all the peoples of the Palestine landbridge, the one whose chariot design was most strongly influenced by the Mitanni design were the Canaanites. An examination of the various types of terrain in which the Canaanites had to fight suggests they chose the Mitanni design for the same reasons the Mitanni had designed it in the first place.

As with so much of our information concerning the Mitanni military, most of our knowledge about the Mitanni charioteer comes from the Nuzi archives. These archives refer to the Mitanni armor as "the armor of Hanigalbat." Scale and lamellar armor appears to have been a Hurrian invention of about the seventeenth century B.C.E. and to have been rapidly adopted by the Mitanni and everyone else in the Near East in a comparatively short time. Evidence for this lies in the fact that all of the terms used for armor by the peoples of the Near East at this time are derived from the Hurrian term *sharyani* or "coat of mail."[22] This term appears in Akkadian as *sariam*, as *saryannni* in Hittite, *shiryon* in Hebrew and Arabic, and *tiryana* in Ugaritic and Egyptian.[23] As described in the Nuzi texts, the armor of the Mitannian charioteer consisted of a mail coat with sleeves and a long skirt covered with individual bronze scale plates called *kursimtu* after the Akkadian, *kursindu*, meaning snake, the analogy with the reptile's scales being obvious. The coat and skirt required almost 1,000 scales to assemble, with the sleeves of the coat alone requiring 200 plates. Two hundred smaller scales sewed over a leather cap served as a *gurpisu* or helmet. Sometimes these helmets had a crest of plaited leather. The most common helmet found among the Mitanni and throughout the Near East was the bronze helmet or *gurpisu siparri*. Sometimes charioteers shaved their heads and wore a linen or leather cap beneath to tighten the fit. The most elaborate helmets were the *gurpisu siparri kursimetu* or great bronze-scale helmet, which offered greater protection than either the leather or sheet bronze models.[24] The charioteer's neck was protected by a high thick bronze collar, a typical feature of the suits of armor of this period. A thick leather belt protected the charioteer's abdomen and helped him bear the weight of the armor. He carried a long dagger in the belt, *patru*, for self-defense should he be forced from his machine.

In contrast to both Hittite and Egyptian practice, the Mitannian chariot driver was equally well equipped, with scale armor and helmet offering the same protection as for the charioteer. In addition, the drivers carried small shields, *aritu*, made of wood and covered sometimes with beaten bronze. Chariot shields seem to have had a double grip, one that could be held in the hand and another consisting of a pair of leather straps through which the driver could slip his arm, permitting him some protection while not interfering with his ability to drive the horses. Chariot horses were prized and expensive military assets, and the Kikulli text (mentioned in the previous chapter) suggests that there was some organized system for acquiring, breeding, and training horses, a surmise supported by the fact that the term for reserve horses, *matru*, has come down to us. Horses began training to the chariot when they were a year old and began pulling chariots by their third year. By their fourth year they became proper chariot horses and usually served until they were nine or ten years old.[25] Cavalry, of course, was unknown, but there is some evidence that certain messengers, *mar shipri*, may have traveled by horseback. The term for horseman was *rakib susi*, suggesting at least that riding horses was not entirely unknown. There is no evidence of horsemen having ever being put to military use, however.

About the infantry, we know next to nothing. That there were infantry units, *shukuthlu*, we can be fairly certain and that there were infantry units of archers and spearmen is reasonably certain as well. Beyond that, we can only say that the infantry was equipped with swords or long dirks for protection and that they wore leather helmets. We have no idea as to how they were employed, but the primary role of the chariot in Mitanni tactical doctrine suggests that the Mitanni may have employed their infantry in a manner similar to that of the Hittites, that is, primarily as a platform of maneuver designed to engage the enemy and fix his position until he could be struck at a vulnerable point by the chariotry. As in other armies of the period, archer units probably provided covering fire for the infantry during its movement to contact and played only a supporting role once the infantry was engaged. Beyond these obvious and general comments, little else is known about Mitanni infantry tactical doctrine.

Although the Mitannian empire was short-lived, Mitanni innovations in warfare were very significant for the future development of warfare. Most important was their introduction, if not invention, of the horse-drawn war chariot and probably the first use of the spoked wheel in war. Mounting an armed man with the composite bow in the chariot gave new flexibility and lethality to a weapon whose impact to this point had been only marginal. The range, mobility, and speed of the chariot wrought a revolution in tactical thinking in the Near East and even shifted the relative power balances among states. One has only to recall, for example, the devastating defeats inflicted upon the Egyptian army by the chariot-equipped Hyksos to appreciate the quantum leap in tactics and lethality that the Mitanni introduction of the war chariot brought about. Within a few short years every major power and even the relatively minor city states of the Near East had reequipped their armed forces with the new chariot weapon, and a new era of mobile warfare dawned upon the armies of the Near East.

NOTES

1. Georges Roux, *Ancient Iraq* (New York: Penguin, 1986), 235.
2. *Cambridge Ancient History*, vol. 2, part 2, 3.
3. See Richard A. Gabriel, *Great Battles of Antiquity* (Westport, Conn.: Greenwood Press, 1994), chap. 2, "Megiddo," for an explanation of Mitanni influence in Syria during the time of Thutmose III.

4. For an excellent account of Suppiluliumas' military campaign see Donald B. Redford, *Akhenaten: The Heretic King* (Princeton, N.J.: Princeton University Press, 1984), 196; see also Roux, 238.

5. This event lends credence to the idea that the Mitanni recognized the priority of the Hurrians as the historically prior settlers in their land.

6. Roux, 238.

7. H.W.F. Saggs, *The Might That Was Assyria* (London: Sidgwick and Jackson, 1984), 38.

8. Roux, 217.

9. Ibid.

10. *Cambridge Ancient History*, vol. 2, part 2, 1.

11. See *Cambridge Ancient History*, vol. 1, part 2, 873; Saggs, 39; Roux, 218.

12. *Cambridge Ancient History*, vol. 1, part 2, 875.

13. Ibid., 874.

14. Roux, 230.

15. O.R. Gurney, *The Hittites* (London: Penguin, 1990), 86.

16. Saggs, 196.

17. Nigel Stillman and Nigel Tallis, *Armies of the Ancient Near East* (Sussex: Flexiprint Ltd., 1984), 24.

18. Ibid.

19. Ibid., 25.

20. Ibid., 139.

21. Ibid., 141.

22. Ibid., 139.

23. Ibid.

24. Ibid., 141.

25. Ibid., 25.

6

The Armies of the Bible
1250–928 B.C.E.

The armies that fought their way into history on the Palestine land-bridge between the thirteenth century and the eighth century B.C.E. occupy an interesting place in military history. Their location here when the Israelites were forging a homeland by force of arms and writing it all down in their great national saga, which Western civilization came to call the Old Testament, ensured that almost everyone at one time or another came to hear of Canaanites, Philistines, and the tales of Joshua, Saul, David, and Solomon, the great generals of the Israelite armies. For more than a millennium our only source of information about these armies was the Old Testament itself, a circumstance that sometimes gave rise to a distorted portrait of these military forces. More recent research has permitted a more accurate portrayal, however, and it remains remarkable that much of what we learned from Old Testament sources proved to be confirmed by new information. Perhaps more importantly, the Old Testament provides the military historian with a rich human context through which to study the armies and wars of the Bible, a dimension of human understanding that is all too frequently absent in more modern accounts of warfare. The great saga of the Israelites was played out against the conflicts of the three major combatants—Canaanites, Philistines, and the Israelites themselves—occupying the same land at the same time and struggling with one another for influence, thereby presenting a unique opportunity to compare the armies, tactics, and military technology of each against the others.

CANAANITES

The period between 1800 to 1550 B.C.E. is called the Middle Canaanite period, when climatic conditions improved and cultural development flourished, permitting the people of Canaan to rebuild their old fortified cities into powerful new urban centers. During this time the first written documents in Canaanite appear, and it is from this period that Canaan as a recognizable entity with its own culture can be said to have truly come into being.[1] Egyptian documents from the time of Senusret II (1897–1878 B.C.E.) tell of a previous time when there were a number of independent Canaanite kingdoms ruled by warrior princes who had learned how to fortify their towns, which then grew into city-states that the Egyptians were forced to deal with militarily. Two of the more famous of these early Canaanite fortified towns, although for very different reasons, were Sodom and Gomorrah. We can deduce from the famous Egyptian story of Sinuwe and his travels in Canaan and Syria that during this time Canaanite society was based upon tribes, each ruled by a warrior chieftain (*melik*) who held his position by virtue of being the fiercest warrior in the tribe. These chiefs maintained household guards (*henkhu*) as part of their personal retinues, which probably constituted the main combat element in tribal wars.

The name Canaan is very old and in antiquity denoted that territory between Gaza in the south and the upper reaches of the Lebanon to Ugarit. To the east the land of Canaan ran to the base of the central mountain massif of later Judah and Samaria, northward through the Jezreel to include the Bekka up to Kadesh. Later in the middle period Canaan was subject to the passage of a group of immigrant tribes originating somewhere in northern Syria, which moved slowly over the land bridge until they entered Egypt itself, settling in the Delta near Avaris and defeating the Egyptians by force of arms. These were the Hyksos. While the origin of the Hyksos remains uncertain, there is no doubt that these militarily sophisticated people introduced their military technology to Canaan,[2] where it was adopted by the rival princes of the Canaanite city-states. The origin of this sophisticated equipment, like the Hyksos themselves, is uncertain as well but may lie in the technology of the Hurrian-Mitannians of the upper Euphrates. (See previous chapter.)

The Hyksos, and later Mitanni, military influence thus brought a number of new weapons to Canaan that revolutionized warfare on the land bridge as it was to do a century later when, having expelled the Hyksos, the Egyptians equipped their own armies with the new military technology. It was from the Hyksos that the Canaanites acquired the chariot and the horse as a new weapon of war. The composite bow, socket axe, and the sickle-sword also made their appearance in Canaan at this time.[3] The coat of mail came into use at approximately the same time, probably worn only by the armed charioteer. Later, we find Canaanite infantry wearing body armor as well.

The new military sophistication of the Canaanites during this period was reflected in another development, the change in the nature of military fortifications of Canaanite cities. Canaanite princes now constructed their cities atop a new kind of massive rampart, a slanted bank of packed earth called a *glacis*. The *glacis* joined an exterior ditch, a *fosse*, obstructing the most likely avenues of approach. The architecture, of course, was a reaction to the wide-spread use of the twin technologies of the chariot and the battering ram in Canaanite warfare. During this time Canaan had extensive contacts with the Mitanni-Hurrians, and it is likely that they now became the predominant influence on the Canaanite method of war. The Mitanni influence in the new architecture, for example, is suggested by the fact that two powerful cities in north Syria, Carchemish and Ebla, possess the same fortifications.[4]

The influence of the Mitanni-Hurrian culture was strongly reflected in the transformation of Canaanite society itself during this period into one based upon the Mitanni model. There now came into existence in Canaan a feudal warrior noble caste based upon heredity and land possession. As in the land of the Mitanni, these warriors were called *maryannu*, and like their Mitanni cousins were an elite group of chariot warriors. This elite ruled over a half-free, Semitic-speaking class of peasants and farmers (*khupshu*) with no middle or merchant class in between.[5] There is even some evidence that the feudal barons were of non-Semitic stock, another similarity with the Mitannian social order. The transformation of Canaanite military technology and social organization produced a society quite able and willing to fight wars, especially in resistance to the aspirations of the great powers to the south (Egypt) and to the north (Hittites and Mitanni).

With the creation of the Egyptian empire under the eighteenth Dynasty, Egypt moved aggressively to strengthen her influence in Canaan, an initiative that met organized resistance from a coalition of Canaanite princes at Megiddo (1479 B.C.E.). In the wake of the Egyptian victory Egypt established garrisons in the major towns of the country including

Ullaza, Sharuhen, Gaza, and Joppa, the last two being major Egyptian administrative centers. Each Canaanite city of any size had an Egyptian "political officer" (*weputy*) and a small staff to oversee economic and political matters, including the collection of intelligence. Egyptian garrisons stationed in major towns were often established as "allies of the king" and could be used to support the Canaanite prince in his local quarrels. The fiction of allies notwithstanding, Egyptian power and influence were real, a fact demonstrated by the Egyptian practice of referring to Canaanite princes as *khazanu* or headman instead of the more prestigious Canaanite title of *melik*.[6]

The presence of foreign influence did not prohibit the Canaanite princes from fortifying their important cities and towns, and by the twelfth century B.C.E. the entire country was heavily fortified and each city-state was ruled by an independent king. Although there was no Canaanite "high king" to direct it, the country-wide Canaanite fortification design was so well integrated as to suggest at least some degree of cooperation among the princes. The purpose of these fortifications was to protect the lucrative trade routes that criss-crossed the country, linking it to Syria and Egypt, and to protect Canaan from the predations of migrating nomadic tribes. Taken together, the system of fortifications was designed to permit the Canaanite princes to mount a mobile defense in depth using mounted chariot warriors. Only as a last resort did Canaanites permit themselves to be besieged in their cities.

Map 6.1 portrays the Canaanite defensive system. The following fortified cities each served as a base for chariot units to disrupt and confront an enemy threat. *Hazor*, the largest of Canaanite cities with a population of 40,000 whose kings ruled over all of northern Canaan, sat astride a key road junction that controlled the route leading to Damascus and the Syrian ports. *Megiddo* controlled the access to the Jezreel Valley from the coastal road (the Way of Horus to the Egyptians; *Via Maris* to the Romans) leading east to the transjordan. *Beth-Shean* stood upon a high mound at the far east exit of the Jezreel Valley and controlled the entrance to the Jordan plain, thereby blocking the logical route of the migrating desert tribes. *Shechem*, in the middle of the country, controlled the cross roads of the lateral routes across the land bridge. Closer to the coast sat *Gezer*, presiding over the southern junction of two ancient trade routes, the Way of Horus connecting Egypt and the main road leading inland up to Jerusalem and the gateway to the central mountains. And *Jerusalem* itself, situated on the northern central ridge, controlled the north-south route running along the spine of the mountains. It also sat astride the continuation of the road leading from the Mediterranean east

Map 6.1
The Canaanite Defensive System

into Jordan.[7] Operating either independently or in concert depending upon the size and nature of the threat, the Canaanite princes were able to mount a fierce defense of their territories from these strategically located urban fortifications. Other important Canaanite cities in the twelfth century B.C.E. were Ammuru, Kinza, Kadesh, Alalakh, Ugarit, Byblos, Tunip, Qatna and Khalba.

By the beginning of the thirteenth century and carrying well on into the twelfth, the Canaanite armies reached the apex of their military effectiveness. Each city-state raised and trained its own armed forces, most of which were very similar in weapons and organization. There was no unified "national" command for there was no "high king" that ruled over all Canaan. But in time of war the engaged city-states were capable of acting in concert and coordinating the movement and deployment of their forces. This had been true when Thutmose III had confronted a coalition of Canaanite princes at Megiddo. From the Ugarit texts the term *resuti* or "subordinate ally" has come down to us, suggesting that within the military coalitions princes were able to permit their forces to act at the orders of a higher commander as, no doubt, had been the case with the Canaanites at Megiddo. The king of the city-state usually took the field as commander-in-chief, but it was not unusual for military command to be delegated to trusted generals in some circumstances. Regular, fully equipped troops called *sabu nagib* were clearly distinguished from militia or irregulars. The term was applied to both infantry and chariotry, suggesting that regular infantry units existed. Field commanders were called *muru-u*, but we do not know the size of units they commanded. It is likely, however, that the decimal system of unit sizing was employed as it was commonly elsewhere. Although Ugarit was among the largest, richest, and most powerful Canaanite states, its military organization was probably quite typical of the other states.

The primary striking arm of the Canaanite armies, their arm of decision, was the elite chariot corps manned by the social elite of feudal nobles serving as chariot warriors called *maryanna*. Each *maryannu* was a professional chariot warrior who—originally at least—maintained his chariot, horses, grooms, driver, runners, and equipment at his own expense. His wealth was derived from the holding of a fief, which although originally conferred by the king, seems over time to have become hereditary.[8] Among the general warrior cast of *marryannu* were an inner elite of "picked men" or *na'arun*, a term that appears in the Ugarit texts. Apparently these elite units were comprised of infantry as well as chariotry. The chariot corps was commanded by the *akil narkabti* or chief of chariotry. A smaller battle guard called the Maryanna of the King also existed. The Canaanite chariot, much like the Mitannian chariot, was heavier than the Egyptian vehicle but lighter than the Hittite machine. Yadin suggests that this was a result of the increased Egyptian influence in Canaanite affairs,[9] but this is unconvincing. The mission of the Egyptian machine as well as the terrain in which it developed were simply different from those that influenced the development of the Canaanite machine. Canaan offered few smooth plains where the opportunity for wide-ranging maneuver and speed would provide dividends. The terrain of Canaan was like that of northern Syria (and the land of the Mitanni), characterized by rocky ground, hills and mountains, forests and glens, conditions that put a premium on surprise, ambush, and shock. The Canaanite chariot was heavier than the Egyptian model, having a six-spoked wheel with the axle moved to the center of the platform to take the weight off the animals. This permitted a larger carrying platform whose floor could be fashioned of wood for strength. One result, of course, was that the machine lost a good part of its maneuverability in a fast turn at top speed, and the endurance of the animals was also compromised to some degree.[10]

The Canaanite chariot warrior, like his Mitanni counterpart, was heavily protected by a mail coat of scale armor. His horse, too, wore a textile or bronze scale coat. These devices, of course, were designed to protect the horse and crew from enemy arrows as they closed in to engage. There is no hard evidence that the driver wore armor, but given the Mitanni influence on Canaanite chariotry it is quite likely that he did. The primary weapons of the Canaanite charioteer were the composite bow, a heavy spear, and a club, the latter, no doubt, to be used only in the direst emergency should the warrior find himself afoot.[11] Depending upon the tactical mission, the Canaanite chariot was quite capable of carrying a three-man crew, a fact suggested by the portrayal of the machine with javelin cases. The first recorded encounter by Israelite troops with Canaanite chariots is *Joshua* 11:5,7–9 where, having defeated the Canaanites near the Waters of Merom (Hula Lake), Joshua "burnt their chariots with fire." In another passage, *Joshua* 17:16–18, the account speaks of the Canaanites possessing "chariots of iron." Michael Grant points out that Canaanite chariots may have had tire rims and perhaps scale armor fashioned of bronze, not iron,[12] as were most of their weapons. Iron weapons at the time of Joshua (1250 B.C.E.?) were still largely peculiar to the Philistines.

Canaanite infantry called *hupshu* had both militia and regular units. Most of the infantry were semitrained militia (*khepetj*) or conscripted and corvee peasantry. These units were lightly armed with bows and spears. There was a long Canaanite tradition dating from tribal days that the infantry supplied their own equipment, but we are uncertain if this tradition persisted into biblical times. The Amarna letters refer to different types of infantry distinguished by their weapons, that is, bows and spears.[13] Canaanite regular infantry were probably well-trained professionals who were heavily armed. These units wore armored corslets for protection, helmets, carried a sword and shield and, probably, the socket-axe. Until the arrival of the Sea Peoples the Canaanites used a shield of Hittite design. Shaped like a figure-8 with a narrow waist, this shield allowed the soldier a greater field of view of his opponent in close combat and permitted a more flexible wielding of the sword. With the coming of the Sea Peoples, the Canaanites adopted the round shield and outfitted their infantry with the spear. At the same time, however, the Canaanite sickle sword was replaced by the straight sword of the Sea Peoples. Scale armor for the regular infantry now became commonplace as well.[14]

Elite units of heavy infantry called *na'arun* appear to have served as the palace guard of the Canaanite kings. The Ugaritic texts mention these units as an inner elite of the general *maryannu* warrior caste. The term itself means "picked men," that is, warriors chosen by their king for loyalty and bravery. Most likely there were special chariot units of "picked men" as well. At Kadesh, Ramses II was rescued in the nick of time by a unit of these elite shock troops, who fell upon the Hittite flank and broke the Hittite encirclement. These *na'arun* were Canaanite mercenaries in the service of the Egyptians. A relief of the battle portrays the Canaanites attacking in phalanx formation line abreast in ten rows, ten-men deep and armed with spears and shields,[15] suggesting that they are elite Canaanite heavy infantry.

The Canaanite kings supplemented their forces with hired freebooters called *Apiru*. The *Apiru* were a class of outcasts, debtors, outlaws, and restless nomads who formed into themselves into wandering groups of raiders, often hiring themselves out to princes and kings for military duty. Often called bandits (*habbatu*) or Dusty Ones, these wandering brigands were a serious threat and often had to be brought to heel by the Canaanite princes by force of arms. One of history's greatest generals, David, was an *apiru* whose reputation as a fierce soldier brought him to the attention of Saul. When forced to leave Saul's court for fear of being killed, David returned to his old mercenary occupation by raising a force of 600 "discontented men" and hiring his soldiers out to one of the Philistine kings. The size and military sophistication of these brigand groups could present a considerable threat to public order. A record from Alalakh tells of a band of *apiru* comprised of 1,436 men, 80 of whom were charioteers and 1,006 *shananu*, probably some kind of archer. Another text records the capture of the town of Allul by a force of 2,000 *apiru*.[16]

Canaanite tactics were similar to those of the Mitanni in that the army relied upon its chariot units to strike the enemy from ambush, catching him while still in the column of march or deploying for open battle. This was precisely the Canaanite plan at Megiddo when they set an ambush for Thutmose III's army along the Ta'anach-Aruna road, hoping to strike as the Egyptian column moved onto the Jezreel plain. If surprise was not possible, Canaanite generals used the chariot to deliver shock against enemy infantry formations. This required that the chariots be accompanied by "chariot runners" or infantry. The Canaanite charioteer engaged the enemy from close range, firing his bow and hurling short spears again and again, relying upon his heavy armor to protect him from enemy fire. In this tactical application infantry phalanxes of spearmen supported by archers would act in support or, if on the defensive, hold their positions, providing the chariots with a platform of maneuver.

The primary role of the chariot, however, was as a strategic weapon. The Canaanite chariots were mobile, sufficiently heavy, well-armored vehicles that could range far from their bases to protect the Canaanite cities from being besieged. Protecting the city itself was at the center of Canaanite strategic thinking, and the chariots were the key element in achieving this goal. Chariots could be used to intercept armies long before they reached the city walls, forcing the enemy to fight on terrain not of its choosing. Chariots were ideal for ambushing enemy patrols, harassing the enemy route of march, keeping interior lines open, and chasing down hired mercenary *apiru*. No infantry force could achieve such a mix of tactical and strategic flexibility. Chariots, of course, were expensive and their crews required extensive training and permanent maintenance at royal expense. The expense was worth it, however, for the chariot allowed the Canaanite kings to erect a strategic defense in depth based upon flexible mobile tactics.

The system of mobile defense worked well for more than two centuries, but Canaan's wealth and strategic position made it too tempting a target for the national predators who wished to control the land bridge. Over time the encroachments, immigrations, settlements, and aggressions of the Egyptians, Aramaens, Sea Peoples, and the Israelites and Philistines took their toll, with the result that by the time of King David the Canaanites had been deprived of three-quarters of their land area and 90 percent of their grain-growing land.[17] All that remained of these proud warrior people was the central Phoenician coastal strip together with its immediate hinterlands. But the legacy of Canaan lived on in the modern world. It was Canaanites who first performed the extraordinary feat of dissecting the sounds of human speech into thirty basic sounds, giving the world its first true alphabet.[18] And it was the Canaanites who were the first to set their language to music. It was they who taught the Hebrews how to set their poetry to music, thereby giving the world one of the greatest gifts of civilization.

PHILISTINES

The penetration of Canaan by the Israelites was already underway when another nation began its assault on the Egyptian province of Canaan: the Philistines. The Philistines came from the west by land and sea. They were the Pelset or the Sea Peoples, and their attempt to conquer Egypt was recorded by Ramses III (1192–1160 B.C.E.) on the great reliefs of Medinet Habu. The Philistines, from which we get the name Palestine, were of Aegean stock and related to both the Minoan and Mycenaean peoples of the Mediterranean islands and mainland Greece, and thus to the later classical Greeks. They probably originated in Cyprus or Crete. Their language was nonsemitic and written in syllabic speech like Carian, but the characters of their script strongly resemble the script of ancient Mycenaean Greece.[19] The Sea Peoples swept down the shores of the southeastern Mediterranean in swift ships accompanied by overland movement of their entire tribes, and with fire and iron swords attempted to capture new lands for settlement. Pharaoh Merneptah (1213–1203 B.C.E.) had fought a battle with them in Canaan, and even before the great battle with Ramses III (1190 B.C.E.), which halted their advance against Egypt, there is evidence to suggest that Philistine elements had already settled in places along the coast of Canaan.

After their defeat by Ramses III, the Philistines settled in significant numbers in the land of Canaan. Whether or not they settled there with the approval of the Egyptians or were simply too numerous and militarily powerful for the Egyptians to eject them, the Philistines seem to have reached some sort of accommodation with the Egyptians.[20] The Egyptians employed Philistine warriors as mercenaries in what might have been an attempt to check the power of both Canaanite and Israelite influence. The Philistines settled themselves along the southern coastal plain of Canaan, a fertile strip forty miles long and fifteen or so miles wide. They inhabited the powerfully fortified cities of Ashkelon, Ashdod, and Gaza on the coast and Gath and Ekron further inland. As Egyptian power weakened, Philistine influence in Canaan increased, and in a short time they became virtually independent and began to push out from their coastal enclaves toward the interior central mountains, which brought them into conflict with the Israelites.

The political structure of the Philistines resembled at least in its broad outlines that of their Greek relatives. Each city was independent and ruled by a prince whose claim to power rested, as in ancient Mycenae, on his royal blood and prowess as a warrior. There was no high king to rule other kings. When the Philistine cities had to act in concert, say to counter a military threat, they met in a council of princes called the *sarney*.[21] Whenever the Philistine city-states took the field in concert, they acted under a unified military command. The armies of the Philistines were mostly comprised of a well-armed professional feudal military caste, and they were the first to employ iron weapons on any scale. Iron weapons had been extant in Palestine in small numbers from at least the time of Pharaoh Merneptah. An iron sword bearing Merneptah's name has come down to us from Ugarit.[22] Bronze weapons, too, remained in use by the Philistines at this time, but they did their best to deny the secret of iron-mongering to both the Canaanites and the Israelites. This monopoly is recorded in 1 Samuel 13: 19–20: "Now there was no smith found throughout all the land of Israel: for the Philistines said, Lest the Hebrews make them swords or spears: but all the Israelites went down to the Philistines to sharpen every man his share, and his coulter, and his axe, and his mattock." The Philistine settlement of Canaan was successful, and in a relatively short time they assimilated into Canaanite culture so thoroughly that their own language was lost and replaced by a Canaanite dialect. Their gods of Aegean origin had their names changed, and the Philistine army adopted the full panoply of Canaanite weapons and techniques of war.[23] With the settlement of the Philistines in Canaan and their introduction of iron weapons, the iron age of military technology can be said to have begun.[24]

The first portrayal of Philistine weapons comes down to us from Ramses III's memorial reliefs of his defeat of the Sea Peoples at Medinet Habu. The Peleset are easily recognizable by their combat dress and weapons. Their soldiers wear a distinctive helmet with a band of what were originally thought to be feathers on the crown. More recent evidence suggest that these were not feathers but a circlet of reeds, stiffened horsehair, or even leather strips.[25] The leather helmet was secured by a chin strap. Body armor was a corslet of bronze or leather shaped in an inverted V, probably indicative of overlapping plates of either material. Shoulder guards to protect the clavicles are in evidence, although it is not certain if this feature is genuine or merely the artist's rendering of strong shoulders. A short kilt like that worn by the Hittites is shown, an item of equipment that may well have been acquired by the Peleset during their wanderings in Asia Minor. The long straight iron sword is the main armament of the soldier, although some Peleset soldiers are portrayed with the short spear somewhat reminiscent of the Greek javelin or *dory* of a much later period. The Peleset shield was round, probably fashioned of wood covered with leather or bronze or, perhaps, an iron rim to ward off sword blows, and was equipped with a boss. We know nothing of the shield's handgrip, but if it was of Aegean origin it is likely that the shield was held by a collection of tethers that met in the center of the shield. With this grip the shield was difficult to maneuver, required great strength to use effectively, and required a high degree of training. Even when the grip was mastered, the shield could not be used to press against an opponent with much force.[26] All of this speaks to the degree of professionalization of the Philistine warrior class, but raises questions about why the round shield was so quickly accepted by Canaanite and especially Israelite armies, which were mostly comprised of semitrained infantry militia.[27] The answer lies in the fact that the round shield was smaller and much lighter than the old full-body shield or figure-eight shields permitting the sword-bearing infantryman much greater speed and mobility on the battlefield. The appearance of the straight sword and light javelin at this time reduced the spear-bearing infantry to a secondary role, permitting the light infantryman to move about the battlefield with increased effectiveness. The light round shield, along with the leather body corslet, was his main protection.

The story of David and Goliath offers yet another glimpse into Philistine weaponry, one that strongly affirms the Aegean origins of the Philistine people. As told by Samuel, "And there came out of the camp of the Philistines a champion named Goliath. . . . And he was armed with a coat of mail. . . . And he had greaves of bronze upon his legs. . . . And the shaft of his spear was like a weaver's beam."[28] There is no mention of Goliath's helmet, but Yadin is probably correct when he suggests that by Saul's time the Philistines had adopted some Canaanite military equipment including the metal helmet, probably of bronze and not iron, with cheek plates.[29] The narrow-blade socket axe also came into wide use among the Philistines as well as the socketed blade for the javelin. It is interesting to point out that both these weapons were probably of bronze since they could be more easily cast in bronze than iron could be worked into this complex shape. Goliath's weapon may well have been a spear as Samuel says, but it is just as likely to have been a javelin, incorporating another Aegean innovation, the loop and cord. Philistine javelins had a slip loop that could be slid over the shaft of the weapon. The loop was attached to a strong cord that was tightly wrapped around the javelin's shaft. When throwing the javelin, the soldier held on to the end of the wrapped cord, pulling it toward him as the weapon was launched, thereby imparting a rotational spin to the shaft. The spin stabilized the weapon in flight, lending it both greater range and accuracy.[30]

The Philistine way of war as portrayed in the Ramses reliefs originally placed its greatest reliance upon infantry, as befits an Aegean people where the war chariot was rarely used in combat. Instead, Greek warriors used chariots as transport, to ride to the battlefield where they dismounted and fought as individual combatants with little in the way of tactical organization. The offer of Goliath's Philistine commander to David that the battle could be decided by combat between two champions, in effect a duel, once more reflects the Aegean attitude toward war as the stage of individual infantry combatants. That having been said, however, once settled in Canaan the Philistines seem to have quickly adopted the primary weapon of Canaanite armies, the war chariot, and transformed some of their warrior caste from heavy infantry into chariot warriors even as the use of Philistine infantry in later battles remained substantial. The first mention of Philistine chariots in the Bible occurs during the time of Saul, more than a century after the Philistines arrived in Canaan, plenty of time to have become acquainted with the Canaanite chariot. At the battle of Michmash, the Bible recounts that "The Philistines also assembled for battle, with three thousand chariots, six thousand horsemen, and foot soldiers as numerous as the sands of the seashore"[31] (1 Samuel 13:5). The reference to horsemen is curious since cavalry at this time was not yet developed. The mention of infantry "as numerous as the sands of the seashore," however, reflects the continued heavy reliance of the Philistines upon trained infantry to a much greater degree than in Canaanite armies. At Mount Gilboa the Bible recounts another example of the Philistine use of chariots: "The battle raged around Saul, and the archers hit him; he was pierced through the abdomen."[32] As Professor Mordechai Gichon has noted, "The outcome of the battle was decided by the Philistine chariots. Saul was forced to retreat up Mount Gilboa . . . the chariot-mounted archers followed close upon his heels up the easily traversable western slope and subjected the Israelites on the flat plateau to constant and effective fire."[33]

Both these battles, a well as accounts of others in the Old Testament, permit some speculation about Philistine tactics. To a much greater degree than Canaanite armies, the Philistines appear to have maintained a large number of heavy infantry of professional quality in contrast to the light infantry of the Canaanites and Israelites. At both Michmash (a Philistine defeat) and Mount Gilboa (a Philistine victory) infantry troops were used in large numbers with the chariots in support. The maintenance of large infantry units made good sense in light of the fact that the main antagonists of the Philistines were Israelites and not the princes of Canaan. As we shall see later, Israelite armies, at least until the time of Solomon, were comprised exclusively of light infantry who specialized in surprise and night attack. In addition, the areas of Israelite-Philistine conflict, at least in the early days, were confined mostly to the mountains of the central massif, terrain highly unfavorable to chariots. Under these conditions, the primary tactical emphasis was placed upon infantry with chariots used in support. At Michmash, for example, the Philistines appear to have used their chariot squadrons to secure the roads leading to and from the battlefield, probably to prevent further reinforcement or retreat of the Israelite armies. At Mount Gilboa, it was Philistine infantry that bore the brunt of Saul's attack, stopping it and driving the Israelites back up the mountain. It was only after the infantry had held its ground that the chariots could maneuver against Saul's flank, subjecting him to *enfilade* fire from their archers. At Aphek-Ebenezer, the battle was joined and carried only by Philistine infantry. They faced the Israelites in a set-piece battle in open terrain, with the result that the Philistines "slew about four thousand men on the battlefield."[34] There is no mention in the second battle that followed of chariots, and once more the Philistines carried the day with their infantry. It appears likely, then, that the armies of the Philistines, while employing a good deal of Canaanite equipment and the war chariot, seem to have stressed infantry far more than did the Canaanites. Whether this was a tactical response to the terrain or to the nature of their infantry-heavy Israelite enemies, or whether it was a people maintaining their traditional military heritage with its emphasis on individual infantry combat cannot be answered here.

Conflict between the Israelites and Philistines grew increasingly frequent as the Philistines pushed out from their main coastal bases and sought to establish trade routes and trading stations that cut across the central mountains into Jordan. The Philistines established a number of trading stations deep in Israelite territory with, we may surmise, small military garrisons to protect them. These stations were seen by the Israelites as a prelude to invasion. From the Philistine perspective, Israelite patrols and occasional forays into the coastal lowlands were seen as a burgeoning threat. Around 1050 B.C.E., the Philistines forced the Israelites into a contest of arms, with the result that the Israelites suffered a terrible defeat at the battle of Aphek. To rally Israelite morale, the Ark of the Covenant itself was brought to the battlefield. A short time later the Israelites were defeated once more by the Philistines. This time the Ark was captured and carried off to Ashdod. The defeat set off a tremendous cry among the Israelites for a national leader who could defeat their enemies and lift the Philistine yoke. The result was the rise of Saul, the first king of Israel.

ISRAELITES

The military history of the Israelites during the biblical period begins with the Exodus (1275–1225 B.C.E.) followed by the invasion of Canaan by the twelve tribes of Israel under Joshua (1225–1200 B.C.E.), followed by the period of the Judges (1200–1050 B.C.E.), the period of Saul (1025–1006 B.C.E.) and David (1006–961 B.C.E.), and ends with Solomon (961–922 B.C.E.). In each of these periods, the army and politico-military structure of the Israelites changed significantly in terms of organization, weapons, and tactics. Evidence from archaeology suggests that the first period, when the Israelites invaded Canaan, was a time of widespread destruction of Canaanite cities and strongpoints, including Hazor, which dovetails nicely with the campaigns of Joshua. Whether this destruction can be attributed to the Israelites seems unlikely, however. The battles of Joshua are conflicts not against Canaanites properly so called, but against rival tribal enemies already settled in Canaan. Most likely the original Israelite penetration of Canaan occurred in areas of sparse settlement in the mountains, where significant opposition was unlikely. As the Israelites settled in, however, it is likely that they came into conflict with other peoples of Canaan, but it is at least as likely that these disputes were settled by negotiation as by war.[35] None of this means, of course, that Joshua did not carry out the successful campaigns described in the Bible. It only implies that the frequency of warfare was far less than one might suppose from reading these accounts.

The Biblical account of the period of the Judges must also be placed in perspective. The Book of Judges recounts the military victories of twelve national Israelite heroes (*shophetim*) whose acts of military bravery forged a national consciousness. These accounts present a number of difficulties. In the first place, none of the Judges were national leaders at all, but local tribal leaders combatting not national enemies but local ones.[36] None of the Judges held any kind of permanent position, but were men called to arms in an emergency and returned their authority to the tribe when the emergency had passed. None of the wars of the Judges involved more than a handful of Israelite tribes, and there was no national Israelite governmental structure. As to the enemies of the Israelites, only one of the wars of this period, Deborah and Barak's victory over Sisera near the Kishron River, was a war against a Canaanite enemy. All the others were against local tribal elements, Midianites, Amelekites, and the Philistines.[37] The pressure from the Philistine threat forced the Israelites to ignore the Canaanites who, after all, shared much of a common culture with the Israelites. A number of Canaanite towns, cities, and fortified places within Israelite territory went unmolested for years by the Israelites while they dealt with the Philistines. It was only during the periods of Saul and David that these places could be brought completely under Israelite control.[38]

The accounts of the Judges remained an oral tradition until around 600 B.C.E. when, along with much of the Old Testament, they were finally compiled in written form. Probably for reasons of ethnic identity and national pride the compilers endowed the oral versions of these accounts with an artificial framework, sequence, and chronology that turned the oral tradition into a great national saga of a people attempting to preserve its national identity and culture against foreign cultural and military influences.[39] Be this as it may, the accounts of the battles of the Judges contain much about the Israelite way of war, including equipment and tactics, that is accurate and from which much may be learned. For purposes of analysis, the period of Joshua and the Judges may be combined in our examination of the military capabilities displayed by the Israelite armies.

The first Israelite military formation, including its means for command and control, is described in the Bible as the Israelites prepared to depart from Sinai and travel to the promised land of Canaan.[40] The Book of Numbers describes in detail the arrangement of the Israelite camp and how it is to assemble and conduct the march. Within the camp each tribe was allocated a fixed area that corresponded to a position in the line of march. Tents were pitched around the tent of the tribal commander, whose standard was displayed to mark his position. The Ark was positioned in the center of the camp under the watchful eyes of the Levite praetorian guard. Command and control over the tribal host in the camp and on the march was accomplished by signals blown into two silver trumpets. A single blast from both trumpets was the command for tribal leaders to gather at the central tent for instructions. A special signal called the Alarm signified the movement of each wing. Although not mentioned, it is likely that a special trumpet call was used to turn the formation from line of march toward any direction to meet a surprise attack, with the noncombatants falling behind the newly assembled battle line for protection. The Israelite organization portrayed in Numbers offers a graphic example of how it was possible to manage the migration of an entire people over long distances while providing for their defense on the march. It is likely that this or similar forms of organization were used by other tribes, as when the nomads of the Jordan invaded the Jezreel, forcing Gideon to defeat them.

The campaigns of Joshua offer some insight into the nature of the Israelite armies. Israelite armies of this period were comprised of tribal levies of semitrained militia configured as light infantry, armed with sickle swords, spears, bows, slings, and daggers. There was no permanent core of professional officers, but tribal units fighting under the command of their own leaders with Joshua in overall command. The lack of an institutionalized military command structure paralleled the absence of a centralized political structure. At this point the Israelites had no king over all the tribes. The leader at any given time was the first among equals of the tribal leaders involved in the battle. Moreover, during the period of the Judges few battles involved more than three or four tribes in confederation. Joshua, presumably, could draw upon the entire tribal host for his manpower. An army of light infantry under Joshua made perfect sense. First, light infantry did not require much training in the use of its simple weapons. Second, the terrain in which the Israelites were fighting favored light infantry. The terrain of Canaan is varied, comprised of mountains, deserts, hills, forests, and rocky glades, with only a few open plains which, if a commander avoided them, permitted maximum effectiveness of light infantry. Joshua was fighting mostly in the hills and mountains of the central massif where light infantry, if employed with tactical skill, could be decisive.

Enemy chariots were useless in the uneven terrain, and even heavy infantry were at a considerable disadvantage in that the terrain made fighting in phalanx very difficult. Moreover, the Israelites had not yet reached a level of military sophistication under Joshua that permitted the use of the chariot. In the battle against the king of Hazor as described in the Book of Joshua, the Israelites captured some enemy chariots. Joshua "houghed their horses (cut their hamstrings) and burnt their chariots with fire."[41] This incident reflects the primitive Israelite technology of war. With no knowledge of how to operate or employ the chariots, Joshua had little choice but to destroy them. Saul's later inability to field chariots at Mount Gilboa cost him his life, and it was not until the end of King David's reign that there is even tentative evidence that the Israelite armies had even a single squadron of chariots. It fell to Solomon to change the nature of the Israelite army completely by introducing large-scale chariot units for the first time. Israelite siegecraft was also primitive. When the Bible recounts Israelite attacks on enemy "fortifications," it usually means tents, the standard solution for which was to set them afire. One of the reasons why so many Canaanite cities and towns were left unmolested by the Israelites until the time of David was because the Israelites had no means to successfully attack them.

The size of Israelite armies remains a matter of some speculation. Deborah, drawing upon only four of the twelve tribes in confederation, put 10,000 men in the field against Sisera if the Bible is to be believed. To relieve the siege of Jabesh-gilead, Saul called upon the entire nation to provide manpower. As was usually the case, tribes far from the area of concern often balked at sending any men at all. To counter this centrifugal tendency, Saul "took a yoke of oxen, and hewed them to pieces, and sent them throughout the coast of Israel . . . saying, Whosoever cometh not forth after Saul and after Samuel, so shall it be done unto his oxen."[42] The population of the Israelite tribes at this time was about 100,000–150,000 people.[43] Calculating the standard ratio of 25 percent of the population of military age suggests that at maximum effort the Israelites could field about 25,000–30,000 men. Under most circumstances, however, Saul would have been fortunate to be able to deploy about a third that number for any given battle. Later, under David and Solomon, the establishment of a centralized political structure led to the establishment of a centralized mechanism for conscription that could more efficiently call up larger levies for national defense.

The most significant military weakness of the armies of Joshua and the Judges was the centrifugal tendencies of a tribal society, which made central direction of any military effort problematical. This weakness eventually produced a catastrophic defeat at Aphr-Ebenezer at the hands of the Philistines in 1050 B.C.E., which resulted in the military occupation of former Israelite territories, the appointment of Philistine governors, disarming of the population, prohibitions against iron-working, and the use of punitive search-and-destroy operations to keep the Israelite population in line.[44] The details of Saul's appointment as king of all Israel by Samuel need not concern us here. Suffice it to say that the circumstances of Philistine control provided the stimulus for the Israelites to form a centralized monarchy for the first time in their history. Under Saul the tribal leaders relinquished some of their authority to the central government, most particularly the ability of the king to levy conscription requirements upon all twelve tribes for military service. Saul defeated the Philistines with the new army in three great battles, and reformed the Israelite army somewhat along Philistine lines.

The presence of standing enemy forces just beyond the Israelite borders emphasized the need for a similar standing force within Israel itself. Saul selected 3,000 warriors to serve as the core of a permanent standing army. As in the Philistine army, some of these men, and probably other units of *apiru*, were mercenaries. David himself came to Saul's court not from the Israelite levy but as the commander of a unit of mercenaries. The Israelite army remained a light infantry force under Saul, although it is not beyond possibility that the professionals were equipped with the protection and arms of heavy infantry. There were no chariot units, however. Saul's army was divided into two divisions, with the smaller one of 1,000 men placed under the command of his son, Jonathan.[45] One of Saul's important innovations was the introduction of the fortified camp for prolonged campaigns. These were well-organized, semipermanent base camps broken into special zones for training, ordinance manufacture, and quartermaster. Each of these zones was overseen by details of specialists. Saul's reforms shaped the character of the Israelite armies for the next fifteen years or so until King David made other changes. Although Saul's reforms made it possible to place larger Israelite armies in the field, they were still underarmed and ill-equipped when compared to Philistine armies. The lack of chariot units, if only for reconnaissance and scouting, was a major disability. The larger size of Israelite armies may have been what tempted Saul to meet the Philistines in open battle near Mount Gilboa, with catastrophic results. The heavy phalanx Philistine infantry held its ground easily against the assault of the lighter Israelite infantry. Philistine chariots then smashed the infantry in a lethal pursuit while other chariot units turned Saul's flank and subjected him and his army to murderous arrow fire, wounding him fatally.

King David's reign was marked by a number of important changes in the Israelite army as he shaped it into an instrument for the acquisition and maintenance of an empire. Map 6.2 outlines David's major campaigns in building the first Israelite empire,[46] the details of which need not concern us here. David's reforms began with establishing firm control over the national tribal levy by requiring military service of every able-bodied male.[47] For tactical purposes the levy was organized into divisions of thousands subdivided into units of hundreds and subunits of fifty and ten, the latter being the smallest unit to have a permanent commander. The recurrence of the number 600 in the Bible with reference to Israelite combat units raises the question of whether this was the standard combat unit or field battalion. The number conveniently divides by four into units of 150 men (the Egyptian system) and by three into units of 200, a system used commonly by other armies of the day. Either or both

Map 6.2
The Wars of David

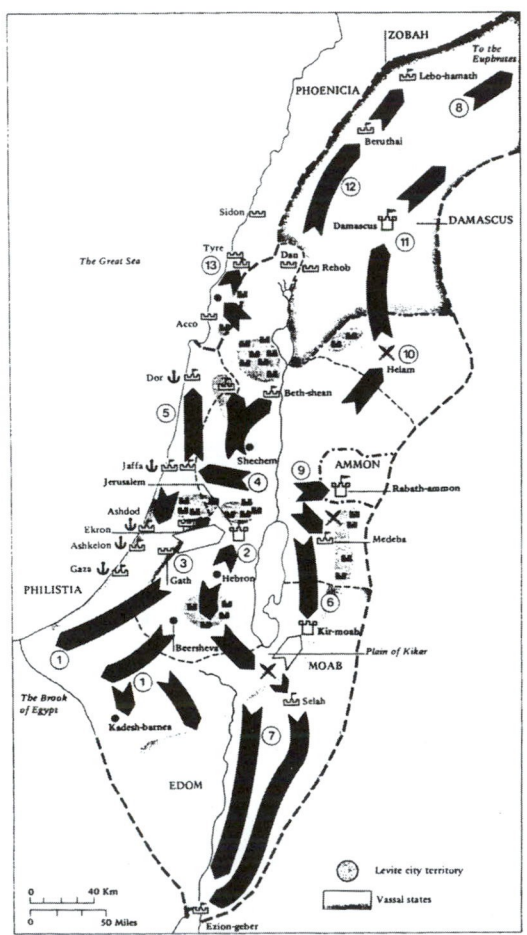

Note: 1: Subjugation of the Negev tribes; 2: The conquest of Jerusalem; 3: Philistine attempts to oust David in the Rephaim Valley; 4: Subjugation of Philistia; 5: Conquest of the Sharon Plain and Valley of Jezreel; 6: The war against Moab; 7: Subjugation of Edom; 8: Trade with the Euphrates region; 9: The war against the Arameans and Ammonites; 10: The defeat of the Arameans in the Edrei gap; 11: Subjugation of Damascus; 12: Extension of the empire to the borders of Hamath and the Euphrates; 13: Establishment of Israelite sovereignty in western Galilee, as far as the Phoenician border.

Source: Chaim Herzog and Mordechai Gichon, *Battles of the Bible* (Jerusalem: Steimatzky's Agency Ltd.), 1978. With the permission of the authors.

systems may have been employed by the Israelite armies under David and later Solomon.

David's conscript army was exclusively an infantry force and a light infantry force at that, just as it had been under Joshua and Saul. While light infantry provided for great flexibility, there remained the problem of how to obtain a proper mix of weapons and other capabilities in sufficient amounts to achieve the overall tactical objective. This was accomplished in the army of David by relying upon tribal units that possessed specific military specialties.[48] In 1 *Chronicles* the Bible records some of the special military proficiencies of the tribes. The Benjaminites, for example, were armed with bows and "could use both the right hand and left hand in hurling stones and shooting arrows out of a bow." Gadites were proficient at "shield and buckler . . . and were as swift as the roes upon the mountains." The sons of Judah "bore shield and spear," as did the Naphtali. The Zebulanites may well have been the Israelite equivalents of rangers for "they were expert in war, with all instruments of war . . . and could keep rank." A bit less clear was the skill of the tribe of Issachar, which was explained as "understanding of the times, to know what Israel ought to do," a description that might suggest scouting and intelligence gathering. Gichon and Herzog have described the importance of these tribal military specialists when brought together in David's army:

In short, David could draw upon the tribal contingents to furnish bowmen and slingers, light and heavy lancers—the former good at fighting in individual combat in difficult terrain, the latter (the children of Judah) forming the closely arrayed heavy phalanx. These were assisted by spearmen, who would hurl their spears before charging the foe with drawn swords. Other tribes were less specialized as far as weaponry was concerned, but were trained to fight in rank and file.[49]

The tribal chiefs were responsible for the basic training of their levies in the use of weapons particular to their clan as well as for maintenance of weapons. Most importantly, they were responsible for providing the tribe's manpower quota to the central army. Alongside this tribal levy was another force comprised of twelve monthly, nontribal and nonterritorial divisions, each of which came on active duty for one month a year. Officered by permanent professional cadre, this provided the king with a large, permanently available cadre of soldiers on one-month service duty every year. This force was expected to take the field immediately in case of emergency and purchase sufficient time for the national levy to be mobilized. A similar system is employed by the Israeli Defense Force today.

The core of the Davidic army was comprised of two corps of professional regular soldiers. The first of these were the "mighty men" of the Bible or *gibborim*, two regiments each built upon a group of special soldiers loyal to David's person called the "Thirty." The first "Thirty" group were the band of loyal followers that had fought with David during his exile. This was a group of hardened combat veterans, whose tales of courage were the subject of Israelite poems and ballads. The second "Thirty" was a group of David's followers who formed around him after he had attained the crown of Judah. These, too, were trusted advisers and combat veterans who, as was David himself, were highly skilled in unconventional warfare and tactical innovation. From the groups of Thirty, David selected his personal bodyguard and many of his high ranking civil and military dignitaries. In this sense, the Thirty were very similar to Alexander's *hetairoi* and Charlemagne's *schara*.[50]

The second corps of regulars in David's army was comprised of mercenaries, including Philistine troops. These hardy professionals were tough combat soldiers whose armament was heavier than most Israelite troops and who could be relied upon to fight well, a not insignificant contribution to morale among soldiers who were for the most part conscripts. That mercenary troops, even Philistines fighting against their own people, could be reliable is evidenced by the fact that David himself, when driven from Saul's court, commanded a mercenary corps that placed itself in the service of one of the Philistine kings. Later, when Saul faced the Philistines at Mount Gilboa, David's unit reported for service among the Philistine troops preparing to do battle. It was the Philistine commander who refused David's help. But there is no doubt that David was quite prepared to fight against his former king and countryman.

Among David's many victories, some came against enemies that deployed chariots against his army in large numbers. The ability to stop charging chariots with infantry alone arrayed on open ground appears to have been one of the Israelite army's special talents, a talent that finds its modern echo in the maxim that the most dangerous enemy of the tank is the individual infantryman. The key to stopping a chariot charge was to engage the machines far forward of the heavy infantry phalanx with light troops using their slings, arrows, and javelins to harass and slow the momentum of the charge until it was no longer sufficient to penetrate the massed heavy infantry phalanx, which then engaged it with spears. Once slowed or stopped, the light infantry, either units in reserve or those recovered from the initial engagement, swarmed over the chariots in close combat, where their swords had the advantage over the charioteer's bow. Whereas in Canaanite and Philistine armies the chariot was used as the primary element to deliver shock, in the infantry armies of the Israelites this role fell to the heavily armored pikeman, most often regulars or mercenaries, arrayed in offensive phalanx.

We have no reliefs or other portrayals of the Israelite infantry soldier at the time of David. But Stillman and Tallis have constructed a portrait of a typical Israelite infantryman from text descriptions. He was called a "valiant man" (*ish hayii*) or a "picked man," (*ish bahur*) or elite troop. Israelite infantry equipment was a mix of Canaanite and Philistine equipment and included a round shield (*magen*), a short thrusting spear (*romah*), a straight sword (*hereb*), and a bronze helmet (*koba*). Regular troops like the *gibborim* probably wore scale or lamellar armor like the Canaanite soldiers, called a *shiryon*. The tribal militia would be even more lightly armed, mostly with javelins, daggers, and slings.[51]

Governing an empire requires trained administrative personnel, and David's court reflected the increased complexity of the Israelite national defense establishment, one that was far larger and more sophisticated than under Saul. David's court had a commandant of the tribal levy (Joab), a commander of mercenary troops (Benaiah), chiefs and high priests of the religious establishment, a superintendent of corvee labor, various high ranking military staff officers and advisors, a chancellor (Jehoshaphat) and an official scribe, who we might imply from the Egyptian model was chief historian and, perhaps, chief of intelligence as well. The whole arrangement bears a striking similarity to the structure of the Egyptian court, although the superintendent of corvee labor is probably derived from the Canaanite practice.[52] David's court and his legitimacy as king rested upon a far more secure foundation that had Saul's. Saul's claim to kingship was based upon Samuel's claim that Saul had been sent by Yahweh. David's claim, by contrast, rested upon no such special claim to grace. Rather, David was made king as a consequence of his military victories and the real power he possessed as head of a conquering army. The two claims, one theological and one constitutional, contested with each other after the death of Solomon, with opponents of the monarchy, often prophets, using the theological claim to undermine the legal legitimacy of the monarchy itself.

David had created an empire and now it was Solomon's task to maintain it. With David's death the national strategy of the Israelites passed over to the defense. An army configured for conquest is not always as well suited for defense. David's defense establishment lacked two important elements: a well-planned system of fortifications and a powerful strategic striking arm, a chariot corps. Solomon immediately turned his attention to these deficiencies. Under Solomon, Israel acquired a corps of chariots, transforming the Israelite army from a light infantry force into an army whose chariots were its arm of decision.[53] The tribal levy remained, but more and more the regular standing army was comprised of professional chariot crews and specialized regular infantry, the "runners," who accompanied the chariots into battle, providing them with strong infantry support in close combat. The regular militia levy probably continued to function as light infantry.[54] The Old Testament gives the size of Solomon's chariot corp at "a thousand and four hundred chariots and twelve thousand horsemen (charioteers)."[55] Information regarding the type of chariots employed by Solomon's army is completely lacking, but it seems reasonable that Israelite chariots would be of Egyptian, Syrian, or Canaanite design since they were the most commonplace machines of the day. It is unclear, however, why 1,400 chariots would require a force of "twelve thousand horsemen." One possibility whose logic is militarily compelling is that the Israelites maintained double crews for each vehicle. This would still leave sufficient manpower to provide a mix of chariot types. Some Israelite chariots may have followed the Egyptian example, being light, fast, and maneuverable machines armed with a driver and an archer. Others, following the Syrian and Canaanite example, might have been heavy machines carrying a crew of three—driver, archer, and lancer/spearman—and used to deliver shock and mounted infantry. The Bible describes the Canaanite chariots as "chariots of iron," and there is no reason to believe that Israelite chariots were clad in armor of some sort as well. Even bronze plate would have been so heavy as to collapse the wooden frame.

Solomon equipped Israel with a system of in-depth fortifications from which the nation could be defended with a mobile strategic defense in depth, the same strategic design employed by the Canaanites two centuries earlier. Major fortifications were built or improved at Hazor, Megiddo, Tamar, Gezer, Baalath, Lower Beth-Horon, and Tadmor (Pallmyra). Each of these "chariot cities" controlled a key road or pass, possessed a good water supply, and offered suitable ground upon which to employ chariots. At Megiddo and Hazor, Solomon replaced the old casement walls with walls of massive stone, this in reaction to the growing use of effective battering rams by armies of the period. A casement wall could be easily collapsed by breaking a hole in its base with a battering ram, using the weight of its rubble fill to press outward against the wall itself. Walls of solid stone blocks cannot be collapsed in this manner. Solomon positioned his chariot forces and regular infantry units in some of these "chariot cities," from which they could react to an enemy threat. These cities, of course, could also be used as bases from which offensive punitive expeditions could be mounted and from which regular combat or reconnaissance patrols could be staged. The guiding strategic concept was to engage the enemy on ground of one's own choosing and to do so before the enemy reached the cities. Like the Canaanites before them, Israelite commanders would permit themselves to be besieged only as a last resort.

The general strategic reserve of Solomon's army was kept in Jerusalem, including the strategic reserve of the chariot corps. To position the reserve in this manner implies that there must have been a network of well-guarded and packed-earth roads leading from Jerusalem to all major defensive positions, otherwise Israelite commanders would have been unable to react in sufficient time. This network of roads would have required road stations, watering points, repair shops, and storage depots along its way and must have run fairly close to existing settlements. Such a system would have had to be maintained on a regular basis, as would the entire military system of defense, and brought into existence a governmental structure centered around Solomon's court that was far more complex and articulated as a response to the growing administrative and military burdens that needed to be dealt with.[56]

Solomon's solution to this increasing complexity was to create a number of commercial monopolies from which the state drew exclusive revenues and to place taxation on a uniform basis, providing a continual and relatively stable source of revenue for the crown from which the governmental and military expenses of the state could be paid. Solomon then rationalized the military logistics system. The country was divided into twelve administrative districts that were only generally identical with the tribal districts. The size of each district varied considerably and was determined with a view to making them equal in productivity and wealth, so that the burden of military supply would not fall too heavily upon any one district. Each district was to supply the food and materials required by the court and military garrisons for one month, thus rotating the burden from district to district while at the same time assuring a continuous and adequate supply of needed materials.[57] Taken together, Solomon's reforms and innovations bequeathed Israel a truly "modern" state in terms of its military, economy, political institutions, and infrastructure. With Solomon, the Israelites cease to be a tribal society and become a national entity for the first time in their history.

Israelite tactics from the time of Joshua until the transformation of the army under Solomon were the result of a simple truth: the Israelites were almost always fighting armies larger and better equipped than they were. Necessity, as the saying goes, is the "mother of invention," and no less so in the design and application of military tactics. Soldier for soldier, there is only so much a light infantry force can do against a superior enemy. If it is to succeed such a force must obtain an advantage in some other way. Israelite tactics during this period were characterized by the following doctrines.

Maximum Use of Terrain. Very often the main problem for a light force is to avoid contact with the enemy until it can choose an optimum location for battle. In the attack on Ai, for example, Joshua moved his army through a cut for fifteen miles, all of it uphill, to position his force without being detected. At the Kishron River in the Jezreel, Deborah used the drainage patterns of the area to her advantage when she enticed the enemy chariots onto the muddy ground, where they bogged down and had to be abandoned.

Swift Approach March to the Objective. David moved his army through the woods of the Rephaim Valley both for concealment and as a way of countering the enemy's heavy weaponry should the army be discovered while moving into position. Knowing that the wind from the sea arrives in Jerusalem about noon, David timed his attack for this hour, knowing that the rustling trees would camouflage the sound of his troops.

Reliance Upon the Night. Joshua moved his army into position against the Amorites to execute a dawn attack. Gideon attacked the nomad camp in the middle of the night, the time when the watch had just changed and the new sentry's eyes had not yet adjusted to the darkness, with 300 men to put the enemy camp to flight.

Division of Forces. While it is a modern military maxim never to divide one's forces, in fact the ability to do so under competent division commanders offers a light force many advantages. Gideon, for example, divided his forces, using a small force to put the enemy camp to flight in the middle of the night and drive it into the anvil of the larger forces waiting on the plain to decimate it.

Use of Surprise. Surprise is perhaps the most commonly displayed characteristic of Israelite battles of the Bible. Time and again the Old Testament tells of commanders moving their forces into position and taking the enemy by surprise or taking him from ambush.

Lethal Pursuit. Once an enemy has been forced into flight, the opportunity for great slaughter presents itself. One of the great innovations in tactics made possible by the introduction of the chariot was the ability to undertake a lethal pursuit, something which had been heretofore a relatively rare occurrence. The remarkable aspect of Israelite tactics was the willingness of Israelite commanders to pursue with infantry. Prior to engaging the Amorites in the second battle around Ai, Joshua marched his men fifteen miles in a night approach over rugged mountainous terrain to fall upon the enemy at daybreak. Defeated, the Amorites withdrew down the defile of the Beth-horon pass, attempting to reach the open country of the Ajalon Valley. Joshua, in Napoleon's famous phrase, "kept the sabre in their back," and pursued them for eleven miles again by night march, dispersing and hunting down the enemy. Before dawn of the next day, thirty miles and forty-five hours after the initial approach had begun, Joshua trapped what was left of the enemy in the valley and defeated them once more.

It is, of course, no accident that such tactical doctrines applied by unconventional commanders are still the hallmark of the modern Israeli Defense Force. Indeed, Israeli officers are still taken into the field to walk the ground fought over by Joshua, Gideon, Deborah, Saul, and David. Here, armed with the Old Testament, the battles of the Bible are fought again and again until the same tactical lessons are learned once more.

NOTES

1. Michael Grant, *The History of Ancient Israel* (New York: Charles Scribner, 1984), 13.
2. Nigel Stillman and Nigel Tallis, *Armies of the Ancient Near East* (Sussex, England: Flexiprint Ltd., 1984), 33.
3. Yigael Yadin, *The Art of Warfare in Biblical Lands in Light of Archaeological Study* (New York: McGraw Hill, 1964), vol. 1, 79.
4. Grant, 16.
5. Ibid.
6. Stillman and Tallis, 35.
7. Grant, 17.
8. Stillman and Tallis, 35.
9. Yadin, 88.
10. Ibid.
11. Stillman and Tallis, 96.
12. Grant, 19.
13. Stillman and Tallis, 35.
14. Yadin, 79–84.
15. Yadin, vol. 2, 108.
16. Stillman and Tallis, 35.
17. Grant, 81.
18. Ibid., 21.
19. Ibid., 67.
20. Chaim Herzog and Mordechai Gichon, *Battles of the Bible* (Jerusalem: Steimatzky's Agency Ltd., 1978), 63.

21. Stillman and Tallis, 38.

22. Yadin, vol. 1, 209.

23. Grant, 68.

24. Yadin, vol. 2, 330.

25. Stillman and Tallis, 149.

26. Richard A. Gabriel and Donald Boose, *The Great Battles of Antiquity: A Strategic and Tactical Guide to the Great Battles That Shaped the Development of War* (Westport, Conn.: Greenwood Press, 1994), 132.

27. The problem of a grip for the round Greek shield was solved in the seventh century B.C.E. with the introduction of the Argive shield. The new grip consisted of two leather loop straps. The forearm was passed through the first loop strap while the second one was grasped firmly by the hand. This arrangement now made it possible for even the common citizen to learn how to use the shield effectively, with the result that a new age of warfare dawned upon classical Greece, characterized by the emergence of the citizen hoplite.

28. 1 Samuel 17:4–7.

29. Yadin, vol. 2, 174.

30. Ibid., 354.

31. 1 Samuel 13:5.

32. 1 Samuel 31:3.

33. Herzog and Gichon, 74.

34. 1 Samuel 4:2.

35. Grant, 55.

36. *Cambridge Ancient History*, vol. 2, part 2, 539.

37. Ibid., 554.

38. Ibid., 559.

39. Grant, 54.

40. Numbers 10:1–10;13–27.

41. Joshua 11:7–9.

42. 1 Samuel 11:7.

43. Lawrence Stager, "The Archaeology of the Family in Ancient Israel," *American School of Oriental Research* 260 (1985): 4–6.

44. *Cambridge Ancient History*, vol. 2, part 2, 571.

45. Herzog and Gichon, 68.

46. Ibid., 76.

47. 1 Samuel 8:11–16.

48. Herzog and Gichon, 85.

49. Ibid.

50. Ibid., 87.

51. Stillman and Tallis, 150.

52. *Cambridge Ancient History*, vol. 2, part 2, 584–85.

53. In 2 Samuel 8:4 the story tells of David capturing a large number of chariots and horses. Keeping only a hundred for himself, he destroyed the other

chariots and houghed the horses. This is taken by some to be an indication that there may have been a small squadron of chariots in David's army.

54. *Cambridge Ancient History*, vol. 2, part 2, 590.
55. 1 Kings 10:26.
56. *Cambridge Ancient History*, vol. 2, part 2, 588.
57. Ibid., 591.

7

The Iron Army of Assyria
890–612 B.C.E.

The Assyrian army of the ninth century B.C.E. was the most sophisticated army of its time in terms of size, weaponry, tactics, siegecraft, innovation, mobility, logistical support, and overall military efficiency. While armies that came after it surpassed it in some limited respects, no army equaled its overall organizational sophistication until the armies of Rome. The Assyrian army was thoroughly integrated into the larger social, political, and economic institutions of the Assyrian state, and much of its success was due to its ability to take maximum advantage of this integration.

Assyria, like the other settlements of the Tigris-Euphrates valley between 1500 and 1200 B.C.E., was a city-state that sat astride important trade routes that the major powers of the day—Egyptians, Hittites, and the Mitanni—sought to control for economic and military reasons. In the twelfth century Hittite power collapsed and Assyria began a 300-year rise to power under the direction of successive powerful kings, which resulted in the establishment of the Assyrian empire in the ninth century B.C.E.

Assyria emerged as the most powerful and successful military empire the world had seen to that time, and its power was unabashedly built upon military force and police terror. Warfare, conquest, and the exploitation of neighboring states became the primary preoccupation of the Assyrian kings. Between 890 and 640 B.C.E., the height of Assyrian power, the Assyrians fought 108 major and minor wars, punitive expeditions, and other significant military operations against neighboring states.[1] During the reign of Sargon II (721–705 B.C.E.), the Assyrians carried out no fewer that ten major wars of conquest or suppression in sixteen years.[2] The result was the establishment of an empire that ran from the Persian Gulf to the Mediterranean Sea, from Armenia and northern Persia to the Arabian desert, and farther west to include parts of the Egyptian Delta. It was the largest military empire in the world, and it was sustained by the largest, best-equipped, best-trained, and cruelest military organization that the world had ever witnessed.

The economic base of the Assyrian empire centered on the three major cities of Nimrud, Nineveh, and Ashur, located on the Tigris River in what is now northwestern Iraq. Like Egypt, Assyria was an alluvial state that depended on agriculture, and its agriculture depended upon the fortunes of a major river. Unlike the Nile, however, the Tigris is not a friendly or gentle river, and its ever-present threat of violent floods required that major irrigation projects be built and maintained. Building and maintaining these massive irrigation networks required large supplies of manpower, which Assyria lacked. Military conquest as a source of slave manpower and the wholesale resettlement of foreign peoples provided the Assyrian solution. The importance of capturing prisoners of war for use as slave labor is reflected in the Assyrian penchant for keeping detailed records of the number of prisoners taken in war. There are several instances when the number of prisoners reported captured runs into the hundreds of thousands.[3]

As long as Assyria could obtain the raw materials and manpower required to sustain the irrigation system, the Assyrian fields could be made to produce at high levels and she could feed her people. Surviving records indicate that successful irrigation produced barley and wheat yields thirty to forty times the amount sown.[4] The area could also be made to yield dates, and the Assyrians developed a substantial agriculture in this area. Cattle, sheep, and goats were raised to provide supplies of cheese and butter (the Assyrians apparently loathed milk). Fishing provided other food sources, as did sesame oil and palm wine.[5] Assyria could support an adequate population, but all was dependent upon sustaining the irrigation system which, in turn, required large numbers of slaves and prisoners to maintain it.

In most other respects, however, Assyria's economic base was insufficient, especially so for a major power. In an age of iron, Assyria possessed few easily available iron deposits for manufacturing modern iron weapons. It also lacked stone for its building projects, most pointedly

Map 7.1
Strategic Threats to Assyria, 900–600 B.C.E.

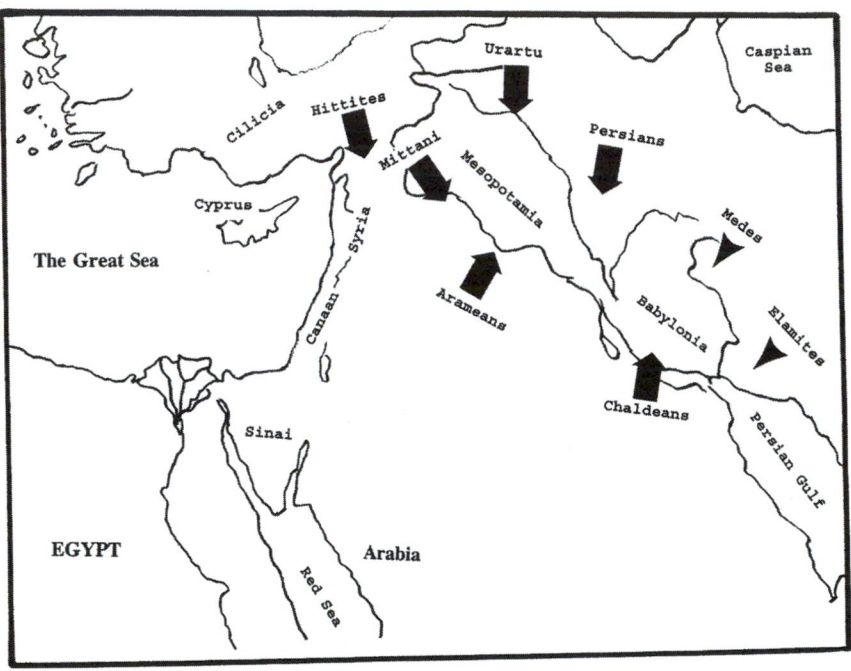

for defensive walls and irrigation projects. Except for the weak and thin wood of the palm tree, Assyria had no wood at all. Long, straight wooden beams were required to construct fortifications, public buildings, and temples, and it was wood from which the Assyrian chariots, forty-foot high siege towers, and vital battering rams were made. In an age of chariot warfare, Assyria had no grasslands on which to breed and train horses. Assyria's geography provided few of the vital strategic materials from which to forge its military strength. The solution was to conquer and occupy the neighboring states to the west, north, and southeast, all of which could provide the raw materials that Assyria required.

Assyria's fragile agricultural infrastructure and lack of military raw materials were aggravated by the country's geographical position on the Tigris, which left it vulnerable to a number of hostile neighboring states whose aggressive designs placed Assyria under constant geopolitical threat. Map 7.1 portrays the geostrategic position of Assyria relative to her hostile neighbors. In the early days (1500–1200 B.C.E.), Assyria was the target of Mitannian, Hittite, and Babylonian expansion and vassalage, and even at the height of Assyrian power, Babylon always had to be watched closely as did her penchant for mischief and hostile alliances. Southwest of Babylon were the Chaldeans, who posed a constant threat to Assyria's southern borders. To the northwest, in the area of modern Armenia, the Urartu posed an even greater threat, as did the Medes in the Zagros Mountains further to the east. Geography placed Assyria in a vulnerable position, surrounded by hostile powers who commonly raided its trade routes, disrupted its economic supply lines, and attacked it outright whenever Assyria was weak. In the Assyrian view, the world was a dangerous place indeed, and there could be no real security unless these neighboring states were brought to heel.

The Assyrian army was forged in the crucible of 200 years of near constant warfare. The rulers of Assyria during this period proved to be strong and talented men who provided the direction needed to sustain a constant reign of conquest and suppression of revolts. Moreover, it was Assyria that gave the world what was to become the imperial system of provincial management of conquered peoples, a system that reached its height under the Romans.[6] The need to respond to a number of new technologies and strategic needs required that the Assyrian army undergo periods of significant reform and reorganization, and to develop new equipment. All these achievements were accomplished by the great warrior kings of the period.

The imperial period witnessed the reigns of six important monarchs, beginning with Assurnasirpal II (883–859 B.C.E.), who was followed by his son Shalmaneser III (858–824 B.C.E.). There then was a period of eighty years in which the archaeological records reveal little about monarchical rule until Tiglath-Pileser III (745–727 B.C.E.) came to power. Six years after his death, the greatest Assyrian ruler and military conqueror, Sargon II (721–705 B.C.E.) ascended the throne. History has accorded this most brutal of Assyrian kings the title of Sargon the Great. He was succeeded by his son Sennacherib (704–681 B.C.E.) and, thirty years later, by his grandson, Ashurbanipal (668–630 B.C.E.). Under three of these monarchs, Assurnasirpal II, Tiglath-Pileser III, and Sargon II, significant reforms of the Assyrian army were carried out that allowed the development of a powerful and modern military machine.

The Assyrian empire was no easy empire to govern. In an age of primitive communications the empire was widely scattered and in some places was geographically isolated by mountain ranges and deserts. It was, moreover, comprised of conquered peoples with strong nationalist feelings often tied to local religious, tribal, and blood loyalties. The Assyrians mastered the administration of this state through the use of a modern bureaucracy, the establishment of a provincial system of authority, the use of auxiliary armies, deportation—sometimes of whole peoples—and the ruthless use of police and military terror, supported by an efficient intelligence system.

With each conquered area a professional civil service ensured that things ran smoothly. Assyrian civil servants were trained in professional schools in a manner similar to the training of Egyptian scribes. The highest-ranking civil servant was a *tartan*, who represented the authority of the king. Next in order came the Overseer of the Palace, the Main Cupbearer, and the Governor. Military men often held high positions in the civil government of conquered areas and, in times of peace, the line between military and civilian authority was often unclear.[7] An interesting aspect of the provincial civil service was the use of former captives in the administration itself; some were freed and permitted to hold minor governmental posts.[8] The Assyrian civil service numbered about 100,000 functionaries.

As efficient as the administrative structure was, no Assyrian monarch was foolish enough to rely upon it alone. Behind the civil service stood a police and intelligence apparatus centered in the personal bodyguard of the king, his "troops of the feet," so called because they stood literally at his feet during battle when he fought from his war chariot. These praetorians, about 1,000 in number, had the task of ensuring the loyalty of the civil service and anyone else in a provincial area who might in any way represent a threat to the royal will.[9] The intelligence service employed spies and other agents to accomplish their task, and it was they who enforced the order for recall, interrogation, or termination of provincial officials who had fallen from the favor of the king.

The control of an empire containing so many disparate peoples required a heavy reliance upon native auxiliary troops. While Tiglath-Pileser III seems to have been the first to use auxiliaries, by the time of Sargon II the practice had been institutionalized. Native auxiliaries were used mostly to garrison the provinces, but after a while they became an integral part of the Assyrian field fighting force.[10]

Behind the imperial system rested the sure knowledge among potential revolutionaries that punishment would be swift and extremely cruel. The Assyrians were the first to practice psychological warfare on a grand scale as a matter of state policy. Assyrian cruelty became legendary. What made the Assyrians different from other conquerors is that they boasted about their cruelty and raised monuments to it as a form of propaganda to convince actual and potential adversaries that resistance was futile and carried terrible penalties. In almost every instance of Assyrian victory the vanquished were dealt severe and public punishment.

Defeated monarchs, generals, and high government officials often met horrible and painful deaths in full view of the newly subjugated population. Assurnasirpal II's vengeance against the city of Susa was a typical example of this Assyrian practice: "I built a pillar over the city gate and I flayed all the chief men who had revolted, and I covered the pillar with their skins; some I walled up within the pillar, some I impaled . . . on stakes." The officers who rebelled were first flayed alive and their limbs were then cut off, "and I spread their skins upon the walls."[11] Sargon II had his main palace hall decorated with particularly brutal reliefs depicting what he had done to his enemies.[12] The room was used specifically for greeting foreign dignitaries, who usually did not miss the point. The king's personal bodyguard also functioned as an intelligence and police force and could be employed to enforce the king's terror at will.

The establishment and maintenance of an empire the size of Assyria's required a military establishment of great size. No accurate figures exist as to the total size of the army, but at the very least the Assyrian army would have to have comprised between 150,000 and 200,000 men.[13] A large part of this force, probably as much as one third, was composed of auxiliary troops used to garrison the provinces. They were called to actual combat service as the need arose. Probably as much as 20 percent of the total army was comprised of reserve troops that functioned in peacetime as local militia but could also be called to national service when needed. An Assyrian combat field army numbered 50,000 men, with various mixes of infantry, chariots, and cavalry.[14] Expressed in modern terms the size of this force would be equivalent to five heavy American divisions or almost eight Soviet field divisions. When arrayed for battle, this force took up an area 2,500 yards across and 100 yards deep,[15] each man occupying a square yard of ground.

An army of this size required considerable manpower, manpower that the Assyrian socioeconomic base could not provide by itself. In the early days of the empire, the army was recruited from the general population by forced conscription. Local provincial vassals sustained feudal militias, which the vassals were required to provide to the king in time of war.[16] Tiglath-Pileser III (745–727 B.C.E.) broke the power of the aristocracy and formed the nucleus of a standing professional army centered around an elite royal guard of a thousand men.[17] Although there are records of the use of auxiliary troops under Assurnasirpal II (883–859 B.C.E.), the practice seems to have been expanded by Tiglath-Pileser. It was formally institutionalized by Sargon II (721–705 B.C.E.), who also expanded the professional army.

Under Sargon II the professional praetorian corps of the army was expanded to several thousand, and an inner elite known as "the companions" or "troops of the feet" formed the spine of the army.[18] Provincial governors were required to raise and support local forces for use in time of war, but the governors were no longer powerful enough to use these forces to resist the king. Yet, local forces were substantial, in at least one instance being comprised of 1,500 cavalry and 20,000 archers.[19] Auxiliary units were thoroughly integrated into the field fighting force but still retained the major function of garrison duty to ensure control of captured populations.

A number of other important reforms increased the fighting power of the army. Assurnasirpal II introduced the first use of cavalry units to the Assyrian army.[20] Indeed, the Assyrians invented cavalry as a new military combat arm. Ashurnasirpal was also the first to employ heavy, mobile siege towers and the mobile battering ram. Under his reign there appears the first use of units of wall-breakers, who specialized in climbing scaling ladders and weakening defensive walls with axes and levers.[21] Cavalry units were integrated into the force structure and eventually replaced the chariot corps as the elite striking arm. In 854 B.C.E. at the battle of Karkar, Shalmaneser III fielded a force of 35,000 men comprised of 20,000 infantry, 1,200 chariots, and 12,000 cavalry![22] Even allowing for exaggeration, what is important are the force ratios. At Karkar, there were ten times as many cavalry as chariots.

By Sargon's time the army had been reorganized into a thoroughly integrated fighting force of infantry, chariots, cavalry, siege machinery, and specialized units of scouts, engineers, intelligence officers, and sappers. Sargon also equipped the army entirely with weapons of iron, thereby producing the first iron army of the period.[23] The Assyrian army was also equipped with iron armor and helmets. The production and storage of iron weapons and other metal materials of war became a central feature of the army's logistical base. A single weapons room in Sargon's palace at Dur-Sharrukin (Fort Sargon) contained 200 tons of iron weapons, helmets, and body armor.[24]

The combat forces of the field army were organized in units of ten formed around national and regional formations, each of which specialized in the weapons and tactics at which it excelled. The ten-man squad under the command of a noncommissioned officer was the smallest fighting unit. The normal tactical unit was the company, which could be tailored into units of 50 to 200 men. The company was commanded by a *kirsu* or captain.[25] In battle, infantry units of spearmen deployed in phalanxes with a ten-man front and files twenty-men deep. These units were highly trained and disciplined in maneuver. Their gradual but persistent movement toward and through enemy ranks, killing as they went, represented a main shock force of the Assyrian army.[26] According to Arnold Toynbee, the Assyrian infantry developed the prototype of the disciplined and courageous foot soldier, which reached its epitome in the Greek hoplite.[27]

Assyrian infantry was divided into three types: spearmen, archers, and slingmen. The spearmen deployed in phalanxes to anchor the main line in the center of the battlefield. Each phalanx was comprised of 200 men, ten ranks across and twenty files deep, commanded by a captain. Assyrian spearmen were heavy infantry armed with a long, double-bladed spear and a straight sword for hand-to-hand combat. The sword was secured to a thick belt that ran around a knee-length coat of iron mail armor. The spearman carried a small iron shield and wore a conical iron helmet with a wool or fabric liner that helped to absorb the energy of a blow and dissipate heat.[28] An important Assyrian innovation was the introduction of knee-high leather boots reinforced with iron plates to protect the shins.[29] The combination of weapons and personal protective equipment slowed the movement of the heavy infantry considerably, and the Assyrians continually experimented with various types of lighter shields to reduce the load carried by the soldier in battle.[30]

Units of archers comprised the second type of Assyrian infantry. The Assyrian composite bow seems to have been of a more advanced type than that usually found in the Near East, and bas-reliefs show that it had to be bent with the knee, often requiring two men to string it.[31] Such a bow would have been very powerful and would have required some form of selection process to obtain strong physical types to use it. Assyrian arrows were iron-tipped and had great penetrating power. Some arrows had an iron tan proceeding backward from the shank to which oil-soaked wool was attached. The wool would be set afire and the arrow used as an incendiary device against buildings and wooden gates.[32]

For protection the archer wore a long coat of mail armor, the weight of which considerably reduced his mobility. Before Tiglath-Pileser, a shield bearer carrying a small round shield was employed to protect the archer from counterfire. Later a larger man-sized shield of braided reeds with a slightly bow-backed top was introduced to provide protection from missiles fired from defensive walls. The Assyrian archer also carried a sword for close combat. The Assyrians increased the rate of fire of their archers by introducing an innovation in the arrow quiver. Carried on the back and secured by a shoulder strap, the quiver had a short rod protruding from the bottom front and opening slightly above the shoulder. This innovation allowed the archer to reach back and pull down on the rod, tipping the quiver forward and bringing the arrows within easy and ready reach. Modern archery experts estimate that this type of quiver might well have increased the rate of fire by as much as 40 percent.[33]

The third type of infantry used by the Assyrians were the slingmen. The sling was probably introduced to the Assyrians by mercenaries or conquered peoples, and the Assyrians were slow to adopt it. While some bas-reliefs show slingmen deployed alongside archers in battle on open terrain, the slingmen saw their primary use in siege warfare. Slingers could direct high-angled parabolic fire against the defenders on the wall.

The Assyrian chariot corps constituted the primary striking arm of the army and gradually underwent major design changes over the imperial period. Originally the Assyrian chariot was used in much the same way as the Egyptian and Mitannian chariot, as a mobile platform for archers. But the Assyrian chariot was always a heavier machine with a stiff and heavy front end, a characteristic that made it less maneuverable at high speed.[34] Originally the crew had consisted of a driver and an archer, with the driver armed with a spear and an axe. The archer wore body armor but had little other protection. The mission of the chariot was to attack massed infantry formations, deliver shock, and then, as the Assyrian infantry clashed at close range, to aid in the pursuit.

Over time the shock role of the chariot increased, and as enemy armies became more developed there was a need to protect the crew in close combat. The result was the development of an even heavier chariot carrying a crew of three, with the third man acting as a shield bearer to protect the archer and driver. By the time of Ashurbanipal, the Assyrian chariot had evolved into a four-man vehicle with a driver, archer, and two shield bearers. The weight of the machine now required three and then four horses to pull it, and the wheels became thicker, requiring eight spokes for strength.[35] All crewmen carried a spear, sword, shield, and axe, a development that turned the chariot corps into mounted infantry. After administering the initial shock to the enemy by mounted charge, the chariot crew dismounted and fought as heavy infantry. The Assyrians maintained a large corps of chariots, but as early as 854 B.C.E. Shalmaneser III had already begun to develop a new combat arm, the cavalry, which eventually eclipsed the chariot corps as the arm of decision of the Assyrian army.

The major advantage of the chariot was that in battles on open terrain it could deliver tremendous shock to massed infantry formations. Its major disadvantage was that in rough terrain its mobility and shock value were severely limited or even lost altogether. As the Assyrian empire grew, the army was required more and more to traverse difficult terrain and to conduct operations in areas where the terrain was not favorable to the chariot. The need to fight in other than open terrain required another combat arm that could maneuver and was capable of delivering firepower. The solution was cavalry.

It was the steppe peoples who lived in the northern areas above the Tigris valley to whom armies owed the development of the horse as a fighting vehicle.[36] At first the horse was too short, light, and weak to carry a mounted rider for any distance and found its primary military use in pulling the light chariot. By the ninth century B.C.E., as a result of breeding and further physical development, the horse had become strong enough to be employed as a new military asset. The presence of Assyrians in Armenia and in the Zagros Mountains most likely brought them into contact with the horse-riding steppe peoples, from whom they obtained the new and stronger breeds of horses.

The introduction of horses and their growing importance to the Assyrian army required that they be obtained in adequate and safe supply. Since Assyria itself, lacking grasslands, offered few of the conditions necessary to breed these animals in sufficient numbers, the Assyrians developed a remarkable logistical and supply organization to insure an adequate supply of horses for the army. The horse recruitment officers, called *musarkisus*, were high-level government officials appointed directly by the king. The fact that they reported directly to the king and not the provincial governors under whom they served testifies to the importance of their function as horse quartermasters. Usually two horse-recruitment officers were assigned to each province. Assisted by a staff of scribes and other officers, they ensured that adequate numbers of horses were assembled and trained for military use.[37]

The *musarkisus* obtained horses on a year-round basis and were responsible for sustaining them in a national system of corrals and stables. Surviving documents indicate that in the city of Nineveh these officers were able to secure 3,000 horses a month arriving on schedules of 100 animals a day! These reports also note that the horses were received from every province of the empire. One report notes that of the 2,911 horses received for a single month, 1,840 were used as yoke horses in the chariot corps, 27 were put to stud, and 787 were riding horses assigned for cavalry use.[38] In addition, the horse-recruitment officers were responsible for securing adequate supplies of mules and camels for use in the logistics train. This efficient logistical apparatus was unknown in any other army of the world at this time.

Originally the Assyrian cavalryman was an ordinary foot soldier equipped with armor, lance, sword, shield, and heavy boots. This great weight severely limited his mobility. Over time the armored coat was reduced to waist length and the shield made smaller. The Assyrians used a blanket, saddle girth, crupper, and breast straps to stabilize the rider.[39] Later, Assyrian cavalrymen learned to control their mounts with their legs and the heel pressure of their boots (the spur had not yet been invented). This made it possible to place archers on horseback as well and gave birth to the first use of mounted archers in the Near East. Writers of the Old Testament called these cavalry archers "hurricanes on horseback."[40]

There is some debate as to the proportionate strength and role of the cavalry in the Assyrian army. Some analysts suggest that the chariot corps remained the primary fighting arm until the end of the empire, and perhaps this is so. Yet, as early as the eighth century B.C.E., Shalmaneser III put ten times more cavalrymen than chariots in the field at Karkar. An Assyrian chariot required at least three horses and sometimes four to deploy in battle. It may well have been that the supply system could not provide the numbers of horses required to sustain both large chariot and cavalry forces. The reports cited earlier suggest that for every horse sent to the cavalry, three had to be sent to the chariot corps, and this does not count replacement horses. A field chariot force of 4,000 machines would require 12,000 horses at the very minimum and 16,000 thousand at the maximum, not counting the ready reserve or the horses supplied to the forces on garrison duty throughout the empire. Add to this the number required of a small cavalry force of 6,000, and the number of horses that had to be acquired and trained for the army's immediate use in time of war was almost 20,000 animals to supply a single field army in battle or on the march to the objective.

A factor that might have worked to keep the cavalry arm relatively small was that the horseshoe had not yet made its appearance. A substantial number of horses on any given march would have gone lame and would have had to be replaced. This would have required that a substantial number of horses, perhaps 5 to 10 percent of the total horse contingent, be held in ready reserve as replacements if fighting strength was to be maintained.[41] A practical solution to these problems would have been to tailor the configuration of the army to the type and location of the battle. On open terrain it would have made sense to deploy the heavy chariots in substantial numbers since they were most effective there. On a long march through mountainous or forested country it would have made sense to reduce the number of chariots to a minimum and increase the number of cavalry. Sargon II seemed to follow precisely this strategy in his campaign against the Urartu in 714 B.C.E.

This campaign required movement over long distances in terrain that was mountainous, forested, and criss-crossed with swift streams and rivers. Mountain passes and gorges filled with snow had to be negotiated as well. We do not know how many chariots were taken along, but after the first engagement with the enemy Sargon sent his chariots home and used only his infantry and cavalry units to complete the campaign. With both types of units Sargon crossed a mountain pass left undefended because the enemy thought the terrain was so difficult that no force of any size could cross it. The Assyrians negotiated the pass, caught the enemy by surprise, fought a major battle, and still had sufficient combat power to capture a fortified city.[42]

The Assyrian army was the first army of the Near East to develop an all-weather capability for ground combat. They fought in winter as well as in summer and even conducted siege operations during the winter months.[43] The fact that the army was almost continually at war somewhere in the empire for more than 200 years provided adequate opportunity for developing field technique by trial and error. And it developed these techniques to a high art indeed. When moving through wooded terrain, for example, the infantry proceeded line abreast in separate ranks. Smaller units were sent ahead as point while others provided flank security. If engaged in battle within heavily forested areas, the spear-bearing infantry was used as the primary striking or defensive force as circumstances warranted. In hilly terrain with light woods the mounted archers and spearmen of the cavalry became the primary striking force. While the cavalry usually moved in column, the infantry provided flank security in line formation.[44] As the army deployed in mountainous terrain, the Assyrians developed the practice of spreading scouts and snipers over wide areas to provide adequate security for the main body. The Assyrians also experimented with mixed units combining infantry, archers, and slingers in a single unit.[45] So adaptable were the Assyrian ground forces that they also fought well in marshlands. Placed aboard light reed boats, they became water-borne marines, using fire arrows and torches to burn out the enemy hiding among the bushes and reeds of the swamp.[46]

In open terrain Assyrian tactics were straightforward and relied upon shock, firepower, and discipline to carry the day. Once the army had been formed for battle, archer and slinger units began firing their missiles from a distance to inflict casualties upon the infantry formations of the enemy. Special archer units were specialists at killing chariot horses and directed their fire at these units.[47] Then Assyrian chariots attacked from as many different directions as the terrain would permit, their archers firing as the machines closed with the enemy infantry. The purpose of the attack was to deliver tremendous shock at a number of different points in an effort to shatter the enemy infantry. As the chariots drove into the mass of infantry their crews dismounted and fought in close combat as infantry. As the enemy mass began to waiver, the phalanxes of Assyrian spearmen, supported by direct fire from archer units, began in disciplined and slow march to close with the enemy. The cavalry, which to this point had been used to pin the enemy flanks, now took up positions to prevent the retreat of the broken enemy, sometimes acting as an anvil against which the infantry and chariot units could drive the fleeing remnants. Once the enemy army broke ranks, the spearmen, archers, charioteers, and cavalry singled out individual targets, rode them down, and killed them.

An army of such size and complexity as Assyria's required a sophisticated logistics apparatus to support and supply it in the field. With few exceptions such as the recruitment of horses mentioned earlier, we know very little about the organization of the logistics system. This being said, however, it is obvious that being forced to fight in so many different climates and types of terrain must have required a high degree of logistical flexibility and planning. The provincial system allowed the Assyrians the advantage of being able to position supplies near their borders in advance of a campaign, but once in enemy territory, like every army until 1860 and the first use of the railway in war, the Assyrian army lived off the land and on captured enemy stores. This need for supplies explains the penchant of early armies to attack cities even when it made little tactical sense for them to do so. And like the armies that came after them, the Assyrians timed campaigns to take maximum advantage of the seasons to assure an adequate supply of food in captured areas.

Even when food and water supplies were adequate, there remained the problem of transport. It is well to recall that at this time there were few roads even in cities and none at all on the campaign. The spine of the supply transport system was the mule and another Assyrian innovation, the military use of the camel. So valuable were these animals that they took high priority as captured loot.[48] In the campaign against Egypt, the Assyrians used camels to cross the Saudi Desert to attack Palestine. The camel served another function as the main transport of the caravan system. As caravan traders themselves, the Assyrians no doubt had maps of every trail, water hole, and oasis of possible military use.

Military power is always a slave to political events, and this fact brought about the end of the Assyrian empire. In 668 B.C.E., Ashurbanipal, the last great Assyrian king, ascended the throne upon the death of his father. He inherited an empire that had grown weary and over-extended from constant border wars and suppressions of domestic revolts. The numerous captive peoples grew increasingly restless under the harsh rule of their Assyrian masters. Political control from the center was weakened as auxiliary forces became more and more unreliable, even as they became more necessary to control almost constant revolts.

In 664 B.C.E. the Elamites sacked Babylon, only to do it again in 653 B.C.E. In 656 B.C.E. Shamash-shum-ukin, the brother of Ashurbanipal, struck at the Assyrian throne by forming an alliance with Babylon, the Elamites, the Arameans, the Arabs, and the Egyptians against his brother. The result was another costly war that tore the army apart and pitted national and regional forces against one another. While records are sparse, the period between 648 and the death of Ashurbanipal in 630 B.C.E. was marked by periods of civil war provoked by Ashurbanipal's sons fighting over the mantle of power.[49] The weakness at the political center encouraged local governors and generals to pursue their own interests through revolts and corruption. The situation was compounded by a number of large-scale popular uprisings that occurred at the same time.

The end came in 612 B.C.E. when a coalition of Medean and Babylonian armies sacked Nineveh and destroyed what was left of the most powerful empire and army the world had seen until that time. The destruction of Nineveh was complete and the terror continued for months as the victorious allies subdued one remnant garrison after another. A terrible vengeance was wrought upon the Assyrians, and their cruelty was revenged with even greater cruelty. A Biblical commentary captured the sense of terrible vengeance for all history.

Cursed be the city of blood, full of lies, full of violence. . . . The sound of the whip is heard, the gallop of horses, the rolling of chariots. An infinity of dead, the dead are everywhere! My anger is on thee, Nineveh, saith Jehovah. . . . I will show thy nakedness to the nations and thy shame to the kingdoms. And then it will be said: Nineveh is destroyed! Who will mourn her?[50]

So complete was the destruction of the Assyrian capital that two centuries later Xenophon and his Greek mercenary army of 10,000 men passed the ruins of Nineveh unaware of what they were passing.[51] Not a single vestige of Assyrian power remained. A people who had lived on the Tigris for more than 2,000 years had literally disappeared from the face of the earth.

NOTES

1. A.T. Olmstead, *The History of Assyria* (Chicago: University of Chicago Press, 1951), 64.

2. *Encyclopedia Britannica*, vol. 21, 1985, 927.

3. W.F. Saggs, "Assyrian Warfare in the Sargonid Period," *Iraq* 25, part 2 (Autumn 1963), 145.

4. Georges Conteneau, *Everyday Life in Babylon and Assyria* (London: Edward Arnold, 1954), 41–42. It is important to note that in the ancient world, references to corn are really references to wheat. Corn is a New World plant not introduced to Europe until after Columbus' discovery of the New World.

5. Ibid., 44–47.

6. Olmstead, 607–8.

7. Ibid., 605–6.

8. *Encyclopedia Britannica*, vol. 21, 1985, p. 930.

9. Olmstead, 607.

10. Ibid., 604.

11. D.D. Luckenbill, *Ancient Records of Assyria and Babylon*, 2 vols. (Chicago: University of Chicago Press, 1926). The quote is taken from vol. 1, 144–45.

12. Pictorial representations of these reliefs appear in Yigael Yadin, *The Art of Warfare in Biblical Lands in Light of Archaeological Study* (New York: McGraw-Hill, 1960), vol. 2, Appendix. See also Saggs, 149.

13. Arther Ferrill, *The Origins of War* (London: Thames and Hudson, 1985), 70. For more accurate figures on the size of the Assyrian army, see Saggs, 145.

14. T.N. Dupuy, *The Evolution of Warfare and Weapons* (New York: Bobbs-Merrill, 1980), 10.

15. Ibid.

16. Olmstead, 603.

17. Robert Laffont, *The Ancient Art of Warfare* (New York: Time-Life Books, 1966), vol. 1, 45. See also Conteneau, 142.

18. Olmstead, 603.

19. Saggs, 145.

20. *Encyclopedia Britannica*, vol. 21, 1985, 925.

21. Ibid.

22. Laffont; see chart, 40.

23. Ferrill, 67.

24. Laffont, 45.

25. Olmstead, 604.

26. T.N. Dupuy, 10.

27. Laffont, 45.

28. Yadin, 94–95.

29. On the subject of boots see Laffont, 45 and Conteneau, 144.

30. I am indebted to Mr. Carl Netsch, a blacksmith in Manchester, N.H., who

helped calculate the weight of Assyrian iron armor and weapons. Hammered iron an eighth-inch thick weighs five pounds per square foot. Accordingly, a soldier in a full suit of Assyrian scale armor, helmet, and iron-shinned boots, armed with a sword and carrying a shield and a spear, would carry a combat load of approximately sixty pounds, or about the same load as carried by a modern soldier.

31. For a description of the Assyrian bow, see Yadin, 295.

32. Conteneau, 61; see also Olmstead, 155.

33. This estimate was provided by several archery enthusiasts. It must be regarded as highly tentative.

34. A good analysis of the Assyrian chariot is found in Yadin, 297–300; as regards the subject of maneuverability, see Conteneau, 145.

35. Yadin, 298–99.

36. *Encyclopedia Britannica*, vol. 21, 1985, 923.

37. The definitive work on this subject remains J.N. Postgate, *Taxation and Conscription in the Assyrian Empire* (Rome: Biblical Institute Press, 1974). See Ferrill as well, 71–73.

38. Ferrill, 72.

39. Laffont, 48.

40. Ibid.

41. These numbers are based upon estimates used by logistics officers in modern armies as they refer to the expected breakdown rate for tanks and trucks.

42. For a detailed account of Sargon II's eighth campaign, see Conteneau, 149–59; see also Richard A. Gabriel, *The Great Captains of Antiquity* (Westport, Conn.: Greenwood Press, 2000), chap. 3.

43. Saggs, 145–46.

44. Yadin, 303.

45. Saggs, 151.

46. Yadin, 303.

47. Saggs, 152.

48. Conteneau, 59.

49. *Encyclopedia Britannica*, vol. 21, 1985, 928–30.

50. Nahum 3: 1–7.

51. Laffont, 49.

8

Chinese Armies: The Shang and Zhou Periods
1750–256 B.C.E.

A student of the art of war in ancient China is faced with the immense richness of the Chinese military heritage. The eminent historian of China, John King Fairbank, once said that "no people before modern times has left so extensive a record of military institutions and exploits."[1] The stage was set for this Chinese saga when civilization emerged in the broad valley of the Yellow River some 4,000 years ago. There, a series of Neolithic cultures developed. With the advent of metalworking and advances in agriculture came a civilization marked by a rich aristocratic culture, splendidly decorated bronze vessels, complex rituals, and a political and administrative structure capable of mobilizing and directing manpower resources organized for war. The three dynasties of early Chinese civilization are the Xia (2200–1750 B.C.E.), the Shang (1750–1100 B.C.E.), and the Zhou (1100–256 B.C.E.), which, each in turn, came to control all of civilized China. No writing has survived from the Xia Dynasty and thus it will not be addressed here. The dates and durations of the more important Chinese dynasties addressed herein appear in Table 8.1

The Shang civilization consisted of one or two hundred clans, one of which constituted a ruling aristocracy from which the king was selected through a complex system of rotation among ten subclans. War was an essential part of the Shang culture and was inextricably linked with hunting, ritual sacrifice, religious observance, political control, and economic

Table 8.1
Chinese Historical Eras

Xia	2200–1750 B.C.
Shang	1750–1100 B.C.
Zhou	1100–256 B.C.
Western Zhou	1100–770 B.C.
Eastern Zhou	771–256 B.C.
Spring & Autumn	771–464 B.C.
(Battle of Chengpu 632 B.C.)	
Warring States	464–221 B.C.
(Battle of Guiling 353 B.C.)	
Qin Empire	221–206 B.C.
(Battle of Jingxing 205 B.C.)	
Han Empire	206 B.C.–220 A.D.

power. The ruling aristocracy derived its legitimacy and authority from military force and religious sanction, while success in war and hunting demonstrated its power. Hunting provided practice for, and was sometimes indistinguishable from, war. Sacrifice helped ensure a favorable outcome for the hunt and victory in war. Hunting and war, in turn, provided animal and human victims for more sacrifices. The hunt contributed to the economy by providing food, while warfare provided plunder and slaves. The Shang aristocracy hunted, warred, and sacrificed on a vast scale. Bone and shell oracle inscriptions speak of hunts in which hundreds of animals were slaughtered, military expeditions by armies of thousands of troops, and sacrificial rituals in which thousands of people were "chastised with the halberd."[2] Tomb excavations have revealed the headless corpses of as many as 600 victims at a single site and multitudes of animals, all slain to consecrate a single house.

The very structure of Shang society was based on war, with the basic social unit, the clan or zi also serving as a military unit.[3] The clan consisted of about a hundred families that lived in a small walled town and fielded a military unit consisting of one man from each family. The zi chief was also a military leader. The royal capital was a larger and more complex version of the clan town and was protected by rammed-earth walls and a standing army supplemented by some of the soldier citizens of a number of zi. In time of war, the rest of the clan fighting men of the capital and other towns throughout the kingdom could be mobilized.

The regular military establishment consisted of the standing army (lu), which was officered by leaders with such titles as "garrison commandant," "frontier commandant," "archer commandant," "horse attendant," and "dog attendant." The army could be commanded by the king, royal princes, or *zi* chiefs, depending upon the circumstances of the conflict. There are even some cases of Shang armies being commanded by royal consorts. At the height of the Shang Dynasty the royal standing army numbered about a thousand men and could be expanded by calling levies from subordinate lineages. Armies mobilized for extended campaigns numbered from as few as 3,000 to 5,000 men for local campaigns against border tribes to tens of thousands for major wars. The mobilized army was divided into three parts: right, center, and left or, an alterative translation, upper, center, and lower.[4]

Armies consisted of chariot forces and infantry. Mounted warriors did not appear in China until at least the fifth century B.C.E., and warhorses in Shang times were used exclusively to pull chariots and supply vehicles. The Shang-era chariot was a two-wheeled contrivance normally pulled by two horses. It had five foot-high wheels and a low-sided wicker or wood body mounted directly on the vehicle's axle. Each chariot was manned by a driver armed with a whip, an archer who rode on the driver's left, and a "striker" who stood on the driver's right and wielded a dagger axe, a wooden haft with a dagger-like blade mounted crosswise near the tip.[5]

The chariot was a costly piece of equipment and a symbol of wealth and power. It appears that in Shang times chariot crews (or at least their commanders) were drawn from the ruling nobility, and while some warrior aristocrats may also have been foot soldiers, most infantry were probably drawn from the peasantry. There is some question as to whether Shang armies fought extensively from chariots or whether the chariot was used primarily as a command platform and to convey warriors into battle. On the basis of fragmentary references to elephants in traditional Shang stories it is at least possible that some Shang armies included war elephants as well. If so, the elephant was not used for long, presumably due to its vulnerability to missile weapons and because Shang warriors soon hunted the wild elephant to extinction.[6]

Shang military organization below army level is largely conjectural, but the generally accepted view is that five infantry soldiers or five chariots and crews made up a "unit of five" or *wu*. This is usually translated into English as "squad," a term that fits well for foot soldiers, but in the case of chariots the five-vehicle *wu* seems more closely equivalent to a modern tank platoon. Groups of three to five chariot platoons formed a "company," each chariot accompanied by a number of foot soldiers prob-

Figure 8.1
Shang Tactical Chariot Organization

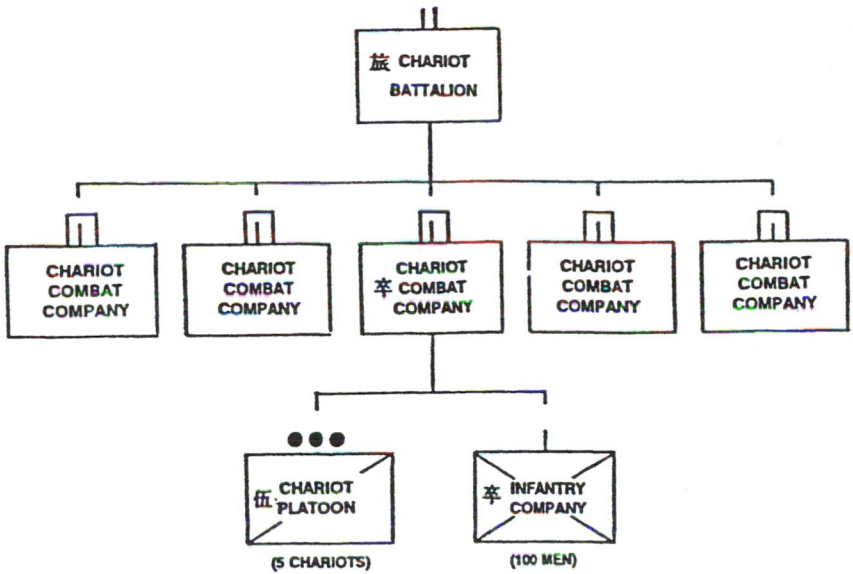

(5 CHARIOTS)   (100 MEN)

ably equivalent to the "chariot runners" of the armies of the Near East. Infantry and archers were organized into 100-man companies, and in later times each five-chariot platoon was supported by an infantry company, forming a sort of company task force or combat company. One chariot company plus the associated three to five infantry companies formed an operational unit equivalent to a battalion. Figure 8.1 depicts the organizational structure of a typical Shang combat battalion.[7]

The basic weapon of the foot soldier was the *ge* or dagger axe, a wooden shaft three to four feet long with a bronze, knife-like blade attached at a right angle at one end. A soldier could wield a *ge* with one or two hands and would swing it down and inward, hooking and cutting the enemy. The "striker" on the chariot crew wielded a similar weapon with a seven-foot shaft. Some soldiers carried the spear or *mao*, which differed from the dagger axe in having a leaf-like bronze blade that formed an extension of the shaft. While the dagger axe was a hooking, slashing, weapon, the spear was a piercing and stabbing weapon used by thrusting or throwing. Battle axes or *fu* with broad, ornate bronze blades have been found in Shang tombs, but they seem to have been used primarily for beheading sacrificial victims.[8]

Archers wielded composite recurved bows about five feet long (about the height of the average Shang soldier!) made of laminations of cattle sinew and horn or of strips of bamboo glued together or bound with silk. Shang arrows had flectched wooden shafts about half the length of a bow and were tipped with stone, bone, shell, horn, or bronze points. Shang armies had no swords, but charioteers and some foot soldiers (presumably officers, guards, and other elite forces) carried hatchets or ornate bronze knives with seven-inch blades sharpened on the lower edge and slightly curved downward like the Gurkha *kukri*. The knife was carried in a sheath tucked into the warrior's belt.[9]

Officers and aristocratic warriors wore silk gowns, helmets, heavy circular bronze neck protectors and armored breastplates made of bronze or leather. Some wore two-piece armor that protected their chests and backs. Their bronze helmets had a rounded crown and the sides and back came down low over the ears and the nape of the neck. Common soldiers wore knee-length hemp gowns gathered at the waist with a belt or length of rope. Their protection in battle was probably limited to shields made of wicker or painted leather stretched over a square or oval wooden frame. Charioteers also carried shields on occasion. These shields were slightly larger than the length of their dagger axes. Infantry shields were slightly smaller than the length of their dagger axes. Oracle inscriptions also show soldiers carrying banners and flags, which may have been used for unit or clan identification or signalling.[10]

While civil wars among the Shang clans were not uncommon, most Shang warfare was directed against partially civilized and barbarian peoples on the borders. On occasion these operations involved armies of substantial size operating over long distances. Although no evidence of Shang supply and transport units or practices has survived, we can reasonably infer the existence of a large, complex, and well-administered logistical organization. Military expeditions increased the area under Shang control and by the thirteenth century B.C.E. Shang armies had pushed west into the Yellow and Wei river valleys. This brought the Shang into contact and conflict with the Zhou, a people who shared aspects of the Shang and barbarian cultures and whose military equipment and capability rivaled those of the Shang. Sometime around 1100 B.C.E., the Shang king, weakened by successive military reverses, succumbed to a Zhou revolt.

The early Zhou kings exerted control over China through a system of decentralized domains ruled by royal relatives, loyal retainers, and native leaders who had submitted to the Zhou. This system of vassalage governed by rulers tied by oaths of loyalty to the Zhou king was akin to European feudalism. While the Zhou kings could field armies from the lands under their direct control, they had to depend on levies from the vassal states to mount large expeditions. Each vassal provided from one to three "armies" or units of military levy, depending on the size and wealth of his domain. A single vassal army might be as large as 3,000 chariots and 30,000 infantry divided into three divisions. The early Zhou army apparently retained the Shang organization of three-man chariot crews, five-man chariot platoons, and five-platoon companies.[11]

Zhou military equipment was generally similar to that of the Shang, with some notable improvements. While the chariot remained the primary shock and mobility weapon, the two-horse Shang chariot gave way to the four-horse chariot with larger, stronger wheels. The *ge* or dagger axe developed into a longer, two-handed weapon with an oval shaft so that it would not twist in the hand. In some cases the dagger blade was lengthened so that the weapon could be used more effectively to slash and cut. Although not yet widely used, swords began to make their appearance, initially as lengthened versions of the Shang knife. The armor of the early Zhou period was made of rhinoceros or buffalo hide or leather, either solid layers formed over a wooden mold or leather plates laced together. Hide or leather was also formed into helmets shaped similarly to those of the Shang era.[12]

The system of vassals and fiefs based on ties of kinship and loyalty was reinforced by Zhou cultural dominance and the use of religious ideology, including the concept of the "Mandate of Heaven" in which the ruler's legitimacy is bestowed by a supreme deity. Over time the Zhou system of government began to break down as a consequence of the spread of new military technology, the disintegration of the old clan system, and the pull of self-interest that weakened the loyalty of the powerful vassals. By the eighth century B.C.E., the Zhou could no longer rely on the vassal states. When the government came under military pressure from the western barbarians in 771 B.C.E., rebellious vassals joined with the invaders and brought down the Zhou state. The king was killed and his successor moved the capital to another city where the Zhou lived on, but only as vassals. Historians refer to the period after 771 B.C.E. as the "Eastern Zhou," the first part of which, 770 to 464 B.C.E., is called the "Spring and Autumn" era, one of the most militarily active and violent periods in all Chinese history.[13]

The Shang era linkage of war, hunting, and ritual sacrifice continued into the Spring and Autumn period, although human sacrifice became somewhat less frequent. Sanctioned violence was at the heart of the Chinese political and social structure during this time. Mark Lewis has noted in this regard that "during the seventh and sixth centuries B.C.E., China was dominated by a warrior aristocracy whose privileged status was

Figure 8.2
Field Army Organization (Notional): Spring and Autumn Era

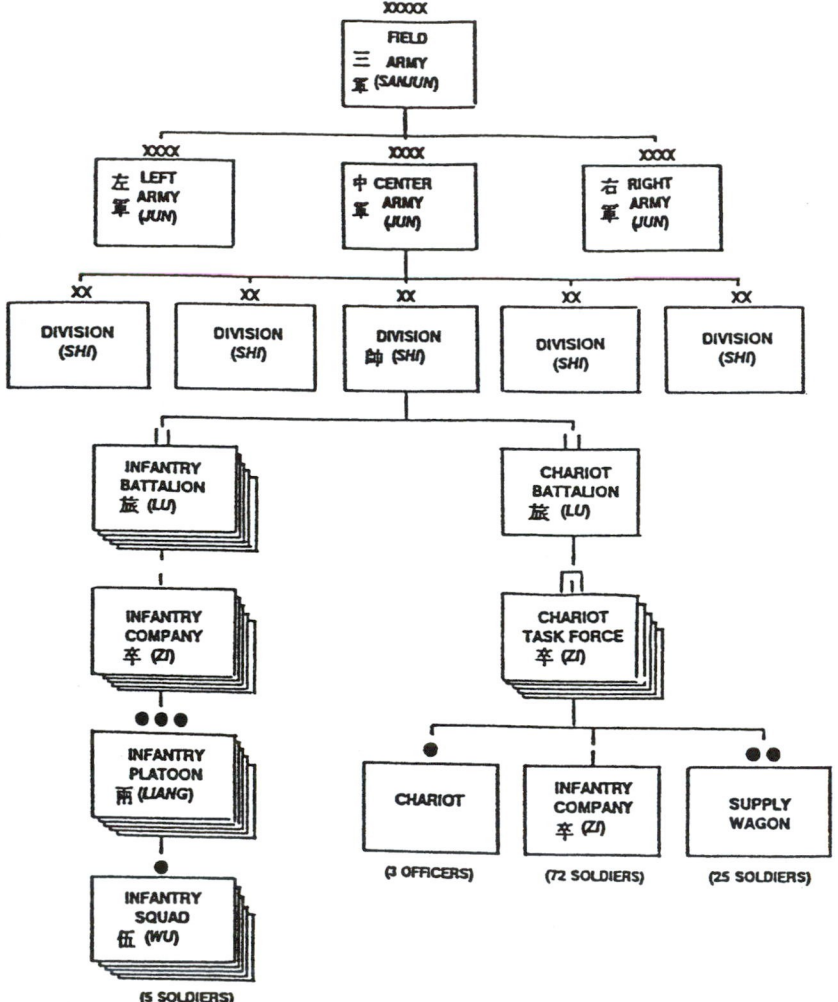

marked by its monopoly of ritually directed violence. Sanctioned killing in the form of sacrifice, warfare, and hunting constituted the central rites of the cults of ancestors and the state altars, and the performance of these rites set the aristocracy apart from the common people."[14] At the beginning of the Spring and Autumn period there were about 170 lineage-based familial city-states of various sizes within the former realm of the Zhou. The larger and more powerful gradually absorbed the weaker states through war, alliances, diplomacy, and treachery, becoming in the process genuine states with clear boundaries, a sense of national identity, and significantly large populations under effective administrative control. The battle of Chengpu (632 B.C.E.) provides an example of the armies and warfare of this period.

The two armies that faced each other at Chengpu were generally similar in organization, equipment, doctrine, and tactics. The Jin field army under Duke Wen is said to have included 700 chariots supported by an army of 22,000 to as many as 52,000 men. The field army (*sanjun*) was divided into the usual three armies (*jun*) of the left, center, and right.[15] This was the heyday of the chariot, the strength of the various states being measured by how many vehicles they could put into the field. The war chariot of the Spring and Autumn period was sturdier, armored with thick leather, and had a shorter race pole than previous models. Some models had foot-long bronze blades attached to the axles to cut down enemy foot soldiers who came too close. The chariot carried the traditional crew of three (driver, archer, and striker). Whatever the social status of the charioteer during the Shang era, by the Spring and Autumn period the chariot crews were comprised exclusively of aristocrat warriors.

Tactically, the chariot was the centerpiece of a combined arms team in which one chariot was accompanied into battle by 30 to 75 infantry soldiers. The basic and larger chariot element of the Spring and Autumn armies was the 100-man combat chariot and combined arms company or *zi* consisting of 1 chariot, 72 infantry organized into 3 platoons (*liang*), and a supply vehicle or cart with a support staff of 25 men.[16] Along with their weapons, the chariot crew carried on board drum, bell, gong, and flag to relay tactical commands to the rest of the company. Zhou era texts suggest that infantry units, which constituted the bulk of the fighting forces during this period, consisted of 5-man squads (*wu*) in a 25-man platoon (*liang*) four of which comprised a one hundred-man infantry company (*zi*). Five companies constituted a 500-man battalion (*lu*) and 5 battalions made up a 2,500–man division or *shi*. Five divisions constituted a 12,500–man army (*jun*), 3 to 5 of which comprised a field army. At Chengpu, the size of the army was about 40,000 men.[17]

The exact proportion of chariots to infantry in a field army is unknown. Figure 8.2 offers a depiction of a notional infantry-heavy field army of the Spring and Autumn period. Texts make a tactical distinction between armies advancing in formal marches with drums beating and armies infiltrating by stealth to conduct raids. One text describes a three-*jun* field army on the march as consisting of an advance guard, follow-up units, and the main armies, with a ten-mile interval between armies.

Various tactical formations were used in battle, although information on specifics is scanty. Infantry usually deployed five-men deep and could be used in conjunction with chariots or massed as a center phalanx with chariots at the flanks. Sometimes men with spears and dagger-axes were deployed in front of the main force as skirmish infantry, with archers in the rear firing over their heads.[18]

Weapons of the Spring and Autumn era were much like those of the previous period augmented by significant changes in military technology. Short swords were more widely used in this period, and the crossbow made its appearance. The heavy one- or two-piece bronze or leather cuirasses had been generally replaced by lighter, more flexible laminar armor made of overlapping rows of hard, lacquered leather plates usually painted black or red. The one-piece bronze breastplate was relegated to ceremonial use. Armor still seems to have been mostly limited to the aristocratic officer class, with the commoners in the infantry making do with the traditional leather or wooden shields. The chests of the chariot horses were protected by mantelets constructed of overlapping leather plates. At Chengpu, one commander covered his horses with tiger skins, perhaps to protect them and make them look more ferocious and intimidating to the enemy.[19]

To Chinese military thinkers of this period, a battle had three distinct phases. Phase 1, planning and preparation, included rituals of divination and sacrifice to assure success, the gathering of intelligence, the seeking of allies, moving the armies into position, making the decision to fight or withdraw, and demonstrations of valor by individual warriors and chariot teams against the enemy. One very important occurrence was the razing of the prebattle campsite as a symbolic gesture that there was no turning back. Phase 2, combat operations, included a decision to take the initiative or to receive the enemy's attack and the clash of arms itself. Phase 3, exploitation and consolidation, included exploitation of victory or, for the loser, flight, submission, or suicide, redeployment from the battlefield, final accounting of dead and wounded, including cutting off the ears of the enemy dead for an accurate body count, and disposition of prisoners. While human sacrifice of prisoners of war had declined, it had by no means disappeared. Texts contain references to the slaughter of prisoners of war and to smearing their blood on the war drums. The last step in phase 3 was an analysis and evaluation of the new set of circumstances that victory had brought about.

There is no clear dividing line between the Spring and Autumn period and the era of the Warring States that followed it. But by the middle of the fifth century B.C.E., major changes had taken place in almost every aspect of Chinese life, particularly in war, politics, and the underlying intellectual and philosophical framework that drove them both. Of the many lineage-based states at the beginning of the Spring and Autumn period, only seven major states contended for power. These were the so-called Central States or *Zhongguo* from which the Chinese name for China is derived. More important was the transformation of the political, economic, and military structure of the Warring States. Everything was now on a larger scale. The populations of the major cities had grown to hundreds of thousands. These large populations could now be adequately fed because of advances in administrative control, vast amounts of new land under cultivation, and technological improvements in agriculture and irrigation. During the Spring and Autumn period the viscount of Li had said that the great affairs of state were war and sacrifice. In the new Warring States era, Lord Shang could say with some justification that the means by which a state arises are war and agriculture.[20]

The state was now administered by a bureaucracy selected for talent rather than for family ties and had become the overarching political unit, displacing all the others. Instead of vassals, central rulers now appointed magistrates (*xian zhang*) to administer political subdivisions. These were civil servants obedient to and dependent upon the central government. The ability of the state to control its people was enhanced by the division of the population into households, neighborhoods, and districts, each of which had collective responsibility for the actions of its members for surveillance, collection of taxes, and the mobilization of manpower and other resources. Whether for public works or war, each household was required to provide one man, and each neighborhood provided an additional five-man squad. So it was that the "army was lodged among the people."[21]

The people of the Warring States were wall builders, constructing walled cities, fortresses, and border walls between the states and along the barbarian frontiers. These huge structures, like the irrigation works and armies, stimulated improvements in the ability to mobilize and control large numbers of people. Over time, the conquered peoples along the borders were brought under the control of the central realm, further increasing the number of men and resources that could be mobilized for war. A number of major military improvements occurred at this time— including the widespread introduction of the crossbow, straight sword, and horse cavalry—that greatly increased the killing power of armies. Many of these new technologies were adopted from the barbarians.[22]

The various aspects of "sanctioned violence"—war, sacrifice, blood covenants, and vendettas—were transformed during this period. Instead of clashes between hot-blooded aristocrats and levies led by essentially civil officials, wars during the period of the Warring States were now fought by mass armies led by professional officers. The last vestiges of human sacrifice and the blood covenant gave way to symbolic ritual, and oaths of loyalty replaced blood loyalties as the cement that bound officers and armies to the state. Codes of vengeance evolved into codes of law for the administration of the state and the maintenance of the armies.

The increasing intensity and magnitude of war, the technological developments accompanying the dawn of the Iron Age in China, the large populations, and the challenges of administering and controlling the Warring States created a demand for a professional corps of advisors to help rulers cope with the challenges of national leadership. This coincided with the rise of the professional civil servant, whose claim to authority rested in his special knowledge and expertise. This development brought about the appearance of itinerant philosophers who wandered with their bands of disciples seeking employment as political counselors, diplomatic envoys, and military advisors. These sages lived at about the same time as the Greek philosophers of the Classical period. This was the period of the "hundred schools" of philosophy. While the Daoists, Mohists, and Legalists along with the followers of Confucius grappled with the man's relationship with the universe and lectured on political and ethical philosophy, another group was concerned with the theory and practice of war. The most famous of these military philosophers was Master Sun of the state of Wu (*Wu Sun Tzu*) who became known to history as Sun Tzu. A contemporary of Confucius, he lived sometime between 544 and 496 B.C.E. His writings on national strategy and war collected in *Sun Tzu's Art of War* remains required reading in the world's military colleges to this day.

The standing professional army of a Warring State could be quickly expanded by the mobilization of the peasantry using the system of the "army lodged among the people." This arrangement could mobilize great numbers of men already organized into squads, platoons, companies, and battalions. Even the smaller states could mobilize armies of tens of thousands. Some documents tell of armies of a million men during major wars. Given the Chinese population of the time, the excellent administrative system, and the logistics base, such a number, if only at maximum effort, was not impossible although unlikely.[23] The Warring State armies were organized in a manner similar to those of the Spring and Autumn period with the addition of developed tactical and strategic doctrine under the command of professional military commanders. The term *sanjun* was still used to refer to the entire army or the army in the field, although the field army might consist of any number of armies. The ideal formation for a field army on the march was a division of five: the advance guard army, left and right flank armies, commander-in-chief and command group with one army in the center, and a rear guard army. The operational organization of the army was still five divisions (*shi*) each of five *lu* or battalions, each of five 100-man companies (*zi*) comprised of five twenty-five-man platoons or *liang* each of five five-man squads or *wu*.[24] As warfare expanded beyond the flat north China plain, the limitations of the chariot in irregular terrain became more and more obvious. The armies of the Warring States were primarily infantry armies. Chariots were still used for transport, command vehicles, and for mobility and rapid reaction, and when the terrain was favorable, for shock action in combat. It was during this period, however, that the chariot began to be replaced by mounted warriors. Both the cavalry warhorse and trousers (much more suitable for horse-mounted warriors than Chinese silk gowns!) were adopted from the barbarians and integrated into Chinese military formations. Cavalry in China seems to have been in at least limited use by the fourth century B.C.E., but its widespread use did not begin until at least the third century B.C.E.[25]

Iron working had been introduced to China by the fifth century B.C.E.[26] Iron eventually replaced bronze but did so over a much longer period than in the Near East. Bronze was still superior for edged weapons and less brittle than iron. The major technological innovations of the Warring States period were the cross-bow and the straight sword. Chinese soldiers had carried long knives into battle since time immemorial, but the first true sword with a blade substantially longer than the hilt did not make its appearance until the Spring and Autumn period. As infantry gained in importance in the battlefield equation, an effective close-combat weapon became essential. By the battle of Guiling in 353 B.C.E., a well-balanced bronze sword with a blade shaped for both cutting and slashing had become the standard weapon of the infantry armies of the Warring States. Sometime around 500 B.C.E. the crossbow made its appearance in China, probably adopted from the southern barbarians. Within a hundred years it had developed into an exceptionally deadly weapon, accurate and powerful enough to penetrate the armor of the period with little difficulty. The trigger was fabricated of cast bronze parts, and the bow was cocked by the bowman standing on the bow and drawing the bowstring back to the lock with both hands.[27] The traditional long weapons, the dagger-axe and spear, were still in use, but were now supplemented by another innovation: a combination of spear and dagger-axe known as the *ji*. The *ji* was a two-pronged spear (or dagger-axe with a knife on its end) that could be used for piercing, slashing, or hooking an opponent, the latter capability of great use in an age of mounted horsemen. The closest Western weapon of similar design and use was the Swiss halberd.[28]

In Warring States armies even ordinary foot soldiers wore armor. Leather molded into cuirasses or fashioned into plates laced together were the most common types of body protection.[29] Chariot crews wore long, cumbersome armor coats, while infantry, who often marched in their armor and had to be more agile on the battlefield, wore shorter tunics. Helmets were of the bronze or molded leather style that had been around for years.[30] Uniform markings, as well as banners used to identify different units, were in use and usually depicted heraldic animals like tigers, dragons, and phoenixes. One writer, Sun Bin, makes reference to several tactical formations although the specific disposition of troops in these formations is unknown.

The penetration is used to assault firm dispositions and destroy elite units. The wild geese formation is used to strike his flank and respond. . . . Mighty crossbow units and rapid-fire troops (probably archers) are used to block the enemy and prolong the battle. . . . The use of the eight formations in making war is to avail oneself of the advantages of terrain in order to seek appropriate dispositions.[31]

Sun Bin goes on to note that in combat only one third of the force is to be employed at any one time with two thirds being held in reserve. This is the reverse of the old Western infantry commander's rule of thumb of "two up and one back."

The advent of extensive fortifications and walled cities during the Warring States era led to developments in siegecraft, including the use of specialized equipment such as chariots with large shields, wheeled siege towers, battering rams, movable ladders, catapults, and powerful crossbows that could fire multiple bolts at the same time.[32] On campaign it became customary for field armies to establish fortified base camps from which to conduct operations or from which to conduct a defense. These camps were constructed much like miniature Chinese cities, with rammed earth walls and intersecting streets that permitted interlocking fields of fire for archers and crossbowmen. The commander's headquarters was at the center of the camp, surrounded by the tents of his staff and bodyguard.[33]

In 221 B.C.E., after another period of civil war, King Zheng of Qin proclaimed himself *Qin Shi-huangdi*, the first "emperor of China," and immediately set about consolidating his rule over the vast expanse of a unified China.[34] Rejecting the old feudal system, the first emperor divided the empire into thirty-six political-military administrative districts called commanderies or *jun*. Each commandery was ruled by a triumvirate comprised of a civil governor, a military commander, and an inspector general, who was the direct representative of the emperor. Each commandery was subdivided into counties. All administrative posts were filled by centrally appointed, salaried officials subject to recall by the emperor. The old hereditary ruling families were pensioned off and kept under close surveillance. The walls of cities and other military obstacles, remnants of the civil wars and old divisions, were leveled and all weapons except those used by the imperial army were confiscated and destroyed. The first emperor imposed a draconian legal code, standardization of the Chinese language, a system of standardized weights and measures, a national network of roads, and the suppression of any subversive thought by the destruction of thousands of historical and philosophical texts. To make the point even clearer, the emperor had several hundred scholars publicly executed.

The reforms of Qin Shihunagdi were immediately threatened by renewed civil war on his death in 210 B.C.E., which ultimately led to the establishment of the Han Dynasty less than a decade later. Warfare during this period was much as it had been during the Warring States era with a number of significant changes, however. The military doctrines and techniques preached by the itinerant military philosophers of the previous period had been thoroughly absorbed by military commanders, with the result that both strategy and tactics became more sophisticated. The powerful crossbow now reached the height of its influence. Larger and larger units of crossbowmen were deployed in battle, with the consequence of putting an end to the domination of the battlefield by the chariot. Armies now consisted almost entirely of infantry and cavalry. Weapons, armor, and other equipment of the infantry remained essentially unchanged. A substantial part of the new armies now consisted of cavalry, and although the effective use of the horse as an instrument of shock would have to await the invention of the stirrup, horses did provide limited shock action and greater mobility than the chariot. In texts of the time, cavalry are often referred to as being within the *qi* mode of warfare, that is, tactical applications characterized by unorthodox applications, stealth, and surprise, suggesting that cavalry as an instrument of shock (the most common way it was thought of in the West at this time) was subordinate to more irregular tactical applications.

The result of the civil wars was the establishment of the Han Empire, which lasted for 400 years and stretched from the Korean peninsula in the east to the steppes of Central Asia in the west, and from the grasslands of what is now Mongolia in the north to the Indochina peninsula in the south. The Han Empire existed at about the same time as the Roman Empire and was about as large. In 36 B.C.E., a Chinese army overran a Hun city on the Talas River in what is now Kyrgyzstan and captured more than a hundred Roman soldiers! These were mercenaries in the pay of the Hun leader. The captives were later settled as a military colony on the Silk Road, where they married Chinese women.[35] In 97 C.E., a Han general in Central Asia dispatched an envoy to Daqin, the Chinese name for the Roman Orient. Unfortunately, the envoy got no further than Parthia, [36] the border realm that separated the outposts of Roman influence from the Orient proper. Two of the world's greatest empires reached out and almost touched.[37]

NOTES

1. John King Fairbank, "The Varieties of the Chinese Military Experience," in Frank A. Kierman and John K. Fairbank, *Chinese Ways in Warfare* (Cambridge, Mass.: Harvard University Press, 1974), 2.

2. Richard A. Gabriel and Donald W. Boose, Jr., *The Great Battles of Antiquity* (Westport, Conn.: Greenwood Press, 1994), 176. Although our work was a collaborative effort, Boose was responsible for the chapter on China. I am grateful to my colleague for once more consenting to make his research available to me so that substantial parts of it may appear in this work.

3. Chang Kwang-chih, *Shang Civilization* (New Haven, Conn.: Yale University Press, 1980), 163.

4. Ibid.

5. Herrlee G. Creel, *The Origins of Statecraft in China*, vol. 1: *The Western Chou Empire* (Chicago: University of Chicago Press, 1970), 276–80.

6. C.J. Peers and Angus McBride, *Ancient Chinese Armies, 1500–200 B.C.E.* (London: Osprey, 1990), 7–8.

7. See Chang, 196; Ralph D. Sawyer, *The Seven Military Classics of Ancient China* (Boulder, Colo.: Westview Press, 1993), 5, 373–74.

8. Peers and McBride, 6; also E.T.C. Werner, *Chinese Weapons* (Singapore: Graham Brash, 1989), 2–11.

9. Sawyer, 4; also see Chang, who provides illustrations of Chinese military weapons and other military paraphenalia.

10. Sawyer, 4; Chang, 198.

11. Creel, 284–93; Peers and McBride, 10.

12. Peers and McBride, 8–10.

13. Joseph Needham, *Science and Civilization in China*, vol. 1: *Introductory Orientations* (Cambridge: Cambridge University Press, 1954), 3.

14. Mark Edward Lewis, *Sanctioned Violence in Early China* (Albany: State University of New York Press, 1990), 15.

15. This description relies heavily on Kiernan. See also Henri Maspero, *China in Antiquity* (Boston: University of Massachusetts Press, 1978), 195–96 and Richard Walker, *The Multi-State System of Ancient China* (Hamden, Conn.: The Shoestring Press, 1953), 41–42.

16. Sawyer, 373–74.

17. Edmund Balmforth, "A Chinese Military Strategist of the Warring States: Sun Pin" (Ph.D. dissertation, Rutgers University, 1979), 54–55, 85–86.

18. Ibid.

19. Peers and McBride, 13–14.

20. Quoted in Lewis, 64.

21. Ibid., 55.

22. Arthur Waldron, *The Great Wall of China: From History to Myth* (Cambridge: Cambridge University Press, 1990), 13–15,18–21.

23. Balmforth, 58.

24. Ibid., 56.

25. Ibid., 361.

26. Needham, 5, 93.

27. Roger Ames, *Sun-Tzu: The Art of War* (New York: Ballantine Books, 1993), 24.

28. Balmforth, 160.

29. Peers and McBride, 22, 44–46.

30. Ibid.

31. Balmforth, 339.

32. Ibid., 346; see also Sawyer, 364.

33. Samuel B. Griffith, *Sun Tzu: The Art of War* (London: Oxford University Press, 1971), 37.

34. Denis Twitchett and Michael Loewe, eds., *The Cambridge History of China*, vol. 1, *The Ch'in and Han Empires, 221 B.C.–A.D. 220* (Cambridge: Cambridge University Press, 1986), 52–72.

35. Needham, 237.

36. Twitchett and Loewe, 580.

37. I am indebted to Donald Boose for this vignette.

9

Persia and the Art of Logistics
546–330 B.C.E.

At its zenith the Persian empire stretched from the Aegean Sea in the west to the Indus River in the east, a distance of 2,500 miles. From north to south the empire encompassed the territory from the grasslands surrounding the Aral Sea to the deserts of Libya and reached as far west as Thrace and Macedonia. The Persians introduced armies the size of which the world had never seen, rivaling those of the Napoleonic era in tactical flexibility and logistical support. Persia invented the science of naval warfare and applied it with consummate skill,[1] invented the javelin, and developed the new combat arm of cavalry to its full military potential.[2]

Credit is usually given to the Medean king, Cyaxares (625–585 B.C.E.), for forging the first army out of the rival tribes of the Zagros Mountains in Iran.[3] He also organized the Medean army into units of bowmen, spearmen, and cavalry. In 584 B.C.E., Astyages succeeded his father to the throne. Although Astyages strengthened the loose tribal coalition that comprised the heart of what would become the Persian empire, he was destined to be the last Medean monarch.

The Persians were only one tribe in this larger coalition and were governed by seven royal families, of which the Achaemenians were the first among equals.[4] In 546 B.C.E., Cyrus II (Cyrus the Great) acceded to the throne of Persia and in a series of short wars conquered the Medes in 549 B.C.E., forming the core of the Persian empire. With his hold on the Persian throne secure, Cyrus set about expanding Persian rule.

Cyrus' first move was against Lydia, a state that occupied the Anatolian Peninsula and blocked a Persian outlet to the Mediterranean. In 546 B.C.E., Cyrus defeated King Croesus (the wealthy Croesus of Greek legend) at a battle on the Halys River. Within a year the Greek city-states along the western coast of Asia Minor had also been subdued. The Persian sphere of influence now reached to the Mediterranean coast and brought the Persians into direct contact with the Greeks.

Between 545 and 539 B.C.E. Cyrus turned his attention to the east and suppressed a number of rebellions among the tribes of the confederation, extending the empire farther toward the Indus River. With his rear secure, Cyrus moved against Babylon, the only major power to the south. In 538 B.C.E. Babylon fell to Cyrus's armies and with its capture, the Persians assumed control of Assyrian possessions in Syria, Lebanon, and Palestine. Only Egypt remained outside the Persian sphere of control. Cyrus's attention for the next ten years was occupied with events in other areas of the empire, where he spent most of his time putting down tribal and national rebellions and warding off incursions along the vast imperial border. In 529 B.C.E., in one of these border wars, Cyrus the Great met a soldier's death while battling the armies of the Massagetae. To his heir he bequeathed an empire complete except for the inclusion of Egypt. Cyrus's son, Cambyses, inherited the throne and immediately implemented his father's plan for the conquest of Egypt. Using the army built by his father, Cambyses defeated the Egyptians at the battle of Pelusium in 525 B.C.E. Persia now controlled all the territory from the Mediterranean to the Persian Gulf. Its newly acquired territories stretched along the Mediterranean coast from Egypt to the Black Sea.

In 522 B.C.E. Darius I (Darius the Great) came to power and faced the problem of governing an empire that comprised no fewer than forty-seven different nations. To enforce Persian rule he established the *satrap* system of imperial administration, designed to prevent the formation of parochial loyalties among the provinces by tying them tightly to the Persian center. The empire was divided into twenty (later 28) *satraps*, each ruled by a governor, a general, and a secretary of state. Each official was independent of the others, and each reported directly to the capital. Besides using the ambitions of these government officials to check each other, inspectors (literally, "the eyes of the king") were sent from the capital at irregular intervals. They had the power to investigate any aspect of provincial government. The inspectors also possessed the authority to punish any provincial official found guilty of corruption. To enforce their edicts the inspectors were accompanied by large bodies of royal troops.

The Persian Empire was tied together by a system of royal roads that facilitated trade, communication, and military movement among the provinces. This road system made it possible to move large military units quickly to any point within the empire to suppress civil unrest or to react to border incursions. An efficient postal service also enhanced the intelligence function of keeping tabs on domestic dissidents and hostile neighbors. The most famous of these royal roads ran from Sardis on the Mediterranean to the Persian capital of Susa, a distance of 1,500 miles. A messenger could travel the distance in less than fifteen days using a series of horse relay stations. Without the road, the journey would have taken three months.[5] Darius also extended the empire into India and pressed the imperial borders to the Indus River. The gold deposits of this new Indian territory were enormous and constituted a substantial portion of the financial wealth of the imperial government.

Darius was the first Persian monarch to coin money, and the gold *daric* coin quickly became the world financial standard of the day.[6] Each *satrap* was assessed taxes on the basis of its ability to pay. Taxes were assessed partly in gold and silver, the ancient metal standards of value, and partly in kind. In addition the provinces were required to defray the costs of the governor's court and the national military forces stationed within their boundaries. By stabilizing tax collections on a regular basis and keeping the burden reasonable, Darius became the first monarch to employ a rudimentary national budget as an instrument of domestic policy. The ability to plan financial and material expenditures against anticipated income and to use coinage as a commonly accepted mechanism of exchange provided the king with a number of military advantages, about which more will be said shortly.

The aggressive policy of the Greek city-states of the classical period to attempt to detach the city-states of Asia Minor from the empire provoked numerous Persian diplomatic and military responses over the next hundred years that led to one military engagement after another between Persians and Greeks. Xerxes' (486–465 B.C.E.) attempt to invade Greece and put an end to the trouble once and for all ended in disaster at the battle of Platea and the Persian naval defeat at Mycale in 479 B.C.E. The period 464–404 B.C.E. witnessed the Persian empire racked by rebellions and decentralization. On the Mediterranean rim the Greeks fomented one revolt after another, often providing political, financial, and even troop support to the rebels. Persia, in turn, became more deeply involved in the political affairs of the mainland city-states in a failed attempt to play one state off against the other as a way of containing Greek ambitions in Asia Minor.

In 401 B.C.E., Cyrus the Younger revolted against the Persian king in a struggle for the Persian throne. His army was largely comprised of Greek mercenary troops. Cyrus was killed at the battle of Cunaxa in 401 B.C.E., but the Greek force of heavy infantry (one unit of which was commanded by Xenophon) destroyed the larger Persian army, once again revealing Persian weakness on the battlefield.[7] The next seventy years saw increased Greek interference in Persia's Mediterranean frontier. Action was met with reaction, while revolts by *satraps* in the border areas and in Egypt further weakened Persian military strength. In the end the Persian empire succumbed to Greek military power in a manner more like a *coup de grace* than a genuine military defeat. At Granicus and Arbela Alexander defeated the Persians, and in 330 B.C.E. he burned the city of Persepolis, marking the end of the Persian empire.

The fall of the empire was due far less to the superiority of Greek arms than to the military and political weakness engendered by Persian social instability. Harem politics, battles of royal succession, domestic wars, rebellions, assassinations, and the need to maintain an empire and army larger than the world had seen to that time was simply too great a task. After Cyrus the Younger's introduction of Greek mercenary soldiers into the Persian army, the practice continued, often leading to disaster and betrayal as the Persians had to contend with a military fifth column in their midst. Persian military prowess was far greater than that achieved by any Greek city-state of the day. Even the empire of Alexander in many respects paled by comparison.

The Persian army was initially formed by Cyrus the Great as an instrument of personal ambition to prosecute his war against the Medes and gain the imperial throne for Persia. It was this army that later formed the core of the imperial force, comprised of over forty different tribal armies that fought under Persian direction. The Persians themselves always remained a minority in the vast tribal empire as well as in the army itself.

The centerpiece of the imperial army was a force of 10,000 called "The Immortals." In Persian they were called *amarata*, literally "those without death." Originally restricted to Persians, this force later allowed Medes and Elamites to join as both their loyalty and valor to the empire was proven. The name "Immortals" was derived from the fact that the force was never permitted to go below 10,000 men. A dead, wounded, or ill soldier was immediately replaced in the ranks so that the force was always maintained at full strength.[8] Augmenting the Immortals was the king's bodyguard of 2,000 foot soldiers and 6,000 cavalry horsemen.[9] These Persian forces comprised a substantial part of the national standing army. Core units were stationed in each of the *satraps*, where they maintained royal garrisons. Originally these units were under the direct command of Persian officers appointed directly by the king. As the *satraps* became more reliable under Darius, these forces were transferred to *satrap* generals and augmented by local forces drawn from the different nationalities of the empire. Among nationality forces within the provinces, Persian officers served as advisers and were responsible for training and other military duties, most notably the provision of supplies.[10]

Cyrus introduced universal military training among the Persians. The Greek historian Strabo records that Persian youths underwent at least ten years of military training before being enlisted in the regular army. Training was vigorous and included physical conditioning, instruction in the bow and javelin, and, most important, horsemanship. Recruits were trained to hunt on horseback, make weapons, and forage for food.[11] In the early wars against the Medes, the Persians had no cavalry units of their own and had to rely upon those provided by other tribes. Cyrus recognized the importance of cavalry and set about making horsemanship the central element in the Persian army. He encouraged all Persians to learn horsemanship as a pride of place in the empire, and soon no Persian would walk anywhere if he could ride a horse.

All Persian males were required to serve in the military under a form of universal conscription. These soldiers formed the bulk of the regular army and were paid on a regular schedule. In addition, each *satrap* was required to maintain a force of specified size armed and organized along its own traditional national lines. In times of war these forces were levied and expected to serve for the duration of the conflict. With this system the Persian king could raise an army of 300,000 men.[12] Armies of this great size introduced a new dimension of warfare, and the Persians fielded armies of this size time and time again.

The Assyrian army of 50,000 men discussed in a previous chapter was, by Persian standards, not very large at all. Darius' army in the Scythian campaign numbered 200,000 men, and the force deployed by Xerxes against the Greeks comprised 300,000 men and 60,000 horsemen.[13] Although Herodotus suggests the size of the force—including naval units and quartermaster troops—was over 5 million, clearly an exaggeration, General Sykes calculates that the army of Xerxes closely approached 1 million men in any case.[14] At the battle of Marathon, the

Greeks were able to put only 10,000 men in the field while the Persians easily put 50,000 men in opposition for what the Persians regarded as merely a skirmish. In 480 B.C.E., the Persian general, Mardonius, was placed in command of 80,000 troops to secure the subjugation of Thrace and Macedonia and, in 479 B.C.E., at Platea, the Persians put 250,000 men in the field. Even near the end of the empire the Persians were able to deploy large forces. In 331 B.C.E., shortly before Alexander destroyed the empire at the battle of Arbela, Darius III fielded a force comprised of 300,000 men, 40,000 cavalry, 250 chariots, and 50 elephants.[15]

The Persian army was well-organized, with a clear chain of command. The smallest unit was a six-man section led by a corporal. Two of these units formed a squad of ten men and two corporals led by a sergeant. Two squads formed a platoon of twenty-four men commanded by a lieutenant, and four platoons comprised a company led by a captain. Ten companies comprised a thousand-man regiment commanded by a colonel. The regiment was the main fighting unit of the Persian army. Ten regiments constituted a brigade of 10,000 men, comprising a *myriad* commanded by a general. The *myriad* was the largest combat unit in the army.[16]

The levied national forces that augmented this well-organized regular force were by no means equally as well-organized or trained. For the most part national forces received only limited training, wore different uniforms, carried different weapons, spoke a variety of languages, and fought in very different ways. Most often they were commanded by their own chiefs and could be highly unreliable, especially if one of their tribal chiefs was killed. It was the Persian practice to occupy the center of the line with their own reliable infantry, position their cavalry at the rear, and on the flanks form a kind of tactical container within which national units were deployed to ensure that these tribal contingents did not break and run when in battle.

The Persian army was comprised of infantry, cavalry, charioteers, archers, engineers, and naphtha throwers. In its early days, Cyrus's army had few cavalry, and the normal mix of infantry to cavalry was 90 percent to 10 percent. After Cyrus the ratio changed to 80 percent infantry to 20 percent cavalry, with the Persians and Medes comprising the bulk of the heavy cavalry as the elite striking arm.[17] Cyrus realized the importance of cavalry to an army that had to move quickly over long distances and fight in many different types of terrain. He personally forged the Persians into the largest cavalry army in the world at that time. The greatest number of Persian cavalry were light cavalry armed with the simple bow (noncomposite) and comprised mostly of irregular nationality troops, sometimes officered by Persians. The tactical role of this light infantry was to harass the enemy and draw it into battle.

The elite of the Persian army was the heavy cavalry, made up almost exclusively of Persian regular units. In its early days the cavalry was armed with the standard weapons of the Persian infantryman, the bow, battleaxe, and oval shield. Later heavy cavalry was equipped with the short stabbing and throwing javelin. Long lances made of wood or entirely of metal, oval shields, and spears were also used. The javelin, properly named, was invented by the Persians and later adopted by Alexander for use by his Greek cavalry. The original Persian word for javelin is *zhubin*, a variant of the word *chubin*, meaning "wooden." It was a short spear about a yard long made of date-palm wood, thick reed, or the wood of the jujube tree. It was tipped with bronze or iron. The Persian javelin could be thrown like a spear, used as a stabbing weapon, or even thrown end-over-end.[18] Each heavy cavalryman carried two javelins as a basic combat load.

Cavalrymen wore body armor made of a heavy leather coat covered with overlapping disks of bronze, iron, and sometimes gold. Armor was often colored in order to distinguish one unit from another. Leather greaves protected the cavalryman's legs. Personal protection was augmented by a small oval shield made of leather with a metal rim. Two holes were pierced in the upper shield near the top rim to permit the soldier to see through the shield when engaged in battle. This simple innovation increased the killing power of the Persian cavalryman by allowing him to see his target when using the javelin.[19]

The Persians experimented with the use of camel cavalry. In his campaign against Croesus of Lydia, Cyrus used his baggage-train camels on the front line and deployed them opposite the Lydian cavalry. The strange smell of the camels spooked the Lydian horses, forcing the enemy cavalry into disarray.[20] While other attempts were made to use camels as fighting vehicles, for the most part the animals proved to be useless, and further attempts were abandoned. Cyrus had made horsemanship such a badge of Persian national identity, honor, and social prestige that no one of any station would volunteer for service in the camel cavalry units.[21] After conquests in India, the Persians introduced elephants into their armies. While they initially struck terror into the hearts of the Macedonians, the Greeks quickly learned to deal with this new weapon of war. When Darius III used them against the Greeks they proved to be of little value on the battlefield.

Persian infantry was of the light and heavy variety. Soldiers in the light infantry were armed with the bow and sling, weapons that made them excellent at harassment and mobility but weak in killing power. The fact that light infantrymen carried no short-range weapons or protections made it impossible for them to close with the enemy with any lethal effect. Cyrus corrected this deficiency by requiring the infantry to carry spears and swords and training the soldiers in close order battle. Soldiers of the heavy infantry carried the long spear, short sword, and battle axe, all weapons designed for maximum lethality at close range. Interestingly, the heavy infantrymen wore black hoods over their heads and faces when engaged in close combat. Whether this practice was based on some strange custom of the Persians, or whether some genius reckoned that a hood would reduce the sounds of close-order battle in the ears of the soldier and thus reduce one of the more compelling elements of fear, is unknown. When arrayed for battle, men in the front rank of the phalanx often would carry a tall wicker shield and a single spear while those in the ranks behind them carried two spears and no shields, presumably one for throwing before contact and the other for close order fighting. Elite Persian infantry was trained to advance in mass and to do so in silence, a rather striking departure from the normal practice of the day, which held that yelling struck terror in the hearts of the enemy.[22]

The Persian chariot corps was small compared to those employed by Egypt and Assyria, and under Cyrus reached a peak strength of only 300 machines. Initially the Persians attempted to improve the chariot by making it heavier, higher, and of larger platform. They also thickened the wheels, used heavier axles, and increased the number of wheel spokes. The result was that four horses were required to pull the vehicle.[23] Since the chariot required a driver and mounted only a single archer or spearman, it required considerable man and animal power for very little firepower in return. The Persian use of the simple bow further reduced the lethality of the chariot-borne archer, and the weight of the machine made transport and movement over rough terrain difficult.

Cyrus tried to increase the lethality and shock power of the chariots by introducing the scythed chariot. Metal scythes attached to each of the chariot's main axles extended outward two yards in length away from the sides of the machine. The idea was to drive the chariots through massed infantry and cavalry formations, letting the scythes do the work of killing as they went. The idea proved to be less effective than originally believed. While they worked well enough against light infantry or against the undisciplined tribal armies of rebellious national leaders, they were useless against a disciplined infantry or cavalry unit. As long as the infantry phalanx held its ground in packed formation, the horses would not charge through the wall of spears and shields. Although Darius III used the scythed chariot at the battle of Gaugamalea against Alexander, he put only 200 machines in the field, apparently to no effect.

The Persians also introduced the use of wheeled mobile siegetowers constructed of wood. These towers were three stories high (about 24 feet) and were pulled along by sixteen oxen linked by four shafts. Xenophon recorded that the weight of the tower was such that each of the 16 oxen was required to pull a load equal to 15 talents or about 870 pounds figured at 58 pounds per talent.[24] Each tower weighed 13,920 pounds or 7 tons fully manned with men and equipment. Each story of the tower was manned with 20 archers who, because of their vantage point above the battlefield, could rain down a hail of arrows upon the enemy with little difficulty.[25] The battle commander could also use the tower as a command and control center, its height providing him with an excellent view of the entire battlefield.

The Persian army used special squads of naphtha throwers in its siege tactics. Cotton soaked in naphtha was attached to arrows and fired against wooden fortifications. The most famous use of this technique was against the Greeks, when Xerxes used it to burn the wooden walls of Athens and the roof of the Acropolis. Persian engineers were excellent and, like the combat engineers of today, often traveled ahead of the main body of the army preparing roads, building bridges, digging ditches, and constructing marine jetties for use by the navy. Like the Assyrians before them, Persian engineers mastered the technique of using inflated animal skins and pontoon boats as floats for bridges.

A cavalry-heavy army has special needs, and it fell to Persian engineers to accommodate them. When crossing water obstacles or steep defiles, horses and pack animals often panic if they can see the water or ground below. The Persians became expert at constructing bridges with covered sides and tops to prevent the animals from seeing down. Persian engineers were expert at diverting the course of rivers and streams to deprive a fleet of its draft or a city of its water supply, tricks they performed against Egypt on one occasion. In the Babylonian War, military engineers diverted the course of the river running through the city to allow a Persian infantry force to gain entrance to the city by moving along the dry riverbed.

Supplying an army of 300,000 men and 60,000 horses is no easy task even for a modern army, but the Persians managed it again and again. On the march it was Persian practice to divide the commissariat in two. In advance of the army, squads of supply officers ranged ahead in search of campsites, water sources, and grazing fields. To the rear of the army was a second commissariat that transported and managed expendable military supplies, arrows, bows, armor, naphtha and other items.[26]

The Persians had a number of advantages in supplying their armies in the field. First, most military sorties enjoyed the advantage of internal lines of communication that led to the empire's rim. Second, each *satrap* was required to maintain specified amounts of military supplies on hand to make supply along these internal lines relatively easy. Taxes paid to the king were paid in gold and silver and in kind, the latter usually in the form of militarily usable supplies. By creating a uniform monetary system based on gold coinage and stabilizing tax rates and collections on the basis of each *satrap*'s ability to pay, the Persian empire became the first state of antiquity to operate on an annual budget. This permitted it to plan expenditures for military purposes in advance.

Among the most effective instruments for provisioning the army in the field was the use of hard currency. Darius I was the first Persian monarch to coin money, using as a standard the *daric* coin weighing 130 grains of gold.[27] Supported by the enormous Persian gold reserves, the *daric* became famous for its purity and stability. It became the only gold currency of the ancient world and could be spent anywhere. The use of a precise standard of weights and measures needed for coinage also had an effect in terms of the ability to obtain military supplies in precise amounts and weights. Unlike earlier times when armies on the march confiscated what they needed to the detriment of the local economy, the Persians could purchase what they needed with a universally accepted currency. Supplying the military soon became big business in which regular suppliers established themselves as providers of military stores. The passage of a military force through an area was often welcomed by cities and towns as an economic boom.

Logistics were also made easier by the existence of a number of all-weather government roads. Those running east and west were kept in the best repair, although it must be remembered that these were not paved roads but earth-packed tracks and trails.[28] These roads were wide and solid enough to permit the passage of wooden mobile siegetowers, which weighed almost seven tons. Compared to moving these devices with sixteen oxen lashed four abreast, the movement of supply carts along these roads must have appeared easy.

Movement of military supplies was also accomplished by large corps of oxen, horses, mules, and camels. According to Xenophon, the normal pack load for a single ox-drawn cart was twenty-five talents or approximately 1,450 pounds.[29] Not to be overlooked was the ability of the soldier to carry his own supplies and equipment. Because the Persian light infantry was so lightly armed, its soldiers could easily be pressed into service to carry other supplies. Horse cavalry, of course, could also carry 100 pounds slung over the saddle.

The Persian navy could move large bodies of troops, animals, and supplies to support military operations on rivers and in coastal provinces. During Xerxes' expedition against the Greek states in 481 B.C.E., Herodotus tells us that the Persians deployed 3,000 transport ships, not counting fighting ships of the line.[30] The Persians were, not surprisingly, not much as sailors themselves but knew how to take full advantage of the shipbuilding and other maritime skills of their coastal provinces along the Mediterranean. They closely supervised the design of special ships and commissioned specially designed long transports powered by fifty oarsmen to transport horses and troops. Smaller thirty-oar ships were used as supply vessels, and shallow draft boats were used on rivers.[31] Taken in historical perspective, the Persian armies were larger and more effective than any army the world had seen to that point. With the exception of the Roman army, no military force would equal the Persian army's ability to support its forces in the field over such long distances until the armies of the Napoleonic era.

It is somewhat paradoxical that a people of the mountains and plains of Iran should have deployed the world's first large standing naval force. The Persians seem to have been the first to use naval vessels on a grand scale, primarily in support of ground operations, to prosecute their grand strategy of empire in the Aegean sector. The ability of these mountain and plains people to recognize the importance of a new weapon heretofore beyond their experience and to utilize it so well ought to give pause to those who suggest that the military minds of the past were less skilled than those of the present.

It is unclear if the Phoenicians or the Greeks invented the first ship designed only to fight other ships. By the time of Cyrus, however, the first fighting ship, the *trireme*, had made its appearance in the Mediterranean.[32] Cyrus was quick to appreciate the importance of these new implements of war and is regarded as the father of the Persian navy. Darius I seems to have been the first to commission the construction of ships for specific military tasks—ships of the line, transports, horse carriers, supply ships—and shortly thereafter the Persians had fully integrated the use of naval warfare and tactics into their grand strategy, designed to counter Greek power in the Aegean and Mediterranean.

As a ship of the line, the *trireme* represented the ultimate combat ship of its time. It was essentially a decked galley about 120 feet long and 15 feet wide, was powered by 170 oarsmen, and could carry 30 combat marines, often archers, on its top deck. Steering was accomplished by a large oar on each side of the stern. The front of the ship mounted a 10-foot iron spike placed just at the waterline. In attempting to sink an enemy vessel, the ship aimed the spike to ram into the opponent's broadside. A *trireme* could reach full speed in about thirty seconds from a dead stop and had a maximum speed of eleven knots. It is important to note that the *trireme* was specifically designed for naval combat and was too crowded for normal seafaring. It did not, for example, have sufficient room to carry its own supplies, not even sufficient water and food for its crew, and the crews normally disembarked for the shore each evening to eat and sleep.[33] The Persian genius lay in the ability to recognize the importance of this new weapon, commission the construction of ships for specific military purposes, secure the foreign crews to man them, build the ships in larger numbers than ever before, and then fully integrate them into large-scale battle strategies to provide maximum naval support for ground operations.

The main weakness of the Persian military machine lay in the fact that its army was always a hodgepodge of tribes and nationalities of varying degrees of military effectiveness. The well-trained and well-disciplined Persian national force was always in a minority within the army itself. Although Persians formed the core of the field army, the spirit and expertise of this elite never truly succeeded in changing the relatively unsophisticated fighting abilities of the national mixture that comprised the main source of manpower for war. The Persian army was not a tactically integrated fighting force in the sense that all units of the army were trained in the same weapons and tactics. As such, it could not be deployed in very many tactically different ways nor be relied upon to fight efficiently as a whole.

The sophistication of the Persian army in deploying infantry, cavalry, and chariot units disguised its weakness in possessing few heavy infantry units. For the most part armies formed up in opposing lines with the light infantry and archers acting as skirmishers in the front, trying to inflict as much damage with their missiles and javelins as possible. As the two lines clashed, the Persians would attempt to strike the flanks and rear with their cavalry and chariots to scatter the enemy, using their usually large numerical advantage to attack from several directions at once. Once enemy infantry began to scatter, cavalry could ride it down and finish it off with lance and javelin. The success of this simple tactical design depended upon the inability of the enemy infantry to withstand the Persian assault. Usually the Persian advantage in numbers served to carry the day.

Any objective analysis of Persian military effectiveness must conclude that, for the most part, Persian armies fought opponents that normally would not present much of a problem. Once the empire was forged, most of the engagements of the Persian army were against rebellious nationalities on the eastern rim of the empire whose level of military skill, tactics, logistics, armament, training, and strength was far below that of the Persians. Under these circumstances the Persian army's lack of tactical integration and, most important, its lack of heavy infantry did not matter very much since its enemies also lacked these assets.

Where this deficiency did matter, of course, was in Persia's wars with the Greek city-states. In every major engagement with Greek armies— Platea, Marathon, Cunaxa, and others—the Persians were defeated or badly mauled. In almost every engagement against the Greeks, the Persians lost despite their great advantage in manpower. The ability of Greek hoplite armies to field tactically integrated forces of heavy infantry buttressed by discipline and excellent military technique acquired through training exploited the main weaknesses of the Persian army to their maximum. At Marathon, for example, the Greek commander was able to completely negate the Persian numerical advantage by forcing battle on terrain that confined the armies to a narrow front along which combat was forced to occur, thereby forcing the Persian commander to commit his units piecemeal. Regardless of the greater size of the Persian forces behind the battle, at the *schwerpunkt* the terrain forced both Greek and Persian units to engage at relatively equal strengths. The Persian weaknesses, disguised by centuries of Persian military success albeit against equally flawed enemies, in the end brought the great empire to its knees before the skill and dedication of Greek heavy infantry and cavalry under the brilliant command of Alexander the Great.

NOTES

1. Arthur Ferrill, *The Origins of War* (London: Thames and Hudson, 1985), 85.

2. Yaha Zoka, *The Imperial Iranian Army from Cyrus to Pahlavi* (Teheran: Ministry of Culture and Arts Press, 1971), 62.

3. *Encyclopedia Britannica*, vol. 21, 1985, 868–69.

4. General Sir Percy Sykes, *A History of Persia* (London: Macmillan, 1958), vol. 1, 140. See also p. 143 for a complete lineage of the Archemenians from Cyrus to Darius III.

5. Robert Laffont, *The Ancient Art of War* (New York: Time-Life Books, 1966), vol. 1, 56. Laffont calculates that the royal road from Sardis to Susa was 1,243 miles long, and the distance could be covered by a rider in a week. Sykes, 164–65, says it was 1,500 miles and would take fifteen days to traverse.

6. Darius may have been the first monarch to coin money. The Greek claim that Croesus was the first king to coin money may have been due to Greek support for Croesus in his war against the Persians.

7. The Greek force of 10,000 men under Xenophon conducted an incredible retreat from the battle of Cunaxa and fought its way back to Greece after a journey of almost 1,100 miles. This great trek is recorded in detail by the commander, Xenophon, in his work, the *Anabasis*.

8. Zoka, 10–11.

9. Laffont, 56.

10. Zoka, 12–13.

11. Strabo, *Geography*, 15. Ch. 3, 18–19.

12. Ferrill, 82 and Laffont, 58 on the size of the Persian army.

13. These figures are taken from Plato's account of the war and are considerably less than those offered by Herodotus, who places the size of the Persian army at 2,641,640 fighting men.

14. Sykes, 196–98.

15. See the chart on comparative battle strengths of ancient armies in Laffont, 38–39.

16. Zoka's description of the organizational structure of the Persian army is excellent and highly recommended. Zoka, 33–36.

17. Zoka, 19.

18. Ibid., 62.

19. Ibid., 54–56.

20. Sykes, 146.

21. Zoka, 29.

22. Xenophon notes this practice in the *Anabasis*, part 1, book 8, 10–11.

23. Zoka, 21–23.

24. Xenophon records the number of talents normally carried by an ox in the *Cyropaedia*, 6, 50–55. The weight of a talent in the ancient world varied widely by time and place. However, in no instance did a talent equal less than fifty-eight pounds. It is this minimal weight that I have used as the basis for the calculations presented herein.

25. Zoka, 27–28.

26. Ibid., 33.

27. Sykes, 163–64.

28. The most important aspects of these roads were the bridges that crossed terrain obstacles. It was probably the ability to traverse these obstacles rapidly more than the quality of the road surface per se that reduced the travel time.

29. Xenophon, the *Cyropaedia*, 6: 50–55.

30. Herodotus, book 7, 89–97.

31. Ibid. See also Zoka, 94.

32. R.E. Dupuy and Trevor N. Dupuy, *The Encyclopedia of Military History* (New York: Harper and Row, 1970), 18–19.

33. Ibid.

10

The Greek Way of War: Classical and Imperial Periods

500–323 B.C.E.

From Sumer to Persia, in the Near East, China, and India, the art of war developed in an unbroken progression for almost 3,000 years. This level of social and military development was not, however, characteristic of the societies of Europe, which lagged considerably behind these other civilizations in almost all aspects of human development including warfare. In Greece, neither the classical period (500–359 B.C.E.) nor the imperial period (359–323 B.C.E.) reached the level of military sophistication already evident in the Near East more than five centuries earlier.

Greek military development began in the archaic age from 1500 to 1200 B.C.E. During this time a warlike people, the Achaeans, occupied the territory of mainland Greece. It is probable that the practice of war in ancient Greece reflected the predominant influence of neighboring Near East armies, but did so to a limited degree. Our earlier analysis of the Philistine armies suggests exactly this. In most respects the armies, technologies, and conduct of war in Greece were far less sophisticated than those of other armies of the Near East during this same period.

Achaean armies used bronze weapons and armor but developed forms of combat that were very different from earlier armies. The ancient Greeks, for example, used archers in a far less sophisticated way, even though there is some evidence that the composite bow may have been available.[1] There is, however, no evidence that Greek armies used chariot-borne archers or military formations of archers in any way. When used at all, the bow was employed by the individual soldier fighting in solitary combat against another soldier. While horses were known in ancient Greece, they were not employed as cavalry or for any other military purpose that we can discern. The armies of ancient Greece achieved only a modest level of sophistication in constructing defensive fortifications. That such primitive defensive works could not easily be overcome by Achaean military forces demonstrates the low level of skill at siegecraft of the ancient Greeks. It was not until Alexander's time in the third century B.C.E. that Greek siegecraft approached the level of sophistication and effectiveness shown by the Assyrians or Persians and only after imitating the proven techniques of these earlier armies.

Warfare among the ancient Greeks consisted of localized battles between loose assemblies of individual combatants who fought for plunder, glory, and fame. Armies were small, usually fewer than a thousand men. There is no evidence of the development of tactics or the ability to coordinate even small groups of soldiers to achieve battlefield objectives. Nor is there any evidence of the development of the various combat arms—infantry, cavalry, chariots, archers, siege trains—or of the art of coordinating these forces with one another. Logistics was also unknown to the Achaean Greeks, and wars tended to be one-day affairs involving unorganized scuffles between groups of warriors fighting as individuals on battlefields chosen in advance by both sides.

Nevertheless, this period is important to the development of warfare in later classical Greece, for it was precisely this military legacy that was transmitted to and influenced the conduct of warfare in the later period. The transition, however, was difficult. Between 1200 and 1000 B.C.E., Achaean Greece was subject to a number of invasions by mysterious peoples who completely destroyed its civilization. It was probably this invasion that set the Aegean peoples in motion, sending some of them, the Peleset, to Anatolia and Canaan. So complete was the destruction of ancient Greece that even writing disappeared.[2] For 400 years, until the eighth century B.C.E., Greece endured a dark age about which we know almost nothing. While the invasions destroyed most aspects of Achaean social, economic, and political developments to that time, the dark age of Greece nevertheless had a profound effect on future Greek military development. The invasions cut off whatever contact the Greeks had with other more advanced armies of the period, severing the continuous line of military development and technique that had been occurring in the Near East for the past 3,000 years. The already rudimentary Greek practice of war under the Achaeans was frozen as if in amber and remained largely unaffected by military developments elsewhere. It was this ancient Greek tradition of war that was eventually passed to classical Greece when the culture reemerged in the eighth century B.C.E.

Greek warfare developed along a separate path and is correctly viewed as *sui generis*. The links with the past that remained were links to Achaean Greece, and the Greek idea of war that emerged in the classical period emulated those forms and methods passed to it through the Homeric sagas. The importance of the Homeric sagas from the military perspective was that they served as the main mechanism through which the classical Greeks rediscovered how to conduct war. And probably more important than the pragmatics of war, these sagas bequeathed a notion of war that linked its practice to the development of the human spirit expressed in moral terms. It was the Greeks who introduced the West to the myth of glory.

The early classical period (800–600 B.C.E.) saw Greece reemerge into recorded history in the form of a number of small agricultural states ruled by feudal landed aristocracies. While the inhabitants of Greece now shared a common language and similar gods, these small states were geographically isolated from one another and developed very different social and political forms. As these communities depended entirely upon the production of scarce agricultural land for survival, the defense of local territories became imperative, with the result that loyalties were closely tied to specific city-states rather than to any concept of a larger people or nation. One consequence was the emergence of a number of independent city-states that engaged in almost constant war with each other.

The conduct of war in the early classical period was much the same as it had been in the earlier Achaean period. For the most part warfare was limited to the nobility, which provided its own weapons and, in true Homeric tradition, fought for glory and fame. As in the earlier period, there were no tactics, no formations, no combat arms, and no attempt to orchestrate battles in a coordinated way. By this time bronze had given way to iron, but the sophistication of warfare remained far behind that of other armies of the time. The cost of weapons was sufficiently high to prevent the arming of the lower classes, which, in any case, were exempted from war by the nobility's fear that an armed peasantry was politically dangerous.

In a strict sense it is inaccurate to speak of Greek armies in this period. Wars were fought between rival clans, whose ability to put armed men in the field was severely limited by the social structure of the city-states. Rarely could an "army" deploy more than a few hundred men. Greek armies of this period were really part-time groups of warriors with not even a semisolid organizational structure. There were no rank structure, no regular soldiers, no pay, no administrative structure, no training schools, and no logistical apparatus at all. It took almost 200 years before the social and political structure of the city-states evolved to the point where the Greek practice of war was definable for cogent military analysis.

By the seventh century B.C.E. the Greek states had acquired populations made more diverse by social differentiation among skills and classes. These changes were accompanied by demands on the part of various elements of the population for a greater voice in political life, demands that led to conflicts with the ruling aristocracies. Over time, these aristocracies gave way to warrior classes (Sparta) and, ultimately in some states, to the middle classes (Athens), which eventually achieved political power. The mark of full citizenship throughout this two-century-long process of change was military service.[3] States gradually extended this privilege to more and more elements of the population, which now had a stake in defending the state. By the seventh century B.C.E., the city-state was the predominant form of sociopolitical organization of Greek society, and along with it came the rise of the citizen army.

Perhaps nowhere in the history of war does one find a subject that has been more romanticized and had more effect on modern armies over the years than the idealized notion of the Greek soldier. It was the Greeks who first developed the idea that warfare ennobled the human spirit, the idea that only in combat are the highest values of man—courage, bravery, endurance, skill, and sacrifice—made manifest. To die fearlessly with sword in hand in the face of the enemy has ever since been a part of the lore of the soldier in the West—for over twenty-six centuries. The appearance of this idealized notion of war in classical Greece marked the emergence of a major new dimension of warfare. The notion that men fight for ideas was in itself a new idea, a powerful psychological engine that has driven men over the centuries to regard the practice of war as worthy of greatness. The emergence of this idea marked a very important turning point in the evolution of war.

The Greek notion of war as the ennoblement of the human spirit had its roots in the Homeric sagas and their tales of heroes who performed feats of military valor. It is probable, though not certain, that Homer wrote during the eighth century B.C.E. and was recounting an idealized version of actual events that occurred during the Achaean age.[4] Because these sagas were written in a language all Greeks could understand, the sagas became seminal sources of Greek military tradition, thought, and practice. The heroes of the Greek narratives became the ideal for Greeks to emulate in war. The Greek religious pantheon supported the idea of war as heroism as well. Greek warriors sought the favor of the gods before going into battle, and it was not uncommon to promise the gods the human sacrifice of prisoners of war.[5] Greek natural science and philosophy, paradoxically, supported the idea as well. Drawing upon Thales' feat of systematizing the use of the mind through reason,[6] the Greeks evolved the great edifice of natural law wherein human nature was perceived as possessing potentialities that could be developed by human action. By the mid-seventh century B.C.E., reason had joined myth and religion to support the Greek ideal of military glory.

By the beginning of the sixth century B.C.E., the social, economic, and political development of Greek culture had reached a point where the city-state had become the basic form of social organization. The increased size and complexity of the populations of these states made it possible to enlist classes other than the nobility in the conduct of war. At this time, originally in Corinth and then shortly thereafter in Athens, there appeared a military innovation that greatly affected the practice of war and laid the basis for the rise of the most famous fighting man in history—the Greek hoplite.

This revolutionary development was the invention of the Argive shield grip.[7] The old shield was held by a collection of leather tethers that met at a ring in the center of the shield. The ability to maneuver the shield with this grip required both strength and a great deal of training. Even when the shield was mastered, it could not be pressed against the opponent with much force. The great military innovation of the sixth century B.C.E. was the replacement of the group of tethers in the center of the shield with a single loop through which the forearm passed and with another loop at the shield's rim that could be held by the hand in a strong grip. At the same time the cost of manufacturing these shields became cheaper, making them widely affordable. As Greek soldiers were always required to purchase their own weapons, greater availability brought these weapons within the reach of the middle classes. The new grip meant as well that the average citizen could easily master the use of the shield with little training, a development that made it easier to enroll the citizenry of the city-states in the practice of war. Now the emergence of the heavy infantry phalanx was possible, and very quickly the practice of war shifted from the contest of noble champions to battles between highly disciplined groups of citizen soldiers armed as heavy infantry.

The armies of the Greek city-states were citizen armies in the sense that members of the politically enfranchised classes had an obligation to perform military service. In some states, such as Athens, the upper and middle classes provided the bulk of military manpower while in others, notably Sparta, a warrior class constituted the political and military elite and monopolized military service. Slaves and noncitizens usually did not perform military service, removing at least one third of the population from the military manpower pool. By the fifth century B.C.E. every Greek city-state also had a cadre of professional mercenary soldiers brought into being by a general manpower shortage.

The armies of the Greek city-states were quite small by almost any historical standard. Thucydides noted that at the start of the Peloponnesian War in 431 B.C.E., Athens had a population of 100,000 free men and 140,000 slaves and aliens. The Athenian army of this time was comprised of 13,000 hoplites, 16,000 older garrison soldiers, 1,200 mounted men, and 1,600 archers. This force of almost 30,000 men represented a supreme military effort on Athens' part. Thucydides noted that eleven years later, when the military situation had stabilized and Athens returned to normal military manpower standards, Athens could muster only 1,300 hoplites and 1,000 horsemen. In addition it could field 1,400 recruits. Most of the Athenian army in 420 B.C.E., some 9,500 men, were not Athenians at all but metics and aliens.[8] Battles of the Greek classical period usually involved no more than 20,000 men on both sides and, more often, involved forces of less than 10,000 men.

As military service was expected of all participating citizens, providing, of course, that they were wealthy enough to purchase their own armor and weapons, all young men underwent military training. In Athens boys were trained in games, running, wrestling, bow, and javelin at private camps (*palestra*). At age eighteen, healthy males were taken into the militia for military training. Upon completion of this training, the young soldier was sent for a year's tour of duty to a garrison. After the second year the soldier remained a member of the active reserve until age forty-nine and was subject to immediate call to service. After that, until age sixty, the soldier became a *presbytatos*, literally "an older soldier," and served as a territorial, guarding camps and forts.

In Sparta the entire state was organized along military lines and governed by an elite caste of warriors. Political power was concentrated in the hands of a warrior class, the "equals," who comprised one tenth of the population. Each warrior drew his income and sustenance from a landed estate worked by a class of perpetual sharecroppers called *helots*. Because the *helots* outnumbered the warrior class by nine to one and had little in the way of rights, Spartan society was organized both for war and suppressing domestic revolts. *Helots* usually served as valets for warriors in times of war and, when manpower became a problem for the Spartans in later years, even served as hoplites in battle. If they served well, they were freed.[9]

Regardless of the method of recruitment or degree of military training, all Greek armies of the classical period carried the same equipment. The primary striking arm of the Greek armies was the hoplite heavy infantryman. The basic weapon of the hoplite was the *dory*, a wooden-shaft spear six to nine feet long with a metal point at each end. The hoplite also carried a sword with a blade approximately eighteen inches long and two inches wide. Used mainly as a cutting weapon, the Greek sword was used only if the spear was broken or lost. The primary defensive weapon of the hoplite was the Argive shield. Greek soldiers wore leather or bronze helmets, a neck guard of leather, and leather greaves that covered their shins to ankle length. Armor was also worn on the forearms. In the eighth century B.C.E., armor was originally a body cuirass made of bronze which, by the sixth century, had been replaced by the linen cuirass made of layers of stiffly glued fabric. Hoplites sometimes wore a semicircular bronze plate hung from the belt to protect the abdomen. The complete military kit was called a *panoply* and weighed seventy-five pounds.[10]

Greek armies organized themselves for battle in essentially the same way. The basic combat formation was the infantry phalanx, comprised of hoplites. Since ancient times the standard depth of the phalanx was eight men deep, the archaic *lochos*. After the fifth century B.C.E., as a reaction to the Theban innovation of using deeper ranks, most city-states adopted thicker formations. In some cases the depth of the phalanx reached twenty-five men. The smallest unit of the phalanx was the *enomotia*, comprised of three files of twelve men. This could also be employed with a six-man front with six men deep. Two *enomotiai* comprised a *pentekostys* of seventy-two men, while two *pentekostyai* comprised a *lochoi*, the basic unit of the phalanx, commanded by a company commander. Four such *lochi* comprised a *mora* of 576 men commanded by a regimental officer. Every phalanx had an elite *mora* comprised of its best warriors. This unit usually anchored the right wing of the battle line. It was Spartan practice to place all officers in the front rank, so that they were the first to come into contact with the enemy and could set the standard for bravery.[11]

The hoplite infantry was drawn mainly from the middle and upper classes. Cavalry remained the province of the nobility, if only for the reason that it alone could bear the cost of horse and equipment. Auxiliary light infantry was drawn from the lower classes but was haphazardly organized and of little use. While the Greeks used some cavalry and light infantry formations prior to the Persian wars, it was their experience with the excellent cavalry and light infantry of the Persians that finally caused the Greeks to pay some attention to these combat arms.[12] In the fourth century B.C.E. Iphicrates reorganized the light infantry into an important combat arm, the *peltasts*.

This new soldier carried a light crescent-shaped shield made of wicker and covered with a hide or *pelta*, thus the name *peltasts*. The shield had a special strap so that it could be slung over the back, allowing the *peltast* maximum mobility on the run. The *peltasts* wore no armor, relying instead on speed to get out of harm's way. Armed with two javelins, the *peltasts* acted as a skirmish line for the phalanx. Deployed to the front, the *peltasts* could rush the enemy phalanx, hurl their javelins into the packed ranks, and then retreat. They could also be used to protect the flanks of the phalanx against cavalry attack or, in the offensive, to attack the exposed flanks of the enemy phalanx. With this new force Iphicrates destroyed an entire Spartan regiment of hoplites during the Corinthian War (394–386 B.C.E.).[13]

Greek cavalry never reached the level it had under the Assyrians or Persians and never became an important combat arm of Greek armies during the classical period. This may have been due to the rugged geography of the land and its patterns of farming, both of which limited the employment of cavalry in large numbers. The short distances between city-states and, thus, battlefields, also worked against the need for mobility over long distances. The individual horse-borne soldier of the eighth through sixth centuries B.C.E. had almost been driven from the field by the emergence of the hoplite phalanx. Cavalry during the classical period was still comprised of the nobility but was used largely for flank security, as skirmishers, and, in rare cases, for pursuit.

The Greek cavalrymen of the classical period rode small unshod horses without a saddle. They rode on a blanket held by a single strap around the animal's belly. Control was managed by means of bit and reins. Armed with a javelin and a sword, the cavalryman of this period was not a formidable threat to the phalanx. After the Persian wars the Athenians created a cavalry force of a thousand men, but these famous "Knights of Athens" were used mostly in traditional roles as skirmishers and marauders. Even during the Peloponnesian War this force was never a significant combat asset.

The Greeks never developed corps of archers to any level of combat effectiveness and, aside from a company of Scythian mercenaries armed with composite bows in the pay of Athens during the Peloponnesian War, the horse-borne archer was unknown.[14] The failure to develop the combat arm of archery is surprising for two reasons. First, the Greek national hero, Hercules, was an archer whose exploits with the bow were well known through the Homeric sagas. Second, the Greeks certainly had sufficient experience during the Persian wars to know about the killing power of massed archers. Perhaps the Greek victories over the Persians ensconced the myth that the phalanx was simply superior to other arms, and blunted further development of archery.

There is, perhaps, another reason. Greek ideas of chivalry required that men distinguish themselves in personal combat in which the better-trained man defeated and killed the lesser opponent, who met his death with honor. The bow, however, killed from afar and did not permit the victim even the opportunity to see his opponent, much less face him and come to grips with him. Fired in salvo, arrows fell among the packed mass of warriors and killed indiscriminately, felling brave and coward alike. In the *Iliad* the bow is presented as being the weapon of cowards or men of evil character. It is the weapon of the treacherous Pandarus or the cowardly Paris, who slay from ambush.[15] Finally, the bow was more likely to wound than to kill, providing no opportunity for the hero's death. With an arrow wound, death came by lingering pain and infection. For these reasons the Greeks of the classical period held a negative moral perspective of the bow and never developed its use in combat to any great degree.[16]

Slingers, who had been around since Neolithic times in Greece as in almost all areas of the Mediterranean, did not come into major military use in Greece until the period immediately following the Persian wars, when small specialty units of slinger infantry appeared. Greek slingers easily outranged the bow and fired stone, clay, bronze, and lead shot.[17] These missiles, averaging between twenty and fifty grams in weight, could be flung up to 300 feet and inflicted terrible wounds. Slinger units were invariably small and used as skirmishers or against light infantry. Their effect on the massed phalanx of heavy infantry, however, was usually negligible.

The logistics apparatus of the armies of classical Greece was rudimentary even by the standards of a Bronze Age army. By Iron Age standards, they were even more primitive. The armies of classical Greece possessed no logistical capabilities in any meaningful military sense of the word. The short distances between city-states worked against the development of logistics. In most cases the battlefield was less than three-day's march away, and battles were short-lived events. There may have appeared no real need for a logistical capability. The failure to develop such a capability, however, had enormous implications, for without the ability to sustain a significant force in the field for long periods it became impossible for any single city-state to subdue all of Greece by force of arms. Under these circumstances, no sense of Greek national identity could develop.

Ox carts were the standard transport of the baggage train, and special units of pioneers cleared the way with axes, sickles, and other tools. With most food carried by the soldier himself, the baggage train carried other items, including harnesses, straps for weapons, files for sharpening weapons, shafts for extra spears, and wood for making field repairs on the wagons themselves. These baggage trains were slow, inflexible, and easily subject to attack. But the Greek tactics of the period did not require mobility or flexibility, and the achievement of battlefield surprise or an attack on a baggage train with a phalanx was almost impossible.[18]

The approach march and the battle itself were accompanied by large numbers of attendants. The general rule was one attendant per soldier, but quite often as many as six or seven attendants might accompany a single soldier. Thus, a fighting force of 5,000 men would usually have with it 5,000 or more attendants. Although these attendants were often slaves, many, especially in Athens, were brothers or relatives of the citizen-soldier and had some degree of military training.[19] The attendants might carry a club or dagger that could, in an extreme emergency, be put to military use. Sometimes these attendants were used as flank security on the march or, more rarely, as skirmishers. They could be employed to help move baggage, treat the wounded, or pick up fallen weapons when the battle was over.

Among the more interesting military aspects of classical Greece was the emergence of military medical personnel on the battlefield. Treatment of soldiers on the battlefield began long before the rise of Greece and can trace its roots back to ancient Sumer. There is little doubt that the Greeks were readily familiar with different types of combat wounds. The *Iliad* mentions no fewer than 140 different types of combat injuries. Physicians in earlier armies had been mostly priests and other religious practitioners. The Greek emphasis on reason made it possible for Greek physicians to bring an empirical and systematic medical protocol to the battlefield in dealing with injuries. The result was a number of analytical treatises that explained the functioning of the body and mind in empirical terms. Alcmaeon of Crotona (500 B.C.E.) was probably the first to experiment with the brains of animals and develop a physiologically based theory of human thought. His work influenced Hippocrates (460–377

B.C.E.), who was the first to combine the speculations of medical theorists with observations from bedside experience.[20] His skeptical insistence on rational thinking and observation as the basis for diagnosis and treatment remain the guiding principle of modern medicine.

The Greeks did not have a military medical service per se. But in a country built on citizen armies, where attendants accompanied soldiers to the battlefield, Greek physicians were in attendance to treat the wounded. The Greeks also made important strides in the field of psychiatry, which they applied to soldiers suffering from combat shock. It is likely that they observed the full range of battle shock psychiatric syndromes that have affected soldiers since the advent of war.[21] The Homeric legends noted that Ajax, driven mad by war, waded into a flock of sheep and slaughtered them, thinking them the enemy. Greek physicians understood the calmative properties of smoking hemp and opium and prescribed them for maladies requiring relaxation. Greek medicine passed directly to Rome in later centuries, and when the Romans established the world's first military medical system, they staffed it largely with Greek physicians.

Greek tactics never reached the degree of sophistication found in the armies of other countries of the same period. The sociopolitical constitution of the city-state could provide only small citizen-armies with little time for training. This required that tactics be kept simple and that the skills demanded of the soldier in battle formations remain uncomplicated.[22] The result was the continuous use of the infantry phalanx for 300 years without serious modification. The phalanx battle formation consisted of opposing masses of infantry aligned in simple rectangles several hundred feet long and thirty feet thick. Opposing phalanxes marched toward one another until their front ranks clashed. Once engaged, only the first two ranks could wield their weapons as the second soldier in each file stepped into the gap, separating the first rank of combatants. As the front ranks met, those in the rear ranks pressed forward with their shields in a compact mass in an attempt to force the enemy formation to flex or break. While these tactics required a highly disciplined soldier who could stand the stress of close combat, they did not require a high degree of military skill.

It is common to assume that battles involving this type of close combat were horrifically bloody; in fact they were rarely so. For the most part, only the first two ranks could actually engage in combat and, in most battles, one side usually gave way within minutes of the initial contact so that the rear ranks rarely encountered any real fighting. The purpose of the massed formation behind the front ranks was to enforce both a physical and moral pressure on the cutting front edge of the battle formation to prevent panic. It has been estimated that the phalanx could remain engaged in actual fighting for less than thirty minutes before severe exhaustion took its toll on the fighting men.[23] Soldiers in the front ranks would be quite fortunate to remain in contact for half that time without collapsing.

The need to retain the organizational integrity of the phalanx even after the other side broke, as well as the inability of the phalanx to move rapidly over uneven terrain without losing its integrity, meant that pursuit was out of the question. Once a unit broke contact, the killing usually stopped and the vanquished were permitted to escape. The rudimentary nature of Greek cavalry during this period prevented its use as a major killing arm in the pursuit. Unless an army found itself trapped by a successful double envelopment, or its retreat limited by the terrain, once panic set in and one side began to run, most of the killing stopped.

The pressure of the mass within the phalanx itself forced soldiers to move to their right as the battle raged. Protected on the left by his shield, every soldier moved closer to the shield of the man on his right to secure greater protection from his comrade's shield.[24] As the space between men closed, the soldier could still employ his spear in an overhand or underhand thrust in the small angle between his shield and that of the next man. But this situation made the use of the sword very difficult, a fact that contributed to the Greek failure to develop this weapon to its potential. As the pressure to the right increased, the whole phalanx began to rotate in a counterclockwise direction. The guiding tactical principle was to have the right wing break to the left and achieve a single envelopment, forcing the enemy in on itself from the flank. The rotation prevented the exposure of any clear points of attack for either cavalry or light infantry.

Greek battle tactics remained unchanged for 300 years until 371 B.C.E., when the Theban commander Epaminondas introduced a decisive new idea against the Spartans at the battle of Leuctra. Epaminondas altered the usual tactical deployment of the phalanx by massing his strongest force on the left wing of his army directly across from the enemy's strongest right wing. The left wing was strengthened to comprise forty-eight files, each fifty-men deep. This arrangement provided Epaminondas with force opposite the enemy right that was four times as great as the enemy's depth. With his right wing weakened, Epaminondas deployed it in an oblique echelon, thereby "refusing" it, and protected it with cavalry and light infantry. Epaminondas introduced another innovation, the deployment of a reserve composed of elite Theban infantry, the fa-

Figure 10.1
Battle of Leuctra, 371 B.C.E., Decisive Action

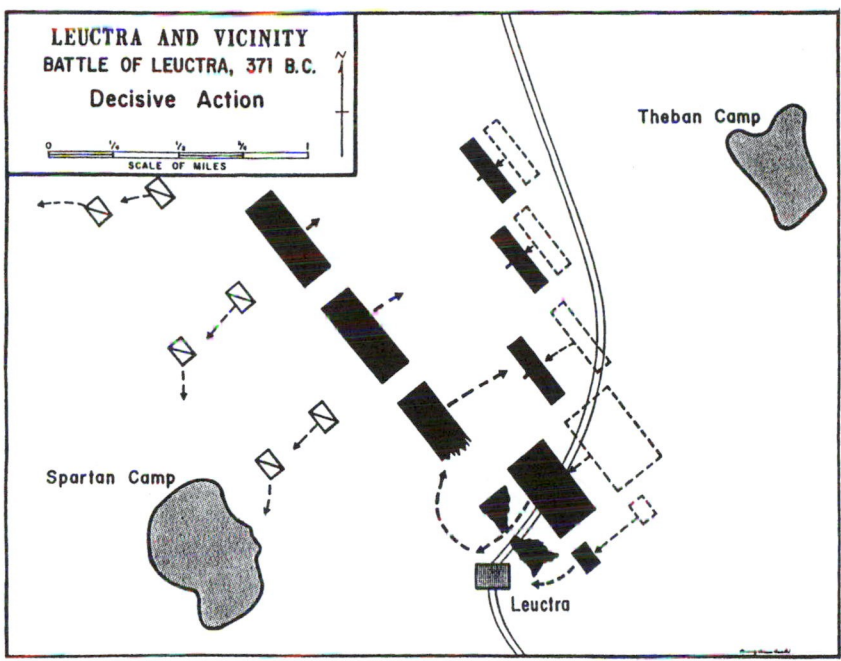

mous Sacred Band. With his left anchored as a platform of maneuver, Epaminondas swung his right wing on a hinge and caught the Spartans in an envelopment.[25] Figure 10.1 depicts Epaminondas' tactical design. The battle of Leuctra represented the first significant change in Greek tactics in 300 years. The use of cavalry and light infantry in direct co-ordination with heavy infantry marked the first use of combined arms integration in the classical period. The use of the oblique formation to refuse a portion of the line represented the first attempt by the classical Greeks to use heavy infantry as a platform of maneuver for other combat arms. All of these innovations, however, came too late to affect warfare in this period to any significant degree.

As with all other elements of Greek military skill during this time, Greek siegecraft and fortification remained hopelessly primitive. Greek armies had no siege trains and relied primarily upon blockade and starvation to subdue cities. The absence of siege towers and archers to neutralize the defense atop the walls made a successful siege very difficult indeed.

Despite the rudimentary nature of warfare in the classical period, its impact on the development of war in later periods of the West was important. The Greeks were the first western army to develop the combat arm of heavy infantry and to use it in a way that later armies of the period, notably the Romans, would emulate. The most important contribution of the classical Greeks was sociological. The classical Greeks contributed a unique view of the role of war in human development. It is correct to say that the Greeks introduced a new morality of war, a morality that placed the conduct of war at the center of human activity as the primary means to ennoble the human personality. The Greek idea of heroism and warfare entered the mainstream of Western civilization and remained the main intellectual force that shaped professional perceptions of war over the next two millennia. Western military development also owes the embryonic beginnings of military medicine to the Greeks. The Greek empirical view of the universe made possible the development and application of empirical medical techniques for treating battle wounds. The attendance of Greek physicians on the battlefield for the first time in the West introduced the idea that soldiers could be salvaged in a systematic manner for use in later battles.

Although the Greeks had no military academies in which to train their officers, they were the first to produce systematic military treatises on tactics and strategy.[26] Xenophon's *Anabasis* was the first work in the West to analyze systematically the nature and conduct of war. His *Cyropaedia* is a study of the strategic relationship between war and politics. The first comprehensive work in Western literature on military theory stressing purely pragmatic applications to the battlefield was written in 357 B.C.E. by Stymphalian Aeneas. The Greeks wrote in a language that all could understand, so what they wrote received wide distribution. More importantly, they wrote in a form that was understandable to other cultures. The result was to introduce Greek military thought into the mainstream of Western civilization.

The unification of Greece could not be accomplished as a prelude to empire without a military revolution in the means required to bring it about. The establishment of the Imperial Age (359–323 B.C.E.) of Greece was preceded by a military revolution of tremendous proportions. The military revolution that brought about this period was the product of two men, Philip II of Macedon (359–337 B.C.E.) and his son, Alexander (337–323 B.C.E.). Philip forged a new army, complete with new battle formations and tactics, and then used it to unify Greece for the first time in history by defeating the combined armies of the city-states at the battle of Chaeronea in 338 B.C.E. His military innovations completely revolutionized the conduct of war in Greece and raised the level of Greek military sophistication to new heights. His son, Alexander the Great, used the new military instrument to establish an empire. He invaded and defeated the Persian empire by force of arms.

Philip's desires to conquer Greece and establish an empire were contingent upon his ability to develop a military instrument that could succeed against both the classical Greek and Persian methods of war. To defeat the Greeks, Philip had to discover a way of dealing with the heavy infantry phalanx, no easy task for Macedonians, who lacked a tradition of heavy infantry and relied mostly upon cavalry. Dealing with the Persian army was a far more complex problem. Any attempt at empire would require the development of several new capabilities, all of which were absent from the Macedonian military. First, if his army was to remain in the field for long periods of time and move over great distances, it required a logistics system. Second, an army operating in foreign territory required more efficient ways to subdue cities. Third, because of the strength of Persian cavalry, Philip had to develop heavy infantry to serve as a platform of maneuver for his own cavalry. Fourth, mobility on the battlefield had to be improved, and heavy cavalry had to be developed to counter the excellent light infantry of the Persians. Finally, new tactical doctrines were required if the new combat arms were to be utilized in a coordinated way.

The military development of Macedonia was different from that of the rest of classical Greece. Macedonia had long experience in fighting from horseback as units rather than as individual combatants and no tradition of infantry fighting, conditions exactly the reverse of the rest of the city-state armies of classical Greece. In Macedonia what infantry there was was generally drawn from the peasantry on a part-time basis, was generally less organized and trained, and was armed more lightly than the hoplite infantry of Sparta or Athens. Philip's first task was to strengthen his infantry.

Philip's first reform was to require that all able-bodied men serve in the army under a system of regular pay and training, thus turning the Macedonian military from a part-time force into a standing army of professional regulars.[27] Philip discarded the Greek tradition of permitting attendants to accompany the army and forced the soldier to carry his rations and equipment. The Macedonian soldier carried fifteen days' rations, almost double the Greek norm. To increase the speed of his ground forces on the march, Philip banned the use of wheeled transport, using pack mules and horses instead. This allowed more rapid movement and increased the ability of the army to move over heavy terrain.

Philip shaped the infantry into a new, stronger phalanx formation. The

Figure 10.2
The Macedonian Phalanx

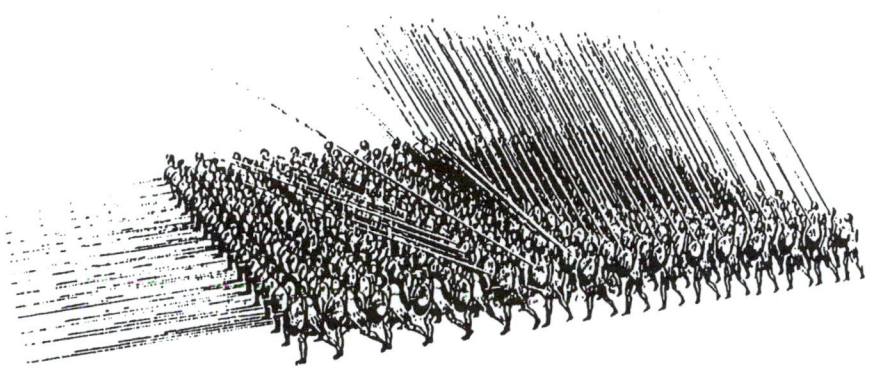

smallest combat unit of the phalanx was a 64-man platoon or *tetarchia*, two of which formed a *taxiarchia* or company of 128 men. The basic combat unit was the battalion or *syntagma* of 256 men. Regiments or *chiliarchia* were comprised of four battalions (1,024 men), and a phalanx infantry division was comprised of four regiments or 4,096 men. The Macedonian infantry division, unlike earlier Greek units of the classical period, was a self-contained fighting unit augmented by organic light infantry and cavalry units. At full strength, a field division also included 2,048 *peltasts*, 1,024 *psiloi* or skirmishers, and a cavalry regiment of 1,024 horsemen. The total force numbered 8,192 men. The field army was comprised of four divisions for a strength of 32,000 men.[28]

The infantry deployed in a phalanx sixteen-men deep, or twice the depth of the normal Greek phalanx of this period. Macedonian infantry was armed with a new weapon, a 13-foot-long spear made of cornel wood with a point at one end and a pointed butt plate on the other to give it balance. This new weapon or *sarissa* weighed approximately eighteen pounds. The infantryman was protected by the standard helmet and armor common to the Greek hoplite and carried a three-foot in diameter, round, rimless shield secured to his body by a forearm grip and a shoulder strap.[29] This arrangement freed both hands to wield the *sarissa*. Philip named this heavy infantry *pezeteri* or "foot companions" to give it the prestige that had traditionally accompanied the cavalry warriors of the nobility, called the "companions of the king." Figure 10.2 depicts the Macedonian infantry phalanx deployed for battle.

Although Philip trained his phalanxes in a number of maneuver drills—oblique, rear, flank march, crescent, and circular formations—the Macedonian heavy phalanx was actually less maneuverable over uneven ground than was the regular Greek phalanx. Moreover, it was more vulnerable at the flanks since the long spears made it difficult to turn toward a new direction of attack. In close combat the phalanx was most vulnerable since the *sarissa* could not be easily used at close range, and the lack of a handgrip at the rim of the shield made it difficult to protect oneself against close-in attack. Discipline and drill could compensate for some of these problems, but the other vulnerabilities remained. Against a unit of swordsmen—the Roman *maniple* for example—the Macedonian "pin-cushion" was very vulnerable indeed.

Philip's design of a new infantry formation was based on new concepts of tactical employment and, indeed, the Macedonian phalanx had been designed from the beginning to accommodate the new tactical thinking. The infantry was no longer the primary killing arm as it was in other Greek armies. Its purpose was to anchor the center of the line and act as a platform for the maneuver and striking power of the other combat arms, most notably the Macedonian heavy cavalry. When formed with the other arms for battle, the phalanx was not the foremost frontal point of the line, but usually held back obliquely in the center. Here the influence of Epaminondas is evident. Philip had spent several years as a young man at the Theban court, where he studied the tactics of the great and innovative Greek general. The heavy cavalry deployed in strength on the right linked to the infantry phalanx by a hinge of heavy elite infantry called *hypaspists* (literally, "shield bearers"). The idea was to engage the enemy on the flank, forcing him to turn toward the attack. As the enemy did so and the cavalry continued to press the right, the slower infantry advanced in hedgehog formation against the opponent's center. If the enemy flank broke, the cavalry could either envelop or press the attack through the enemy formation while the infantry closed, using the phalanx as an anvil against which to hammer the enemy. If the opponent's flank held the cavalry in check, now he had to deal with the shock of the phalanx falling upon his center. Philip's contribution to Greek infantry lay not only in a new design for it, but even more in devising a new tactical doctrine of how to employ it.

The elite striking force of the Macedonian army, its arm of decision, was the heavy cavalry or "mounted companions," armed with sword, shield, and javelin. Organized into squadrons of 300 strong, the cavalry attacked with the javelin held overhand and resting on the shoulder to execute a downward stabbing thrust. This technique was necessary to prevent the rider from being unhorsed by the shock of impact for the stirrup had not yet made its appearance in the West. Once a victim had been impaled, the javelin was abandoned and the cavalry fought on with

sword and shield. Macedonian cavalry usually attacked in a wedge formation like an inverted cone, with the wide end to the front. This formation maximized shock, but left little with which to exploit a
breakthrough. Alexander's Thessalian cavalry were trained to attack in
diamond formation so that if the point penetrated, the body of the formation provided greater impact and shock, allowing the cavalry to explode through the enemy formation.[30] The ratio of cavalry to infantry in
Philip's army was one to six, making it the largest integrated cavalry
force ever fielded by a Greek army. The use of cavalry in lethal pursuit
to effect a strategic decision beyond the tactical victory by completely
destroying the enemy army was also introduced by Philip at this time.

While the army of Philip and Alexander was certainly tactically superior to the Greek armies and a good match for the Persians, by itself
it would have been a useless instrument for constructing a far-flung empire. The Macedonian army would have remained a force fit only for
obtaining limited strategic objectives had Philip not turned his genius to
creating a new logistics capability and the means for rapidly subduing
fortified cities. Among the most important contributions of Philip and
Alexander was the design of logistics and siegecraft capabilities, which
set the standard for future Western armies.

Philip greatly increased the logistics capabilities of his army. First, he
discarded the Greek tradition that allowed each soldier to bring along an
attendant on military operations. He allowed only one attendant for every
ten infantry soldiers and one for every four cavalrymen. Second, he reduced the size of his noncombat contingent by forbidding soldiers to
take along wives and other women, mostly prostitutes and cooks. Third,
Philip discontinued the use of drawn carts except for a few used as field
ambulances and as transport for siege machinery. Most importantly, he
prohibited the use of oxen in his baggage trains, utilizing only horses
and mules as pack animals.[31] As simple as these innovations appear, the
impact on the speed and mobility of the army was enormous.

Reducing the number of attendants and excluding women cut the number of people to be fed on the march by almost two-thirds! Under the
old system a 30,000-man combat force would have been accompanied
by 30,000 attendants and at least 10,000 women, all of whom greatly
increased the logistics burden and, more importantly, slowed the rate of
march for the combat army. The army of Alexander could march thirteen
miles a day while separate units, such as a cavalry squadron, could do
forty miles a day.[32] These rates of movement were impossible under the
old system.

Forbidding the use of ox-drawn carts more than tripled the army's rate of movement. A two-oxen cart could haul 1,000 pounds. The use of neck harnesses (the horse collar had not yet been invented) pressed on the animal's windpipes so that larger loads were not practical. An ox team required 100 pounds of feed a day, and under the best of conditions an ox-cart could make two miles per hour for only five hours before the animals were exhausted.[33] In contrast, five horses could carry the load of an ox-cart and make four miles per hour for eight hours over any type of terrain. Five horses required only half the amount of forage needed to feed a team of oxen.[34] Thus, the ox could move 1,000 pound load only ten miles per day while the horse team could move the same load thirty-two miles per day on half the food and at twice the speed. In barren areas where forage had to be carried by the supply train itself, the useful carrying load of the horse increased by 50 percent.

Without carts the Macedonian soldier became a beast of burden. Ten days' rations (three pounds of grain per day per soldier) weighed thirty pounds. In addition, the soldier's weapon, shield, armor, and bedding weighed another fifty pounds for a combined load of eighty pounds. But the ability of the soldier to carry his own food and equipment considerably reduced the overall logistical burden on the army. For example, an army of 50,000 men that used animals to carry only a third of the load carried on the back of the Macedonian soldier would require 6,000 additional pack animals! An additional 240 animals would be required to carry feed that would nourish the other animals for only a single day.[35] By requiring the soldier to carry his own equipment, Alexander created the lightest, most mobile, and most versatile military force the West had ever seen.

A mobile army risked ruin in enemy territory if it could not quickly subdue the walled garrisons of the enemy. Philip introduced the use of modern siege operations and equipment into the Macedonian army. It was Philip who first organized a special group of artillery engineers to design and build catapults. The specific aspects of Greek siege machinery need not be considered here.[36] For the most part it consisted of equipment that had been used by both the Assyrians and Persians, including siege towers, battering rams, fire arrows, and the *testudo*. What was more important than the machinery, however, was that the Macedonian army was the first Greek army to fully integrate siegecraft into its organization and to train its troops in coordinated attack, much as the Persians and Assyrians had done centuries before. The larger impact of the Macedonian use of siegecraft was that it allowed Greek science, mathematics, and engineering an opportunity to contribute to the Greek art of war. By the time of Demetrios I (305 B.C.E.), known by his nickname of *Polio-*

cretes or The Besieger, Greek inventiveness in military engineering was the most sophisticated in the West.[37]

An important contribution of Greek military engineering under Philip and Alexander was the invention of artillery, the earliest of which took the form of catapults and torsion-fired missiles. The earliest example dates from the fourth century B.C.E. and was called a *gastraphetes*, literally, "belly shooter." It was a form of crossbow that fired a wooden bolt on a flat trajectory along a slot in the aiming rod. Later, weapons fired by torsion bars powered by horsehair and ox tendon (the Greeks called this material *neuron*) springs could fire arrows, rocks, and pots of burning pitch along a parabolic arc. Some of these machines were quite large and mounted on wheels. One such weapon, the *palintonon*, could fire an eight-pound stone over 300 yards. Philip was the first to employ these weapons as a regular part of his siege train. But it was Alexander who made them lighter and more mobile. Alexander's army on the Persian campaign carried prefabricated catapults weighing only eighty-five pounds. But it was the manner in which Alexander employed these weapons that was truly innovative. He used them in a completely new way, as covering artillery.[38]

The importance of Greece in the development of warfare rests in its geographic position and its location in time. Both combined to make Greece a major transmission belt for the transfer of important concepts and technologies of war to the West. Once incorporated into the Roman empire, the Greek contribution to war was readily transmitted throughout western culture. Perhaps the most significant Greek contribution was the attitudinal perspective that war ennobled the human spirit. This idea became the foundation upon which a new civic religion was erected, which saw war as a vital aspect of modern civilization. It was the Greeks who introduced the notion of military service as a moral obligation of citizenship that rests at the base of nationalism. Without this, the modern nation state could not have emerged in the form that it did.

The armies of Philip and Alexander were not genuinely innovative when viewed against the background of the military tradition of the Near East. Armies of earlier periods performed the same feats with similar and better technologies. But these armies and empires had little or no contact with developments in the West. The value of Greece lay in the fact that when it finally achieved a level of military sophistication evident in earlier armies, it did so precisely at a time and place that permitted it to transmit these developments directly into European culture. Had the development of war been left entirely to the Greeks, however, it is likely that it would have progressed only marginally from Philip's day. The fragmented nature of Greek society during the classical period militated against any sustained progress, while the personal and unstable nature of Alexander's empire leaves in doubt the degree to which the Greeks could ever have developed the social mechanisms required to sustain it for very long. It fell to others to bring into being the means for improving the Greek way of war.

NOTES

1. It would have been strange indeed if the Achaeans did not possess the composite bow, given their contact with Assyria. By the classical period, however, the bow seems to have reverted to the simple bow in Greece. Athens' special corps of Scythian bowmen deployed in the Peloponnesian war did use the composite bow, as did Cretan archers.

2. Arthur Ferrill, *The Origins of War* (London: Thames and Hudson, 1985), 98.

3. The thesis that political emancipation gave rise to the phalanx is by no means universally accepted by classicists. Some would argue that it was the revolution in weapons that came first, which then made it possible to enlist the lower classes for war, who in turn demanded political rights as a reward for military service.

4. J.K. Anderson, "Wars and Military Science: Greece," in Michael Grant and Rachel Kitzinger, eds., *Civilization of the Ancient Mediterranean* (New York: Charles Scribner, 1988), vol. 1, 679–80, notes that a number of these sites mentioned in the sagas can be identified with real places, but the point is in much dispute.

5. Robert Laffont, *The Ancient Art of War* (New York: Time-Life Books, 1966), vol. 1, 57–58.

6. It should not be assumed that Thales was the only person in this period utilizing logical analysis. Most of the surviving texts of the period present events in the form of rebuttals, clearly suggesting that there were others writing on similar subjects.

7. For an examination of the Argive shield, see Peter Connolly, *Greece and Rome at War* (Englewood Cliffs, N.J.: Prentice-Hall, 1981), 52–53.

8. Thucydides, book 2, p. 13 (Pericles); see also Laffont, 73 and also Hans Delbruck, *History of the Art of War* (Westport, Conn.: Greenwood Press, 1975), vol. 1, 39.

9. An excellent work on the Spartan army is J.F. Lazenby, *The Spartan Army* (Wiltshire: Aris and Philips, 1985). A more extensive analysis of Sparta at war can be found in W. Kenrick Pritchett, *The Greek State At War*, 3 vols. (Berkeley: University of California Press, 1971).

10. See Laffont, 73, for the weight of the panoply. Among the more interesting elements of hoplite armor were the various helmet designs. In the classical

period, helmets of bronze became more sophisticated until they included cheek guards and even full-face casts including moustaches. However, these helmets made it very difficult for the soldier to hear. After a number of attempts to solve this problem by various devices, ear guards disappeared, sacrificing protection to hearing. The result was that a glancing blow to the helmet often produced a severed ear.

11. Anderson, 688.

12. It is noteworthy that in all of Xenophon's accounts of the Persian war, there is not a single positive mention of Persian cavalry.

13. Hans Delbruck, *History of the Art of War* (Westport, Conn.: Greenwood Press, 1975), vol. 1, 151; Laffont, 73; Anderson, 692–93.

14. These Scythians were usually employed as military police and not combat soldiers, a fact that says much about the Greek view of archery in war.

15. *Iliad*, 4:85–140 and 11:368–83.

16. For more about the Greek moral perspective on the bow, see Richard A. Gabriel, "Armaments," in *Italian Encyclopedia of Social Sciences* (Rome: University of Rome, 1990).

17. Connolly, 48; for a more detailed analysis of the development of the sling, see Manfred Korfmann, "The Sling as Weapon," *Scientific American* 229, no. 4 (October 1973): 34–42.

18. It is easy to forget that the ancients had few roads and no maps. Armies often spent considerable time trying to find each other. Roman mapmakers were the best in the world, but with the collapse of Rome and the rise of medieval cartographers whose placement of locations was generally poor and guided by religious beliefs, the problem of finding the opponent became a major headache for commanders in the Middle Ages.

19. Delbruck, 56.

20. Franz G. Alexander and Sheldon T. Selesnick, *The History of Psychiatry* (New York: Mentor Books, 1966), 52–54. Despite its title, his work provides an excellent history of anatomical medicine as well.

21. For a history of psychiatric breakdown in battle from Egypt to the present, see Richard A. Gabriel, *No More Heroes: Madness and Psychiatry in War* (New York: Hill and Wang, 1987), chap. 2.

22. As Aristotle noted, the strength of the phalanx rests in the discipline and courage of the troops, not in their skill. Or, as Xenophon put it, the strength of an army resides in its soul and not in its weapons.

23. Ferrill, 103.

24. Thucydides's account of the battle of Mantinea (book 4, chap. 71, p. 1) describes in detail the tendency of men to crowd to the right, thus forcing the phalanx to rotate.

25. An excellent analysis of the contributions of Epaminondas can be found in Delbruck, chap. 4. The footnotes of this chapter are worthy of serious attention.

26. Delbruck, 159–63.

27. The problem of how to pay for such a force was a constant one. Philip's capture of enemy gold and silver mines early in the war helped, but a continual pursuit of booty was the long-range solution.

28. T.N. Dupuy, *The Evolution of Weapons and Warfare* (New York: Bobbs-Merrill, 1980), 14.

29. Connolly, 78–79.

30. Ibid., 71.

31. A truly extraordinary work on the logistics system of Alexander is found in Donald W. Engels, *Alexander the Great and the Logistics of the Macedonian Army* (Berkeley: University of California Press, 1978), 12.

32. Ibid., Table 7, 153.

33. *Animal Management* (London: British Army Veterinary Department, 1908), 299.

34. Engels, 15.

35. Ibid., 24.

36. A good account of Greek siege machinery is found in Grant and Kitzinger, 330–38.

37. The modern term for the study of siegecraft is poliocretics, named after the famed Greek besieger of the third century B.C.E.

38. Dupuy, 30.

11

Carthaginian Armies
814–146 B.C.E.

C arthage was founded thirty-eight years before the first Olympiad or about 814 B.C.E. as one of a number of colonies established in Sicily, Spain, and North Africa by the Phoenician city-state of Tyre in her effort to expand her influence into the western Mediterranean. Carthage, in Phoenician, was *kart-hadasht*, meaning "new city," and it is likely that Carthage was designed from the beginning to be the leading colony even though others, Utica for example, had been founded earlier.[1] Tyre was a Canaanite city whose name in Greek was *Phoenicia*, meaning "dark skinned,"[2] and by which name modern Lebanon was known in the West during antiquity. The Romans called the people of Carthage *Poeni* or *Puni*, hence the name Punic Wars. By the sixth century Carthage was the richest maritime power in the western Mediterranean, supported by a powerful navy and commercial fleet. In 586 B.C.E., Tyre herself came under siege by the Assyrian king Nebuchadnezzar and the mother-city could no longer provide protection to her colonies in Sicily. The role of protector fell to Carthage, which immediately dispatched troops to counter Greek predations there and in Sardinia. With Roman and Etruscan help as well as aid from other Greek city-states on the island, Carthage successfully checked Greek expansion, gradually bringing Sicily under her control. For the next 300 years the linchpin of Carthaginian foreign policy was to retain control of Sicily and prevent it from becoming a base to interrupt her trade in the Mediterranean or from becoming a strategic platform for the invasion of Africa itself. It was during this time that the other Phoenician colonies on the African coast were compelled to recognize Carthage's primacy and submit to Carthaginian rule. With the exception of Utica, which was permitted to keep its walls, the other cities were required to demolish their fortifications, disband their armies, and pay tribute in the form of money or troop levies to Carthage, who maintained the only standing military force.

Carthage was almost unique among non-Greek states in possessing a constitution. For the first three centuries after its founding it is likely that Carthage followed the Phoenician model and was ruled by kings. As in Tyre and Sidon, however, these kings were not hereditary but elected by a powerful oligarchy of merchant princes. The authority of these kings, moreover, was not absolute and was circumscribed by tradition and legal limitations, including removal by the same oligarchy that elected them. By the fourth century B.C.E., Carthage had evolved an oligarchic republican regime based on an annually elective dual magistracy, that of the *shofets* (in Latin *suffetes*) or, translated into Hebrew, judges; the *Gerousia* or Grand Council, with an inner permanent committee of thirty elders; a high court of 104 judges selected for life by a college of *pentarchs*; and a popular Assembly comprising all citizens who met the minimum property qualifications. All offices were reserved for the aristocracy, so that the basis of political privilege in Carthage was wealth, not heredity.[3] Carthage was a commercial society where war and the military took second place to profit, where military adventures were subjected to the test of cost-benefit analysis, and where generals were distrusted and kept on a short leash.

In 580 B.C.E. Carthage sent troops to put down Greek pretensions in Sicily and Sardinia. Although successful, one of her commanders had performed badly and was refused the right to return to Carthage with his troops. These troops were Carthaginian citizen-levies and refused to obey, threatening to strike at Carthage herself. The revolt was put down by a general named Mago, who then reformed the army and established the first of the great Carthaginian military families. Among these were the Barcas, who produced Hamilcar, Hasdrubal, and, of course, Hannibal. Carthage's newly acquired foreign policy responsibilities of protecting her sister colonies and maintaining her commercial supremacy in the western Mediterranean threw the inadequacy of her citizen-levies to meet these needs into sharp relief. The population of Carthage in the third century B.C.E. probably did not exceed 400,000 counting all classes, a number far too small to provide for her commercial and military manpower needs, even with the addition of levies from the other colonies.[4]

Moreover, Carthage's population was not comprised of hardy agricultural stock whose absence from the land produced only marginal economic disruption. Carthage's population were mostly freemen who were merchants, tradesmen, and artisans, whose absence from economic activity was costly to Carthage's revenue. It was, then, simply a question of economics and numbers. It was cheaper to hire soldiers than to conscript them, and by the fourth century B.C.E. the citizen-levy had been abandoned and replaced with mercenaries.

Carthaginian recruitment agents became a common fixture throughout the Near East, Italy, Greece, Gaul, and Africa, where they hired individual soldiers and complete military units from princes and kings. A small number of Carthaginian citizens continued to serve in the military, but their numbers were insignificant. The last date for which we have evidence of Carthaginian units participating in war outside Africa is in 311 B.C.E.[5] It was around this time that Carthage created a new unit called the Sacred Band, comprised of elite citizen-soldiers. This unit, Polibius tells us, was 3,000 strong and was armed like Greek heavy infantry, by which we suppose he meant the infantry of Alexander and not classical Greece, although we cannot be certain. Other sources suggest the unit was a training battalion for young cavalry officers, but this, too, is uncertain. Whatever its composition, the Carthaginian Sacred Band could not, by law, be employed outside the *chora* of Carthage itself, suggesting that it may have been some sort of praetorian or civic guard.[6] Why this unit was created remains a mystery. One can only say that with Alexander's victories came a desire to imitate Greek forms of warfare.

The mercenary system presented Carthage with a number of problems. First, mercenary armies were expensive. But Carthage was very rich, and as long as her armies protected her trade and metals monopolies throughout the western Mediterranean, the cost was manageable. Carthage also charged her dependencies for the privilege of protecting them, sometimes, as in Iberia and Libya, requiring that they furnish specified numbers of troops and then paying them as mercenaries. Second, mercenary armies must be kept busy or they become ill-disciplined and even mutinous. This was solved by having the army almost constantly occupied somewhere outside of Carthage itself. For more than a century Hanno occupied them with the conquest of North Africa's hinterlands, which Carthage exploited for raw materials and agriculture. Third, mercenary soldiers were one thing, mercenary commanders quite another. Command of the armies was always in the hands of Carthaginian field generals. At first this presented some problems, as a commercial people usually do not produce great military commanders. After the fourth century B.C.E., however, Carthage had begun to establish a handful of powerful families whose sons were experienced military commanders. This new military caste was established by Mago (hence the military dynasty known as the Magonids) and soon produced others. Examined objectively, Carthaginian commanders were some of the best in the western world. Finally, powerful generals in command of mercenary troops can become a serious threat to civilian political authority. The Carthaginians hit upon a novel solution to deal with this problem.

Prior to the reform of the army, Carthaginian commanders had been high ranking political officials. As was the Greek practice, the king's themselves in the early days commanded their armies in battle. After 300 B.C.E., military commanders were no longer permitted to hold public office of any kind. A complete separation of military from civic authority was introduced. Generals and admirals were now appointed only for specific periods of time or for specific conflicts by the Council of 100 judges. Nor was it uncommon for a member of this court or even a senator to accompany the general in the field and report on his performance and, we might reasonably surmise, his political loyalty. Generals could be removed at any time by the council. When Roman ambassadors came to Carthage to demand the removal of Hannibal for his siege of Sargentum, it was to this council and the Carthaginian senate that they appealed. To make certain that its edicts were taken seriously, any Carthaginian commander who failed in the field or who otherwise failed to carry out his orders with diligence could be publicly crucified in the city's main square! The system worked admirably, for with the exception of one Bomilar who in 308 B.C.E. attempted some sort of attack on the city with a small band of elite troops, Carthaginian commanders were completely loyal and presented no risk of praetorianism to the civil authority.

The success of the Carthaginian military system is evident in two respects. First, right to the end Carthage was able to place large forces in the field sufficient to the missions set for their commanders. Second, the quality of Carthaginian commanders was generally excellent, by far superior to Roman commanders, with the notable exception of Publius Scipio. As to the size of the armies, a few examples will suffice. The walls around Carthage were also used as barracks and stalls for animals and supplies. In the two-and-one-half-mile-long wall that protected Carthage from an assault from the mainland, there were stables sufficient for 300 elephants, 4,000 cavalry horses, and barracks for 20,000 infantry and 4,000 cavalry.[7] A force of this size represented the central core of the Carthaginian army, to be expanded in time of crisis. One advantage of a mercenary army is that their commanders could hire troops as they went from the very country within which they were conducting operations. Thus, in 262 B.C.E. at Minoa Heraclea in the battle with Rome in Sicily, the Carthaginian commander had an army of 50,000 foot, 6,000 horses, and 60 elephants. When Hamilcar Barca (Hannibal's father) left Carthage to expand Carthaginian influence in Spain, Polibius tells us he carried only a few elephants and a small army with him. A few years later when Hamilcar was killed by the Oretani in Iberia, his army was 50,000 foot, 6,000 horses, and 200 elephants. When Hannibal moved to cross the Alps, he started with an army of 40,000 foot, 8,000 cavalry, and 37 elephants.[8] While Carthage's military system could produce adequate manpower to deal with most military situations, what it could not do, of course, was fight a war of attrition with a power whose manpower reserves *and* disciplined stubbornness could draw Carthage into a war of attrition. It was in these terms that the wars with Rome were ultimately unwinnable.

As commanders of mercenary armies, Carthaginian commanders could not rely upon a standard tactical or organizational "system of war" such as Roman or Greek commanders could. Mercenary units fought under the command of their own leaders and in their own style and with their own weapons. This forced Carthaginian commanders to become experts at utilizing diverse military specialties in imaginative ways while still orchestrating these specialties to achieve the overall tactical objectives of the army as a whole. This was no easy task, for there was no "system" to enforce or support the commander's will. Carthaginian commanders had to win the loyalty and respect of their men often with their own feats of bravery, comraderie (Hannibal ate and slept with his troops on the ground), or with brutal punishments. On the other hand, Carthaginian commanders were often appointed for the duration of a war and given a free hand with their troops, with the result that Carthage could rely upon a corps of seasoned, experienced professional generals who had the opportunity to train and shape their armies into instruments of their will. Unlike Roman armies, for example, the armies of Carthage were not comprised of marginally trained citizen-levies of short term service led by political generals who swapped command every other day. Instead, they were commanded by wily combat veterans of great experience, skill, and imagination, who held their commands for long periods.

At the end of the Third Punic War the destruction of Carthage was so complete that no Carthaginian records survived. Most of what we know about the composition and weapons of the Carthaginian armies comes from Roman sources like Polibius and Livy, and most of it from the accounts of the Roman war against Hannibal.[9] We can, however, be fairly certain that Hannibal's army was typical of the earlier Carthaginian mercenary armies recounted in Greek sources. Hannibal's army, then, was composed of the usual strange mixture of soldiers from many lands and cultures. The most loyal and talented of Hannibal's soldiers were the heavy infantry of Libya-Phoenicia, who provided the bulk of the Carthaginian armies. The Libyans, in whose land Carthage was founded, were originally reduced to slaves and forced conscripts. But by 480 B.C.E., we hear of them fighting in Sicily. Over the centuries, the Libyans and Phoenicians intermarried (thus Libya-Phoenicians) and the former slaves became loyal participants in the Carthaginian culture. By the third century, however, they remained the only one of Carthage's dependencies that was still required by law to provide manpower. Once conscripted, however, there is evidence that they were as well-paid as the mercenaries. Polibius tells us that troops from this dependency provided the bulk of the cavalry as well as the infantry arms.[10] Prior to the First Punic War the Libya-Phoenicians are described as equipped with iron breastplates and helmets, carrying great white shields that covered most of their body, marching in a slow and orderly fashion (suggesting a phalanx), and supported by the four-horse heavy chariots of Canaanite design that were traditional to Carthaginian warfare. At the beginning of the Punic War, they are equipped quite like the late Greek infantryman, with metal helmet, greaves, linen cuirass, round shield, *sarissa*, and short sword. Most likely they fought in the manner of the Macedonian phalanx of 4,000 men organized in 256 files, each 16-men deep. Hannibal used them in precisely this way until Lake Trasimene when, he inflicted a severe defeat upon the Romans and began to reequip his infantry with captured Roman equipment and weapons. This, of course, would have required training in Roman tactics, where the phalanx was replaced by the Roman *maniple* formation. It is also likely that some Gallic infantry was reequipped in this manner to include the adoption of mail armor and the use of the *pilum* as the primary missile weapon. Libya-Phoenician troops could also be configured as light infantry, where they gained a reputation for fighting from ambush and carrying out swift raids.

Hannibal's "Spanish infantry" came from two groups of tribes, the Iberians themselves and the northern Celt-Iberians, tribes of intermarried Celts and Iberians. Both provided heavy and light infantry forces, but with a somewhat different mix of weapons. The Iberian heavy infantry wore mail armor, helmets, and were protected by a large oblong shield similar to the Roman *scutum*. They carried a thrown javelin, but relied mostly upon the Spanish sword, the *falcata*. The *falcata* was a slightly curved sword, single-edged for the first two thirds of its length (55–63 cm) with the remainder of the blade double-edged. Five centimeters wide at its broadest point, the weapon was cast in one piece with the handle and hilt curving back over the hand, providing good protection. The secret of the *falcata* was in its manufacture, from the finest Spanish steel, which made it so sharp and durable that it would cut through almost any armor and was known to break the Roman sword of this period, a weapon of Greek design and not yet the true *gladius* of later years.[11] So superior was this weapon, that when Scipio captured Cartegena in 209 B.C.E., he captured a number of Spanish ironsmiths and forced them to teach his own smiths how to manufacture the *falcata*, which the Romans then adopted and called the *gladius hispanicus* or sword of Spain. Spanish heavy infantry used the scale, lamellar, or chain mail of the day, the latter an innovation of the Celts and standard issue of the Roman armies of the period. Spanish heavy infantry were fierce and courageous soldiers, every bit the equal of the Roman legionnaire.

Spanish light infantry were armed with the standard kits of darts, javelins, light shields, and slings. One type of Spanish light infantry used a distinctively Spanish round buckler shield of leather, wicker, or wood called the *caetra*, a design that brings the Greek *peltast* to mind. They also carried the *falcata*. Although generally unarmored, their skill at sword play and their agility made them effective combatants even against heavy infantry. Balearic slingers had served in Carthaginian armies at least since 337 B.C.E., when their ability to fire both long- and short-range slings made them a threat against light infantry. Slingers usually carried two slings, one for short range and one for long range. The long-range sling could cast a stone the size of a tennis ball almost 300 yards. Slingers could be deployed in units ranging from 500 to 2,000 strong. When fired in salvo as indirect artillery, sling fire could be deadly to a packed infantry or cavalry formation. Balearic slingers were the finest in the ancient world, and for almost 600 years they were hired by one army after another as mercenaries. They were, however, generally regarded as savages and often demanded to be paid in women rather than gold![12]

The Celt-Iberian infantry served as both heavy and light troops. They used the same standard armor and helmet as their Iberian kin but carried the typical Celtic double-edged slashing sword. They also carried the *soliferreum*, an Iberian weapon, a slim javelin made entirely of iron, about the same size as the *pilum*, and used in generally the same manner. Another Iberian weapon, the *falarica*, was a shaft of pine wood with a long iron head around which the soldier wrapped wool soaked in tar or pitch to be lit and thrown. This incendiary weapon was adopted by the

Romans and converted into an artillery weapon fired by catapults and torsion-fired field guns.

Hannibal recruited large cohorts of Celtic infantry from the Gallic tribes (the Romans called the Celts Gauls) north of the Po River. Celts had fought in Carthaginian armies as mercenaries from at least 340 B.C.E. and were the most enthusiastic of Hannibal's soldiers. The Celts had been at war with the Romans for more than a century before Hannibal's invasion of Italy. It was the Celts that sacked Rome in 390 B.C.E., and it was the Celts that invaded Italy again and again over the next century to check Roman expansion in the north. In 225 B.C.E., only seven years before Hannibal's invasion, 70,000 Celts had invaded Italy once more.

Organized into clans, these tribal warriors served as heavy infantry and lived for war, glory, and plunder. They used the long, double-edged sword as their basic weapon. A slashing weapon, it could be swung from side to side or over the head, bringing it down like an axe. During Brennus' war against Rome, this axe technique split the Roman shields. To counter this, Roman armorers redesigned the shield, placing a rim of iron along the top edge. Originally, the Gauls (or Celts) wore no armor, and sometimes fought stark naked as they charged in wild groups into the enemy formations. It was a sign of valor to fight without armor, and yet it was the Celts who gave the world chain mail armor. Perhaps its great cost made its wide use prohibitive. The Celts in Hannibal's army— who often comprised 40 percent of his army—were equipped with captured Roman armor and helmets. Celtic warriors fought as individuals and were incapable of any field discipline or maneuver. Hannibal often used them as shock troops to strike the enemy line before committing his more valuable African infantry. This, of course, resulted in heavy casualties among Celtic units, but they were generally expendable in any case. To the Celt, however, the opportunity to engage in the most dangerous assaults was seen as a badge of great honor, and for the most part their heavy casualty rate did nothing to reduce either their loyalty or fighting élan.

Hannibal's cavalry, like the rest of his army, was a mixed bag. There was a small number of elite Carthaginian heavy cavalry, probably comprised of professional warriors from Carthage itself. It is also likely that some small contingents came from the upper classes of Libya-Phoenicia. The Celts, too, contributed some heavy cavalry, but only in small numbers. The Spanish contributed the greatest numbers of heavy cavalry. The primary weapon of the Spanish cavalry was the long lance with a leaf-shaped socketed blade. They also carried the *falcata* and the buckler-shield, and wore mail armor, helmet and greaves. Their role was to deliver shock. But their tribal traditions often prompted them, once engaged, to dismount and fight alongside the infantry. Sometimes they carried a light infantryman armed with *falcata* and *caetra* on the back of the horse. When engaged, both would dismount and fight as infantry.[13] Saddles were not widely used, although at times the Hellenistic style is found. Spanish cavalrymen used a broad girth with a blanket, controlling the horse with bridle and snaffle bit.

Hannibal employed large numbers—some 6,000 at Cannae—of Numidian light cavalry. Sometimes enemies of Carthage, sometimes serving out of common interests, but mostly paid mercenaries, these units came from Numidia (called this by the Romans because it was populated by nomads) and began serving in large numbers in Carthaginian armies in the third century B.C.E. They rode bareback and carried short javelins and light spears and sometimes a short sword or dagger. A light round leather or wicker shield served as a defensive weapon. They were specialists in maneuver warfare, often attacking, retreating, maneuvering, and then attacking again from a different place on the battlefield. Specialists at ambush, they often dismounted and fought on foot to complete the destruction of the enemy. The Numidians were the classic light horse and could not deliver sufficient shock by themselves. At Cannae, for example, they were unable to break the Roman allied cavalry on their own. Once it had been broken by the heavy Spanish cavalry, however, it was the Numidians who conducted the pursuit, with great effect.

Other troops fighting with Hannibal included a small unit of Macedonians (4,096 men or a single infantry phalanx) provided by Philip of Macedonia at the battle of Zama, and Italian troops from Rome's rival cities on the Italian peninsula. Livy and Polibius make it a point to argue that the Italian states remained loyal to Rome in the face of Hannibal's enticement of freedom. For the most part, this was true. However, many Italians—Apulians, Bruttians, Lucanians, and Samnites—did side with Hannibal. The Samnites in particular went over in large numbers. They had fought three wars with Rome in less than sixty years, with the final rebellion against Roman influence coming in 269 B.C.E.[14] After Cannae, the Samnites openly supported Hannibal. Southern Italian troops had reputations for fierceness, treachery, and brutality, characteristics that made their efficiency on the battlefield far out of proportion to their numbers, not unlike the Norman troops of a later European period.[15] By 208 B.C.E., more than 40 percent of Hannibal's army was comprised of Italian troops. When Hannibal returned to Africa in 203 B.C.E., most of the 18,000 veteran troops who went with him were Italians. At Zama, 12,000 Italian troops—mostly Bruttians—formed the third line of Hannibal's order of battle. As the rest of the Carthaginian army crumbled around them, these Italian troops stood firm and fought to the death.

Hannibal's army was also equipped with the premier fighting machine of its day, the elephant. Elephants had been in Carthaginian armies since 289 B.C.E., when they were introduced to the battlefield by King Pyrrhus against the Carthaginians, who were fighting a war against Syracuse. Carthaginian commanders were suitably impressed and quickly equipped their armies with this new shock weapon, abandoning their heavy Canaanite chariots in the process. Carthaginian armies first used the elephant against the Romans at Agrigentum in 262 B.C.E. The Carthaginian elephants were not Indian or African bush elephants, both of which are considerably larger, but the now-extinct and much smaller African forest elephant, found then in Morocco and Algeria. Only seven feet at the shoulders, the Carthaginian war elephant was not large enough to carry a turret and archer. Instead, under the steady hand of the *mahout*, the elephant itself was the weapon used to deliver shock and strike fear into the hearts of untrained soldiers and horses.

Hannibal had thirty-seven elephants with him when he crossed the Alps. As an instrument of war, the elephant has a long and generally impressive history. Alexander first encountered them in his wars against the Persians, who probably obtained them from the Indians. During the wars of Alexander's successors (the *Diadochi*), the elephant in war became common among the armies of the Mediterranean area. The elephant frightened those armies that had never seen it. In the reign of Claudius, for example, the Romans took them to Britain to impress the local chieftains. Unless a horse had been trained around them, elephants easily spooked cavalry mounts. Moreover, a charging wall of elephants could deliver shock against an infantry formation quite unlike any other weapon, horse or chariots. In Persia and India elephants carried platforms from which archers could command the battlefield with their fire. Elephants also made excellent anchor for lines of infantry, and their size even made them excellent screens behind which cavalry could be repositioned on the field.

Like all implements of war, however, the elephant came equipped with disadvantages. Light infantry skirmishers could meet the elephants in advance of the infantry line and strike them with darts, swords, and javelins, wounding them into a rage. Torches, too, could be used to frighten the beasts away from their line of advance. Roman units employed specialized units of *velites* who maneuvered behind the animals and cut their hamstring tendons. Enraged elephants were very difficult to control, and on more than one occasion they turned and stampeded over their own formations. To prevent the animals from running over their own troops, the *mahouts* carried a large iron spike and a hammer. If control of the elephant could not be regained, the *mahout* drove the spike behind the animal's ear into its brain, killing it instantly! There are no surviving reports of how well this technique worked.

The armies of Carthage were such a mixture of groups, weapons, tribes, and even languages that they could not be disciplined to a standard tactical system. It is testimony to the brilliance of Carthaginian commanders—of which Hannibal was but one albeit the most notable example—that for more than three centuries they were able to field these kinds of armies and still be very effective in war. Carthaginian field commanders were known for their personal bravery and courage, traits that endeared them to tribal and clan units and to the leaders of the units that fought under them. Carthaginian commanders could also be ruthless in disciplining their troops with beatings and death sentences if they did not perform well. This is hardly surprising for an officer corps well-acquainted with seeing their Carthaginian comrades who failed in war crucified in the public square of Carthage. In a real sense, then, the soldiers of Carthaginian armies often had more to fear from their commanders than from the enemy. The tactical effectiveness of Carthaginian armies and the brilliance of their commanders lay not in the employment of some standard tactical system (as with Rome, for example), but in their ability to employ various types of units creatively in a given battle situation to obtain maximum collective effect. At the same time, of course, the battlefield tapestry had to be woven into some sort of tactical whole if victory was to be achieved. This is no easy task, and modern commanders might well ponder the difficulties involved.

All of the above notwithstanding, it is possible to discern some "tactical constants" or general rules that seem to have governed Hannibal's (and others') battle tactics. The first of these rules was always to maximize shock and surprise. Hannibal frequently engaged the enemy while it was still deployed in column of march. Another rule was to engage only after the enemy was made to work hard to transit some obstacle like a river, stream, hill, or forest. A third rule was to use the terrain to maximum effect, and always tempt the enemy to fight uphill. Fourth, contain the enemy where you can kill him. Hannibal often anchored his lines of infantry with heavy formations of phalanx infantry, forcing the enemy into a smaller and smaller area. Cavalry tactics centered upon the use of this arm to drive the enemy cavalry from the field as a prelude to turning back and staging a shock attack against the rear or flank of the enemy infantry. Above all, if Hannibal was unable to secure any of these advantages, he avoided battle. If he could not fight on his terms, he would not fight at all and conserved his manpower for another day.

Hannibal and other Carthaginian commanders relied upon cavalry as the arm of decision, with infantry used as a platform for maneuver or as shock troops. This development is hardly surprising. Close contacts with the Greeks made the Carthaginians thoroughly familiar with Alexander's military system, one that also used cavalry as the arm of decision and the infantry as a platform for maneuver. Second, for years Carthage had to defend the grain crop of Libya-Phoenicia against the lightning raids of the Numidians. The size of the border was such that fixed fortifications were impractical. Thus, Carthage developed its own indigenous cavalry to deal with the problem. One consequence was the development of a tactical doctrine that stressed the use of the horse over infantry, exactly the reverse of the Romans. Taken as a whole, however, Carthaginian armies were fragile entities subject to poor-discipline and fragmentation if events got beyond the control of their commanders. It is a testimony to their training and experience that Carthaginian commanders rarely let this happen.

NOTES

1. B.H. Warmington, *Carthage, A History* (New York: Barnes and Noble, 1993), 42.

2. Terence Wise and Richard Hook, *Armies of the Carthaginian Wars* (Oxford: Osprey, 1982), vol. 4. There is some doubt as to the meaning of term Phoenicia. The *Cambridge Ancient History*, vol. 2, part 2, 1975, 520 notes that the word "Phoenician" is derived from the Greek *phoinix*, meaning "red purple dye," probably denoting that Tyre and its cities were famous as the source of royal purple dye made from the sea creature *murex*. Interestingly, the word "Canaan" is also derived from an older word meaning purple dye which in Hebrew is *kna'ani* which means "merchant." Thus, by the fifteenth century B.C.E., the land of Canaan (Greek Phoenicia) was the "land of the purple dye merchants."

3. Brian Caven, *The Punic Wars* (New York: Barnes and Noble, 1992), 2.

4. Warmington, 133.

5. Ibid., 46.

6. Richard A. Gabriel and Donald Boose, *Great Battles of Antiquity* (Westport, Conn.: Greenwood Press, 1994), 290.

7. Warmington, 131.

8. Gabriel and Boose, 290.

9. Ibid.

10. Wise, 7.

11. Ibid., 19.
12. Warmington, 46–47.
13. Gabriel and Boose, 291.
14. Wise, 22.
15. Warmington, 46.

Armies of Ancient India: Vedic and Imperial Periods
1200–120 B.C.E.

Indian military history in the ancient period began thousands of miles away from India itself, on the great steppeland that stretches from Poland to Central Asia. Around 2000 B.C.E. this land was inhabited by a semipastoral, stockbreeding, warlike tribal people who even at this early date had tamed the horse and, perhaps, invented a chariot whose spoked wheels, light cart, and team of horses made it far superior to the ass-drawn, solid-wheeled, wooden platform vehicles extant in Sumer during the same period. Sometime in the early part of the second millennium, perhaps around 1500 B.C.E., these people, which history came to call Indo-Europeans or Aryans, began to migrate westward, southward, and eastward, probably under the pressure of desiccation of the land or overpopulation. It was these people who invaded Anatolia and imposed themselves as a warrior aristocracy upon the natives and became the Hittites, and who imposed themselves on the native Hurrians and became the Mitanni. Over several more centuries they moved further eastward, invading Iran and eventually India, a process that took several centuries.[1]

Most of the population of India at this time was comprised of stone-age aboriginal peoples. The exception was the relatively advanced Harappa culture of the Indus Valley, dating from circa 3000 B.C.E. The Harappa civilization had been under pressure from the aboriginal peoples for more than a millennium, and by the time of the Aryan invasions of

India (circa 1200 B.C.E.) the Harappa culture had almost completely disintegrated.[2] For the next 500 years, beginning in the northwest of India, the Aryans spread out throughout the Indian continent, gradually displacing the original Indian population and becoming the dominant culture. This period of war and conquest (1200–700 B.C.E.) was the time of the *Rigveda*, the great collection of epic and heroic myths and tales chronicling the battles and settlement of the Aryans. The most famous of these epic poems is the *Mahabharata*. Composed as an oral poem like the *Iliad* and comprised of 90,000 verses, the *Mahabharata* is the longest single poem in the world[3] and falls into the same category as the great Irish and Icelandic sagas, telling the tale of a warrior people. The Aryans (also called Vedics) imposed their culture, societal structure, martial values, and military technique on the original Indian population, completely transforming it into a martial culture.

The Aryan-Vedic social order imposed on the Indians was tribal and ruled by a warrior aristocracy. The Vedic king was a warrior-chief whose skill at war and bloodline provided legitimacy for his claim to rule. His first obligation was to protect the tribal kingdom (*rashtra*), and there was at this early date no notion of the king being divine, something that would develop over the next 500 years. The *rashtra* was comprised of tribes (*jana*), tribal units (*vish*), and villages (*grama*). The nucleus of the tribe was the family (*kula*), with the eldest male as its head (*kulapa*). The warrior king was called the *raja*, a term closely related to the Latin *rex*.[4] The king was assisted in governing by a council of elders (*sabha*) and other advisors like the *purohita* or chief priest and astrologer, the *senani* or military commander (although it was the king who personally led the army into battle), and the charioteer, often the king's oldest military comrade, who drove his chariot into battle.[5]

Vedic society was divided into four groups: the military aristocracy, originally *rajanya*, but more commonly *kshatriya*; the priests or *brahmins*; the more prosperous land owners and traders, the *vaishyas*; and the agricultural cultivators or *shudras*. The Vedics erected early prohibitions against eating with and marrying the darker aboriginal peoples, probably as a way of maintaining their status as rulers over a vast majority of indigenous peoples. Based on skin color, these prohibitions gradually evolved into the Indian caste system evident to this day. The Vedic tribal social order lasted until circa 700 B.C.E., when it gave way to larger, more stable societies of regional scope even as it preserved its essential social and governing institutions within the new monarchies and republics. The result was that by 600 B.C.E., northern India was divided into sixteen such states, all constantly at war with one another.

Map 12.1
The Sixteen Major States of Northern India, c. 600 B.C.E.

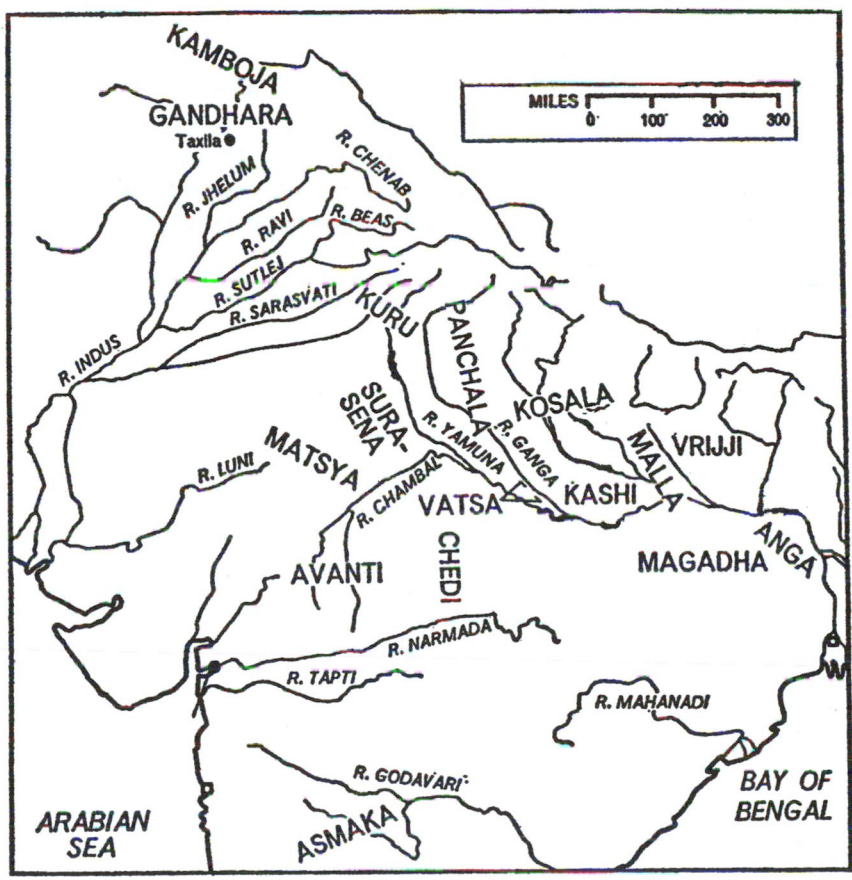

The Aryan-Vedic martial tradition continued unabated. Map 12.1 depicts these states and their locations.

Perhaps as a consequence of the caste system, which permitted the warrior class to maintain its hold on power for the next millennium, the martial values of the Aryan-Vedics struck deep roots in Indian culture and persisted until the modern era. In the Indian tradition, war was the normal activity of the state, and as soon as a king gained power he was expected to begin to attack his neighbors. In the Indian view, war was essentially a large tournament and was fought for honor and glory of the king and great warriors. A well-developed code of chivalrous conduct existed, unchanged from Vedic days. Cowardice in battle dishonored the soldier and his lord while bravery and fighting to the death were rewarded with immediate entry into heaven. A defeated king might even follow the ideal of *jauhar*, in which the king, his family, and closest advisors were burned to death in the innermost chambers of his great hall while his men fought to the end on the battlements. Even the conduct of battle was governed by chivalrous ideals. A warrior fighting from a chariot might not strike at a soldier fighting on foot. A wounded soldier, one disarmed, or one who offered surrender, might not be killed. For the king the true reward of battle was honor and glory and the homage of the defeated king who, not surprisingly, immediately began planning his revenge.

This last point is important, for it explains much as to why the Vedic martial tradition persisted for as long as it did. In Indian thinking, there were three kinds of conquest: righteous conquest, conquest for greed, and demonic conquest. The first, righteous conquest, involved defeating the rival king on the battlefield and then making him a vassal. Whatever booty was taken was minimal, and the defeated king was permitted to continue to rule his own land as long as he paid homage to the superior king. Conquest for greed, as the name implies, levied great burdens on the defeated to provide money, materials, or manpower to the victor. But once again the defeated king was permitted to remain in power and govern his state. The third type of conquest, demonic conquest, occurred when the enemy's lands were ravaged, the king deposed, and his territory incorporated into the victor's realm, politically destroying the losing state.[6] From the time of the Aryan-Vedics, the last two—greed and demonic conquest—were discouraged as being without moral standing as, one surmises, clearly befitted a warrior society wherein even rival kings were members of the same aristocratic class and even ethnic identity. Such a system of warfare permitted the rival aristocracies to survive even military defeat and never wrought destruction of such a magnitude that would permit the overthrow of the Vedic social order by the lower classes or indigenous peoples. As with the kings and aristocracies of absolutist Europe, who had more in common with one another than with the peoples they governed (thus French as the language of "international" diplomacy), war fought for glory was never permitted to destroy the system as such. For the system to change, both Europe and India would require someone whose martial values did not include a sense of societal limit, someone from outside the royal class and of low birth. In Europe this person was Napoleon. In India, it was Chandragupta Maurya.

The very martial tradition that encouraged warfare in India at the same time prohibited warfare on such a scale and of such scope as to effect a strategic decision, permitting a strong leader to unify the nation. Derived from the early conquests and cattle raids, the Vedic ideal of war was not unlike that found in the *Iliad*, with exactly the same result. Indian warfare finds its parallel in Greece, where the ideal of war as individual combatants seeking glory led to a social order (city-states) and military agency (citizen-hoplites) that guaranteed constant warfare without ever permitting a strategic decision that would have permitted the social order to advance beyond tribal warfare. There was frequent war, but no social change. It was Philip II of Macedon who developed the military instrument to fight war on a scale that could effect a strategic decision. The result was the unification of Greece for the first time in its history and the emergence of a scale of warfare that could produce an empire. Exactly the same set of circumstances emerged in India and, interestingly, at about the same time as in Greece.

Our understanding of warfare in Vedic times is clouded by a lack of hard information. We are forced to deduce much of what we know from descriptions on a few reliefs and the lines of the *Mahabharata*, which, because it was written down long after the events portrayed in it, is not a reliable source. This aside, some approximation of the tribal warfare conducted by Aryan chiefs against the indigenous peoples and each other can be assembled. First, the Aryans were horse and chariot people, and their large chestnut horses must have terrified the natives of the Indus Valley, who had never seen the animal, just as the horses of the *conquistadors* later terrified the Incas and Aztecs.[7] The chariot provided such a great military advantage against a people barely out of the stone age that the newcomers must have quickly established their dominance on the plains of the Indus, driving the aboriginal peoples into the jungles and forests. The Aryan chariot was a light, two-man vehicle drawn by a two-horse team, probably (like the early Hurrian model of the same period) with its axle still forward of the rear wheel. The chariot was used only by the warrior aristocracy, while the common members of the tribe—warfare was a tribal activity involving all social classes—fought on foot. The chariot warriors probably wore armor, perhaps leather or scale plate, but there is no evidence of the helmet until much later.[8] The chariot warrior carried a lance, spear, or javelin. The simple bamboo bow was used extensively in this period by footsoldiers and was probably adopted from the local model. The chariot warrior, when he used a bow, most likely used the composite bow fashioned of animal horn.

Swords, axes, and slings were used as well by infantry. The Aryans were a bronze-age culture and were adept at fashioning weapons of bronze. At the time of the Aryan invasion, however, the indigenous peoples of India had only recently (the Harappa excepted) exited the stone

Figure 12.1
Ravana in Full Battle Array

RAVANA.

Note: 1: dagger axe; 2: club; 3: mace; 4: lasso; 5: metal trident spear; 6: crescent axe;
7: cane arrow; 8: incendiary arrow; 9: unknown; 10: bronze leaf-point javelin; 11:
iron-tipped spear; 12: sickle-sword; 13: sword; 14: battle-axe; 15: trident dagger;
16: club; 17: stimulum (?); 18: composite bow.

age. Their only metals technology was copper. Iron did not make its
appearance in India until around 800 B.C.E. [9] We know nothing of Aryan
tactical doctrine during this period, but on the plains at least it could not
have been very much different from that of the Mitanni, essentially
clashes of chariot-borne warriors in individual combat as the rest of the
scuffle raged around them, every man fighting for himself with no coordination with other combatants. At least this is the impression one
receives from the epic literature of the time. Figure 12.1 depicts Ravana,
the monster king of Ceylon and southern India in full battle array, car-

rying a fine selection of the weapons commonly employed by the armies of the day.[10]

The chariot had originally been the spine of the Aryan armies. Over time, however, the chariot gave way to the war elephant and the ridden warhorse as the primary mounts of the warrior aristocracy. By the sixth century B.C.E., armies contained cavalry contingents in the thousands. In true tribal fashion, the warhorse was held in almost mystical esteem, and the *Rigveda* endowed the animal with divinity. Below is the *Rigveda*'s description of *Dadhikra*, a divine warhorse.

> Rushing to glory, to the capture of the herds,
> swooping down as a hungry falcon,
> eager to be first, he darts amid the ranks of the chariots,
> happy as a bridegroom making a garland,
> spurning the dust and champing at the bit.
>
> And the victorious steed and faithful,
> his body obedient in battle,
> speeding through the melee,
> stirs up the dust to fall on his brows.
>
> And at his deep neigh, like the thunder of heaven,
> the foemen tremble in fear,
> for he fights against thousands, and none can resist him,
> so terrible is his charge.[11]

The chariot seems to have disappeared as a true implement of war, probably circa 650 B.C.E. The Chinese pilgrim, Hiuen Tsan, writing of his travels in India, described the Indian army as having chariots. He noted that "the army is composed of foot, horse, chariot, and elephant soldiers. . . . The chariot in which an officer sits is drawn by four horses, whilst infantry guard it on both sides."[12] This description is not of a war chariot, but a field command vehicle in which the officer *sits* while guarded by infantry. During a later visit the same Chinese author wrote again of the Indian army, this time completely omitting any mention of the chariot, suggesting that the chariot as a fighting vehicle was fast disappearing from the ranks. In 493 B.C.E. during the sixteen-year war between Ajatashatru of Magadha and the Vrijis, two new weapons appeared for the first time on the Indian battlefield. One of these, the *mahashilakantaka*, was a large catapult for hurling heavy stone shot, and the other, the *rathamushala*, was a two-horse spoked wheel chariot with scythe blades attached to the hubs, designed to be driven through infantry formations.[13] Both these weapons were likely the result of increased Persian influence as a consequence of Persian imperial incursions into the northwest of India. Barely fifty years earlier (530 B.C.E.) Cyrus, the Achaemenid emperor of Persia, had crossed into the Hindu Kush and extracted tribute from the tribes of the northwest region, the prelude to a much larger incursion to come. Darius I made northwest India part of his empire, and Herodotus reports that Indian troops equipped with reed bows, cane arrows, iron-tipped spears and even chariots, fought in the Persian army against the Greeks in the wars of 486–465 B.C.E.[14] In any event, there is no further mention of these chariots. About a century later in the army of Chandragupta Maurya (321–297 B.C.E.) there was mention of cavalry, foot, and elephants, but no chariots. At the battle of the Hydaspes in 326 B.C.E. Porus put 4,000 cavalry and 200 war elephants in the field along with his 30,000 foot, but deployed only 300 chariots, all of the four-horse variety, carrying six men each.[15] They were not fighting vehicles. As in the Near East, the chariot probably gave way to cavalry in India because of its greater ability to traverse and maneuver over difficult terrain. But there was another reason for replacing the chariot. The primary role of the chariot in ancient warfare was to deliver shock. And nothing could quite deliver shock like an elephant.

As late as the eighth century B.C.E. the elephant was mentioned in Indian literature as the *mrigahastin* or "the beast with a hand," a description that suggests the animal was still a wild beast and not yet domesticated.[16] It was probably not until the sixth century B.C.E. or so that the animal was tamed, and probably another fifty years before it made its appearance on the Indian battlefield. The first mention of the elephant as an instrument of war appears in the account of one Sung Yun, a Chinese traveler who visited the kingdom of the Hunas in the early sixth century B.C.E. His report speaks of fighting elephants with swords fastened to their trunks, which produce great carnage, but there is no other mention of this practice elsewhere.[17] The report of another Chinese traveler noted earlier, Hiuen Tsan, of about the same time makes mention of "war elephants covered with a coat of mail [probably scale armor], and his tusks are pointed with sharp barbs [metal tips]. On him rides the commander in chief who has a soldier on each side to manage the elephant."[18] By the end of the sixth century B.C.E., the elephant had replaced the chariot as a major combat arm and had become the backbone of Indian armies.

The Indian elephant was much larger than its African forest cousin used by the Seleucid Greeks and Carthaginian armies three centuries later. The Indian elephant is ten to eleven feet high at the shoulders and carries tusks averaging more than six feet in length. They were trained and cared for with great reverence by their *mahouts* or handlers, who rode them into battle. Their great bulk made them an excellent instrument for shock, and they were often employed in the van of the army, using their great strength to break enemy ranks, smash palisades, gates, and other defenses. They could even be employed next to one another in a line like a living bridge over which troops walked to cross a stream or river. Elephants were often equipped with leather, textile, or scale armor to protect against arrows and pikes. They were usually employed with a basic combat load of the *mahout* and three other soldiers equipped with composite bows, javelins, and a long spear to ward off any attackers. Like modern tanks, elephants in the Indian tactical scheme of things were rarely deployed alone and were usually accompanied by a small infantry contingent whose task it was to protect the animal from attack by infantry. The animals were trained diligently for war, often with great success. Porus' elephants at the battle of the Hydaspes retained their discipline in the face of massed infantry advancing with long pikes pointed at the animals' eyes. Calmly, the animals retreated one step at a time, retaining formation and composure as they went.[19] In other cases, however, they simply broke and ran stampeding over everything in their way. No matter how great the number of instances where the animal panicked or otherwise proved useless, Indian commanders continued to place great faith in the war elephant, often to their regret. Centuries later, the Muslim rulers of India placed the same heavy reliance on them, only to be equally disappointed.

By the beginning of the fifth century B.C.E. the regional monarchies and republics had become the dominant form of sociopolitical life in northern India. Far larger, richer, and more populated than any of the old tribal fiefdoms of the Vedic age, these states battled each other for predominance for more than a hundred years. Four northern states— Magadha, Kashi, Kosala, and Vrijis—struggled with one another until around 550 B.C.E., when Bimbisara succeeded in bringing two of them to heel. His son, Ajatashatru, took over from his father in 493 B.C.E. and conquered the Vrijis state. Ajatashatru died in 461 B.C.E. and was followed by five kings, all of whom gained the throne by parricide. In 413 B.C.E. a usurper, Mahapadma Nanda, came to the Magadha throne and established a short-lived dynasty. In the space of fifty years, however, the Nandas proved themselves powerful and capable kings who expanded Magadha control and introduced the first attempt at an Indian empire in the north. In 321 B.C.E., the Nandas were overthrown by another usurper, Chandragupta Maurya, who established the first and last genuine Indian empire of any significant size. It lasted less than 200 years.

There is a legend concerning Chandragupta Maurya that as a young man he traveled to Taxilia in the north where he met Alexander the Great, who had conquered the city and made it his base of operations. It was as a result of this meeting that Chandragupta resolved to become a powerful prince. Seven years later, at the age of twenty-five, Chandragupta defeated the last Nanda king of Magadha and usurped the throne. A second legend has it that at his side was a powerful brahmin, Kautilya, who guided the young prince in matters of statecraft. Kautilya is supposedly the author of one of the most important works on statecraft produced in India, the *Arthasastra* or Treatise on Polity. Like a combination of Machiavelli's *The Prince* and Plato's *Republic*, the *Arthasastra* is both a theoretical and practical dissertation on how to organize a state and its army and how to employ both successfully in foreign policy.[20] It provides us with a good deal of our information on the political and military organization of the Mauryan imperial state.

Chandragupta moved quickly against the Greek governors and allies that Alexander left behind, reducing them by force of arms. He then extended his control to both the Indus and Ganges plains and further northward into Afghanistan, the largest territory ever controlled by a single Indian monarch. In 303 B.C.E., the Seleucid Greeks under Seleucus Nikator attempted to invade India once again but were rebuffed by Chandragupta's army in a series of battles and eventually withdrew. In 297 B.C.E., as legend has it, Chandragupta relinquished his throne, became a Jainist monk, and slowly starved himself to death. His son, Bindusara assumed the throne. Known to the Greeks as Amitrochates because of his title, *amitraghata* or Destroyer of Foes, Bindusara continued his father's policy of armed conquest, bringing all of the subcontinent under the Mauryan empire except for the Kalinga state on the east coast. Bindusara's son, Ashoka, came to the throne in 272 B.C.E. and immediately attacked Kalinga, bringing it within the imperial realm. The imperial idea had become a reality in India for the first time in its history. Ashoka ruled for thirty-seven years. After his death, decline set in almost immediately, and by 180 B.C.E., the empire began to collapse.

Chandragupta governed a true monarchical imperial state. The king ruled with the help of a small body of elder statesmen, the *mantri-parisad*, that functioned as advisors. This privy council is said to have been as small as seven members or as large as thirty-seven and included an inner core of very powerful advisors. These included the Great Councilor or *mantrin*, the *purohita* or chief priest, the treasurer or *sannidhatr*, the chief tax collector, *samahartr*, the minister of military affairs, *sandhivigrahika*, the *senapati* or chief military advisor or general, and the chief secretary or *mahaksapatalika*.[21] Below this council the state was governed on a day-to-day basis through powerful individuals called superintendents, who oversaw various government departments. Although every effort was made by Chandragupta and his successors to select competent people to fill government positions, in a very short time these offices became virtually hereditary and, over time, the quality of government officials declined. The Indian imperial state never developed a permanent bureaucratic system staffed by officials selected for merit and competence. As a consequence, the administrative system of imperial India never rose above the competence expected of a group of the king's personal retainers. The military system itself was controlled by high ranking civilian superintendents who oversaw the operations of state armories where all military equipment and weapons were manufactured, as well as supply depots, cavalry, elephants, chariot corps, and infantry, including provisions, training, and general combat readiness. According to Megasthenes, the Seleucid ambassador to Ashoka's court, the imperial army itself was run by a committee of thirty of these superintendents while each branch or department—infantry, cavalry, elephants, chariots, navy, commissariat, etc.—was run by a committee of five men.[22] It is likely that these committees reported directly to the chief military man, the *senapati*, who then reported to the king. It is interesting to note that despite the increased bureaucratization of the military under the Mauryas, the old martial ideals survived unchanged, and it was still the common practice for the kings themselves to take the field with the army, sometimes in the van.

There were six types of troops in the Mauryan imperial army: the *ksatriya* or troops of the hereditary warrior class, who formed the spine of the professional army; mercenaries and freebooters hired as individuals, seeking military adventure; troops provided by corporations or guilds; troops supplied by subordinate allies; deserters from the enemy; and wild forest and hill tribesmen used in much the same manner as the French and British used Native American tribes in their wars in North America. The troops of the corporations are little understood and may have been units maintained by the guilds to guard their caravan routes and trade stations. Such units were later found in the armies of medieval Europe. Or it might simply have been that certain occupations were required to provide troop levies in times of war, perhaps in much the same manner as certain occupations provided membership regiments for the European armies of World War I.[23] The imperial armies, then, were not conscript armies. In Vedic times, warfighting was the responsibility of all members of the tribe. But the development of the caste system prevented the various classes from associating even in war, thus relieving the largest manpower pool, the cultivators, from military service. By the time of the Mauryas, whatever sort of conscription had once existed earlier had disappeared, and the imperial armies were armies of professional warrior aristocrats and other professionals fed, equipped, trained, paid, and otherwise maintained at great cost to the state.[24]

The Mauryan army was quite large. Classical sources (Pliny) state that the size of the army of the last Nanda king was 200,000 infantry, 20,000 cavalry, 2,000 chariots, and 3,000 elephants, and it was overwhelmed by Chandragupta's force of 600,000 infantry, 30,000 cavalry, and 9,000 elephants. When Alexander confronted Porus on the banks of the Hydaspes he faced an army of 30,000 foot, 4,000 cavalry, 300 chariots, and 200 war elephants, an army of considerable size to be deployed by a minor king of a minor state in the Jhelum region.[25] Less than a year later Alexander confronted the army of the Malavas state, another minor regional entity, and faced an army of 80,000 well-equipped infantry, 10,000 cavalry, and 800 chariots.[26] Even accounting for the exaggeration common in ancient accounts, it is by no means unlikely that these armies were this large. The population of India during this period was somewhere between 120,000,000 to 180,000,000 people. Even excluding the lower social orders, the Mauryan empire possessed an enormous manpower pool. Moreover, India was rich in gold and metals and the skills to produce weapons in great quantities in state armories. The Ganges plain and other areas further north were excellent for breeding mounts for the cavalry. Whatever the true size of the imperial armies, they are all recorded as smaller than those said to have existed during the later Medieval and Muslim periods of Indian history.[27]

The tactical organization of the Mauryan army may have been influenced somewhat by the Chinese innovation of combining several combat arms within a single tactical unit and training it to fight together as a unit, employing their arms in concert. Indian armies of this period had within them a basic unit called the *patti*, a mixed platoon comprised of one elephant carrying three archers or spearman and a *mahout*, three horse cavalrymen armed with javelins, round buckler, and spear, and five infantry soldiers armed with shield and broad sword or bow. This fifteen-man unit when assembled in three units formed a *senamukha* or company. Three of these formed together comprised a *gulma* or battalion. Units were added in multiples of three, forming an *aksauhini* or army comprised of 21,870 *patti*.[28] Sources also speak of military units formed around multiples of ten, and there were no doubt units of single arms that could be employed individually or in concert with other arms. Thus, the *Arthasastra* mentions a unit called the *samavyuha* or battle array that was about the size of a Roman legion (5,000 men). This unit comprised of five subunits joined together, each subunit containing 45 chariots, 45 elephants, 225 cavalry, and 675 infantrymen each.[29] It goes without saying that managing such units in battle requires a high degree of tactical sophistication.

The military equipment of the Mauryan imperial army was essentially the same as it had been for the previous 500 years. A relatively complete portrayal of personal weaponry can be found in Figure 12.1. The Indian bow was made of bamboo, was between five and six feet long, and fired a long cane arrow with metal or bone tips. Nearchus, the Cretan chronicler who accompanied Alexander into India, noted that the bowman had to rest the bow on the ground and steady it with his left foot in order to draw it full length. The arrow fired from the bamboo bow could penetrate any armor.[30] At the Hydaspes, the battle took place over muddy ground, which prevented the archers from steadying their bows in this manner and rendered them useless. The composite bow or *sarnga* was also used, but probably far less so and not by cavalry. When Alexander's cavalry at the Hydaspes attacked the Indian cavalry with bow and arrows, the Indian cavalry took heavy losses and had no means of returning fire. It is unlikely that the Indian cavalry ever became proficient with the bow, relying completely upon lance and javelin, the weapons of light cavalry. If the Mauryan army possessed heavy cavalry, they appear to have done so in small numbers, with the greater number of cavalry units being of the light variety.

Infantrymen carried a long narrow shield made of raw oxhide stretched over a wooden or wicker frame that protected almost the entire body, unlike the small round buckler carried by the cavalry. Armed with lance, bow, and javelin, the infantry tended mostly to be of the light variety. Heavy infantry carried the *nistrimsa* or long two-handed slashing sword, while others were armed with iron maces, dagger-axes, battle axes, and clubs. A special long lance, the *tomara*, was carried by infantry mounted on the backs of elephants and used to counter any enemy infantry that had fought its way through the elephant's infantry screen to attack the animal itself at close range. What evidence we have suggests that from Vedic times until the coming of the Greeks, only slight use was made of body armor, and most of that was of the leather or textile variety. With Alexander's invasion, however, the use of metal and lamellar armor became more widespread as did the use of scale plate armor for horses and elephants.[31] The helmet did not come into wide use until well after the Common Era, and for most of the ancient period the soldier relied mostly upon the thick folds of his turban to protect his head.

By the Mauryan period the Indians possessed most of the ancient world's siege and artillery equipment including catapults, ballistas, battering rams, and other siege engines. A distinguishing characteristic of Indian siege and artillery practice was a heavy reliance upon incendiary devices such as fire arrows, pitch pots, and fireballs. There was even a manual instructing how to equip birds and monkeys with the ability to carry fire inside buildings and on to rooftops.[32] This was not surprising in a country whose military fortifications and buildings were made mostly of wood. Megasthenes described the fortifications of the Mauryan capital as a "mighty wooden wall with 570 towers and 64 gates." Most cities and towns were surrounded by wooden palisades, and the supporting structures of gates were mostly wood as well. Fire was such a constant threat to Indian towns that thousands of water containers and buckets were required to be kept full of water and placed outside of dwellings at all times to extinguish fires. All citizens were required by law to assist in fighting fires, and it was even required that people sleep in the room nearest the street exit to escape fire more easily and to be quickly available to help in fighting them. So serious was the concern for fire that the punishment for arson was death by burning alive![33]

While the *Arthasastra* offers much advice on how to prepare for battle, there is nothing on the tactics that shaped the conduct of the battle itself. We may be relatively certain, however, that an army of such size and complexity as the Mauryan imperial army, with its thousands of attendants, merchants, family members, elephants, horses, etc., would hardly have been able to move quickly. The *Arthasastra* declares that a good army can march two *yojanas* a day and that a bad army can only manage one. This amounts to a rate of march for an effective army of about ten miles a day, considerably below what the armies of the Near East could manage during the same period.[34] It is likely that the Mauryan army followed the age-old practice from Vedic times of agreeing with the enemy as to the location of a battlefield in advance. Under these conditions, surprise was likely to have been a rare event.

Much of the advice offered by the *Arthasastra*, at least from the tactical perspective, seems to be of the same variety as that proffered by Sun-Tsu, that is, more a set of maxims designed to make the commander think than a set of rules to be applied in certain circumstances. That is why to the Western mind such maxims often appear obvious. For example, the injunction that "armies in good locations will defeat armies in bad," is designed to get the commander to consider terrain in the tactical equation. Likewise, "Strike the enemy when he is caught in unfavorable terrain," has the same purpose.[35] Some specific tactical applications do appear, however. Thus, "the army's back should always be to the sun," or "When a defeated army resumes its attack, it cares not whether it lives or dies, its fury cannot be resisted; let a defeated army flee."[36] Hints of a tactical system appear in the suggestion that whether the attack is from the center, right, or left, it should always be led by the strongest troops. The weakest troops are to be kept in reserve. But the reserve is very important. The king should always station himself with the reserve to exploit any enemy failure and a king should "never fight without a reserve."[37]

The only detailed tactical description of an Indian army in battle comes to us from Arrian's description of the battle of the Hydaspes between Porus and Alexander. We might examine that battle somewhat speculatively in an effort to deduce what tactical capabilities might have characterized Indian armies of the imperial period. Porus had deployed his army in a line, awaiting Alexander's attack. A line of elephants ran across the entire front with infantry deployed behind it. Chariot units and cavalry anchored the wings. One can deduce from this deployment that Porus expected Alexander to attack the center of his line with his infantry. In response, Porus might then unleash his elephants against the phalanx, break it, and then attack the shattered infantry with one or both of his cavalry wings, following up with his infantry all along the line. Porus' deployment lacked flexibility. Alexander arrived on the battlefield without his infantry, who were still struggling to catch up after a long march. Porus might well have attacked Alexander then or even while his infantry was arriving and still in column of march. Porus did neither.

Alexander began the battle with a strong cavalry attack against Porus' left wing. Outnumbered, Porus showed tactical maneuver by ordering elements of his cavalry on his right wing to redeploy to his left by riding behind the battle line. This they accomplished with success, stopping Alexander's attack in its tracks. Alexander now ordered fresh cavalry units into the attack, ordering them to extend to Porus' left and ride around the flank and turn it. With an excellent tactical eye, Porus ordered his left wing to break contact, form in order of march, and extend further to the left to stop the envelopment. This was an excellent but risky response. Alexander's cavalry now stopped their advance around the flank and turned inward and struck Porus' left wing in the middle of its redeployment. At the same time, Macedonian cavalry, which had followed Porus' right wing cavalry behind the battle line, arrived behind the redeploying left wing, striking it from behind. It was at this point that Porus's army demonstrated its discipline and training. Under attack from two directions, Porus ordered the cavalry wing to deploy front to back and engage the Macedonians from two directions. Once more Alexander's brilliant maneuver had been stymied by Porus' excellent tactical response.

Alexander now ordered his infantry phalanx into the attack. They moved slowly toward the Indian center, with *sarissae* extended. This pinned the elephant line in place, making it impossible for Porus to bring his infantry, deployed behind the elephant line, into action. The elephants kept their discipline and retreated step by step before the Macedonian pikes. Pushed back against the infantry, the elephants were vulnerable to attack by Thracian javelin men and the Agrianian swordsmen, who proceeded to decimate the elephant line. Gradually the Macedonian infantry began to encircle the Indian army. On the left flank, the Indian cavalry found its spirit and made one more attack only to have it repulsed. Alexander's cavalry now pressed the Indian cavalry back on the infantry and elephants into one great mass. The Macedonian infantry pressed against the mass "with great slaughter." For eight hours the armies fought hand-to-hand. Much to the credit of the Indian army, it fought on and never lost its discipline.

This summary of the battle of the Hydaspes reveals an Indian army that was every bit as tactically sophisticated as any army anywhere during this period. It was an army capable of integrating combined arms into a tactical whole, and very capable indeed of tactical flexibility after it was engaged. Moving thousands of cavalrymen across the entire battlefront in response to an attack on the opposite wing is no easy maneuver. Even more difficult was the ability of Porus' cavalry to engage the enemy attack from two directions at once after itself being struck from the rear. These are the tactical characteristics of a well-trained professional army. Even the war elephants revealed a high degree of training. Under attack from the *sarissa* and swordsmen of the Macedonian infantry, the animals did not break. They held their ground, backing up slowly and in formation. Even when there was nowhere to go, the elephants stood their ground. If we remind ourselves that Porus was but a minor king as Indian kings went, we are led to the conclusion that the level of tactical sophistication of the imperial army of a few years later surely equalled that of Porus' army and in all probability even surpassed it. If so, it is a fair conclusion that the Indian armies of the imperial period were no less accomplished than any other army of the period, including the most effective army of the time, the army of Alexander the Great.

NOTES

1. A.L. Basham, *The Wonder That Was India* (New York: Grove Press, 1954), 29–33.

2. Romila Thapar, *A History of India* (Middlesex, England: Penguin Books, 1966), 24.

3. Ibid., 31.

4. Basham, 33.

5. Thapar, 36; see also Basham, 33.

6. Basham, 124.

7. The Aztecs and Incas thought the horse and man were a single being and were frightened when they saw the Spanish soldiers dismount and the single being become two animals!

8. *Cambridge History of India* (Delhi: Cambridge University Press, 1968) vol. 1, 88.

9. Ibid., 89.

10. A.V. Williams Jackson, *History of India* (London: The Grolier Society, 1906), vol. 1, 121.

11. Basham, 36. Poetry translation reprinted with permission.

12. *Oxford History of India*, 3rd ed. (Oxford: Clarendon Press, 1958), 105.

13. Thapar, 56.

14. Herodotus, book 7, 65.

15. *Oxford History of India*, 105.

16. Thapar, 35.

17. Basham, 129.

18. *Oxford History of India*, 105. Italics mine.

19. Richard A. Gabriel and Donald Boose, Jr. "The Campaigns of Alexander: Battle of the Hydaspes," in *The Great Battles of Antiquity* (Westport, CT: Greenwood Press, 1994).

20. Thapar, 70.

21. Basham, 99–100.

22. Ibid., 132.

23. *Cambridge History of India*, 441 for information on Indian guild armies.

24. Bashram, 129.

25. *Oxford History of India*, 87; see also Gabriel and Boose.

26. Ibid.

27. Thapar, 79.

28. Basham, 131.

29. Ibid., 131.

30. From Nearchus as quoted in *Cambridge History of India*, 370.

31. Basham, 133.

32. If such an idea seems silly, it ought to be kept in mind that the American back-up plan to the destruction of Japan by the A-bomb was a plan to attach small incendiary devices to millions of bats and drop them over Japanese cities.

The idea was that the bats would roost in the eves and corners of Japanese houses and buildings, which were made largely of wood and lacquered paper. At a set time the incendiary devices attached to the bats would ignite, setting fire to thousands of Japanese structures.

33. *Cambridge History of India*, 429–30.

34. Basham, 135.

35. Quoted in Alfred S. Bradford, *With Arrow, Sword and Spear* (Westport, Conn.: Greenwood Press, 2001), 126.

36. Ibid.

37. Ibid.

13

Rome: The Armies of the Caesars

753 B.C.E.–378 C.E.

T he Roman army was the longest-lived political institution in the West. Beginning in the eighth century B.C.E., the army of Rome survived until 478 C.E., the date commonly accepted as marking the collapse of the Roman empire in the West. However, the Roman army continued in existence under the direction of the eastern empire of Constantinople, where it survived for another thousand years until the capital fell to Moslem armies in 1453 C.E. From its inception until its demise, the army of Rome survived more than 2,000 years. As a social institution it was unique in the world, and its contribution to the pattern of warfare in the West was enormous.

The history of the Roman army begins in the seventh century B.C.E., shortly after the mythical date of 753 B.C.E., commonly accepted as marking the founding of Rome.[1] The Roman state was organized on the basis of tribes and powerful families, and this social order was also the foundation of the army. Each tribe and family contributed a certain number of infantry and cavalry soldiers to the army, even then called the *legio*. The strength of the army was about 3,000 infantrymen and 300 cavalrymen, the latter comprised of the wealthiest nobility. Roman military organization and weaponry of this period were strongly influenced by the Etruscans, who in turn were influenced by Etruria's contacts with the Greeks.[2] The same hoplite revolution that produced the weapons, formations, and tactics of the Greek phalanx was therefore largely repeated in Rome.

The armament of the early Roman soldier consisted of a bronze helmet with padded liner, cuirass, shield, sword, and spear. The round shield, although of Italian origin, looked very much like the Argive shield of Greece except that it retained the central handgrip. The Roman oval shield, the *scutum*, appeared in prototype among other Italian tribes (most likely the Samnites) at about this time, but was not adopted by the Romans until later. The Roman sword of the day was the antennae type and varied in length from thirty-three to fifty-six centimeters. The Roman javelin had a thin metal shaft cast into the blade with the shaft inserted into a wooden shaft, the forerunner of the famous *pilum* (also possessed by the Samnites of this period). The basic fighting formation of the army was a variant of the archaic Greek *lochos* phalanx, but one that permitted a somewhat freer style of fighting in which the soldier could wield his axe, sword, and spear more easily.

With the establishment of the Roman Republic in 510 B.C.E., Rome began 200 years of almost constant war against its rivals in Italy, which ultimately resulted in Roman domination of the entire mainland. The war against the *Veii* lasted twenty years and resulted in important changes in the Roman army. Camillus reorganized the army on the basis of age and experience rather than on the traditional basis of wealth and social position, with the best and most experienced soldiers placed in the front ranks. Camillus introduced regular pay, and a number of weapons were standardized. Under Camillus the soldier was still required to purchase his own weapons, but now did so from the state, which oversaw their manufacture in state armories.[3] It is likely, too, that Camillus may have introduced a new weapon, the Roman-style *pilum*. The old javelin was comprised of a wooden shaft and a cast bronze, socketed blade. The new *pilum* had a long iron blade almost three inches wide affixed to a wooden shaft by two rivets. Within a century this weapon had become a basic weapon of Roman infantry and remained so in one form or another for more than a thousand years.[4]

In 386 B.C.E. a large army of Gauls (Celts) crossed the Alps intent on attacking Rome. Commanded by a ferocious tribal warrior chief named Brennus, the Gallic army was organized around a force of heavy infantry armed with slashing broadswords and augmented by excellent heavy cavalry. Tactically, the Gauls attacked in a free-wheeling infantry formation using infantry and cavalry in concert to deliver maximum shock.[5] The two armies met on the Alia River eleven miles from the gates of Rome. The Romans deployed an army of 15,000 men, the largest Roman army ever put into the field. Deployed in the old Greek phalanx formation with spear infantry arrayed in front, the Romans were no match for the highly mobile and flexible Gallic army. The phalanx cracked under the first attack and broke completely under a cavalry envelopment. The Gallic cavalry undertook a ruthless pursuit, driving the Roman infantry into the river where almost the entire army was either drowned or slain by arms. It was the worst military defeat in Rome's history.

The Romans never forgot this catastrophe at the hands of the Gauls, and it has been suggested that the psychological influence of this defeat was what accounted for the ferocious cruelty that Roman armies later showed against the Gauls in the many battles between the two in later years. The immediate Roman response, however, was to fortify Rome itself. The old earthen wall erected by Tullius was replaced. Employing Greek engineers, the Romans constructed a wall of volcanic stone twelve feet thick and twenty-four feet high around an area of 4,000 acres, twice the size of the old city. The enclosed area made Rome the largest fortified city in Italy.[6]

The defeat on the Alia had demonstrated that the old phalanx was too brittle and lacked the flexibility and mobility to deal with a force of heavy infantry and cavalry capable of maneuver. The Romans abandoned the old Greek phalanx and replaced it with a looser organization that permitted the individual soldier more maneuvering room in close combat. Eventually, this formation developed into the manipular legion. The Romans also abandoned the old thrusting spear and replaced it with the *pilum*. The first two lines were armed with the thrown *pilum* while only the third line retained the spear, with which to mount a final line of defense against a breakthrough. The longer sword was replaced with a shorter iron sword designed for thrusting rather than slashing, and training was reformed to emphasize the swordplay of the individual soldier.

New tactical doctrines were introduced. The first two lines of the infantry were trained to hurl their *pila* against the enemy charge to break its momentum and lessen the impact of the shock of contact. Once the formations closed, the Roman soldier brought his sword into play. This was made more effective by increasing the spacing within the formation to allow the soldier somewhat greater room to wield his sword. Roman doctrine aimed at permitting the soldier to act independently within the larger tactical formation while retaining the tactical integrity of the overall formation. The soldier was permitted to move freely over five square yards of ground, seeking and destroying individual targets. Looser tactical formations permitted greater flexibility and maneuverability but, unlike the old Greek phalanx, required a much higher degree of training and skill on the part of the individual soldier to make it work. Roman combat training programs were adapted accordingly.

Almost immediately after 380 B.C.E., the Romans began a policy of expansion against the Latin League of city-states, and within fifty years Rome had succeeded in subduing her rivals. By granting either full or limited citizenship to her former rivals, Rome was able to incorporate them into the Roman realm while remaining preeminent. Her former rivals were now required to make troops available for "the common defense," a convenient fiction that permitted these troops to be used at the direction of Rome. This policy permitted Rome access to a very large manpower pool for military purposes so that by 338 B.C.E. Roman influence extended over an area of 4,500 square miles and encompassed a population of more than a million people.[7]

The next phase of Roman military development began with the Samnite Wars (327–290 B.C.E.). The center of Samnite power was the region of the Appenine Mountains, which rise above the Liri River and overlook one of Italy's richest agricultural areas, the Campanian plain. It is also an area of very difficult terrain.[8] For over forty years the Romans fought battle after battle against the Samnites, and in the early stages suffered defeat after defeat. At the battle of Caudine Forks in 321 B.C.E., an entire Roman army was trapped, forced to surrender, and made to walk under the yoke. The basic Roman problem was that their formations were still too inflexible to maneuver in rugged terrain. The Romans eventually defeated the Samnites by 290 B.C.E., and with the experience gained from these wars launched yet another military reorganization of the army.

Among the most important Roman innovations to emerge from these wars was the military road. The main front against the Samnites was at Capua, some 132 miles from Rome. To support their armies so far from the capital, the Romans built the Via Appia, a paved road that ran through the coastal plain from Rome to Capua. The Romans built bridges to cross streams and paved fords at low spots in the rivers. Marshlands were crossed by raised roads built in the fashion of aqueducts. As Rome established her hegemony over Italy and, eventually over the Western world, it connected the empire with a network of military roads. The Romans built over 250,000 miles of roads, including 50,000 miles of paved permanent roadways.[9] To place this achievement in perspective, the U.S. interstate highway system consists of 44,000 miles of paved roads.[10] The Roman road net not only provided Rome with internal lines of communication, but increased the speed with which military units could move. On dry unpaved roads an army of 6,000 men could move

Figure 13.1
The Manipular Legion

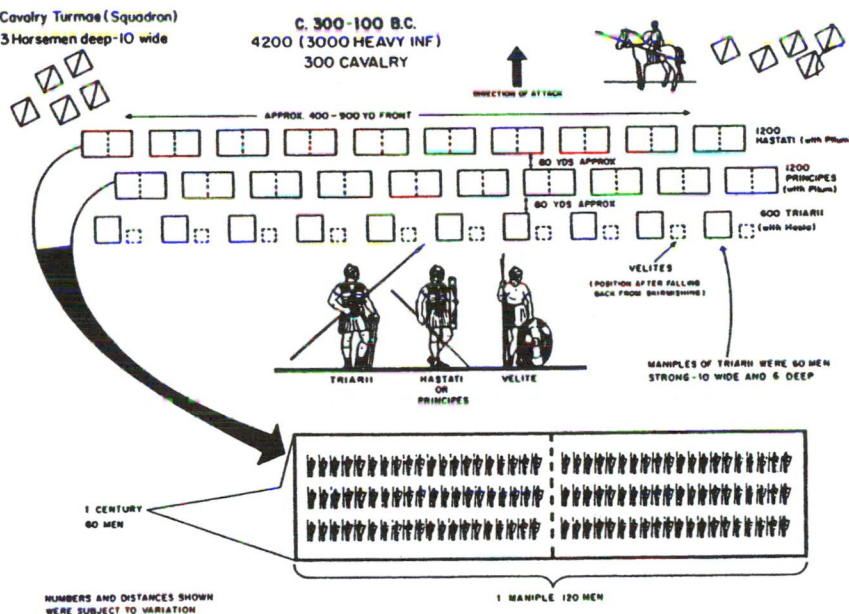

no more than eight miles a day. In wet weather movement was almost impossible at any speed. On paved roads, however, a legion could move thirty miles a day in all kinds of weather.[11] Roman military roads revolutionized logistics and commercial transport as well.

During the Samnite wars the phalanx legion was replaced by the manipular legion (Figure 13.1). It was also at this time that the Romans replaced their heavy Argive-style shield with the larger, lighter, wooden *scutum* shield. The Romans also adopted the Samnite-style *pilum* which, along with the *scutum*, remained standard Roman issue until the end of the imperial period. The manipular legion was the basic fighting formation of the Roman army throughout the Punic Wars. However, Scipio Africanus found that the new legion was sometimes too fragile to withstand the attacks of Hannibal's Spanish heavy infantry and gradually increased the strength of the maniples, increasing their numbers to 600 men. These new *cohorts* gradually replaced the maniples until, around 100 B.C.E., the Romans adopted the cohortal legion as their basic fighting unit.

The army was also reorganized on the basis of age and experience. The youngest, most agile, and least trained men served as light infantry or *velites*. Armed with darts and javelins, they acted as skirmishers. The front line of the legion was comprised of older and more experienced soldiers, the *hastati*. Armed with the sword, two *pila*, and *scutum* shield, they formed the first line of heavy infantry. The center line was comprised of the best and most experienced veterans, the *principes*. Averaging thirty years old, these were Rome's battle-hardened veterans. The legion's last line was comprised of older men, the *triarii*, and constituted the last line of defense. Armed with the spear, they lent stability to the formation. In times of retreat, the *triarii* remained in place and covered the passage of the other ranks through their lines.[12]

The basic tactical unit of the new Roman army was the maniple (literally, "handful"), somewhat equivalent to the modern infantry company with a strength of 120 men. The maniple was divided vertically into two centuries (literally, "one hundred") equivalent to platoons of sixty to eighty men each. Originally, as the name implies, the centuries had been comprised of 100 men, but that number proved too large to be effectively controlled by a single officer. The number was reduced to eighty men although the name was retained.

The key to the flexibility of the legion lay in the relationship between the maniples within each line and between the lines of heavy infantry. Each maniple deployed as a small independent phalanx, with a twenty-man front and a six-man depth. The spacing between soldiers was greater than in the old phalanx, allowing independent movement and fighting room within an area of five square yards. Each maniple was laterally separated from the next by about twenty yards, a distance equal to the frontage of the maniple itself. The maniples in each line were staggered, with the second and third lines covering the gaps in the lines to their front. Each line of infantry was separated from the next by an interval of approximately 100 yards. This *quincunx* or checkerboard formation (see Figure 13.1) provided maximum flexibility for each maniple and for each soldier within it.

Flexibility was increased by the relationship between the lines of infantry. If, after the first line engaged, it was unable to break the enemy formation or grew tired, it would retire in good order through the gaps left in the second line.[13] The second line then moved to the front and continued the attack while the first rank rested and regrouped. This maneuver could be repeated several times, with the effect that the Roman front line was always comprised of rested fighting men. The *triarii* remained in place in the last rank resting on one knee, their spears angled upwards. The *triarii* were the legion's organic reserve, to be employed at the commander's will.

The ability to pass through the lines of infantry in planned and disciplined fashion offered another advantage. In most armies of the past, defeat of the front ranks often turned the battle into a rout. Until the Romans no army had learned how to break contact and conduct a tactical retreat in good order. The manipular formation made a disciplined retreat possible. Upon command, the first line of infantry formed into close-order maniples, turned, and withdrew to the rear through the gaps left in the other two lines. The second rank would follow. The *triarii* then covered the retreat with their spears as the *velite* light infantry deployed to the front of the *triarii* to engage and delay the enemy by skirmishing, while the main body withdrew in good order. The ability to conduct a tactical retreat represented a major revolution in tactics.

Tactical flexibility was enhanced by the ability of each maniple, if need be, to fight and maneuver independently. This flexibility allowed Roman commanders to make good use of the element of surprise. A commander could position a few spare maniples in hidden positions, often at the flanks, or even attempt to insert them into the rear of the enemy. Once the main forces engaged, these maniples could be brought into action by flag signal, surprising the enemy with an attack from an entirely different direction. Often the sight of a few maniples marching on the main force from an unexpected direction was sufficient to cause it to panic.[14] Once more the maniple added a new tactical dimension to warfare.

It was during the Samnite Wars that the *pilum* became a major weapon of the Roman army. This weapon was of Italian origin and had been around in one form or another for two centuries. It was made of a wooden shaft about four feet long in which was inlaid an iron rod and blade of about equal length. The total length of the weapon was about six feet. Each soldier in the first two ranks carried two *pila*, one light and one heavy.[15] The iron and wooden parts of the *pilum* were held together by iron pins. Later, when Marius again reformed the legions, one of these pins was also made of wood so that the iron shaft would break off and remain embedded in the shield or body of the enemy. In Caesar's time, the shaft was made of soft metal so that it would bend upon impact. Both innovations were designed to prevent the enemy from throwing the *pila* back, one of the great drawbacks of the spear in antiquity! A broken or bent *pilum* stuck in an enemy shield rendered it useless for protection and provided the Roman swordsman with a significant advantage in close combat.

The Roman soldier was the first soldier in antiquity to fight within a combat formation while at the same time remaining somewhat independent of its movements as a unit. He was also the first soldier to rely primarily upon the sword instead of the spear or javelin. The Roman sword of this period was a short, slashing sword of Italian origin. After the Punic Wars, the legions adopted the famous *gladius*, a short sword incorporating many of the features of the Spanish *falcata*. The *gladius* was twenty inches long and approximately three inches wide and made of tough Toledo steel. It was stronger in composition than any other existing sword, and because it would not break provided a psychological advantage to the Roman soldier. To use it well, however, required skill and a high level of training.

In 264 B.C.E., the Romans introduced military training programs in the use of the new *gladius*. Interestingly, at this same time Rome introduced gladiatorial contests as public games, and it is likely that some gladiatorial training techniques were adopted by the army. As with the gladiators, the shield parry followed by a sharp underthrust to the chest became the killing trademark of the Roman soldier. In the hands of Roman legionnaires, the *gladius* became the most destructive weapon until the advent of the firearm. More soldiers died of wounds inflicted by the *gladius* than were killed by an other infantry weapon in antiquity.[16] If the spear- and javelin-bearing phalanx formations of past armies can be said to have resembled spiked pincushions, then the Roman legion, with its reliance upon the *gladius*, resembled a buzzsaw.

A Roman legion had a strength of approximately 5,000 men and usually took the field with an allied counterpart of the same size, organization, and weaponry, except that the allied unit usually contained a heavier cavalry section of approximately 600 horsemen. Deployed for battle, the legion had a combined strength of 10,000 men, including 900 cavalry. Two legions and two allied legions comprised a consular army commanded by one of Rome's two elected consuls. A consular army numbered between 18,000 and 20,000 men and deployed across a combat front of one-and-one-half miles.

The legion commander had a staff of professional officers who handled administrative, supply, and other planning matters. Combat command rested in the hands of six tribunes, two for each infantry line. Below the tribunes were the combat unit commanders of the maniples— sixty centurions, two for each maniple. Real combat leadership was provided by the centurions. While other military posts became subject to political appointment and corruption, the centurions of the legion always remained the best and most experienced combat soldiers. Promotion through the ranks was based on demonstrated bravery and competence. The most respected soldiers of Rome were the first centurions or *primus pilum* (literally, "the first spear") of the legions, and right to the end they remained the best combat commanders the nation could field.

The Roman legion had two significant weaknesses. The first was the lack of a professional senior officer corps. Roman senior officers were civilians, often state officials or politicians, appointed to command the legions during time of war. To make matters worse, this consular system required that the same army appoint senior commanders who rotated field command each day. Despite the best military organization in the ancient world, the practice of divided command often made it impossible for the legions to maintain command direction. Changing command every other day made it impossible for the legion to become the effective instrument of the commander's will. Hannibal frequently chose the time of battle to coincide with the daily command of a specific adversary who, he reckoned, had some flaw that provided Hannibal with an advantage. Other weaknesses were the failure to provide for security while encamped, and poor security on the march. During the wars against Pyrrhus and the Gauls, the Romans were often caught in morning and evening surprise attacks while in camp. The result, which came later, was the famous Roman fortified camp. The Romans were also slow to learn the need for security while on the march, and in the early battles against Hannibal they were often surprised and taken while still in column of march.

The second major weakness was the poor quality of Roman cavalry. Like the Greeks, the Romans regarded service in the cavalry as little better than tending animals. The best soldiers from the best families refused to serve in the cavalry, and it was the most poorly trained of the combat arms. Even through the Punic Wars, Roman cavalry often retained their old habit of using their mounts to arrive at the battlefield only to dismount and join the fray as infantry. Roman cavalry seemed ill-suited to maintain the direction of the charge and showed a tendency to break up into small clusters of loose formations and wander all over the battlefield. They used no special armament, preferring instead to carry the weapons of the infantry. Hannibal's arm of decision, on the other hand, was his superbly trained cavalry. In battle after battle he drove the Roman cavalry from the field, turned, and massacred the Roman infantry. Eventually the Romans gave up trying to develop their own cavalry and simply hired it from allied units.

With the Roman army at peak fighting strength after the Samnite Wars, Rome turned its attention to the last remaining competitor for influence in Italy, the Greek colonies on the Italian mainland. Foremost among these was the city of Tarentum, which appealed to King Pyrrhus of Epirus for help in warding off Roman intentions. Pyrrhus landed in Italy with a force of 25,000 Greek professional mercenaries, the most highly esteemed fighting men of their day. At Heraclea the citizen army of Rome fought well against these professionals, but was defeated when Pyrrhus's elephants frightened the Roman horses and drove the cavalry from the field. Pyrrhus then used his elephants to charge and shatter the Roman formations. A year later the Greek phalanx and Roman legion clashed at Ausculum. This time the Romans held out longer and inflicted so many casualties on the Greeks that ever since a victory won at high cost has been called a "Pyrrhic victory." In 275 B.C.E., at Beneventum, the two armies fought again. This time the Romans had learned how to neutralize the elephants by wounding them with their *pila.* Pyrrhus was forced from the field and withdrew to Tarentum. A short time later he returned with his army to Greece.

This short war marked a turning point in Roman history. First, it demonstrated that the armies of the Greek phalanx, the most renowned armies of their day, were no match for the new Roman legions. Second, the war marked the first of a series of foreign wars that eventually led to the establishment of a worldwide Roman empire. Third, Rome was now master of all Italy. Only Sicily remained unconquered, and Roman aspirations there brought Rome into direct conflict with Carthage, the foremost military power of the western Mediterranean. The result was the Punic Wars.

The first Punic War lasted from 264 to 241 B.C.E. and saw Rome emerge as a naval power as she built hundreds of copies of a captured *quinquereme* and trained sailors to man them. But Roman military power rested on infantry, and in typically pragmatic fashion Rome introduced two innovations that permitted her to bring infantry power to bear at sea. These were the grappling hook and the *corvus* or Raven. The *corvus* was a swiveling boarding platform with a grappling spike on the end. As the Roman ships closed with the enemy, grappling hooks were used to pull the ships into contact with each other. Then the *corvus* was swung over the side and dropped on the enemy's deck, held fast by the spike. Roman infantry poured onto the enemy's ship and slaughtered its crew and defenders. So effective were these new tactics that in five years Rome won five naval engagements against the superior navy of Carthage.[17]

The next ten years of war at sea marked the emergence of a new dimension of warfare in antiquity. Empires of the past had shown themselves incapable of sustained military effort. Past empires often crumbled after a single defeat. Rome's effort in the Punic Wars demonstrated that the new social organization of the state lent greater military staying power to a nation with the moral and political will to use it. In 255 B.C.E., a Roman fleet of 248 ships was sunk in a storm off Cape Pachynus with a loss of more than 100,000 men, a number equal to fifteen percent of the able-bodied men in all of Italy.[18] Rome's response was to build another fleet which, in 252 B.C.E., was destroyed in a storm, with another horrendous loss of life. Again and again Carthage defeated large Roman fleets, only to have Rome construct and outfit another and send it to sea. In 242 B.C.E., Rome defeated Carthage off the Aegates Islands by once more putting a greater number of ships to sea than her adversary and ending the First Punic War.

Polibius called this war the bloodiest in history, and it is probable that the loss of life on both sides, most of it Roman, approached 400,000 men, a number almost equal to all the men lost by the United States in World War II.[19] No state or empire before Rome could have sustained such losses and survived. Rome had mastered the challenge of strategic endurance, of mobilizing enormous resources for a national military conflict and, in doing so, set a pattern that was to be replicated by the modern industrial state.

In 219 B.C.E., Carthage's attempts to extend its power in Spain forced a confrontation with Roman interests there, causing the outbreak of the Second Punic War. The brilliant Hannibal brought the war directly to Italy, and in 218 B.C.E. crossed the Alps with a force of 38,000 men and thirty-seven elephants. Hannibal's strategic design required that he succeed at enticing a number of Italian city-states, along with the Gauls, to defect and supply manpower and logistical support to his army.[20] The Romans reacted to Hannibal's presence in northern Italy by sending an army of 40,000 to intercept him. In 218 B.C.E., at the Trebia River, Hannibal ambushed the Romans, killing 30,000. A year later Rome sent another army. This time the Roman army was trapped in a defile surrounded by hills near the shores of Lake Trasimene. Once more almost the entire Roman force was killed, including its commanding general.[21] In two short years, all of northern Italy was in Hannibal's hands and the road to Rome was open.

The manpower loss of almost 100,000 men forced Rome to go over to the defensive. While Hannibal waited, Rome rebuilt its army, this time placing an army of 80,000 men, the largest Roman army ever to take the field, under the command of Fabius Maximus. Unable to force Hannibal to battle, the Roman army followed him around Italy for two years, destroying the countryside to deprive Hannibal of a logistics base. This policy to this day is called "Fabian tactics" in honor of the Roman general who invented it. Hannibal understood that he could never bring the war to a conclusion unless he destroyed the Roman army as a means of weakening Roman political will. In 216 B.C.E. Hannibal enticed the Roman army into battle at Cannae and trapped them in a double-envelopment. Of the Roman force of 80,000 men, 70,000 were killed and the rest taken prisoner. Hannibal lost 5,500 men.[22] It was the worst defeat in Rome's history. Taken together, the three defeats at Hannibal's hands had cost the Romans over 150,000 men. On the verge of manpower exhaustion, Rome raised two more armies and set out after Hannibal again, this time on two fronts.[23]

Unable to defeat Hannibal in Italy, Rome struck at Carthage itself. In 204 B.C.E., Scipio Africanus landed in North Africa with an army of 37,000 men, intent on attacking Carthage. The presence of a Roman army in North Africa forced Hannibal to abandon Italy and return to Carthage to take command of the city's defense.[24] In 202 B.C.E., the two great commanders fought each other on the plains at Zama. The battle raged all day, finally resolving itself when the Roman allied cavalry (Numidians) broke off its pursuit of Hannibal's cavalry, turned, and attacked the rear of Hannibal's army as the Roman infantry chewed on it from the front. When the battle was over, 20,000 Carthaginians lay dead and another 15,000 had been taken prisoner. With the defeat of Carthage, Rome became master of the western Mediterranean.

After the battle of Cannae, Philip V of Macedonia had sought to take advantage of Roman weakness by signing a mutual assistance treaty with Hannibal. Seventeen years later, in 197 B.C.E., Rome avenged the insult by invading Macedonia and meeting the Macedonian army at Cynoscephalae, the Dog's Head. The Roman army that marched into Greece with the objective of destroying the army of Philip V was essentially the same army that for twenty years had fought Hannibal. Its experience had made it the most reliable killing machine in the era of muscle-powered warfare. Its superbly trained legions of swordsmen relied upon an excellent logistics system that kept the soldier physically fit and well-fed while in the field. The army of Rome was a well-integrated triad of ferocity, skill, and efficiency.

The war with Hannibal forced the first reforms in recruitment, which expanded the manpower base of the Roman army away from the aristocracy to the landed middle classes. Roman skill at diplomacy and her willingness to extend citizenship to her allies in Italy further expanded the manpower recruiting base. Polibius records that at the time of the war with Macedonia, Rome's military manpower stood at 700,000 legionnaires and 70,000 cavalry.[25] Roman training, typically with weapons and shields twice their normal weight, and the psychological disposition that may have resulted from the introduction of training methods associated with gladiatorial contests, produced a skilled, cold-blooded fighting man accustomed to death and killing. The horrible wounds inflicted by the *gladius*, a murderous little meat cleaver, often shocked the enemy. The Roman aptitude for war often had a devastating psychological effect upon the adversary. Livy records an incident where some of Philip V's units skirmished with a Roman patrol and got the worst of it. Hoping to build morale among his troops, Philip ordered the bodies of the Greek dead brought into camp and a funeral held for them. The Macedonians, accustomed only to neat wounds inflicted by javelins and spears, were not prepared for the sight of what was left of their countrymen after meeting the Roman buzzsaw. Livy recorded the horror of the Macedonians on seeing their dead. "When they had seen bodies chopped to pieces by the Spanish sword, arms torn away, shoulders and all, or heads separated from bodies . . . or vitals laid open . . . they realized in a general panic with what weapons, and what men, they had to fight."[26]

The two armies, each about 26,000 strong, met in a dense fog on uneven ground. The soldiers of Greece were regarded as the best in the world. Heirs of Alexander, they fought in the traditional Macedonian phalanx. The Roman army was led by a brilliant twenty-nine year old general, Titus Quinctius Flaminius. When it was over, 8,000 Greeks lay dead and another 5,000 had been taken prisoner. The famed phalanx of Alexander had proven no match for the flexibility of the Roman legion. The era of the *sarissa* was gone, and in its place the age of the *gladius* had begun. And with it, the future belonged to Rome.

In 189 B.C.E. Rome dealt the Seleucid empire a major defeat at Magnesia on the Ionian Peninsula, giving Rome a free hand in the Aegean. Twenty years later Rome clashed with the Macedonians for the last time at Pydna, slaughtering its army and removing Macedonia as a major power. Within the space of a single generation, two of the three most powerful Greek states had been defeated by Roman armies. In 146 B.C.E. Rome destroyed Corinth, demonstrating her determination to remain in Greece. In the same year, on the flimsy pretext that Antiochus had given refuge to Hannibal, Rome destroyed Carthage, giving Rome mastery of the Mediterranean, which the Romans now called *Mare Nostrum*, literally "our sea." But years of war had brought Rome to the brink of exhaustion. Military manpower was in such short supply that in 171 B.C.E. all retired centurions under the age of fifty were recalled to active duty.[27] In an effort to stave off revolts by the soldiery pay was raised, rations improved, and the death penalty for lapses in military discipline repealed.[28] Still, revolts broke out among Roman garrisons.

In 107 B.C.E. Gaius Marius was elected consul and obtained command of the army.[29] He brought about the most significant series of military reforms that the Roman army had seen in 250 years. His most important reform was to change the basis of military recruitment. The traditional landowning middle-class, which had provided the base of military manpower from the very founding of Rome, could no longer meet the expanded requirements of Rome's military efforts. Marius opened up the ranks of the army to the propertyless of Rome. Roman citizenship was still required, but after the Social Wars (90 B.C.E.), citizenship had been extended to all Italians, expanding the manpower base further. Marius was careful to leaven the new army with veterans and property holders. The quality of manpower drawn from the proletariat was below the hardy peasant stock to which the legions were accustomed. To bring quality up to standard, Marius introduced new drill and training regimens. Every training program from sword drill to road marches was upgraded, and a strict discipline was imposed. In 105 B.C.E. the training methods used in Roman gladiatorial schools were officially incorporated into the army.[30] The result of these reforms was a tough, disciplined, professional soldier. The old militia army was allowed to die a natural death.

Prior to Marius, the legions were assembled on an *ad hoc* basis as military necessity required. Marius made the legion organizations into permanent structures and provided each legion with its own standard. The standing legions were filled out as requirements demanded, but the legion organization was now permanent in times of peace. Later, Caesar provided each legion with a number and, under Augustus, each legion acquired a name. Marius also introduced major tactical innovations. The decline in the quality of military manpower along with the experience of Scipio in Spain and later with the Gauls and Celts had shown that the maniple had to be sturdier to withstand attack.[31] Marius combined the maniples into cohorts so that three maniples now formed a 600-man cohort. Ten cohorts comprised a legion of 6,000 men. All soldiers were armed with the same weapons—*pilum*, *gladius*, and *scutum*. The cohorts could still fight in open or closed order, and the checkerboard (*quincunx*) formation was retained. Instead of the old battle order of three lines, the cohort was trained to assemble in any combination of lines. Its more massive size permitted it to form in lines, squares, rectangles, or circles, while the use of the same weaponry allowed it to confront an attack in any of these formations with the same type and level of combat power. The result was the cohortal legion (Figure 13.2), which increased its combat power while retaining and even increasing its flexibility and maneuverability.

Figure 13.2
The Cohortal Legion

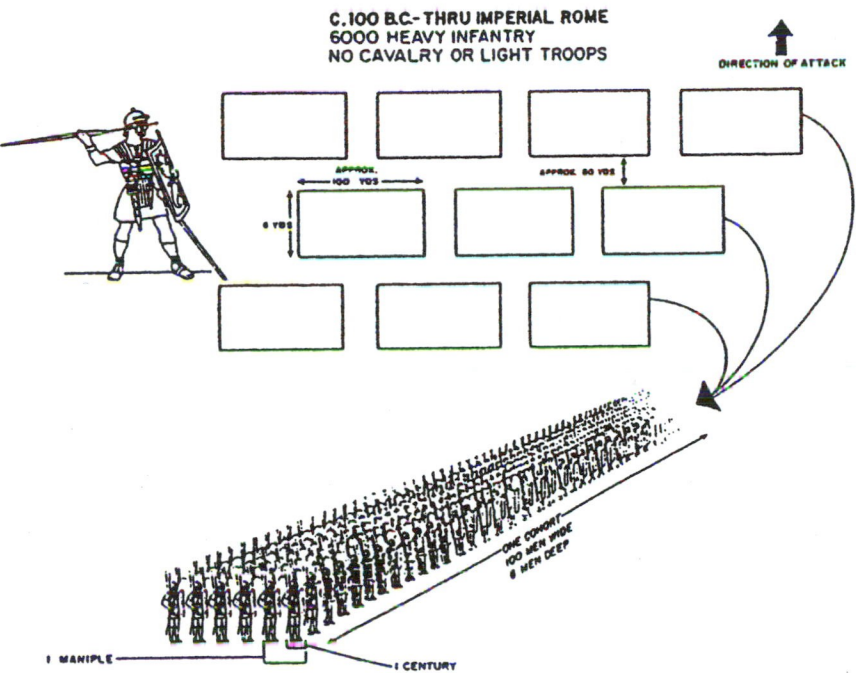

Marius' logistical reforms closely paralleled those introduced by Philip of Macedon two centuries earlier. Baggage trains were reduced by the simple expedient of requiring the troops to carry most of their rations and equipment. A soldier carried fourteen days rations instead of the usual three-day supply. He also carried two sharpened wooden stakes used in building the military camp each night. Armor and helmets were worn on the march, and the soldier carried his own weapons and other military equipment. The complete pack of the Roman legionary was sixty pounds, and they called themselves "Marius's mules." Marius leaned out the baggage train further by the extensive use of mules, horses, and even camels. A legion had a standard complement of 500 mules, a very small number by even Alexander's standards.[32] Boots of a new design were issued to reduce foot injuries. Marius positioned the small baggage train directly behind each legion in the line of march, a practice that did much to reduce the vulnerability of the supply train to attack.

The Marian reforms concentrated the combat power of the legion in the heavy infantry to the almost total neglect of cavalry and light infantry. The Roman army became a one-armed fighting machine. It is one of the curious aspects of Roman military history that, for a people who loved horse racing and raising horses, the Romans never developed cavalry into a significant combat arm. Also interesting is that Italy, a country surrounded on three sides by water, never developed a serious naval arm either. The legion had approximately 300 cavalry divided into ten squadrons (*turma*) of thirty horsemen organically attached to it. Each squadron was commanded by a *decurio*. The squadrons deployed in either line or checkerboard formations in the same manner as the infantry. The troopers were armed in Greek fashion with helmet, armor, shield, spear, and sword. The heavy cavalry charge perfected by Alexander, in which engagement occurred in mass and at the gallop to deliver maximum shock, was unknown to the Romans. Instead, cavalry usually engaged at a walk or brisk trot, foregoing any shock value. Worse, cavalrymen preferred to dismount and fight alongside the infantry. Despite Roman experience in the Punic Wars and in the wars against the Greeks, Roman cavalry never developed into an arm of decision. It was used in the traditional manner, to protect infantry flanks, to reconnoiter, forage, and sometimes, to pursue. It remains a paradox of the first order that such great Roman generals as Scipio, Sulla, Marius, and even Caesar himself never saw the need to develop Roman cavalry to a level where it could be a decisive combat asset.

Marius introduced the practice of hiring the standard military mechanics of the Mediterranean—Balearic slingers, Cretan archers, and other specialized military practitioners—and integrating them into the legions. The old practice of utilizing Italian allied legions in concert with Roman legions was abandoned. The extension of citizenship to all the peoples of Italy made it possible to form legions entirely of Romans. Perhaps because of his own experience against tribal armies, Marius gave considerable attention to the problem of preventing surprise attack. The combat formations of pre-Roman armies were reflections of a less sophisticated style of warfare that was mostly incapable of surprise attack. It is not surprising, then, that these armies did not develop the art of castrametation—building fortified camps while in the field—to a high art. The Roman era changed war considerably, and the size, diversity, and mobility of the armies against which Rome fought made the prospect of surprise attack a horrifying reality.[33] The Romans introduced the practice of constructing a fortified encampment at the end of each day's march. The camp provided the commander the advantage of choosing between offensive or defensive action if attacked, and provided a secure rallying point around which a routed legion or army could regroup.

A typical Roman field camp (see Figure 13.3) was an 800-meter

Figure 13.3
Roman Field Camp under Construction

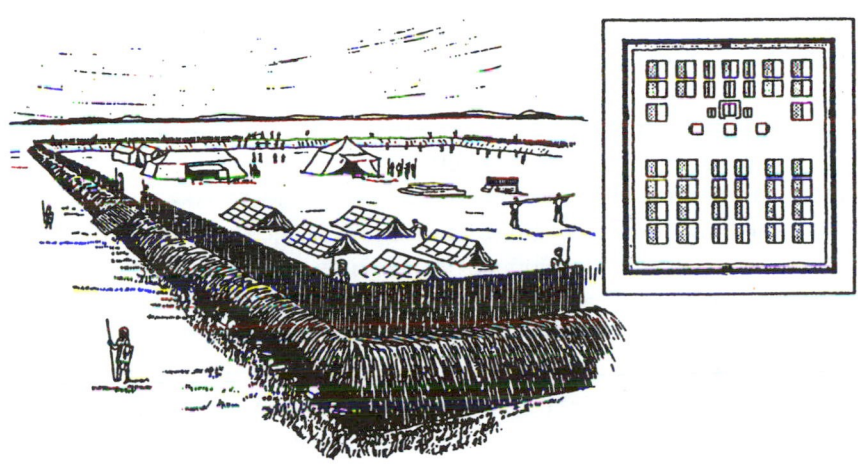

square or rectangle with rounded corners surrounded by a ditch twelve feet wide and nine feet deep. The earth from the ditch was used to construct a three-foot high parapet. Three-and-a-half-foot long sharpened wooden stakes were inserted into the parapet, providing the wall with a spiked front. Inside the perimeter the soldiers' tents were arranged in symmetrical fashion. Each unit always occupied the same location in the camp, and units were grouped into their normal combat formations for rapid deployment in case of attack. The ability to protect their armies while in the field gave the Romans a major military advantage.[34]

The organizational structure of the Roman army was thoroughly modern. War had become so complex that complex organizational structures were required to fight it. Each senior officer had a small administrative staff responsible for paperwork. Just like modern armies, the army of Rome generated great amounts of paperwork. Each soldier, for example, had an administrative file containing his full history, awards, physical examinations, medical record, training record, and pay record. Legion staffs included sections dealing with intelligence, supply, medical care, pay, engineers, artillery, siegers, and veterinary affairs.[35] There was hardly any function that would not be immediately recognizable to a modern staff officer.

The combat command organization remained the centerpiece of the legion's fighting ability. The Roman legion was led by a curious combination of professional noncommissioned officers and politically appointed semiprofessional officers. The spine of the legion's combat command were the centurions, the only permanent unit commanders the legion possessed. They were career officers who functioned like company commanders. Promoted from the ranks on the basis of merit, experience, and demonstrated performance, the centurions often spent twenty-five years in the same legion. When units were sent to replace losses in another legion, the centurions went with their men. The Romans had discovered the secret of effective military leadership: selecting and retaining the best soldiers for combat command and keeping them in place for long periods of time. In contrast to the centurions, all legion officers were political appointees of varying degrees of experience and ability including the legion's six tribunes, who served one or two tours of duty and then moved on to political careers. The rationale for having political appointees as officers was to prevent the legions from developing officers who might be tempted to use military force to threaten the Roman state. The ability of the Roman army to fight so well with a semiprofessional officer corps seem proof enough of the proposition that the fighting ability of an army rests not in its officer corps, but in the leadership and cohesion of its small units.

While the armies of the past, most notably the Greeks, had doctors in attendance on the battlefield, the Romans were the first to systematize the provision of medical services to the soldier. In the process, they established some of the basic principles of military medical care, which are still used by armies today. War produced so many casualties that the Romans began attempting to evacuate their casualties to rear-area hospitals. Many wounded died in transit. To improve the survival rate, the Romans established a series of military hospitals located along the major roads off the empire.[36] The Romans were the first to implement the principle of proximity of treatment as close to the battlefront as possible. By practicing triage, treating the wounded quickly, and returning them to service, the Roman army established the three basic principles—proximity, triage, and expectancy of return to the unit—that remain the basis of modern military medical practice.

Roman military medicine began by ensuring the health of the soldier when in garrison. The military diet was excellent and provided sufficient calories and wide variety. The army's logistical system provided fresh fruits, seafood, birds, and exotic foods by transporting them to Roman garrisons as far away as Germany and Britain.[37] Exercise and physical conditioning kept the solider in good condition. Roman military garrisons were models of cleanliness and field hygiene, with safe water supplies, running-water latrines, baths, heated barracks, and other amenities that prevented epidemics and illness. Each legion had a full complement of medical doctors and supporting staff, including a corps of medical orderlies who served as combat medics (*capsari*). Each legion fort had its own hospital for treating the sick and wounded. These hospitals were large insulated structures with ventilation to ensure comfortable temperatures for the patients. Insulated wardrooms, some with their own latrines, were designed to ensure quiet surroundings. A Roman military hospital could usually accommodate sixty beds. The army trained its own physicians, and many of the doctors were Greeks.[38]

Hundreds of medical treatises on how to treat certain battlewounds and illnesses were produced, and the frequent wars provided opportunity to develop surgical and other treatment procedures for a wide variety of combat wounds. Special instruments, such as the arrow extractor, suture, and tourniquet, were developed. Roman physicians developed special forceps and probes for extracting different kinds of missiles from the body. Field orderlies carried bandage boxes with different types of dressings and were expert at stopping bleeding and setting bones.[39] Field surgery, complete with sterilized instruments, reached a very high level of skill, certainly as high as if not higher than that practiced in the American Civil War.

The Roman genius for war lay more in organization, application, and endurance than in invention, as in the case of siegecraft and artillery. The Roman contribution to siegecraft was to improve the old Greek machines. The major innovation was to use them in a consistent, organized manner so as almost always to succeed. The Romans employed armored siege towers made of wood, some as high as twenty-four meters, massive iron battering rams, large iron hooks to dislodge stones, covered platforms to protect miners, tunnelers, and assault teams, and bridges, drawbridges, and elevators mounted on towers to swing assault teams over the walls. Roman catapults were much larger than the old Greek models and were powered by torsion devices and springs made of sinew kept supple in oil. The largest of these devices, the *onager* (called the "wild ass" because of its kick!) could, as Josephus reports, hurl a 100-pound stone over 400 yards.[40] Smaller versions of this machine were also used. Vegetius noted that each legion had ten *onagi*, one per cohort, drawn by ox-carts, that were organic to the legion's organization.[41]

Roman advances in the design, mobility, and firepower of artillery were significant. Smaller versions of siege machines, such as the scorpion and *ballista*, were compact enough to be transported by mule or horse. These machines could fire seven- to ten-pound shot over three hundred yards. Caesar required that each legion carry thirty of these small machines, giving the legion an organic mobile artillery capability.[42]

Small machines fired iron-tipped wooden bolts. Designed much like large crossbows mounted on small platforms or legs, these devices could be used as rapid-fire field guns against enemy formations. They weighed about 85 pounds and fired bolts approximately 26 inches long over a range of 300 yards.[43] One version of this machine fired small leaden shot that could easily kill a man at 100 yards and hit a small group of men at 200 yards. It was common for the Romans to open a battle by subjecting their enemy to a long-range artillery barrage. With a maximum range of 450 to 500 yards, the small *petrobolos*, literally "stone thrower," was more accurate than the flintlock musket of later times. Slightly larger versions were mounted on a wheeled frame. The smaller versions required a two-man crew to operate, while the larger machines needed a crew of ten. These machines could fire two to three rounds a minute and were used to lay down a barrage of fire against enemy troop concentrations.

Overall, the strength of the Roman army lay in its training, discipline, and organization. Tactically, it was a one-armed army in that its emphasis on heavy infantry led it to neglect the development of cavalry. Its failure to develop trustworthy cavalry forced it to rely upon the shovel for tactical security when in the field, and the necessity to construct a field camp every evening reduced its ability to cover ground on the march by four to five hours a day. When in the field, the logistical system had difficulty keeping up with the army, often forcing a reliance upon foraging. Where the level of economic development was high, in Gaul for example, foraging worked adequately. But where economic development was marginal, as in Germany, the army was forced to rely upon its own logistical resources, often with poor results.

The legions of Rome produced by Marius' reforms proved equal to the task of battle when Caesar used them to subdue Gaul. But the Marian reforms had changed the basis of loyalty of the legions from the state to their *condottieri* commanders, to whom they looked for pay and booty. Caesar used them to seize power, initiating the death throes of the Roman Republic. Caesar's military rule came to an end at the point of a dagger when he was assassinated in 44 B.C.E. The struggle for power among several factions degenerated into a fifteen-year civil war in which the best soldiers in the world fought each other in support of the political ambitions of their commanders. The civil war ended at the battle of Actium (31 B.C.E.) with Augustus' defeat of Mark Antony, and ushered in the age of imperial Rome. The period from 27 B.C.E. to 180 C.E. is called the *Pax Romana*, a time when Rome conferred on its empire a time of unparalleled peace, stability, and development. Rome thus brought about a golden age in which economic, literary, artistic, and engineering development grew rapidly. The architect of this peace was Caesar Augustus.

Augustus reduced the imperial army to 25 legions, about 150,000 men, but retained a force of auxiliary troops of about the same number, or a total military force of about 300,000 out of a population of almost 100 million.[44] The force structure was driven by a new strategic concept that relied upon a small force of high cohesion, discipline, mobility, and technology to defend the imperial borders. Reducing the size of the army and stationing it on the frontiers of the empire was possible only because Augustus reasoned that the nature of the threat had changed. Spain and Africa had been pacified. Redrawing the security frontier in Asia had reduced the Parthian threat and made the frontier more militarily defensible. The tribes beyond the Rhine and Danube were also at peace with Rome, and the reestablishment of the civil peace permitted the removal of the legions from Italy itself, where they were no longer needed as a civil police force. The new strategic concept depended upon Roman diplomacy preventing the emergence of more than one threat at a time. Without a central reserve, the empire could only be strengthened at one point at a time without risking weakening its defenses elsewhere. To facilitate the rapid movement of troops to the imperial frontiers, Augustus began the construction of a superb road network that connected Roman military bases with the imperial frontiers. This road net was the substitute for a strategic reserve.

Augustus demobilized the veteran armies of the civil wars and standardized the new system of recruitment to stabilize the supply of military manpower. Military service was now a career. In order to meet the demands of the demobilized soldiery after the civil war, Augustus established a policy of granting veterans land throughout the empire, often as military towns. These settlements provided groups of loyal veteran soldiers that could be called to arms in an emergency. Many veterans started farms from which Roman forts and units contracted for supplies. The sons of the veterans often followed their fathers into the military, often serving in the same legions. Augustus established a special fund, the *aerarium militare*, supported by death and auction taxes, to ensure an adequate treasury from which to pay retirement benefits to legionnaires. A normal military career spanned twenty-five years.[45]

One effect of these reforms was to change the social composition of the legions. From Augustus's time forward, more and more legionnaires were of non-Italian stock. The division of the empire into the Greek-speaking east and the Latin-speaking west was manifested in the recruitment of the legions. The western legions were recruited in Italy and the romanized provinces of Gaul. The legions of the east were drawn almost entirely from that area, while the legions stationed along the Danube had a mixture of Latin and Greek soldiers. Permitting non-Romans to serve in the legions was facilitated by a change in the law that permitted the legitimization of children born to legionnaires and their non-Roman wives, and the removal of any bars to inheritance for the child. This permitted the sons of legionnaires to join the legions and become citizens. Stabilizing the legions in one place for long periods (sometimes centuries!) meant that generation after generation established strong Roman loyalties in the area and supported the identification of the local population as being a part of the great empire of Rome. It was not unusual for a soldier to remain assigned to the same legion, century, and cohort for his entire career, and he might spend all of his military life in the same camp.

The prolonged period of peace allowed Augustus to standardize the size of the legion. In Caesar's day, cohorts varied in size by as much as a few hundred, and the number of cohorts per legion varied as well. The Augustan legion was standardized at 6,000 men composed of ten cohorts. The first and tenth cohort had 1,000 men each, while the remaining eight were 500 strong. The reason for this arrangement is unclear. Weaponry, training, logistics, and tactics remained essentially as they had been in Caesar's day. The most important reform of the legion was the close integration of provincial troops, *auxilia*, within the battle formations of the imperial legions themselves. Irregular units first became important during Caesar's wars, and during the civil wars large contingents of troops were drawn from the provinces and fought under their national commanders. By the Augustan age, fully half the imperial army, approximately 150,000 soldiers, was drawn from the provincial forces.

Auxiliary units were organized in infantry and cavalry cohorts of 500-men strong. Early on, these provincial units were permitted to fight under the command of their own chiefs and use their own weaponry. This created two major problems. First, as provincials they naturally identified with their homeland and were reluctant to serve anywhere but in that homeland. Second, their national identity and loyalty made the possibility of mutiny very real. Rome attempted to solve these problems by making the national chiefs Roman citizens in the hope that this would encourage their loyalty to Rome. This often worked. The case of Arminius, however, was a dismal failure. Often a mixed national unit would be assigned a veteran legionnaire, perhaps a retired *primus pilum*, as a commander whose task it was to whip the unit into shape and keep it loyal to the imperial standard.

Throughout the age of Augustus the Romans never found a genuine solution to the problem, and unit mutinies and tribal revolts (like the one in the Teutoburg Forest) remained a real concern. Over time, however, provincial units were shifted around from province to province to dilute traditional loyalties. By Trajan's time, it had become standard practice to create standing units of auxiliaries, comparable to legion cohorts, where nationalities were deliberately mixed to reduce tribal identifications. These units were known by their numbers and were given the general designation of *numeri*. One effect was that large numbers of barbarians gained military experience and familiarity with the Roman system of war. Since few of the men in the numeri served for a career, they became a source of military expertise that was used to improve the military capabilities of the barbarian tribes, sometimes to Rome's regret.[46]

From the time of the Republic, the Romans had always taken great care to assure that the command arrangements of the army did not threaten the aristocratic nature of the Roman state. As such, civil control of the military (the magistracy) and frequent rotation of commanders were the mechanisms to achieve this goal. The result was that Rome never produced a professional senior officer corps, nor did it develop any military colleges. The senior officer corps was always chosen for its political credentials rather than its military ones, which were often completely lacking to begin with. The civil war increased the Roman fear of *condottieri* generals, and Augustus introduced a command system that assured civil control of the army. The higher officers of the legions were anything but military professionals. The Augustan legions were commanded by a new type of public official, the *legatus*, an office created by Augustus. Caesar had begun a similar practice by placing command of sections of his army under the control of officials loyal to him personally. Augustus institutionalized the practice.

The *legatus* was a public official with a sufficient political reputation for loyalty to the state and was appointed by the emperor to legion command. The *legatus* served only one or two years with the legion, at which time he returned to Rome to hold another public post or was transferred to one of the provincial governorships or other posts for men of praetorian rank. Such a system of short tenure and rotation of office served to prevent the rise of senior commanders who might use their military posts to strike at the state. At the same time, however, it made it impossible for the army to develop senior career officers. A young man might gain some military experience by being appointed a *tribunus militum*, which permitted military service for a short time. Despite its name, the post under Augustus was a minor one and held none of the traditional powers associated with the old tribunate under the Republic. For the most part, senior officers assumed legion command with little or no military experience at all.

This arrangement might well prove workable at the strategic or theater level of operations, but could easily lead to disaster at the tactical level where senior officers might actually have to lead their men into battle. This essential amateurism of the senior officer corps was offset by the institution of the centurionate. Each legion had sixty centurions, six attached to each of the legion's ten cohorts. The centurions began life in the ranks and were promoted on the basis of performance, which, as Livy says, was defined by leadership and courage.[47] They served for life with the same unit, and were true and well-respected professional soldiers. It was within the centurionate that the professional combat leadership of the legion resided.

Although technically noncommissioned officers, the centurions acted more like modern company commanders in both tactical and leadership responsibilities. A tradition had grown up in the Roman army in which it was customary for the legion commander to consult with a group of senior centurions before taking the legion into battle. This group of senior centurions was called the *primi ordines* and consisted (probably) of the centurions of the first cohort (usually the first to engage and the anchor of the infantry line) and the senior centurions of each of the remaining cohorts. This meeting functioned much like the modern commander's conference, and it afforded the inexperienced legion commander the opportunity to seek and receive advice from men much more experienced in war. Given the success of the Augustan legions, it seems reasonable to conclude that despite inexperienced senior commanders, most were intelligent enough to take the advice of the legion's combat veterans in planning and executing military operations.

One of Augustus' important contributions to Roman military power was his recognition of the navy as an important instrument of national policy. Early in his reign Augustus ordered the construction of two naval bases, one at Misenum on the Bay of Naples and the other at Ravenna, near the mouth of the river Po. These two bases served as the headquarters of the Roman fleets for centuries afterward. Smaller fleets were constructed and stationed at critical ports throughout the empire. The major rivers had regular squadrons assigned to them to patrol their waters. It required almost another century after Augustus for Rome to produce a truly modern navy. But it was Augustus who first recognized naval power as an important element in Roman grand strategy.[48]

The Roman armies of the Augustan age were the most proficient and professional soldiers that Roman society had ever produced. Their strength, as always, lay in disciplined infantry, good training, and superb logistics. Their weakness, as always, lay in their failure to develop disciplined cavalry and integrate it into an overall tactical doctrine. The Romans simply hired cavalry when they needed it and always employed it as a minor combat arm. Man for man, unit for unit, however, there was not another army in the world—and perhaps had never been—that could go head to head with the legions of Rome and emerge victorious. When they came up short, as the legions sometimes did, it was most often due to poor leadership rather than to the quality of the Roman soldier.

By the time of Trajan (98–117 C.E.) Roman military policy had succeeded for more than a century in keeping the imperial borders secure. The great length of the imperial borders forced Trajan to conduct one preemptive raid after another against the border tribes to maintain the security of the frontiers. Even so, the legions were stretched thin. Hadrian (117–38 C.E.) adjusted the frontiers to coincide with extant military capabilities and adjusted the legions' positions to take maximum advantage of natural barriers. In Germany, for example, the lines of defense ran along the Rhine and, further east, along the Danube. The area between the upper Rhine and upper Danube was fortified by a ten-foot high, 200-mile long wooden palisade complete with guard towers and forts along which the legions deployed. In places where natural barriers were insufficient, Hadrian constructed them as he did in England with Hadrian's Wall. Behind the border posts Hadrian improved the network of connecting roads to permit the legions to move quickly to any point of attack. As under Augustus, there was no central strategic reserve. As long as Rome did not have to fight on two fronts at once, as long as the legions remained of high quality, and as long as the prestige of the Roman army was sufficient to give any tribal leader sufficient pause, Roman grand strategy worked well.

The army of Hadrian's time comprised about 157,000 legionnaires organized into 28 legions augmented by 227,000 auxiliary troops, the *auxilia* first introduced by Augustus. By the middle of the second century C.E. there were 257 cohorts of auxiliary troops, of which 130 were mixed cohorts. These mixed units, first used by Caesar against the Gauls at Alexia, were comprised of infantry supported by a small cavalry squad-

Figure 13.4
Roman Body Armor and Helmets

Lorica Segmenta
First Century A.D.

Roman Cavalry Chain Mail
Adrianople, 378 A.D.

Roman Port Helmet
3rd Century

Roman Cavalry Helmet
1st Century

Intercisa Helmet
378 A.D.

Source: Courtesy of J. Dunn.

ron at a ratio of 4 infantry to every 1 cavalryman, with the cavalry comprising 120 horses. In addition, there were 40 milliary units (units of 1,000 men) of which 22 were mixed. This new type of unit was introduced by the Flavians in the east. There were 82 ordinary cavalry regiments and eight milliary cavalry regiments. The total Roman army of this period was approximately 384,000 men, of whom 71,000 were mounted.[49]

The equipment of the legionnaire changed during this period (see Figure 13.4). The Roman helmet was now made in arms factories in Gaul to take advantage of Celtic skill in iron-making. A new helmet called the Port type was introduced, originating in the Alpine area. Its distinguishing feature was its extended neck guard, which gave substantially greater protection down to the shoulders. Body armor also underwent important changes. The chain mail worn for centuries by the Roman legionnaire gave way to the new *lorica segmenta*. This, too, was a Celtic innovation, and consisted of connected steel bands held around the body by straps and hooks. The new armor weighed only twenty pounds compared to more than thirty pounds for the chain mail.[50]

The traditional oval Roman *scutum*, which had been in use for more than four centuries, was replaced by a shorter rectangular shield of the same name. Constructed like a half cylinder with straight sides, the new shield was made of laminated wood covered with leather. It was reenforced with metal around the edges, an innovation probably first introduced during the Gallic wars to counter the downward blow of the Gallic broadsword, and was reenforced with an iron boss and a protected hand grip. The new shield weighed about twelve pounds. The straight sides of the shield permitted a tighter interlocking of shields with less exposed space between each one, a considerable advantage when fighting either infantry or cavalry whose primary weapon was the stabbing spear, the most common weapon of the tribal armies. The traditional *pilum* remained, but underwent several design changes, sometimes becoming heavier and then lighter. One heavier model had a plumb weight at the base of the striking point to give it greater force in penetrating the enemy shield. As the Roman legions came more and more to face cavalry and spear-carrying infantry, the *pilum* gradually gave way to the spear, a more effective instrument against both types of adversaries.[51]

The Roman sword underwent changes that made it lighter and shorter. The *gladius* remained essentially the same weapon, but what was changing was the nature and armament of the adversary, which, in turn, forced a change in infantry tactics. More and more, the legions fought in closed lines rather than in the open formations of the past. Gradually, the *gladius* gave way to the barbarian sword, the *spatha*. Derived from the Celtic long sword, the *spatha* had a blade of sixty to seventy centimeters in length, and functioned as a cutting, not a stabbing, weapon. Its adoption, besides being a response to changing tactics, also reflected the fact that more and more barbarian infantry was being used in the legions, infantry whose native weapon was the *spatha*.

Roman cavalry underwent significant changes during the second century C.E. It was during Hadrian's time that the traditional Roman neglect of cavalry began to change. The arrival of the Roxolani along the Danube introduced the Romans to a new type of cavalry first developed in the East. These *cataphracti* were heavy cavalry in which both the horse and cavalryman were armored. The cavalryman carried the *contus* or lance. Hadrian was the first Roman emperor to introduce units of *cataphracti* into the Roman army. These new units did not, however, change the traditional Roman emphasis on infantry. Most Roman cavalry of this period were hired units, and the role of cavalry in Roman tactics remained essentially unchanged. Traditional Roman cavalry rode small horses (almost ponies, averaging 14 hands high) that carried no armor.

The cavalryman wore chain mail armor, a helmet that covered the whole head except for the eyes and nose, and carried the long Celtic *spatha* as his main weapon. The standard cavalry shield was a flat oval-shaped device. The saddle appeared among Roman cavalry for the first time in the late first century, as did the horseshoe, another Celtic innovation in war. There is no evidence of the use of the stirrup by the Romans. The armament of Roman cavalry during this period clearly reflected its limited tactical role in support of infantry. Its armament reflected the earlier Greek pattern of cavalry employment in conjunction with the infantry phalanx. It was not an independent combat arm of great power.[52]

By the middle of the fourth century C.E., Roman military equipment had undergone further changes as a result of the changing nature of the army itself and because of the kinds of enemies with which it had to deal. In general, Roman military equipment became more like that of the barbarian armies the Romans fought. By the battle of Adrianople (378 C.E.), the *gladius* had disappeared from the kit of the Roman infantryman, replaced by the barbarian *spatha*. As Roman infantry was expected more and more to act as a barrier to barbarian cavalry charges, the thrown *pilum* was replaced by the stabbing spear, a weapon much more suited for use in a wall of pikes. The straight-sided cylindrical *scutum*, a shield designed to repel infantry attack, was replaced by the light oval-shaped shield characteristic of barbarian cavalry. This shield permitted the soldier more striking area with his spear. As Roman heavy infantry increasingly became light infantry valued for its mobility more than its combat weight, body armor fell into disuse, so that by the time of Adrianople most Roman legionnaires went into battle with little or no body armor. The characteristic Roman helmet finally gave way to the lighter, cheaper, barbarian helmet known as the *Intercisa* type, and even the military belt, the very symbol of the legionnaire for centuries, was discarded in favor of a single broad belt with a leather baldric for holding the sword.[53]

By the beginning of the third century the threat to Rome came not from without, but from political turmoil within. The murder of Emperor Commodus, presumably with the concurrence of the Praetorians, began a period of marked domestic instability that weakened the empire. At first the corrosive effects of political murder had little effect. Septimius Severus (193–211 C.E.) even took a more active military role, raising three new legions to deal with the Parthian problem and adding a Mesopotamian province to the empire. He disbanded the Praetorian Guard and replaced it with a new unit of ten cohorts of double strength (30,000 men) recruited from the frontier legions. This army was the forerunner of the later Roman mobile reserve, which was intended to reenforce frontier armies as well as suppress any military rebellions that might occur among the frontier legions.

From 235 to 297 C.E., when Diocletian finally put down the last surviving pretender to the Roman mantle, Rome suffered through sixty years of civil war in which no fewer than sixteen emperors and more than thirty would-be emperors were felled by the dagger or the sword. As the legions supported the political ambitions of their *condottieri* commanders by fighting among themselves, the frontier defenses were left in shambles. Much of the trained manpower of the legions fell in battles with one another. As political instability ruined the legions, across the frontiers the barbarians began to form tribal confederations and to act in concert militarily. The Germans began making forays along the Rhine, and the Goths pressed along the Danubian border. In the Near East, Persia began its rise to power, replacing the old Parthian Empire as a worthy competitor willing to do battle with Rome.

Increased pressure on the frontiers revealed the shortcomings of the Roman army, weakened by political war. The old preclusive defensive strategy was no longer possible, and Rome changed to a more elastic system of defense. The frontier legions, border garrisons, and strong points were retained, but it was now recognized that the quality of the legions and the multiplicity of highly mobile cavalry threats required increased mobility if the defenders were to contain the barbarian penetrations. The legions acquired stronger cavalry components designed to run down enemy horsemen and engage them until the legion infantry could be brought to bear. Credit is usually given to Gallienus (253–268 C.E.) for creating the first large-scale Roman cavalry force, which was used as a central reserve to reenforce the border infantry garrisons. After Gallienus, a number of strong emperors—Claudius, Aurelian, and Probus—won major victories against the invaders and managed to stabilize the Roman frontiers. In 284 C.E. Diocletian assumed the purple. He reigned until 305 C.E., the longest reign of any Roman emperor since Antoninus Pius.

The major reforms of the Roman army came during the reigns of Diocletian (284–305 C.E.) and Constantine (306–337 C.E.). Since it remains a matter of some debate as to what reforms were introduced by which emperor, the reigns of the two are treated here as a single period in which to trace the outlines of the reforms of the Roman army. Diocletian restored the imperial borders in a series of vigorous campaigns on several fronts. To manage the empire more efficiently, Diocletian created the post of vice-emperor. In 293 C.E. he reorganized the empire for administrative purposes by creating a number of smaller provinces out of the larger ones. The frontiers were organized into four military sectors, each of which had it own legions, cavalry detachments, and mobile cavalry reserve. To tie the system of forts and unit deployments together and make rapid reenforcement possible, Diocletian spent a fortune on roads, bridges, and strong points.

Under Diocletian the army grew from the 300,000 men who served under Severus to about 400,000 men. The number of legions was doubled from thirty-three to almost seventy, but in some instances the number of men per legion was reduced to only 1,000. Constantine reduced the strength of each legion even further. The overall increase in manpower came in the increased number of *auxilia* and the creation of new types of infantry units, with the result that the old legionary infantry became a smaller proportion of the overall army. At the same time Diocletian expanded the number of cavalry units, almost all of which were drawn from German and other barbarian tribes. A large variety of these units—*cunei, alae, vexillationes*—were raised from other segments of the army. The old legionary cavalry disappeared, replaced by the new types of barbarian units. Despite these changes, it is important to note that under both Diocletian and Constantine the Roman army was still predominantly an infantry army. Whereas in the early days of the empire the ratio of cavalry to infantry was approximately one to ten or twelve, by the time of Adrianople it was one to three.[54]

The armies were now reorganized to make the new strategic concept of elastic defense work properly. Diocletian stopped the tradition of awarding military commands to powerful political personages, most often provincial governors. Command was now offered to professional soldiers. Under Constantine the separation of career paths became permanent. The remnants of the old legions were posted in fixed positions at key border or river points for frontier defense. Over time their quality declined as the better soldiers chose to serve in the elite units. The legion remnants were redesignated as *limitanei* (border guards) and *riparienses* (river guards), and were usually deployed in "legions" of 1,000 men. Diocletian formed the *comitatenses*, or mobile imperial army units, comprised largely of provincials from Germany, Illyrium, and the Danube, directly under the command of the emperor himself. These units were stationed near the major cities and roads of the interior of the empire and functioned as a strategic rapid reaction force to expel border penetrations. Infantry contingents within these units were largely light infantry and of provincial or barbarian origin. The cavalry contingents were divided into 500 horse regiments called *vexillationes*, and the infantry, although still called "legions," was assembled into brigades of 1,000 men. At the end of the fourth century C.E., there were a total of 170 legions in the field. Between the *comitatenses* and the field legions there was another rapid-reaction cavalry force called the *pseudo-comitatenses*, used to fill the gaps as the occasion arose.

Although Diocletian began the reforms of the army in the third century, it was Constantine who formalized and systematized the new army into a coherent military system supporting a new military strategy. The mobile reaction strategy recognized that most barbarian incursions were not wholesale tribal movements seeking resettlement within the empire. This pattern of tribal migration began decades after Adrianople, only after the empire revealed itself to be much weaker at resisting wholesale tribal migration. Moreover, the Roman practice of recruiting entire barbarian armies along with their families for service in the imperial armies encouraged migration. At the time of Constantine, however, most border incursions were carried out by relatively small bands of raiders seeking plunder. Against such raiders, the Roman policy of mobile reaction worked relatively well. Infantry posts and border strongpoints served as pockets of resistance until larger mobile forces could arrive. Since most of the raiders were horseborne, Roman reaction forces were cavalry and light infantry. As long as the tribal incursions were sporadic and of relatively small size, these reaction forces were adequate. Once they became tribal migrations intent on settling down within the imperial borders, Roman military strategy proved inadequate.

Roman tactics changed to accommodate both the new strategy and the nature of the new threat. Legion infantry now fought in smaller contingents (about 1,000 strong compared to the old 5,000-man legion) armed with spear and light shield. Roman infantry required mobility and flexibility to deal with the barbarian cavalry and had to be capable of stopping a barbarian cavalry charge. To accomplish this, Roman infantry now deployed in compact lines rather than in the open *quincunx* formation and functioned more like the old precohortal phalanx, with a wall of spears to stop enemy cavalry. The infantry's role was to stop and fix the enemy cavalry until Roman cavalry could engage and deal with it directly. Infantry was still the largest and strongest combat arm of the army by far, but was transformed from the arm of decision into a tactical platform of maneuver for the cavalry in much the same way as infantry had been for Alexander.

The defeat of the Roman legions at Adrianople in 378 C.E. was the beginning of the end for the empire of Rome. The victory of Gothic cavalry, followed by the demands for resettlement of the Goths within the imperial borders, marked a dramatic change in the nature of the strategic threat now confronted by Rome. And it was a threat that Rome could not deal with successfully. The fact that the Roman empire eventually collapsed in the west has often obscured the fact of its remarkable survival in the east against incredible odds for almost a millennium. It is by no means clear that even a modern nation state equipped with modern armies and weapons could have done any better at keeping the empire alive. Certainly the experience of the colonial empires of the nineteenh century suggests that they could not.

The military collapse of the Roman armies is far more understandable in terms of the erosion of their psychological base than in any other terms. The men who came to comprise the legions near the end simply had no attachment to any common past or expectations of a common future. The almost mystical attachment to Rome that had motivated the old legions was gone. Incessant reorganizations and transfers of the legion and unit personnel destroyed any common focus of identification for their membership. There was left no anchor of psychological stability and no cultural identification to which the recruit could be socialized. The proud traditions and histories of the legions were no more.

It may well have been that the demands made upon the armies of Rome in the late imperial period were simply too great and that a collapse was inevitable. Perhaps so. But the collapse of the Roman armies cannot be seen as some sudden military catastrophe. The gradual process of collapse is really a study in military disintegration, itself the product of many other factors. After all, the collapse of the empire was accompanied by an overall decline in Roman social, economic, civic, artistic, and literary life, much of which was already destroyed or in shambles even as the armies sought to defend the corpse. And, in a very real sense, the empire after the third century was Roman in name only. Its substance had fled a century before. The empire collapsed because of a general decline of things Roman in almost all areas of life. The fact that the armies stood to the last is a remarkable testament to their greatness. No nation before or since has ever accomplished what the Roman armies accomplished, and given the nature of modern weapons, probably no nation ever will. The time of the Roman legions, the armies of the Caesars, may represent a historical singularity.

NOTES

1. The date of 753 B.C.E. is archaeologically too late to mark the first settlement of Rome and too early to mark the beginning of true urbanization. The

date seems to have come into common usage as a consequence of a squabble among ancient historians. For more on this point see Michael Grant, *History of Rome* (New York: Charles Scribner, 1978), 10.

2. A good history of early Italian military systems is found in Peter Connolly, *Greece and Rome at War* (Englewood Cliffs, N.J.: Prentice-Hall, 1981), 90–126.

3. This policy resulted in the rise of a state arms industry. It is noteworthy that Egypt, Assyria, and Persia all had centralized arms industries, while Greece never developed the institution.

4. Robert Laffont, *The Ancient Art of War* (New York: Time-Life Books, 1961), vol. 1, 94, argues that the Romans acquired the *pilum* from the Samnites. Archaeological evidence reveals a wall painting on a tomb in Gigioli, Italy of a *pilum* that dates from the fourth century B.C.E., 200 years before the Roman wars with the Samnites.

5. Robert O'Connell, "The Roman Killing Machine," *Quarterly Journal of Military History* (Autumn 1988): 38.

6. Grant, 55.

7. Ibid., 57–58.

8. The author's forebears came from the same region of Italy as did Marius, indeed from the same town of Arpinum. After the Roman conquest of the area, the once proud Samnites manufactured sandals for the Roman army. The name of the local dialect, "ciocciari," became identified with the military sandal itself.

9. Grant, 264.

10. *Statistical Abstract of the United States* (Washington, D.C.: Government Printing Office, 1988), 572.

11. "Roman Empire and Military Airlift," *Wall Street Journal,* 9 December 1988, A7.

12. T.N. Dupuy, *The Evolution of Weapons and Warfare* (New York: Bobbs-Merrill, 1980), 18.

13. Leaving gaps in the formations effectively solved the problem of fragility inherent in the phalanx, which could not retain its overall integrity if any section of it broke.

14. The term *maniple* can be translated literally as a "handful" of men, a meaning that indicates the organized yet independent manner in which the maniple fought.

15. The heavy *pilum* differed from the light in that it had a weight just behind the base of the metal shaft. This weight increased the weapon's penetrating power. If the angle of descent was forty-five degrees, a heavy *pilum* could pierce armor and helmet. A light pilum could be thrown about sixty feet. Sometimes a throwing cord was used to impart rotational velocity to the weapon, increasing its stability and range.

16. O'Connell, 38. This statement might make an interesting Ph.D. dissertation.

17. Ibid., 42.

18. Ibid.

19. The United States lost approximately 440,000 men in World War II.

20. A testimony to Rome's political skill in bonding its Latin allies to itself was seen in the fact that few Italian states defected to Hannibal despite his repeated successes.

21. We can put more faith in Roman records of killed and wounded than we can in accounts for more ancient armies. The organizational nature of the Roman army required accurate accounts, while those of previous armies usually did not and were used to glorify the deeds of their kings.

22. For an excellent modern account of the battle of Cannae, see General Sir John Hackett, *Great Battlefields of the World* (New York: Macmillan, 1984), 10–13. Of course the accounts by Livy and Polibius are better.

23. This rate of movement provides a striking example of the military impact of paved roads on the mobility of an army.

24. Hannibal sustained his forces in Italy for more than thirteen years!

25. Richard A. Gabriel and Donald Boose, Jr., *Great Battles of Antiquity* (Westport, Conn.: Greenwood Press, 1994), 331.

26. Livy, as quoted in Gabriel and Boose, 332.

27. Laffont, 111.

28. This is the first time in history that a military force abolished the death penalty. The practice of decimation for units that performed dishonorably continued to be used, however.

29. Arpinum is modern-day Arpino and also the birthplace of Cicero.

30. Watson, G.R. *The Roman Soldier* (Ithaca, N.Y.: Cornell University Press, 1969), 56.

31. The use of the heavy broadsword swung overhead by these tribal armies at first caused serious problems for the Roman infantryman. Later he was trained to step into the descending blow of the sword, take its impact with the shield held over his head, and thrust upward with his own sword into the belly of the enemy.

32. T.N. Dupuy, *The Encyclopedia of Military History* (New York: Harper and Row, 1970), 100.

33. The nature of the tribal military organizations of these armies made them extremely flexible. The lack of a strong organizational structure and small baggage trains made them capable of rapid mobility and surprise attack, especially when fighting in rugged or wooded terrain. Armenius destroyed three Roman legions in the Teutoborg Forest by surprise attack.

34. For accounts of the Roman camps see G.R. Watson, 66–68 and Connolly, 135–42. Both are based on Vegetius' famous account.

35. For the Roman staff organization, see Connolly, 223. See also Dupuy, 98–101.

36. Richard A. Gabriel, *No More Heroes: Madness and Psychiatry in War* (New York: Hill and Wang, 1987), 49–51. See also Richard A. Gabriel and Karen S. Metz, *History of Military Medicine*, vol. 1, *Rome*.

37. On the Roman military diet see *Encyclopedia Britannica*, s.v., "The Roman Military Diet."

38. Graham Webster, *The Roman Imperial Army*, 3rd ed. (Toronto: Barnes and Noble, 1985), 262. See also Gabriel and Metz.

39. Webster, 261.

40. Ibid., 240–43; Josephus (7:1, 6, 3).

41. Vegetius, ii, 25.

42. Dupuy, 24.

43. Ibid., 30.

44. Grant, 247. The population was probably somewhere between 75 and 100 million.

45. Ibid., 256

46. Gabriel and Boose, 412.

47. Ibid., 413.

48. For an account of the military reforms of Augustus, including the navy, see Richard A. Gabriel, *Great Captains of Antiquity* (Westport, Conn.: Greenwood Press, 2000), chapter on Augustus.

49. Gabriel and Boose, 436.

50. Ibid.

51. Ibid., 438.

52. Ibid., 438–39.

53. Ibid.

54. Ibid., 442.

14

Barbarian Armies: Iberians, Gauls, Germans, and Goths

250 B.C.E.–378 C.E.

This chapter examines the barbarian armies—Iberians, Gauls, Germans, and Goths—that fought against Rome again and again from the time of Hannibal's invasion of Spain until the Roman defeat at Adrianople in 378 C.E. at the hands of the Goths. All these armies were tribal in nature, the Gauls of Caesar's time being a partial exception insofar as they were a settled people who practiced extensive agriculture and mining and developed a socioeconomic infrastructure of roads, bridges, schools, etc. Armies are always creatures of the larger social orders that give them life, and this is no more starkly evident in the contrast between the armies of Rome and the barbarian armies. In tribal societies, however, the connection between structure, tactics, organization, and even weaponry and the social order is much closer than in advanced societies, if for no other reason than because tribal societies produce fewer resources that can be spared for military adventures. Indeed, it is precisely the necessary proximity of this connection that defines barbarian armies as such, far more than their military ability. The analysis that follows proceeds from the nature of the Gallic, German, and Gothic social structures as determinative of the military structures of their respective armies.

As contact between the more advanced Roman society and the tribal societies of the barbarians increased over time, both the tribal social orders and the armies of the barbarians changed dramatically. Under

Augustus, Rome made an enormous investment in Gaul with the precise objective of "romanizing" the population, so that by the second century C.E., Gaul was no less a modern, urban, and sophisticated society than Italy itself. So, too, with the Goths and, to a lesser extent, the Germans west of the Rhine. Many Goth and German tribes served in the Roman army as *foederati* and *auxilia*, with the effect that they became familiar with Roman weapons and the Roman way of war, conditions that led to changes in their social orders as well. The Iberians, after centuries of Roman occupation, abandoned their old tribal social structures and armies to become just another group of Roman provincials participating in the Roman imperial culture. A previously presented analysis of the army of the Iberian tribes during Hannibal's time will not be repeated here. The reader is referred to chapter 11 for a description of the army of the Iberian tribes.

GAULS

In Caesar's day Gaul included the whole of France and Belgium and parts of Holland, Switzerland, and all of Germany west of the Rhine. The population was of mixed origin, although the Celts were probably in the majority, and probably numbered between 15 and 20 million people. The population was divided into 2–300 tribes, with some tribes held as vassals—what Caesar called *clientelae*—to the larger ones.[1] These tribes lived in villages scattered around a central town that was often fortified, although usually without a moat. These towns were often located on appropriately high ground for defense. The Gauls practiced extensive agriculture and cattle breeding, and their tribes were more stable than the largely nomadic and pastoral Germanic tribes across the Rhine.[2] The country itself was relatively well developed in terms of infrastructure, possessing many bridges, dirt roads, frequently used river fordings, docks, and relatively heavy river traffic. Caesar drew heavily upon this extant transportation and economic infrastructure to sustain his armies during his campaigns in Gaul.

The success of Caesar's armies against the Gauls was due in no small measure to the fact that the Gallic enemy was simply not very proficient at waging war. Caesar was fortunate, for example, that the Gauls never developed a truly effective cavalry fighting arm even though cavalry was the preferred branch of combat for the Gallic nobility. Moreover, the Gallic propensity to conduct undisciplined frontal assaults against combat-hardened Roman infantry squandered numerical superiority time and time again. Tribal armies tended as well to bring along the whole tribe when they went to war, a consequence of their social values and structure. As a result, a battlefield defeat often exposed the entire tribe to massacre. The practice of bringing the entire tribe to the battlefield was common to Gauls, Germans, Iberians, and Goths alike, more so if the tribes were on the move in search of new homes or seasonal pasture and happened to encounter the Roman army, often with catastrophic consequences. In 58 B.C.E., Caesar attacked the Helvetii during one of their migrations, with the result that 238,000 men, women, and children of a tribe of 368,000 were slain. Two years later, Caesar put an end to a German migration that had crossed the Rhine into Gaul. At the junction of the Moselle and Rhine rivers, Caesar trapped and slaughtered the entire tribe to a man! By his account, 430,000 Germans were slain, a deliberately calculated act of political butchery designed to send a message to any other tribal people who might consider resisting the will of Rome. Even in Rome the massacre provoked shock and outrage. One writer of the day called the slaughter "unquestionably the most atrocious act of which any civilized man has ever been guilty."[3]

The military organization of the Gauls was a reflection of their larger social structure. Gallic society was governed by an aristocracy of nobles surrounded by groups of retainers who acted as a warrior class, not unlike the warrior retinues of the European Middle Ages. Most of the rest of the social order was composed of various types of free landholders and tenant farmers, a large portion of whom had been reduced to serf status. The Druidic priesthood constituted another social caste but, while influential, it was unable to act as an organizer for Gallic society outside of its religious functions.[4] Unlike Germany, however, the Gallic social order was not primarily that of a warrior society. The Gauls were a relatively advanced people who practiced extensive agriculture, constructed forts, bridges, and roads, and used currency rather than the more primitive barter as a means of economic interchange. The constant jockeying for power and shifting alliances among the rival nobilities further precluded any significant degree of national integration to confront the common Roman enemy. One consequence was the lack of any national army or any genuine level of military sophistication that could be marshaled to defend Gaul against the Roman invasion.

Among most of the tribes of Gaul the primary fighting arm of the tribal armies was cavalry. Although the chariot had been used in Gaul for centuries, it was probably used primarily to transport individual combatants to the battlefield, rather than as a fighting vehicle per se. In any case, the chariot seems to have disappeared—except among the tribes in Britain—sometime prior to Caesar's arrival in Gaul. As the Gallic warrior nobility increased its control over other segments of the population, the chariot was replaced by the horse, so that cavalry became the primary combat arm of the nobility. Caesar called these horseborne nobles *equites* or "knights," and they typically constituted the tribal command structure for war. Gallic armies had spent centuries fighting one another, with the consequence that there was little outside influence to encourage the development of weapons, tactics, or style of warfare. Gallic armies at the time of Caesar remained what they had always been for centuries, coteries of ill-disciplined combatants with little in the way of tactical skill or sophisticated weaponry.[5] This was certainly true of the cavalry, which was accustomed to fighting as individual combatants rather than as a true combat arm capable of being employed in concert with other arms. Even when combined with infantry, significant coordination in battle was rarely achieved.

In a social order divided feudally between warrior knights on horseback and tenant farmers, serfs, and freeholders, it is hardly surprising that Gallic infantry amounted to little more than an untrained, temporarily assembled mob of armed rabble incapable of any degree of tactical sophistication, discipline, or direction on the battlefield. The typical Gallic foot soldier was a light infantryman armed with the long cutting sword as his chief weapon, which he typically wielded as an individual combatant rather than as part of a unit.[6] Little use seems to have been made of spearmen or archers, although Caesar occasionally encountered javeliners and slingers. Both infantry and cavalry carried wooden or wattle shields, and Caesar recorded that some Gallic troops fought stripped to the waist. In other instances he recorded that the nobility sometimes wore bronze cuirasses, chain mail, and highly decorated helmets, but these items seem to have been more signs of military rank and status than genuinely defensive implements. Thus it was that although the Celts of Gaul had invented chain mail armor more than a century before Caesar's arrival, its use among common soldiers was almost nonexistent, while it was often employed by the warrior nobility. Roman commanders immediately recognized the value of chain mail and quickly equipped all their troops with it.

The Helvetii and the Nervii, the tribes against which Caesar fought most of his important infantry battles in Gaul, were exceptions to the generally poor quality of Gallic infantry.[7] It is the accounts of Caesar's battles with these two tribes that have led historians often to attribute their excellent fighting abilities to all the other tribes as well when it is not accurate to do so. The Helvetii had refined their art of war through centuries of running battles on their borders with the Germans. This experience caused them to develop excellent infantry, which fought in disciplined formations under generally good combat commanders. The Helvetii also seem to have acquired some of the German skill at cavalry. The Nervii of the Sambre Valley were entirely an infantry force of high skill and discipline, and possessed no cavalry at all. In all of Caesar's battles in Gaul, it was only the Helvetii and Nervii who dared challenge the legions of Rome to infantry combat in open field. And when they did, they consistently gave a good account of themselves against the superior Roman force.

These exceptions aside, the conduct of war by the Gallic tribes left much to be desired, especially when confronting the Roman enemy, whose strong suit was organization. The Gauls had almost no permanent military organization to speak of. Centuries of tribal civil wars made any military coalition a fragile entity, and Caesar was a master of playing off one tribe against another to prevent a concentration of superior forces against him. So fragile were these battlefield coalitions that often a defeat of a single contingent was sufficient to cause other contingents to think better of continuing the fight and simply leave the field. The inability of the Gallic tribes to sustain a political coalition for any length of time made the creation of a national Gallic army capable of sustained military operations even against the common Roman enemy an impossibility.[8]

The Gauls lacked any significant military organization even within the individual tribes. When the tribe went to war, the whole tribe went as well, including women, children, and the old. While we might well regard Caesar's accounts of these tribes numbering in the hundreds of thousands with some suspicion, nevertheless it is quite likely that a tribe might arrive on the field of battle with 5,000 warriors and 60,000 noncombatants in tow. With no logistical system to speak of, Gallic armies were incapable of remaining in the field for more than a few days before they had consumed whatever supplies they carried with them or could ravage from the countryside. Without a commissariat, the Gallic armies were incapable of sustained strategic and tactical direction, conditions that conceded great advantages in sustainability and tactical maneuver to the Roman enemy.

Encumbered with thousands of noncombatants, a Gallic army usually anchored itself around a ring of wagons—a *laager*—when in the field. Women, children, and supplies were concentrated with the *laager* for protection. This practice proved to be a terrible advantage in defeat. Contingents defeated on the field of battle would tend to gather around the *laager* for protection and, perhaps, a final stand, thereby bringing the battle to the noncombatants and exposing them to capture and massacre.

On a number of occasions, as already noted, Caesar defeated the Gallic warriors only to surround, capture, and enslave entire tribes. In other instances, he massacred entire peoples trapped in this manner.

In battle, the Gauls usually demonstrated no discernible tactical system of engagement. Led by their mounted nobles, the mob of unorganized infantry launched a frontal attack, hoping to overwhelm their enemy with sheer numbers and ferocity of the assault.[9] Such attacks were not carried out by units but by individuals fighting as individuals, which was, after all, precisely the point when tribes fought tribes. It was individual combat that provided the opportunity to demonstrate bravery or acquire status through one's actions. The overall consequence of such a system of war was not victory or defeat, but demonstrated military courage. Unorganized or not, however, these infantry attacks were not to be ignored. On more than one occasion, the assault of Gallic infantry shattered Roman cohorts. The Gauls were a big people, perhaps as much as seven inches taller on average than the Romans. Naked to the waist, their faces colored with paint, and their hair plastered straight up with a mixture of ash and water, the howling Gallic infantry could take a terrible toll. They fought with their broadswords swung over their heads and brought down with great force upon the heads of the shorter Roman infantry. The Roman shield of Caesar's time was made entirely of wood, and the force of a Gallic sword was often sufficient to split the shield in two.[10]

All this aside, it is difficult not to read Caesar's *Commentaries* without being tempted by the conclusion that much of Caesar's brilliance in command in his campaigns against the Gauls had to do with exploiting the obvious weaknesses of Gallic armies to good effect. It is difficult to escape the obvious truth that Caesar was almost always fighting armies that were technologically and organizationally primitive by Roman standards, often lacking even the most rudimentary military capabilities. The Gallic armies that took the field against Caesar were mostly indistinguishable from the armies of Brennus that had destroyed the Roman legions 300 years earlier. Only now the armies of Rome were vastly different, and the armies of the tribal Gauls had changed hardly at all.

GERMANS

Rome's first encounter with the *Teutones* or German barbarians occurred in 113 B.C.E. when mass migrations of the *Cimbri* (which translates as "plunderers") and *Teutones* crossed the Rhine and moved through what is now Switzerland to southern Gaul. Four years later these Germanic tribes invaded the Rhone valley as a first step in breaching the

Roman security frontier protecting northern Italy. Rome sent an army to stop the invasion, but it was defeated. After several further attempts to deflect the German line of migration, Mallius Maximus led a Roman army of 80,000 men against the Germans in 105 B.C.E. At the battle of Arausio, the Roman army was virtually annihilated along with 40,000 noncombatants.[11] Arausio was one of the worst disasters ever to befall Roman arms, and it left the road to Italy open.

For unknown reasons, the Germans changed direction and moved toward Spain, where they encountered strong resistance from the native Celtiberians in the Pyrenean mountain passes and were repulsed. The Germans now turned back toward Italy. But the Romans used the time between the battle of Arausio and the redirection of the German advance to raise another army. This was also the time of the Marian reforms. Marius himself led the Roman army into Gaul to stop the German advance. In 102 B.C.E. Marius drew the *Teutones* into battle at Acquae Sextae (modern Aix-en-Provence) and slaughtered 90,000 men, women, and children while taking another 20,000 prisoner. Meanwhile the *Cimbri* had crossed the Brenner and defeated another Roman army in the Po valley. Marius redeployed to the south and in 101 B.C.E. defeated the *Cimbri* at the battle of Vercellae, in which 140,000 men, women, and children were slain and another 60,000 taken prisoner. With these two battles, the German storm died as suddenly as it had arisen.

For over forty years the Germans remained quiet behind the Rhine. In 58 B.C.E., Caesar defeated another German menace by the name of Ariovistus, who crossed the Rhine at the invitation of some Gallic tribes that were opposing Caesar, and the German threat receded once again. A year later, Caesar defeated the Germanic tribes on the west bank of the Rhine and established Roman power there as a buffer to any German crossing. Caesar then crossed the Rhine on a spoiling expedition and ravaged German territory before withdrawing. Caesar's successful campaign in Gaul established the Rhine as the Roman northern security frontier. This frontier remained quiet throughout the great Roman civil war and, when Augustus became emperor of Rome, the Rhine frontier was still undisturbed.

Augustus undertook to extend the Roman northern frontier cross the Rhine to the Elbe, with the result that in 9 C.E., a German army under Arminius destroyed three legions in the Teutoburg Forest, putting an end to Roman expansion in Germany forever.[12] As a result, the lands beyond the Rhine remained wild, tribal, and Germanic, untouched by the romanization that so strongly shaped Gaul and the rest of the western empire. Had this division of rival and hostile cultures not occurred, there would have been no Germanic tribes to gradually migrate to Britain and bring with them the Germanic roots of the English language. Had Germany between the Rhine and the Elbe been successfully romanized, one culture, not two in unending conflict would have dominated the West. There would have been no rival and barbarian culture to eventually destroy Rome and plunge Europe into the Dark Ages. J.F.C. Fuller sums up the importance of the Roman defeat in the Teutoburg Forest on Western history when he notes, "There would have been no Franco-German problem, or at least a totally different one. There would have been no Charlemagne, no Louis XIV, no Napoleon, no Kaiser Wilhelm II, and no Hitler."[13] He might have added that there would have been no military destruction of the Roman Empire at the hands of barbarians.

The German armies that the Romans encountered in their efforts to subdue the land between the Rhine and the Elbe were products of a social order far less developed than the Gauls that Caesar had fought fifty years earlier. It is an axiom of military history that the nature and structure of armies is determined strongly by the nature and structure of the larger social orders that give them life. In this regard, then, it can be said that the social order of the Germanic tribes was essentially premodern in that it was not strongly or clearly articulated and lacked clear specification of social roles. The bonded male warrior group became the dominant form of military organization. In Germanic society, every male was first and foremost a warrior, and the entire society was formed around the conduct of war. Prowess in war was the road to social advancement, and behavior on the battlefield was the primary determinant of social rank and status.[14]

Tacitus' description of the Germans as "fierce looking with blue eyes, reddish hair, and big frames," recalls earlier Roman descriptions of the Gauls, and it is likely that, like the Gauls, the average German was much taller than the average Roman.[15] The Germans had not yet reached a level of political development where state institutions had come into existence. Instead, the Germanic peoples were divided into tribes or *Volkerschaften*. Twenty-three different tribes inhabited the land between the Rhine and the Elbe. The average tribe numbered about 25,000 people living on a land area of approximately 2,000 square miles. Some of the larger tribes possessed 35–40,000 people and occupied a proportionally larger land area. These tribes were divided into extended family-clans called "hundreds" or *Hundertschaften* comprising 400 to 1,000 people living in a single village on a land area of 20 square miles.[16]

Agriculture was not extensively practiced by the Germans, and what cultivation was undertaken was done by the women, the men contributing to the food supply by hunting and fishing. Even their housing structures were primitive, at times little more than holes in the ground covered by animal skins. Roman commanders found them unfit for quartering Roman troops. Land was held in common, as were some cattle herds, and their utilization was determined by the head of the community, the *hunno* or *Altermann*. Within each tribe were a small number of wealthier noble families who met in assembly with the clan *hunni* to address major issues, including war and peace. In wartime, however, it was common for the council to select a war chief, usually from the most powerful warrior noble families, to command the tribal army. An average German tribe could put 5–7,000 warriors in the field under the command of the war chief. The actual fighting units, however, were centered around the clans, and a Germanic army of 5,000 warriors would have at least twenty and as many as fifty subordinate unit leaders, the clan chiefs, commanding the troops.[17]

Germanic tribes were first and foremost warrior societies in which all other social roles were defined or influenced by the warrior ethos. Thus, German men did not farm because it was beneath them (women's work), but they hunted because hunting improved their combat skills. The relationship between a man and his wife and family was also conditioned by the warrior ethos. It was the woman who, as a gift of her dowry, brought weapons to her husband. German women acted as the tribe's military medical corps, and it was these *wilde Weiber* (literally "wild women") that the wounded turned to for medical aid. The role of the German wife in war is linguistically preserved in the modern German military term for sergeant or *feldwebel*, which translates literally as "field wife." German women accompanied their men into battle, urging them on to greater efforts by reminding them of the cost of enslavement to themselves and their children. German society existed to support the professional warrior, whose very social existence was defined by his ability to fight.

In times of war, each clan provided its own coterie of warriors under the leadership of the village *hunno*, who was also the civic leader of the clan in peacetime. The solidarity and cohesion of the family and clan was extended to and defined the warrior group, with the result that German small combat units were highly cohesive, strongly disciplined, self-motivated, well-led, and well-trained in the skills of individual close combat. These units could be relied upon to undertake murderous charges upon command and to fight well in dispersed small groups. While blood ties usually assured that clan units remained loyal to the larger tribal military field command, in fact there was probably only the most rudimentary command and control exercised by the war chief over the maneuver of the individual clan units. Once the tribal levy had been assembled and a general battle plan decided upon, implementation was left to local units with little in the way of any ability to direct the battle. Curiously, many centuries later, the German Army General Staff after 1850 seems to have rediscovered this traditional loose relationship between combat units and their field commanders when they developed the "new" tactical doctrine of *Auftragstaktik*, a tactical system in which field commanders drew up only general plans that assigned lower-level combat units specific objectives and then permitted the lower level combat unit a full range of individual initiative to achieve its objectives. So it was with the German tribes. Once the tribal levy had been assembled and a general battle plan decided upon, implementation was left to local units, which had little in the way of ability to direct the battle.

German weapons were the consequence of many years of intertribal warfare, the lack of contact (until much later) with any other culture from which new weapons could be acquired, and, as Tacitus tells us, the German difficulty in working with iron. Tacitus does not tell us why the Germans were such poor iron smiths, but it is clear that they were far behind the Celts and Gauls, who, in the second century B.C.E., were making chain mail armor superior to the Roman armor. Roman sources record that only a few of the German warriors, probably their nobles or fiercest warriors, wore body armor or helmets. Basic body protection was afforded by a large shield made of wood or braided reeds covered with leather. Some troops wore a covering of leather or hide on their head as well, providing a rough facsimile of a helmet. The basic weapon of the German soldier was the *framea*, a seven-to-ten-foot spear tipped with a short but very sharp blade, which could be thrown or used in close combat.[18] Some German units seem to have also used longer spears, which were employed by the front ranks of the unit to either stop the charge of the enemy or, in the offensive, to break through the enemy formation. Once inside the enemy formation, the *framea* was the primary killing weapon. The sword was known in Germany, but was relatively rare and not commonly used by German combat units until much later, when German units serving in the Roman army became familiar with it. By the second century C.E., there was also a thriving illegal weapons trade with the Germans, which allowed them to obtain Roman weapons and armor. The German warrior also carried an assortment of short wooden javelins with fire-hardened tips, which, as Tacitus tells us, they could hurl long distances. Other missiles, stones, and sharpened sticks were also salvoed at the enemy. Although some German tribes later developed excellent cavalry, for the most part German cavalry of the first and second century C.E. moved at such a slow pace in the attack (perhaps a trot or even a walk) that the infantry had little difficulty in dealing with it. The age-old tendency of tribal warriors to dismount from the horses and fight as infantry was also evident. As the Romans learned more than once to their chagrin, the primary strength of the German tribal levy was infantry.

German infantry fought in a formation that the Romans called a *cuneus* or wedge. Vegetius, writing two centuries after the battle of the Teutoburg Forest, described the *cuneus* as "a mass of men on foot, in close formation, narrower in front, wider in the rear, that moves forward and breaks the ranks of the enemy."[19] This formation, also called the Boar's Head formation by the Romans, was not a wedge with a pointed front such as Alexander's cavalry wedge formation. Rather, it more resembled a trapezoid, with a shorter line in front followed by a thick formation of closely packed troops, with a rear rank somewhat longer than the front rank. Commanded from the front by the *hunno*, this wedge formation was designed primarily to deliver shock and to carry the formation through to a penetration of the enemy ranks.

The use of the wedge against the Roman open phalanx explains other Germanic battlefield habits. For example, if the object of the wedge was penetration, then there was no need to armor the men in the center of the wedge. Body armor and helmets were worn only by the warriors in the front rank and on the outside files of the wedge. A thousand years later the Swiss adopted a similar practice and armored only the front rank and outside files, while the men in the center of the Swiss pike phalanx (itself a resurrection of the Macedonian phalanx) wore only leather armor or none at all.[20] Moreover, if the wedge did its job and broke the enemy formation, then the fight was reduced to either a pursuit or a scramble of individual combats. Under these circumstances, the troops least encumbered by armor and other weighty equipment had the advantage.

Against the Roman cohort, however, the Germanic wedge was at a disadvantage. First, the thinner Roman depth meant that more Roman weapons could be employed on the first battle line than could be presented by the *cuneus*. Moreover, if the wedge did not succeed in penetrating the Roman formation, it was overlapped by the longer Roman line and easily enveloped. Once this occurred, the Roman swordsman operating from open formation against a packed body of spearmen could wreak havoc. A single stroke often sliced the blade from the Germanic *framea*, leaving the warrior all but defenseless. Finally, the open Roman formation could move more easily over broken terrain than could the massed Germanic wedge, and conferred the advantage of greater tactical mobility upon the Roman cohort. Add to this the ability of Roman field commanders to exercise greater direction over the armies as a whole than could the German war chiefs, and it is obvious that in a set-piece battle (Arminius' victory in the Teutoburg was from ambush), the Roman legions were likely to carry the day.

The German strength lay in the highly disciplined and cohesive nature of its clan combat groups or *Kampfgruppen*. These groups could move quickly through the forests and swamps and could fall with terrible ferocity upon an enemy not yet deployed for battle. They could break contact and withdraw just as rapidly, for group discipline was central to the clan fighting unit. German warriors were particularly competent in scattered combat, surprise attacks, ambushes, feigned withdrawals, rapid assembly, and most other aspects of guerrilla war. But it took the insight of a new type of tribal war chief to use the combat abilities in a manner that produced a major battlefield victory against an army that was in almost every way superior to the Germans. With the single exception of Arminius and his victory over the Romans, the Germans produced no warrior chiefs with the imagination required to defeat the legions of Rome.

The tribal threat to the imperial frontiers from Augustus' time to the end of the empire came primarily from the growing military power of Germanic tribes. The term *Germanic* covers a wide range of peoples that lived north of the Rhine-Danube, line beginning on the North Sea and extending eastward toward the Black Sea. These peoples varied in the degree of their social and military development and even spoke completely different languages. Their increased pressure against the imperial frontiers over the centuries was due to three factors. First, many of these tribal societies were warrior societies, so that war with the Romans fulfilled their requirements for social status, prestige, and entertainment obtained through raiding and plunder. Second, at various times tribes moved toward the imperial frontiers in a simple effort to better their lives, a situation paralleled somewhat by the popular migrations of the present day of peoples of East Europe seeking better living conditions in the West. In this regard, tribal warriors often served in Roman frontier units for fixed terms. On returning to their tribes, they passed on knowledge of the better living conditions in the West, which probably helped stimulate a greater desire of the tribe to migrate. Third, as was the case with the Goths in 376 C.E., encroachment on tribal lands by stronger tribal invaders forced the Goths nearest the imperial frontiers to attempt to cross borders in search of safety. The result was the battle of Adrianople. Given the great length of the imperial borders and the strength of the stimuli pressing tribal migrations, it is no surprise that from the middle of the third century C.E. until the end of the empire, these frequent tribal penetrations constituted the primary strategic threat that Rome had to confront on its borders.

GOTHS

The Goths probably originated in Scandinavia and then migrated to the upper Vistula, gradually moving south toward the middle Danube and then east toward the upper rim of the Black Sea.[21] By the third century C.E., the Romans distinguished two Gothic kingdoms in this area. North of the Danube in the former Roman province of Dacia lived the Visigoths, also called the West Goths. North and east of them in southern Russia north of the Black Sea were the Ostrogoths or East Goths. Early in the fourth century, the Goths were converted to Arian Christianity, and the translation of the scriptures into Gothic turned the barbarian Gothic tongue into a literary language.[22] The first serious Roman contact with these seminomadic peoples came in 238 C.E. in the province of Moesia (northern Bulgaria), where the Roman legate Gaius Trajanus Decius defeated the Goths in a series of running battles that lasted for four years.

In 250 C.E., the Goths under King Cniva attempted a large invasion of the same area. Cniva crossed the Danube in force and defeated a Roman army at Philippopolis, plundering the entire area and killing more than 100,000 people, by Roman accounts. Decius, now emperor, marched against the Goths, and in two major battles drove them back to the marshes south of the Danube mouth. Having backed the Goths into a corner, Decius pressed the campaign to exterminate the Gothic threat once and for all. At the battle of Forum Treboni in 252 C.E., the Goths trapped the Roman army under Gallus and defeated it. Decius himself was killed. Gallus became emperor and concluded a truce with the Goths in which the Goths were permitted to keep their booty and retreat back across the Danube in return for a Gothic promise not to undertake further border incursions. The Romans agreed as well to pay the Goths an annual monetary tribute.

In 258 C.E., the Goths raided Circassia and Georgia, and four years later they mounted sea and amphibious raids against Moesia, Thrace, and northern Asia Minor. They even sacked Ephesus, where they destroyed the Temple of Diana, one of the seven wonders of the ancient world.

Five years later, with 500 boats, they passed through the Bosphorus and occupied the area around Byzantium, laying waste to Corinth, Sparta, Argolis, and Athens. The Greeks met the attack and destroyed the Gothic ships, forcing the invaders to retreat overland through Macedonia. In 268 C.E., Marcus Aurelius Claudius, having commanded the armies that held the Danube frontiers under three emperors, himself became Emperor Claudius II. He marched his armies into Thrace to deal with the Gothic threat. In 269 C.E., at the battle of Naissus, Claudius isolated and slaughtered the Gothic army, costing it 50,000 men. The Goths were driven back behind the mountain passes and starved into submission. Claudius compelled the Goths to enter military service as *foederati*, and he was awarded the appellation *Gothicus* for his great victory. With the death of Claudius, the Goths once again tested Roman resolve and once more crossed the Danube. The new emperor, Aurelian, attacked and drove the Goths completely out of Moesia and back across the Danube. The peace he concluded with the Goths lasted almost a hundred years until, under pressure from the movement of other tribes, the Goths once more crossed the Danube and met and defeated the Roman army at Adrianople in 378 C.E.

As with the Germans, Celts, and Iberians, the social structure of the Goths strongly influenced the organization, tactics, and overall combat capabilities of the Gothic armies. The Goths lived a semiagricultural existence centered around the village in which hunting, cattle raising, and a pastoral style of life predominated. The Gothic social order centered about the clan—the *hunno* or hundred, headed by the *alderman*, the civic head of the clan, who conducted most of the important political and social functions of the village.[23] As with other Germanic tribes with which the Romans were familiar, tribal leadership was conducted by an oligarchy of nobles. There is, however, some evidence that a monarchy may have developed among the Ostrogoths at this time, but that is uncertain. What seems certain is that the Visigoths at least had reached this level of social articulation and that the monarchy was in evidence. During wartime, a tribal assembly, presumably comprised of the *hunni* and nobles, selected a war chief who conducted the campaign. It is also probable that during periods of war the Goths organized their military commands into units of 10, 100, and even 1,000 men, the latter under the command of a *comites* or count or, perhaps, a *dux* or duke.[24] If so, it is likely that such an arrangement may have resulted from Gothic contact with the West, wherein they might have gained knowledge of such an organizational schema. If combat units of this large size were to be supported logistically, some organizational unit or units would have been required. However, we have no evidence that they existed. In all probability a Gothic army on the move took its households with it, living off the land or their livestock and whatever provisions they were able to carry.

The size of the Gothic armies of the third and fourth century C.E. was clearly not as large as the ancient commentators would have us believe. Eunapius, for example, recorded that the Gothic army that crossed the Danube in 376 C.E. prior to the battle of Adrianople consisted of 200,000 warriors. A century earlier, Trebillius Pollio gave 320,000 as the size of the Gothic army that crossed the Danube in 267 C.E. While it is likely that by the fourth century the Goths were among the most numerous and powerful of the Germanic tribes, it is unlikely that they could muster more than 12,000 or 15,000 warriors under arms. Delbruck's analysis of the Gothic army's route and rate of march prior to Adrianople concluded that the Gothic host probably had 15,000 fighting men, another 45,000 noncombatant men, women, and children, and, perhaps, another 10,000 slaves, or a body of people 70,000 strong.[25]

The fighting power of Gothic combat units was probably quite good. Unlike the earlier Germanic tribes, many of the Goths who fought at Adrianople had served in the Roman army in one capacity or another. Goths had been serving in Roman units for more than a century and were as well armed as the Roman soldiers. It was this opportunity to serve with (and fight against) the Roman imperial army that permitted the Goths to develop a powerful and highly competent class of warrior nobles and retainers under the leadership of their war chiefs. As a consequence, the combat leadership of the Gothic army was experienced and tough.

Oman argues that of all the Germanic tribes, the Goths were the first to place their main military reliance upon the horse.[26] To the Goth, it was more honorable to fight on horseback than on foot. Gothic heavy cavalry relied upon experienced horsemen armed with the lance and sword. Horses and military equipment were expensive, however, and it is unlikely that the Gothic cavalry contingents were very large relative to the large mass of infantry with which they fought. It is very likely that some Gothic cavalry had served in the Roman army as hired cavalry and were familiar with Roman cavalry doctrine. Gothic cavalry used the saddle, but there is no evidence of the stirrup.

Most of the Gothic army was infantry. Unlike the infantry of its earlier Germanic ancestors who fought as light infantry with spear and javelin, Gothic infantry was well-armed heavy infantry. The infantry carried the shield and sometimes a pike. Its major arms were the short sword or

scamasax or the long cutting sword, the *spatha*. Some infantry carried the *fransica*, a single-bladed battle-axe that could be wielded or thrown and could easily split Roman armor, shield, and helmet.[27] As best as can be determined, Gothic infantry did not fight with body armor, although it is likely that some Roman shirt mail must have made its way into the Gothic army. Like their ancestors, the Goths fought in a fluid wedge formation designed more for its ability to be led by the combat chief than for its military effectiveness.

The army of the Goths moved with and around its wagon forts or *laager*. These wagons carried the army's food supply for the soldiers and their families, and whatever other logistical items were required for the campaign. At the end of each day, the wagons were drawn into a circle to form a wagon fort behind which a camp could be constructed. The wagon fort served as the base from which the entire army could fight. In dire circumstances, the Gothic army could fall back upon the *laager* in retreat to regroup its forces or offer a last stand of resistance. The way in which the Goths used the *laager* strongly paralleled the functions that the Roman field camp served for the Roman army.

The Roman experience with the Goths had generally not been a pleasant one over the century leading up to Adrianople. In a number of instances, the Goths had massacred Roman armies and ravaged the provinces of the empire. Their peculiar habit of cutting off the right hand—the hand needed to work the plow—of Roman provincial farmers was particularly irksome. On balance, however, it was the Romans who had won more battles and killed more Goths than the reverse. At Adrianople, the Goths redressed the balance.

NOTES

1. J.F.C. Fuller, *Julius Caesar: Man, Soldier, Tyrant* (New York: DaCapo, 1965), 95.

2. Ibid. See also Peter Wilcox and Rafael Trevino, *Barbarians Against Rome* (London: Osprey Publishing, 2000), 54–58.

3. Richard A. Gabriel and Donald Boose, Jr., *Great Battles of Antiquity* (Westport, Conn.: Greenwood Press, 1994), 355.

4. Fuller, 98.

5. Ibid., 99.

6. Ibid.

7. Ibid.

8. Ibid.

9. Wilcox, 59.

10. Ibid., 60.

11. Gabriel and Boose, 398.

12. Gabriel and Boose, "Battle of the Teutoburg Forest," in *Great Battles of Antiquity*, 397–428 for a detailed account of this battle, including tactical and strategic implications for Roman policy in Germany.

13. J.F.C. Fuller, *A Military History of the Western World* (New York: DaCapo, 1954), vol. 1, 253.

14. Hans Delbruck, *History of the Art of War: The Barbarian Invasions* (Lincoln: University of Nebraska Press, 1990), vol. 2, 303.

15. Tacitus, *The Germania* (London: Penguin Books, 1970), 104.

16. Gabriel and Boose, 415; see also Walter Goffart, *Barbarians and Romans: The Techniques of Accomodation* (Princeton, N.J.: Princeton University Press, 1980), for a more comprehensive examination of German tribal society at this time.

17. Delbruck, 304; Tacitus, 106–8.

18. Tacitus, 105.

19. Delbruck, 305.

20. See Gabriel and Boose, "The Swiss Way of War," in *Great Battles of Antiquity*, 611–42.

21. Gabriel and Boose, 446–47.

22. Ibid.

23. Delbruck, 307.

24. Ibid., 314; see also Wilcox, 11–15.

25. Delbruck, 286–289; see also Tim Newark, *The Barbarians* (London: Blandford Press, 1985), chap. 2.

26. C.W.C. Oman, *The Art of War in the Middle Ages* (Ithaca, N.Y.: Cornell University Press, 1982), 5.

27. Ibid., 3.

15

The Army of Byzantium
476–1453 C.E.

Byzantine history is not for the squeamish. The imperial chronicles are a gruesome record of murders, blindings, mutilations, and paranoid conspiracies conducted by a line of ruthless emperors dedicated to the protection of the state, its official religion, and their own absolute power. Despite this (or, perhaps, because of it), the Eastern Roman Empire held the frontiers of civilization against the barbarian onslaught of Slavs, Turks, Germans, Goths, Franks, Normans, Persians, and Arabs for almost 1,000 years after the empire in the West had ceased to exist. Byzantium was the heir and protector of the Romano-Hellenistic culture that had been inundated and destroyed by waves of barbarian invasions and settlements in the West. Byzantium's libraries, churches, and universities preserved the ancient texts of Greece and Rome and kept the intellectual and material culture of its civilization alive until it was passed to the West by the Arab invasions, where it was "rediscovered" during the European Renaissance. Right to the end, Byzantines never thought of themselves as anything but the continuation of the Roman empire. Greek came to replace Latin as the language of administration, but the titles of the military units remained almost exclusively Latin. Byzantines thought of themselves as Roman citizens and their capital, Constantinople, as *Nova Roma*, the New Rome.[1]

The eastern part of the empire of Rome was wealthier than the west, containing the granary of Egypt, the manpower of Anatolia and Thrace, and the great cities of Antioch, Alexandria, and Athens from which it controlled the lucrative trade routes to Asia. The west, by contrast, was increasingly dominated by Germanic culture and tribes who settled within the imperial borders, transforming the old Graeco-Roman world into a cultural, economic, and technological backwater. Much that had been Rome—its intellectual life, its engineering, its social and political institutions—was gradually destroyed, replaced by tribal versions of these same institutions. The armies of the west became tribal and then feudal armies, little more than mobs of armed thugs devoid of tactics and strategy, led by heroic tribal chiefs whose main goals were personal glory and plunder. At the same time, Byzantine armies were sophisticated instruments of war capable of combined arms operations under the direction of generals who had developed a genuine science of warfare and applied it well. For almost 1,000 years the armies of Byzantium fought outnumbered, usually won, and succeeded in defending civilization against the tribal onslaughts of barbarian invaders. Byzantium kept the light of western civilization alive until it was extinguished by the Moslem victory over the great capital itself in 1453 C.E.[2] As the light went out, the embers of European culture in the West had been once more beginning to catch fire and Graeco-Roman civilization was beginning to be reborn.

The design of the Byzantine army as an identifiable military entity can be traced to the reforms of Justinian (527–565 C.E.). With the removal of the last Roman emperor in the West, Romulus Augustulus, by the German military commander, Odoacer, in 476 C.E., the last vestiges of the Roman imperium in the West came to an end. The empire lived on in the East, and the citizens of Constantinople still considered themselves Romans, spoke Latin for another two centuries as the official language, and thought of their city as the New Rome. The army that served the Byzantine state during the period from 476 to 565 C.E. was essentially the old army of Diocletian (284–305 C.E.)[3] and Constantine (306–337 C.E.),[4] with its emphasis on horse-born mobile forces and the widespread use of barbarian soldiers and war chiefs. In practice, however, the army had fallen into decay. Unable to recruit sufficient manpower of good quality, the old infantry units, the *limitani*, had been reduced to little more than armed farmers serving as militia. The shortage of manpower had reduced the strength of these units from legions to little more than cohorts. Even the famous *comitatensis*, the highly mobile cavalry field armies that had served as the enforcers of imperial authority, had declined as a consequence of the increasing use of barbarian tribal contingents (*foederati*) serving under their own chiefs. The loyalty of these units was always in doubt, and they remained a potential threat to imperial authority until 400 C.E. On 12 July of that year a local riot in Constantinople turned into a national policy of ridding the empire of German allies. Within a month, 35,000 barbarian troops were slain and the rest chased over the borders, thus ridding the Byzantine armies of its barbarian elements and forcing the authorities to recruit mostly Byzantine citizens for the armies.[5] Fired by the desire to reunite the old empire of Rome, Justinian reformed the army further into a credible instrument of military power.

The centerpiece of Justinian's new army was the *comitatus*, or personal army, an army in which the troops swore loyalty to those who recruited them rather than to the state. The army was paid by booty provided by commanders. These armies were throwbacks to the days of Rome before the imperium, when *condottiere* generals like Caesar and Pompey raised armies for profit and personal ambition, although it is more likely that the example that Justinian had in mind was drawn from Constantine. Constantine had accelerated the practice of enlisting barbarian warriors commanded by their own chiefs, whose loyalty was sworn to Constantine himself and supported by allotments of booty. Under Justinian, the most important elements of the new armies were the *bucellarii*, or personal armies of the Byzantine noblemen. The nobility swore an oath of loyalty to the emperor, as did the selected army commanders, while the troops swore an oath of loyalty to their commanders. The entire arrangement had a tribal ring to it, and had the army of Byzantium not undergone additional reforms later on, it is probable that the same military-civil feudal arrangement that eventually developed in Western Europe might well have developed in Byzantium as well. The army also had units of *numeri* or regular imperial troops paid and trained by the state. While there were some units of *numeri* that served as cavalry, most were spear-bearing heavy infantry collected into units of 200 to 400 men. Filling out the ranks were the *foederati*, bands of mercenary professionals of barbarian origins. Efforts were made to place Byzantine officers with these units, and their commanders were closely watched for political disloyalty. It is unlikely that the army numbered more than 60,000 to 70,000 men at full mobilization.[6]

The principle fighting arm of Justinian's new army was the heavy cavalry, a further development of the emphasis placed upon cavalry by Constantine. Most of the barbarian enemies along Byzantium's long frontiers were horseborne, requiring the development of cavalry forces to react quickly to frontier penetrations. These heavy cavalry or *cataphracti* were enclosed in mail armor and helmet, carried the bow and the lance, and were protected by a small shield. The light cavalry were horse-archers, who used a larger shield to protect their unarmored bodies. Infantry was heavily armored along the old legion lines and carried the spear. The heavy spear-bearing infantry was used as a platform of maneuver for the cavalry, which had become the arm of decision. It was with armies of this design that Belisarius and Narses restored Byzantine control to larger areas of former Roman territories in the West.[7]

The most important reorganization of the army of Byzantium began less than a century after Justinian when Emperor Maurice (582–602 C.E.) outlined a plan for a thoroughly modern imperial army. He put forth the plan in his famous *Strategikon*, one of the more important works of military theory and practice to emerge during this period. A number of the aphorisms contained within it have survived as common military lore to this day, the most famous of which is Maurice's dictum that "an army of deer commanded by a lion is better than an army of lions commanded by a deer."[8] By Maurice's time the barbarization of the army had grown to alarming proportions, and the reorganization of the army was driven by the realization that it relied far too heavily upon tribal and mercenary forces whose loyalty was suspect. Moreover, without conscription, the army cost far too much in hard cash and was pushing the empire to the brink of financial crisis. Finally, Byzantium was increasingly surrounded by hostile armies, especially by the tribal armies north of the Danube. The empire required a larger, cheaper, more loyal, and more combat-effective military instrument if it was to survive.

Maurice attempted to institute universal military training as a prelude to conscription to replace the old system in which the nobility paid taxes so that the state could hire mercenaries or men of the lower classes. The attempt failed as the nobility refused to serve in the military, although later it was the upper classes who provided much of the raw material for the Byzantine officer corps. Maurice set his reforms in motion, but was unable to follow through to the degree that the army became fit for anything except defensive purposes. It was his successor, Heraclius (610–641 C.E.), who completed Maurice's reforms and placed the recruitment base of the army on an entirely new footing that ensured the empire an adequate supply of military manpower for years to come.

The reforms begun by Maurice and completed by Heraclius and others created a military instrument whose structure, units, weaponry, and tactics remained essentially unchanged for the next 500 years.[9] The basic tactical and administrative unit for both infantry and cavalry was the *banda* (for cavalry) and the *numerus* (for infantry). These were units of 300 to 400 men and were the approximate functional equivalent of a

Figure 15.1
Byzantine Army Organization, 600–1071 C.E.

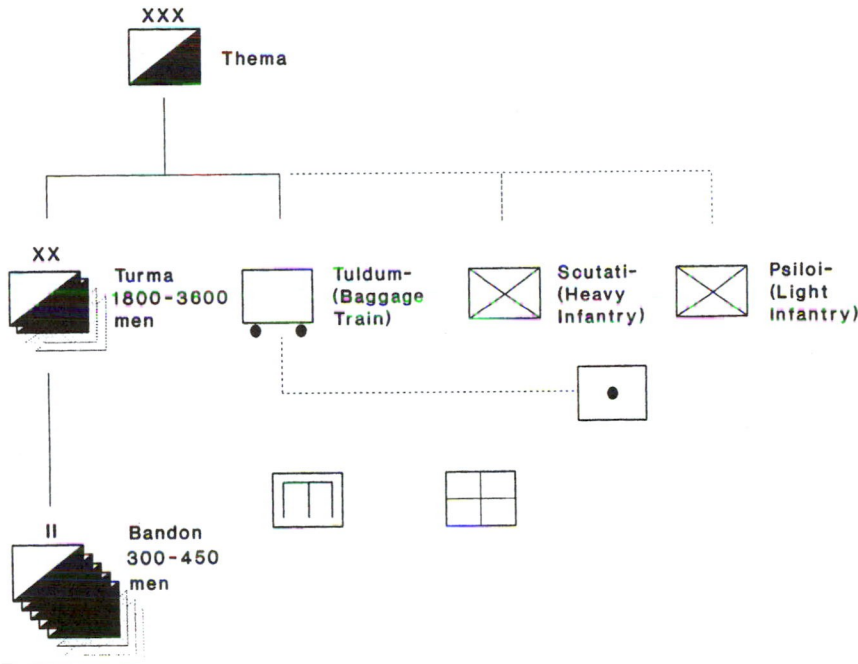

modern battalion. The *banda* was commanded by a tribune or, later, a *drungarios*, or colonel equivalent. Five to eight *banda* constituted a *turma* or division, which served under a *turmach* or duke. Two or three *turmae* made up a *thema* or corps under the command of a *strategos* or general officer. The Byzantines made a deliberate effort to keep units at nonstandard sizes so as to confuse enemy intelligence about the strength of the national army. The total army strength was between 120,000 and 140,000 men. Figure 15.1 portrays the organization of the army during this period.[10]

The most important element in the army, its arm of decision, was the heavy cavalry, the *kavallarios*, which deployed in ranks eight to ten men deep. Fully mailed, armored cavalrymen—the *cataphracti*—became as much a national symbol of the new Byzantine army as the old infantry legionnaires had been for Rome. The cavalryman wore a steel helmet and a long chain mail shirt that ran from his neck to his thighs. High leather boots covered steel shoes, and he wore mail greaves on his forearms and gauntlets on his hands. Often the cavalryman wore a cotton coat over his armor to protect from the heat and to diminish the gleam of the sun reflecting off the armor. The cavalryman's horse, especially those troopers who served in the front ranks, were equipped with steel armor as frontels and poitrals. The horseman carried a small round shield strapped to his forearm, which allowed both hands to be used freely for the bow.[11] While there were companies of lancers, most heavy cavalry carried the lance and the bow. The stirrup made the lancers formidable fighting men, as it increased the stability of the rider and now made possible the cavalry charge at full gallop. Similarly, the stirrup made it possible for the Byzantine to develop the technique—learned from the Sassanid Persians—of standing in the stirrup and firing the bow at the gallop.[12]

The lance or *kontarion* was the primary weapon of the heavy cataphract, but he also carried a broadsword (*spathiou*) and axe. Although not as heavily armored as the European knight, the Byzantine cavalryman was a more formidable fighting man. Because he was lighter, the cataphract was more mobile than the European knight and could fight more efficiently when dismounted. The Byzantine cavalryman also carried more firepower than the European knight, especially in his use of the bow. Byzantine cavalrymen were better trained in drill and maneuver than the European knight, and there was no European equivalent to their use of the bow from horseback. Finally, Byzantine cavalrymen were accustomed to fighting as units and possessed a wider range of tactical formations and maneuvers than did the European knight, who tended to train as an individual for individual combat. Here the legacy of Roman organization in the East can be seen in stark contrast to the barbarian methods of combat now predominant in the West. The Byzantines also had units of light cavalry. These cavalrymen wore mail capes instead of complete suits of armor. Their weapons were the lance, bow, and sword, and they used larger shields.[13]

Byzantine infantry came in heavy and light varieties, with heavy infantry being somewhat more numerous. These heavy infantrymen were called *scutati* after the large round shields they carried, derived originally from the Roman shield or *scutum*. Infantrymen were heavily armored and wore complete suits of chain, plate, or lamellar armor with helmets, gauntlets, and knee-high boots. Over this armor the infantryman often wore a cloth coat that was color-coded to mark his unit on the battlefield. He carried the spear, shield, and short sword for close combat. Some infantry carried a type of axe called the *tzikourion*, which had a standard blade head with a spike in the back of the blade, somewhat like a halberd. If the blade was turned around so that the soldier struck with the spike, there was no known armor that could not be easily pierced by this weapon. It was an excellent weapon for close combat against mounted knights or cataphracts. In the press, the axe was similarly well designed for cutting off the legs of cavalry horses. It may have been the axe and the need for more room to wield it effectively that prompted some infantry units to abandon the old round shield and adopt the kite-shaped shield from the Normans, whom the Byzantines fought in southern Italy. As was done at the battle of Hastings, the kite-shaped shield could be stuck in the ground in front of the soldier while he used both hands to wield his axe.

The light infantry soldier (*psiloi*) carried the bow as a basic weapon and was armed with the dagger and short sword for close combat. His bow was larger and more powerful than the one carried by the cavalry, and his quiver held a basic combat load of forty arrows. Some light infantry carried two or three javelins as well. Although the men of the light infantry wore helmets, they usually wore no armor beyond a padded leather coat. For protection they had a large round shield, which they secured to their belts by means of a strap, creating the effect of a kind of armored turtle.[14]

The Byzantine army paid its soldiers and officers well, and military service was a lucrative career.[15] Unable to enforce conscription, the Byzantine emperors taxed the wealthy for the money to attract and pay good soldiers. It was a small price to pay for having a national army whose loyalty was beyond doubt. While there were still some *foederati* and mercenary units, their numbers were small and never sufficient to constitute a threat. In any case, they were closely monitored by the Byzantine intelligence service. The staff structure of the army was sophisticated and patterned after the Roman model. It possessed the same usual complement of administrative, engineer, supply, and intelligence sections as the Roman staff. The Byzantines were expert planners, and the army had numerous supply depots around the country full of pre-positioned military stores. Byzantine armies had excellent intelligence services, perhaps the best signal service next to the Mongol armies, and organic artillery sections of catapults and *ballistae* to provide artillery support. The military medical service, modeled along Roman lines with some improvements, was the best in the world for its day, and was not surpassed in the West by any army until at least the American Civil War.

On the march the army practiced castrametation with the same skill and discipline as had the Roman legions, and with the same beneficial results. When advancing into hostile territory, the army was preceded by scouts and intelligence units to prevent surprise. Scouting units were expected to locate good campsites and water supplies, while combat engineer units improved the roads and built bridges to speed the army's advance. Under normal conditions cavalry units would lead the way, but in rugged terrain, infantry units led the army toward its objective. Following Caesar's dictum that a commander ought to be seen by his men in battle, Byzantine commanders routinely rode at the head of their troops.

The tactical doctrine of the Byzantine army was very sophisticated compared to other armies of the period, with the exception of the Mongol armies. As a combined arms force, the Byzantine army preferred to deploy and fight in that manner, stressing the interaction between cavalry and infantry. Nonetheless, the army could and often did fight only as a cavalry force, with little or no supporting infantry. The centerpiece of the Byzantine tactical doctrine was its emphasis on the offensive. When circumstances did not permit taking the offensive immediately, Byzantine commanders always prepared their battle plan so that they could go over to the attack as soon as practicable after meeting the enemy assault. Byzantine commanders seemed to have grasped the fact that to truly defeat an enemy, the fight must be carried to him, rather than permitting him to withdraw after he has exhausted his opportunity to attack. The Byzantines were experts at harassing an enemy army in retreat. One tactic, the "shadow war," used in the later days of the empire when manpower was short, permitted a numerically superior enemy to penetrate the country and conduct its raids. Later, when it was loaded down with loot, the Byzantines harassed the retreating army to the border, "dogging and pouncing" upon the enemy, destroying unit after unit until the enemy was defeated and forced to abandon its loot and flee.[16]

Byzantine tactics always envisioned a number of blows delivered in succession against the enemy to force him to react in a manner that the Byzantine commanders could anticipate. In modern terms, Byzantine field commanders were experts at "getting inside the enemy's decision cycle" so that they, not the enemy commander, could orchestrate the tempo of battle while forcing the enemy into a foreseeable situation where a decisive blow, often a double envelopment with heavy cavalry, could be accomplished. Byzantine tactics encompassed five major elements applied in concert. Figure 15.2 portrays a typical Byzantine tactical formation.[17]

Fundamental to Byzantine tactical deployment was a strong front line comprised of heavy infantry (*scutati*). Byzantine infantry never deployed on the field with only a single infantry line, however. The idea was that if a flank was turned or the end of the line overlapped by the enemy, a second line of infantry deployed closely behind the first could deal with

Figure 15.2
Standard Byzantine Battle Formation

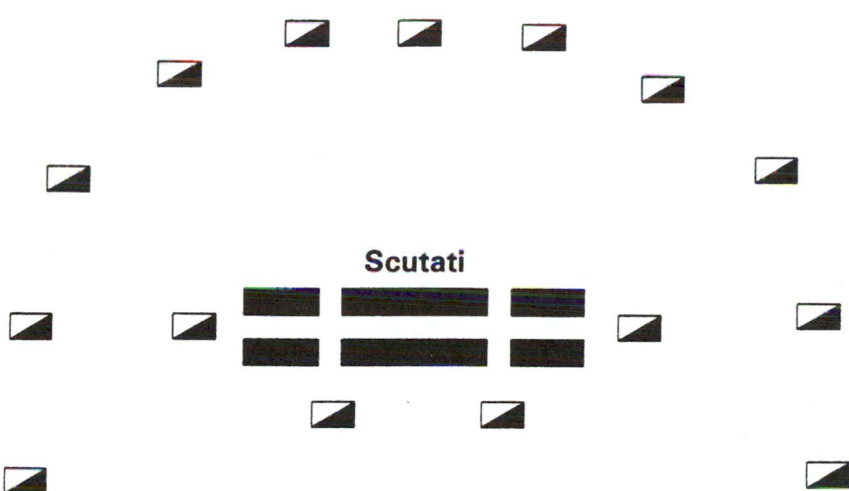

the problem while the first line continued to fight, thus preventing a wholesale collapse of the center. Accordingly, the Byzantines always deployed a second line of infantry close behind the first. Behind the infantry lines and well to the rear stood the rear security/tactical reserve element of the army, normally comprised of heavy cavalry units. This element's first task was to prevent surprise from the rear and to deal with any attempt by enemy cavalry to execute an envelopment of the infantry. This element was also the commander's reserve, and could be thrown into the battle at a propitious moment to contain a deep penetration or exploit a breakthrough by friendly forces. Byzantine commanders always attempted to have a reserve force on hand.[18]

A fourth element of the Byzantine tactical schema was the flank security/envelopment cavalry units. These were deployed close to the flanks of the infantry lines. Their task was to stop any attempt to flank or overlap the infantry line. In coordination with the infantry they played an even more important role in that if the infantry line moved into the attack, it was the flank cavalry units that moved forward with them and attempted to envelop the enemy infantry. If the center held against the enemy attack, the flank cavalry units could move forward and pinch the enemy flanks inward. If things went well, these enemy units could be driven by the cavalry "hammer" against the "anvil" of the heavy infantry and hammered to death.[19]

The fifth element, the distant screening/envelopment units of heavy cavalry, were deployed far forward or far out to the flanks. Their original mission was to harass and disrupt any enemy movements toward the battlefield or around the flanks. Often, sizeable elements of these units were concealed from the enemy until they could be brought into action with sudden surprise. If the enemy commander committed in force against the center, the envelopment/screening units could then be committed in force against the enemy's back. Under ideal conditions, a double envelopment could be achieved. The whole tactical schema depended for its success upon excellent discipline and training that permitted the various elements in the tactical plan to know precisely how and when to strike for maximum effect.[20]

Should things go badly, however, and the center infantry line be forced back, they could retire in old Roman fashion through the gaps in the rear line left there for precisely this purpose. The ability to shift lines confronted the enemy with the need to deal with the fresh troops of the second line at the point of greatest stress (*Schwerpunkt*). If the second line was hard-pressed and enemy penetrations occurred, the rear security/reserve was positioned to deal with the penetrations in piecemeal fashion. But such caution was not the Byzantine way. If a breakthrough of some size occurred, it was more usual for the cavalry reserve to commit in force and attempt a double envelopment of the enemy by riding around the flanks of the engaged infantry lines and taking the enemy in the rear or the flank. Enemy units that penetrated the infantry line could continue to advance to the rear, but were deprived of anyone to fight as the cavalry maneuvered to strike the main enemy force. In this manner the Byzantine commander could render the penetration tactically irrelevant by maneuvering into the attack and bringing the battle to the enemy by going over to the offensive. Such bold tactics clearly required excellent and audacious commanders—the Captains of Constantinople—for whom Byzantium became famous.

There could be any number of variations on this tactical plan, and flexibility was a major characteristic of Byzantine tactics. For example, Figure 15.3 shows the deployment of a Byzantine cavalry *turma* in a battle in which only cavalry elements are present.[21] One notes that the flexibility of the system was a consequence of excellent discipline and training. The figure shows a *turma* of 3,000 to 4,000 horse drawn up in nine *banda*. To the front are three *banda* of 450 cavalrymen each drawn up in lines from five to seven ranks deep. About 250 yards behind these advanced units are four half-bands positioned in the gaps behind the first three *banda*. Another band is deployed in double ranks to fill in the gaps between these bands. Held in reserve on each flank are two half-bands

Figure 15.3
Tactics of a Typical *Turma*

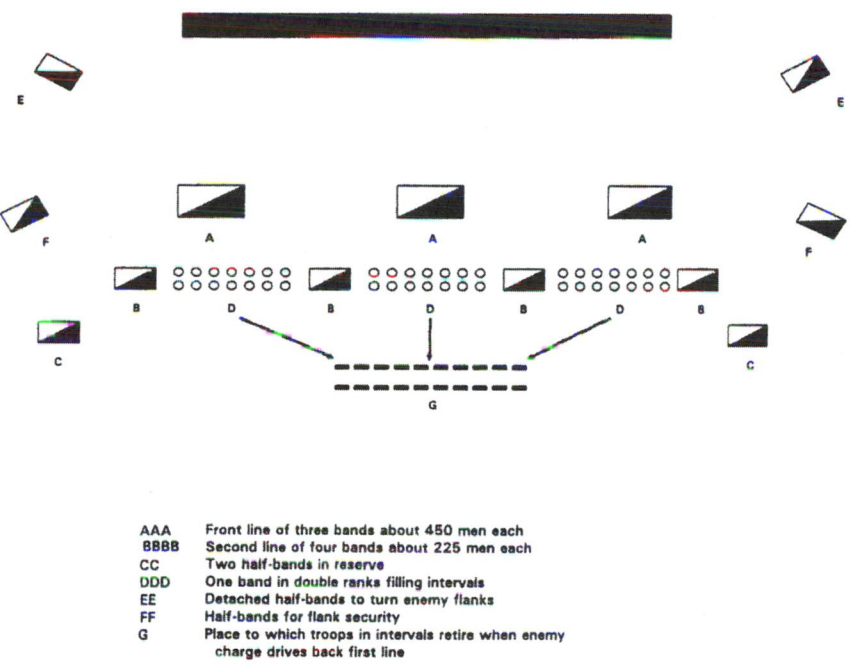

AAA	Front line of three bands about 450 men each
BBBB	Second line of four bands about 225 men each
CC	Two half-bands in reserve
DDD	One band in double ranks filling intervals
EE	Detached half-bands to turn enemy flanks
FF	Half-bands for flank security
G	Place to which troops in intervals retire when enemy charge drives back first line

whose mission is to plug any gaps and contain any penetrations in force. Further out beyond the flanks are two half-bands acting as flank security, while still further out are two additional half-bands acting as scouts. Sometimes the flank security units were concealed, to be used with surprise when an enemy attempted to turn a flank. As complex as this tactical system was, it maximized flexibility and provided the commander with a defense that preserved the tactical option of going rapidly over to the offensive when and if events permitted.

Byzantine tactical doctrine and practice were highly flexible, and in the hands of a competent and imaginative commander, any number of combinations of forces and schemes of employment were possible. The important thing to note, however, is the existence of a standard tactical doctrine that provided the general theme upon which variations might be played by talented commanders. Tactical doctrine emphasized coordinated action between the various combat arms, cavalry, and infantry, as well as with other types of units, artillery, archers, engineers, etc., in orchestrating the battle plan. The emphasis was placed upon the offensive and use of surprise mostly delivered by heavy cavalry. Tactical doctrine also stressed the employment of all fighting forces in a coordinated manner, and always made provision for the use of a reserve committed at the commander's discretion. The emphasis was always upon the attack and forcing the enemy to fight.

It is worth noting that the Byzantine army as portrayed in this analysis was designed in the seventh century and remained unchanged in its essentials for five centuries. It was designed and utilized at a time when infantry in Europe had fallen almost into uselessness as the emergence of the armored knight drove infantry from the field. The medieval armies of Europe at this time were largely cavalry armies, and the ability of these quasibarbarian armies to fight with combined arms was lost. In Byzantium, by contrast, the value and skill of disciplined infantry operating in concert with other arms, the legacy of the Roman way of war, had been refined to a high art and formed the spine of Byzantine tactics. Even under Justinian, spear-bearing, disciplined heavy infantry played an important role in support of cavalry. In Byzantium we find the infantry of old—as good as the infantry of the Roman legions—anchoring the battle line against cavalry attack and serving as a platform of maneuver for the heavy cavalry in the offense. Armed with spear and short sword and capable of fighting in open or closed formation, Byzantine infantry could operate effectively against both infantry and cavalry. Byzantine infantry also operated well in concert with artillery and archers. In close combat the infantry was a formidable force. They attacked at the run and, just before contact, threw their spears at the enemy and closed with swords and daggers. In many ways the Byzantine *scutati* infantry combined the best capabilities of the Roman legion with the old Greek infantry phalanx.

The Byzantine system depended upon discipline and training, which, in turn, depended upon an adequate supply of good-quality manpower that could be forged into good soldiers. The Persian wars (602–627 C.E.) lasted for a quarter century and were terribly costly in terms of men and money. Byzantium lost approximately 200,000 men, and much of the Anatolian peninsula was overrun and devastated. Byzantium faced a critical shortage of manpower, and Emperor Heraclius had to find a way to fill out an army that had been 120,000 strong during the previous century. As Byzantium gradually gained control of the devastated provinces of eastern Anatolia at the end of the Persian wars, it was the army that reestablished effective control in these areas, with generals becoming military governors. When the old provincial system collapsed, the emperor accepted the quasimilitary governmental system as fact and reorganized the empire's territory on a new basis, the *theme*.

The empire was divided into six *themes*, and later a seventh was added to provide manpower for the navy.[22] Each *theme* was a military and administrative district commanded by a *strategos* or general officer. His task was to raise an assigned number of troops, both infantry and cavalry, from within the *theme* that could be used to defend the district in time of war. Within the *theme* there were other military and administrative subdistricts commanded by lower-ranking officers. All officers were appointed by the emperor to assure their loyalty. By the ninth century the number of *themes* had increased to fifteen and still later grew to thirty. The governor-generals in charge of the *themes* were rotated to prevent them from becoming too politically entrenched. The most senior and loyal officers were assigned to the largest and most strategically important *themes*.

The number of troops that could be raised from each *theme* varied from 4,000 to 15,000 depending upon the size and wealth of the area. Each *theme* also maintained a militia home guard to keep order when the main force was away. Each force within a *theme* was designed to be a complete and balanced combat force of infantry and cavalry capable of quick mobilization, rapid movement, and self-defense. When the force was not sufficient to deal with the threat, forces from other *themes* were sent to the area as reenforcement. These forces were usually cavalry units that could move rapidly. Often, the infantry units were left behind or followed on later. The *theme* system provided the Byzantines with a stable supply of manpower over the long term. This, in turn, made it possible to reduce the number of mercenary and foreign contingents in the army to a small number.

The Achilles' heel of the Byzantine army was the demographic base that provided its manpower. Politically, the emperors preferred an army drawn from the homeland as both better motivated and more loyal than mercenaries or recruits drawn from the provinces of the empire. As long as control over the Anatolian peninsula remained secure and the army was not too large (120,000 or so), the armies of Byzantium remained effective, if comparably small, fighting instruments capable of meeting defense requirements. However, fully two-thirds of the entire military manpower supply of the empire was drawn from eastern areas of Anatolia. Should Byzantium ever lose control of this area, as it almost did during the Persian and Arab wars, its manpower base would be seriously weakened.

In 1071 C.E. disaster struck. Emperor Romanus IV lost his entire army of 60,000 men to the Seljuk Turks at the battle of Manzikert in Armenia. Along with the defeat of the army went the loss of the eastern Anatolian provinces, so that the most manpower-rich areas of the empire fell under the occupation of the Turks. This was the beginning of the end. Deprived of its manpower base, the Byzantine armies were forced to rely upon mercenaries and foreign nationals, with the inevitable decline in the size and quality of the army. In 1204 C.E. a Venetian-led Crusader army captured the city by storm, creating in its wake a Latin state that lasted until 1261 C.E. After nearly a millennium of independent existence, the empire of Byzantium had become little more than a Frankish feudal kingdom. During the period of Latin occupation the central imperial structure was fragmented into fiefdoms,[23] and the decentralized military organization characteristic of Western feudalism replaced the old imperial armies. Attempts to recreate the imperial armies after the Byzantine restoration of 1261 C.E. were unsuccessful. Insufficient manpower and finances made the reconstruction of the national armies impossible. The emperors had a difficult time raising even a force of 10,000 from the remaining *themes* they still controlled, and for the last two centuries of their existence the Byzantines never again played the role of a great power in the affairs of Europe or Asia. In 1453 C.E., Constantinople itself was overtaken by the Ottoman Turks, and the last light of the old Graeco-Roman world was extinguished in the East.

NOTES

1. Michael C. Markowitz, "The Thousand-Year Garrison State: The Evolution of the Byzantine Army, 476–1453," *Command* 7 (November–December 1990): 48.

2. Ibid., 48–49.

3. Albert A. Nofi, "The Fall of Rome," *Strategy and Tactics* 39 (July–August 1973): 14–15.

4. Karen C. Huber, "Triumphant Over All People," *Military History* (October 1991): 10–11.

5. Nofi, 20.

6. Hans Delbruck, *History of the Art of War: The Barbarian Invasions* (Lincoln: University of Nebraska Press, 1990), vol. 3, 339–50. See section entitled "Justinian's Military Organization."

7. John Halden, "The Byzantine World," in Kurt Raaflaub and Nathan Rosenstein, eds., *War and Society in the Ancient and Medieval Worlds* (Cambridge, Mass.: Harvard University Press, 1999), 244–47.

8. Markowitz, 57 for this and other aphorisms of Maurice. For other Byzantine treatises on military subjects see George T. Dennis, *Three Byzantine Military Treatises* (Washington, D.C.: Dunbarton Oakes, 1985).

9. C.W.C. Oman, *The Art of War in the Middle Ages* (Ithaca, N.Y.: Cornell University Press, 1953), 47.

10. Halden, 251–57.

11. Tamara Talbot Rice, *Everyday Life in Byzantium* (New York: Dorsett Press, 1967), 113–15.

12. Ibid., 107.

13. Ibid. See also Richard A. Gabriel and Donald Boose, Jr., *Great Battles of Antiquity* (Westport, Conn.: Greenwood Press, 1994), 659.

14. Rice, 107.

15. Warren Threadgold, *Byzantium and Its Army* (Palo Alto, Calif.: Stanford University Press, 1995), see chap. 4.

16. Gabriel and Boose, 662.

17. Ibid., 663.

18. Ibid.

19. Ibid.

20. Ibid., 664.

21. Oman, 52–53; see also Gabriel and Boose, 665.

22. Rice, 116–18.

23. The best work on this period of Byzantine military history is Mark C. Bartusis, *The Late Byzantine Army: Arms and Society, 1204–1453* (Philadelphia: University of Pennsylvania Press, 1992).

16

The Vikings: Raiders from the Open Sea
780–1070 C.E.

Within the Western military experience, perhaps no soldiers have been more maligned in official historical accounts of warfare than the Vikings. Historians of the early middle ages universally portrayed them as heartless, cruel, and inhuman, with no respect for the established conventions and civilities of war. And, these early historians quickly remind us, the Vikings were pagans, a fact that accounts in the minds of these historians for their frequent assaults on churches, monasteries, and clerical estates. In truth, however, it is unlikely that the Viking soldier showed any greater degree of inhumanity in war than any other European soldier of the time. The Franks were known for their brutality, which they amply demonstrated in their frequent massacres of the Jews as their armies passed through Jewish communities, while traveling down the Rhine on the way to the Holy Land to free Jerusalem from the infidels! Angles and Saxons too, those Germanic tribes that left Jutland and Frisia to settle in England and transformed Roman Britain into Germanic England, were harsh combatants. Safe from continental influence in their new island home, the Angles and Saxons retained their old pagan Germanic heroic traditions longer than most continental tribes, a propensity that their early conversion to Christianity did little to dilute.[1] In point of fact, the Viking style of war was no more brutal—and often far less total in its application—than that of any other army of the day. Much of the Viking's bad press was due to accounts written by church historians about a people who were not yet Christianized and who made a habit of plundering church property, not because it was church property but because it was often the richest prize to be had.

The Viking Age is usually reckoned as encompassing the period 780 C.E., the year of the first tentative small scale raids against the English coast, to 1070 C.E., when the last vestiges of Danish rule in England come to an end with the extension of the Norman conquest. The *Anglo Saxon Chronicle* records the first Viking raid on the English coast as occurring in 789 C.E.[2] It is, of course, not surprising that western accounts of Viking attacks focused on their raids against England. In fact, however, Scandinavian trading and military expeditions had been taking place along the German coast two centuries earlier. It was these Viking raids against the Carolingians that forced the major transformation of the Franks away from their traditional reliance on heavy infantry to a reliance upon heavy cavalry. Only heavy cavalry, it seems, could respond rapidly enough to the coastal raids of the Vikings.[3] So effective were Viking raids against France that Charlemagne's successors found it reasonable to offer the Vikings a province of their own along the French coast in return for their promise to stop the attacks. The norsemen promptly took them up on the offer, settled in the province now known as Normandy, and became culturally, linguistically, and militarily French, even to the adoption of the continental style of horseborne warfare. Two centuries later, these settled Vikings, now called Normans, crossed the English Channel under the command of their captain, William the Conqueror, defeated Harold at Hastings, and established the English monarchy that rules to this day. It was Vikings, too, that established the first monarchies in Russia at Kiev, and travelled down the great Russian rivers to Byzantium, where they formed the personal escort of the Emperor, the famous Varingian Guard. It was Danes who established the first professional army in England and established Ireland's most important ports and trading outposts. And it was the Vikings who discovered and settled Greenland and Iceland and who, it now seems likely, may have made landfall in the new world four centuries before Columbus.

We first hear of the Scandinavian peoples in official Roman accounts of the first century B.C.E., when the Romans encountered the Teutons and Cimbri, both Scandinavian peoples who had migrated earlier to northern Germany. Later Augustus Caesar sent a fleet beyond the Rhine mouth north around the coast of Jutland. As a result of this expedition, the Cimbri sent ambassadors to Rome. During Nero's reign (60 C.E.), another Roman fleet traveled to the Baltic, and soon Pliny the Elder was writing in his *Natural History* of a people of great size and fierce courage who lived on a large island in the Baltic, which he called Scandinavia. By 100 C.E. Tacitus was reporting in some detail on this same people. Then, for almost 400 years the historical record falls silent until 493 C.E., when Cassiodoris mentions them again. In his *Origin and Exploits of the Goths* he reports that the Goths were really refugees from Scandinavia who had left their native home centuries before.[4] Jordanes, writing in the sixth century, refers to one of the northern peoples as the Dani, probably the Danes, and another people thought now to be the Swedes.[5] A century later the Viking raids on England began, with the result that accounts of their raids and their society passed commonplace into the historical literature of the period.

The division of the Scandinavian peoples into three separate nations—the Danes, Norwegians, and Swedes—is an invention of medieval chroniclers and probably did not exist in the minds of the warriors of the Viking Age. If the Vikings distinguished themselves from their comrades at all it was mostly likely on the basis of the dialect differences between East and West Norse. Perhaps, too, they saw certain communities in this or that part of Scandinavia as being loyal to a certain powerful chieftain who might call himself king. But of whatever significance such differences may have been, they were overwhelmed by a stronger sense of being one people who shared language, religion, law, social organization, art, general culture and, perhaps most important, the same heroic martial tradition.[6] Certainly, there was no sense of nationhood in the medieval or modern sense of the term. The idea of a national identity different from the Norse folk identity came late to Scandinavia. To be sure the kingdoms established in Denmark at the beginning of the ninth century, in Sweden fifty years later, and Norway fifty years after that, were more cohesive than the petty military kingdoms they replaced. But there was nothing truly "national" about them. They were simply larger personal aggrandizements of territory, wealth, and power, and proved in most instances to be as unstable as the smaller ones they replaced. By 1070 C.E. when the Viking influence in England had finally run its course, there were still only the most embryonic notions of nationality in the kingdoms of Scandinavia, and practically nothing in the way of national institutions of any sort. When the medieval chroniclers speak of the "countries" of Denmark, Norway, and Sweden, then, and their kings, it must be remembered that it is only in a very narrow sense that these institutions bore any resemblance to nominally similar institutions extant in Western Europe during the same period.[7]

Viking society conformed to the old Indo-European pattern of a social division into three classes, the slave (*pir*), the freeman/peasant (*karl*), and their warrior rulers (*jarl*) that had appeared throughout Europe and the Middle East as a consequence of the Indo-European migrations two millennia before.[8] Slavery was essential to Viking society, for clearing and farming the harsh north land was difficult, especially so when the farmers left their land on a regular basis to "go a viking," that is, wandering, trading, fighting each other in clan disputes, or raiding the French and English coasts. It was the slaves who kept the farms going in their absence. Slaves were lucrative business commodities as well, and the Vikings soon controlled the northern slave trade. Sources of slaves included captives taken on raids against the English and Germans along with organized slave hunts in the Slavic areas of East Europe and Russia. Indeed, the very name "slave" is taken from a confusion of medieval Latin and the vulgate, in which the Latin word for "Slav" (*Sclavus*) was idiomatically identical to the Latin word for "slave," or *sclavus*.[9] The free peasant tilling the land was the backbone of Viking agricultural society, and it was the shortage of good land that stimulated the Viking farmers to set sail across the Atlantic in search of more of it. It was also the search for land that turned the Viking raiders against England and France into permanent settlers there, where they became farmers once more. Each agricultural clan community consisted of several score farms (*bygd*) in proximity to other communities. To protect their customary rights and settle disputes, the freemen met in a regular consultative assembly called the *Thyng*. Informally organized, this most typical of Scandinavian political institutions was confined to the locality in which its writ ran. There was no national equivalent of this consultative assembly. Its task was to maintain the customary law, debate the application of new laws, safeguard the rights of the free peasant, and control the constant clan and individual blood feuding by apportioning penalties and compensations.

The elite class of warriors also possessed large estates, and their importance in Scandinavia society (and German society) is signified by the very term for "lord," *Hlaf-ord*, which means "loaf-ward" or "he who controls the bread."[10] In an agricultural society like the Viking society, the position originally derived from agricultural wealth and only later was attributed to military leaders. The relationship of the elite class of Viking warriors to the rest of Scandinavian society was quite different from that found in northern Europe, where early on powerful lords were able to exercise their authority to form large, almost national, political units and use their military might to enforce a degree of social control to limit clan and individual violence.[11] This development came much later in Scandinavia, with the result that Viking society was fragmented into many local clans, chiefdoms, and individual warrior bands that did pretty much as they wished in the absence of some national authority to curtail them. Individual and clan violence came to be seen as the normal way of life for the Viking, so that unbridled violence became character- istic of Viking society until well into the eleventh century. In these cir- cumstances, military training, fighting, and violent death were commonplace and a boy learned early how to use his weapons. Having killed a man in honorable combat was an important mark of status, and some of the Norse sagas tell of warriors who killed their first man at the age of twelve! While most clans were based on blood ties, groups of itinerant warriors, bandits, and criminals often would band together in "artificial clans" based on common interest, loot, and ties of friendship. Many of the early Viking raiding parties were comprised of such artificial clans, often of men banished from certain sections of the land by blood clans for some violent offense. The warriors produced by these social circumstances were first-rate fighting men. As Gywn notes, "Take self- confidence and professional skill, add resources, cunning, no nonsense about fair play, a strong disregard for human life and suffering, especially the other man's, and you have a good soldier."[12] It was thus with good reason that the English *Book of Common Prayer* cries out, "From the fury of the Northmen, oh Lord, deliver us."

There were several reasons why the Vikings began raiding first Europe and then Ireland and England in the sixth century. These include signif- icant overpopulation throughout Scandinavia, a shortage of adequate farm land in the face of increased claimants, the desire to expand the areas for slave hunting and other trading, the heroic warrior tradition that had become even more socially prominent as a result of increased free- lance violence, and the inability of the great lords to ensure social peace. First and foremost, however, the early raiders were warrior adventurers who came to fight and loot. As one analyst has observed, "Loot is loot in any language, and Western Europe was full of it. Ireland, England, France were the Viking's Mexico, with learning, arts, wealth, and a civ- ilization superior to those of their northern *conquistadors*, and a similar inability to defend themselves from a numerically inferior but mobile and energetic foe."[13] But the desire for adventure was, by itself, insuf- ficient, for the lands that the Vikings sought to plunder were across the open sea. Before the Vikings could make good their plans they required the development of a new military technology to transport them to their objective, the sea-going Viking ship.

The reputation of the Vikings as great sailors of the open sea began only in the seventh century with their raids on Ireland and England. Before that Viking ships were little more than coastal *entrepots* or river-going craft. Despite Scandinavia's reputation for fierce weather, in fact most of the coastal areas are accessible by coastal boats almost year round. The west coast of Norway is laved by the Gulf Stream, and hundreds of off-shore islands shelter the inland waters around Denmark and Sweden, making them navigable almost year round. The result was that Scandinavians became excellent coastal sailors but had little experience on the open sea. All this changed when, during the sixth century, the long process of experiment in ship building that had begun in the Bronze Age finally produced a vessel capable of ocean voyages.

The Viking ship was a marvel of technology. The early ships used in the raids on England were fifty feet long, weighed twenty tons, and carried a crew of 32 to 35 raiders. Within fifty years, a captain of some rank could command a ship of 75 feet with a beam of 18 feet that ran a little over 6 feet from the bottom of the keel to the gunwale amidships. Her keel alone might run 57 feet and was fashioned from a single oak timber. Clinker built, she was constructed of sixteen strakes of different thicknesses joined by rivets. Below the waterline, the ship's planks were lashed with spruce root lashings and narrow strips of whale bristle while her seams were caulked with tarred animal hair or wool. This made the Viking ship very flexible indeed, so that she could pitch and roll in heavy ocean seas without risk of breaking apart. Her mast was thirty-five feet tall with a single square sail made of strips of heavy woolen cloth strengthened by a rope network and hoisted on a yard of thirty-seven feet. Steered by a side-rudder oar, the Viking ship was of exceedingly shallow draft, rarely exceeding three-and-one-half feet, which gave her the ability to put into shore along any harborless coast or to sail deep inland along shallow streams and rivers.[14] The height of her sail made it possible for the Vikings to approach land quite closely before the sail could be seen from land. This, and her shallow draft, made it possible for the Vikings to be upon their prey often with less than an hour's warning. Because it was equipped with oars, it has sometimes been believed that the Viking ship was powered primarily by oarpower in the fashion of the ships and galleys of antiquity. Archer Jones in his analysis of the Viking ship seems to hold this view.[15] In fact, the Viking ship of the seventh century was primarily an ocean-going *sailing* ship, with her oars used primarily for moving up narrow rivers or, more importantly, for pulling rapidly away from the shore to avoid pursuers. If becalmed, of course, the ship could move under oar power. But this would be effective only if she were moving along the coast and had only a short distance to travel.

The Viking military tradition was deeply rooted in individual heroic combat between heavy infantrymen. Not surprisingly, this tradition dominated the Viking way of war both at home and abroad. Interestingly, the Viking farmer/soldier was a good horseman and horses were in common use in Scandinavia, but the animal was not used for war. Horses might be used to transport the soldier to the battlefield (although even this was not common), but there never developed a tradition of fighting from horseback. When raiding, however, it was common for the Vikings to steal every horse they could find, mount up, and range far and wide over the English countryside in search of loot. If forced to battle, the Vikings dismounted and fought as heavy infantry. So strong was the tradition of infantry combat that it affected how battles were fought among the Vikings at sea. Naval battles were never fought in the open sea, but always in protected inlets or close to land. There were no naval tactics as such, and ramming and maneuver were unknown. Instead, Viking captains maneuvered their ships close to one another so their soldiers could board and fight it out infantry style on the bloody deck.

The early Viking raiders were not princes, kings, or *jarls*, but a middle ranking type of warrior called the *hersir*, an independent land owner or local chief. Assembled in the command of these captains were the usual collection of adventurers, criminals, and freebooters. It was only later, at the end of the tenth century, that the more powerful *jarls* and chieftains joined the raiding business in search of new land, settlement, and even national identity. The military organization of the Viking raiders was primitive and consisted largely of the traditional Norse warband under the command of a warrior chieftain. The soldiers themselves fought for glory or plunder and, later, for the pay or *Danegeld* of silver coins paid by the English as a fee for not raiding the coastal towns and farms. From time to time an English official would refuse to raise the money to pay off the Danes. To discourage this behavior the Vikings acquired the habit of slitting the nostrils of the recalcitrant official's nose. Unable to raise the money, the official "paid through the nose," thus giving rise to a popular expression in the English language. In general, Viking raiding parties seem to have been the ultimate expression in military free-booting and were usually relatively small, under a few hundred men.[16]

For the wars among themselves, however, the Vikings had a more formal military structure that paralleled their social structure. The clans were led by local chiefs, who formed their men into *sveiter* or detachments. These detachments were sometimes formed into a *fylking* or battalion under the command of a high chief and fought under a common battle standard.[17] The tactical array of the Viking band was quite limited and seems to have included only two identifiable tactical formations. The first of these was the *skjaldborg* or shield wall in which warriors arranged themselves in a circle or square close enough so that each man's shield overlapped that of the man next to him. As each man died, the formation contracted inward, allowing a fierce fight in the defense that could, if required, be to the death. In the offense, the shield wall could have several ranks deployed one behind the other making it, in effect, a phalanx. Armed with the sword and spear in the defense, the *skjaldborg* was a formidable tactical array against both infantry and mounted attack. At the Battle of Stamford Bridge, Harold Hadrada deployed in this manner, ordering his first rank to place the butts of their spears on the ground and aim the points at the horseman's body. The second rank held their spears straight out aimed at the horse's chest. Within the shield wall, the personal body guard of the commander could be used as a mobile reserve to be rushed to any point that threatened to give way.[18]

The second tactical formation used by the Vikings was the *svinfylka* or "Swine's Head" formation. Although the Norse believed that this formation had been given to them by their great war god, Odin, in fact it is more likely to have derived from the fourth- to fifth-century Roman legionary formation called the *porcinum capet* or "swine's head." In his *Germania*, Tacitus describes a similar formation used by the Germans called the "boar's head." The Viking version of the formation assembled the best warriors at the front of a wedged-shaped formation with the first rank formed of two men, the second three, the third four, etc. The wedge would crash at full run against the enemy line, throwing the full force of the ranks behind it to press through or deep into the enemy line, or through a shield wall.[19] Viking tactics were unsophisticated but often successful because of the courage and ferocity of the Viking warrior, who was always mindful that he was fighting for his reputation as well as for loot.

The standard Viking military kit included a conical iron helmet with a nose bridge similar to that worn by the Franks (see Figure 16.1). Some evidence suggests that in earlier times Viking warriors wore more complete and ornamental helmets, but these, like early Viking armor, may have been confined to use by chiefs, more a sign of rank or status than genuine protective combat equipment. The same seems to have pertained to armor. As long as the battles were confined to conflicts among the Scandinavians themselves and were mostly individual combats, Viking armor seems to have been used to a significant extent. But by the end

Figure 16.1
Viking Warrior in Battle Kit

of the eighth century, the old splinted-limb armor of the Viking chieftain appears to have fallen out of favor so that by the time of the raids against Europe, armor was used only sparingly.[20] It may have been that the need to conserve weight aboard ship and to move quickly once ashore led to the thinning down of body armor. When it was used, it was commonly the mail *byrnie*, identical to that used by Harold's troops at Hastings. This mail shirt was short-sleeved and ran to mid-thigh. Sometimes it was slit up the back for greater mobility in wielding weapons.[21] Traditional Viking armor included the *heimskringla*, a body shirt fashioned of thick reindeer hide that was said to be more effective than the mail *hauberk*.[22] There is no evidence of lamellar armor in Scandinavia, nor do we find fabric armor of hardened plates. Both these devices are of Middle Eastern origin, and although the Vikings had extensive contact with Byzantium, these armored styles do not appear to have found their way into wide use in Scandinavia.[23]

The Viking shield ("the round war-board") was round and about twenty-four inches in diameter. Made of wood, it often had a metal rim and boss and possessed an Argive-like grip, which rendered it easy to maneuver. Later Viking warriors are portrayed as carrying the kite-shaped shield shown on the Bayeau Tapestry in the hands of Harold's men at Hastings. Probably of Norman-French design, the kite-shield may have been used as a fashion since by all accounts the small round shield was easier to use with the sword and, in an interesting application, if slid up the arm, the shield freed the warrior's hands so he could wield the terrible Danish war axe. Unlike the war-axe of the Franks, the Danish axe was not meant to be thrown but to be wielded with both hands with such force that it could easily cleave a man, his armor, shield and helmet, in twain. Since the average Viking was likely to be taller and somewhat more physically robust than his opponents in, say, England or France, the heavy Danish axe with its six-foot handle wielded by these fierce warriors was a terrible weapon indeed.[24]

Other Viking weapons included the spear, bow, and sword. If surviving portrayals of Viking warriors can be believed, their spears seem to have been of Carolingian design, with their characteristic broad-leaf blades and wings projecting from where the socket joined the shaft. The design is that of a "boar-spear," where the wings act as a hilt to prevent the weapon from penetrating too far into the body. These wings could also be used as a hook to pull a mounted soldier from his mount.[25] The Viking bow was usually made of elm and was about five feet long, accommodating arrows of two to three feet in length, a length that suggests that the bow was drawn to the ear. Although not commonly thought of as such, Viking warriors were excellent archers, the bow being a favorite weapon of the hunt throughout Scandinavia. Still, it was used sparingly in battle, as would be expected of heavy infantry. Interestingly enough, the Viking bow is remarkably similar to the English longbow of later use, suggesting that the English may have learned a thing or two about archery from the Danes.[26]

The Viking warrior's main weapon was his sword. An object of reverence, swords bloodied in battle were often passed down from father to son, and in some of the Norse sagas swords were even given names. Smelting steel was unknown to the Vikings, but they did know that putting red-hot iron in a charcoal fire (often containing bones) would make it harder. This was due to the transfer of carbon to the iron, turning it into steel. Viking smiths made bars of this case-hardened iron which they cut into strips. These strips were twisted and hammered into the center of the sword blades. Thinner strips of steel were then bent and hammered along the edges of the center blade and hammered flat in a process known as pattern welding. The complete sword blade was then heated and quenched in some liquid to temper it and give it greater strength. Tempering was often done in mud or honey since water turned quickly to steam, drawing off the heat too quickly. Some of the Norse sagas speak of swords that were "quenched in blood," giving rise to the suspicion (unproven!) that some of these swords were tempered by driving them through the body of a slave! Similar notions were said to apply to the manufacture of the Damascene swords of the Islamic warrior. Once again, there is no evidence to support the belief.

A most peculiar Viking military institution was the *beserker* (literally, "bearskin"), a special breed of elite soldier renowned for being transformed by the fever of battle into a fearless killer without regard for his own life. Tales of these warriors stress that when in this battle-trance the *beserkers* possessed great strength and were impervious to pain and wounds. Similar soldiers were called *ulfhednar* (literally, "wolfskin"). Like the old Norse legends of the werewolf (literally, "wolfman"), these elite soldiers were said to become transformed into the animals themselves in some mystical manner, during which they took upon themselves the fighting qualities of the animal itself. *Beserker* and *ulfhednar* are commonly portrayed in the poems and sagas as usually forming into units of twelve men, where they served as special suicidal shock troops. One explanation for their behavior may be that the Vikings had discovered the secret of the *aminita muscaria* mushroom. One authority on this fungus notes that some Norse tribes used the mushroom in religious ceremonies. The mushrooms were fed to sacred reindeer and the animal's urine collected after it had time to metabolize the fungus. The animal's kidneys concentrated the mushrooms into a powerful natural amphetamine. When the reindeer's urine was drunk prior to battle it had the effect of a powerful amphetamine in that it sharpened the senses, quickened the reflexes, reduced susceptibility to pain and fatigue, and accelerated the soldier's mental processes. Whatever the explanation, the behavior of the Viking *berserker* was sufficiently remarkable that its description entered the English language so that when a person was said to be acting violently he was said to have gone berserk.[27]

NOTES

1. C.W.C. Oman, *The Art of War in the Middle Ages* (Ithaca, N.Y.: Cornell University Press, 1953), 22.

2. Mark Harrison, *Viking Warrior* (London: Osprey Publishing, 1993), 4.

3. Oman, 20–21.

4. Gwyn Jones, *The Vikings* (London: Oxford University Press, 1968), 22–23.

5. Harrison, 3.

6. Gwyn Jones, 69.

7. Ibid., 11.

8. Ibid., 67.

9. Ibid., 150.

10. Harrison, 30.

11. Oman, 20.

12. Gwyn Jones, 202.

13. Ibid., 200.

14. Ibid., 190.

15. Archer Jones, *The Art of War in the Western World* (Urbana: University of Illinois Press, 1987), 104.

16. Richard A. Gabriel and Donald W. Boose, Jr., *The Great Battles of Antiquity* (Westport, Conn.: Greenwood Press, 1994), 506.

17. Ibid.

18. Harrison, 13.

19. Ibid.

20. Archer Jones, 105; Harrison, 31.

21. Stephen B. Patrick, "The Dark Ages: A Military Systems Profile, 500 to 1200," *Strategy and Tactics* (March 1993), 7.

22. Harrison, 48.

23. Ibid.

24. Archer Jones, 105.

25. Patrick, 7; Harrison, 50.

26. Patrick, 7.

27. Gabriel and Boose, 507. I am indebted to Professor Lowell Roberts, formerly of St. Anselm College, for the information concerning the *aminita muscaria*.

17

The Arab Armies
600–850 C.E.

This chapter deals with Arab armies, that is, those military forces of Arabian origin that established the empire of Islam through military conquest before being subsumed into the larger Muslim convert population that brought about substantive changes in the original Arab armies. Somewhat arbitrarily, the original Arab armies can be said to have existed from 630 to approximately 842 C.E., the time when the Abbasid caliph, al-Mutasim introduced the "Mameluke Institution"— slave Turk soldiers who replaced the original Arab contingents in the armies of Islam. Until that time, the armies of Mohammed and his immediate successors were almost exclusively comprised of Arabs from Arabia, and between 633 and 656 C.E. these armies invaded and conquered large segments of the Byzantine and Sassanid empires. Over the next 100 years the Arabs fought three civil wars. The first war replaced the original successors of Mohammed with the Umayyad family, who ruled from Syria from 661–750 C.E. The Umayyads survived the second civil war (684–692 C.E.), but were driven from power during the third civil war (744–750 C.E.) and replaced by the Abbasid family, who ruled from Iraq and retained the caliphate, although in much altered form, until 1250 C.E.[1] The Arab invasions set in motion enormous changes and produced a new sociopolitical order that eventually included the whole of the Arabian peninsula, all the Sassanid lands, and the Syrian and Egyptian provinces of the Byzantine Empire.

The emergence of Islam in Arabia between 570 and 632 C.E., the dates of Mohammed's life, brought into being a new social, religious, and military force, which swept out of Arabia on the wings of religious fervor begun by the Prophet himself and collided immediately with the two great powers of the day, the Byzantine and Sassanid empires. The Byzantine Empire ran from East Europe, through the Anatolian peninsula, along the Palestinian landbridge, through Egypt on to Libya, to include Syria. The Sassanids controlled all of Iraq and Iran and large areas stretching eastward into central Asia. One of the more remarkable achievements in military history was the conquest of large areas of these empires by Arab armies that probably never exceeded 5,000 men at any time[2] in less than thirty years time. Both empires were fragile, weakened by long wars between them. From 540 to 629 C.E., the Byzantines and Sassanids fought continuous wars in Syria and Iraq. At one time the Sassanid armies washed their weapons in the Mediterranean, occupying Antioch, Alexandria, and Jerusalem only to be driven back by Emperor Heraclius in 623 C.E. The sapping effect of these wars on the empires' strength was enhanced by religious persecution within the imperial borders. The conflict between Manichaeism and Zoroastrianism, along with the struggles between heretical Christian sects, weakened Sassanid authority, as did the long and bloody persecution of the Monophysites in Egypt by the Christian emperors of Byzantium. Terrible bouts of plague and disease struck both empires on and off for half a century, further weakening imperial will. By the time of the Arab invasions, both empires were mere reflections of their former power and relatively easy pray to the wide-ranging *razzias* (raids) of the Arabs.

The Arab invasions were begun by the Prophet himself who, having come to think of himself as truly God's messenger, sent messages to the emperors of the Sassanids and Byzantines demanding that they accept him and his message. In the absence of an imperial reply, Mohammed began the holy wars near the end of his life by sending an army of 3,000 men to attack the Byzantine frontier near the Dead Sea.[3] This force was defeated at Muta. Undeterred, Mohammed sent another force against the border the next year and succeeded in occupying some small settlements of Christians and Jews near the northwest Arabian border. Legend suggests he was preparing for yet another attack against Byzantium when he died on 7 June 632 C.E.

In 634 C.E. the Arabs attacked the Byzantine border provinces again, this time with three columns moving through Palestine and destroying a Byzantine garrison enroute. At the same time another Arab army attacked Damascus. The Byzantine relief force was engaged and forced to withdraw. In the meantime all of Palestine was left defenseless to Arab raids. A year later Damascus fell to the Arabs. The next year the last remaining Byzantine force in Syria was defeated at the Yamuk River, forcing the Byzantine frontier back to the Amanus Mountains. Two years after Ya-muk, Jerusalem and Caesaria surrendered to the Arabs. Between 639 and 646 C.E. Arab armies proceeded to eradicate the last vestiges of Byz-antine rule in what had been Roman Mesopotamia, destroying the old unity of the Roman Mediterranean world forever.[4] To the east, a series of other Arab victories spelled the end of the Sassanid empire. The Sas-sanids were brought under attack in force in 634 C.E., and within three years Arab armies had pushed to the edge of Iraq. The Sassanids with-drew beyond the Zagros, leaving the door to Persia open. By 641 C.E. a fresh Arab advance across the Tigris was underway and within eight years all of Persia was under Arab rule. Arab armies now prepared to push further eastward across the Oxus, reaching ultimately to India. At this time, far to the West, Egypt and Alexandria became major Arab naval bases, extending the influence of Islam to the Mediterranean sea.[5] In 661 C.E. with the coming of Umayyads, the Arab assault turned west once again, occupying Tunisia and the coast of Morocco. At the end of the century, Arab armies crossed into Spain. In less than forty years Arab armies had grown from little more than tribal coalitions to masters of an empire.

The dream of empire had been conceived in the mind of a single man, Mohammed the Prophet, who set in motion the means and motive for the extensive Arab conquest. At the time of Mohammed's birth, Arabia was a harsh land, home to a tangled coterie of rival clans and tribes. Most were desert wanderers based around tribal control of critical oases. Other tribes lived in small towns. Arab society lived by trading and raiding, a patriarchal society bound together by ties of kinship and the sworn duties of the blood feud. The Arabs of Mohammed's day were pagans intermixed with small communities of Jews and heretical Chris-tians. Arab society was almost totally illiterate. Mohammed was born into this society sometime near 570 C.E. in the town of Mecca of the tribe of Quaraysh.[6] The Quaraysh tribe were traders, but drew much of their income from their protection and control of the *Ka'ba*, an ancient black stone worshipped as sacred by the Arabs. Arab pilgrims made annual visits (*hajj*) to worship at the stone, for which the Quaraysh charged fees. It is one of the more interesting aspects of religious history that Mohammed, the strict monotheist, retained the duty of pilgrimage to Mecca to worship at the old pagan shrine of *Ka'ba* as a central tenet of his new religion of Islam.[7]

Mohammed married the widow of a successful caravan trader and soon was running the family business. At the same time his devotion to his own religious visions grew more intense and he came to believe that he was the messenger of God. Religious and economic conflict with his own tribe in Mecca forced Mohammed to flee to Medina where, after a short time, he gained converts and was made leader of the tribes there. Mohammed and his followers attacked the caravans of Mecca. This led to war, in which Mohammed gained victory in a number of battles. These victories brought his old relatives, the Quaraysh tribe, and other tribal leaders under his rule. This coalition became converts and served as the nucleus of the armies that spread the new religion of Islam. Mohammed's fusion of religious fervor with the traditional Arab practice of raiding and tribal warfare provided the important stimulus that motivated the early Arab armies to conquest. A central tenet of Mohammed's new religion was the belief that those who embrace Islam have a sacred right to war upon those who are unbelievers, to conquer and rule them in the name of the true God. The purpose of holy war is not to convert the conquered to Islam, for the faith prohibits forced conversions. It is, instead, the idea of a *jihad*, a holy war to destroy the infidel, war in which God is always on the side of the army of believers.[8] Mohammed himself is said to have proclaimed the doctrine of holy war on his last visit to Mecca. Tradition has it that his last statement to the faithful was that "Muslims should fight all men until they say, "There is no God but Allah."[9]

The structure of the Arab army reflected the structure of Arab tribal society. Arab society during Mohammed's day and for more than a century afterward never really developed a stable political order that was worthy of the designation "state." There was no state *per se* and therefore no stable administrative structure of government. Arab society remained what it had always been, a tribal society characterized by personal leadership and appointed retainers, which drew no distinction between society, religion, and the army. Indeed, there was never a formal army as such. Instead, there was an alliance of powerful tribal chiefs who led their personal armed retinues in battle. What treasury there was came from gifts and booty obtained in raids. There was no financial system. Government was essentially an enlarged tribal system of negotiated consensus among powerful tribal chieftains, and it was these warrior chiefs who controlled the Arab populace and the army. Government, if it may be called that, was a system of indirect rule through tribal intermediaries. This system of indirect rule plagued the Muslim empire until its end. Power ebbed and flowed from the center of authority, but no caliph was ever able to retain control of the tribal and regional armies for very long.

Revolts and insurrections rooted in jealousy, political interests, religious apostasy, and traditional blood feuds went on for centuries.[10]

Some authorities have argued that the invasion of the Byzantine and Sassanid empires by the Arab tribes was comparable with the invasion of the Western Roman Empire by the German tribes, with the same general result, the establishment over the long term of a number of separate states ruled by powerful national kings.[11] It seems more correct to say, however, that the Arab invasions were different. Unlike the tribal invasions of the Western Roman Empire, the Arab invasions were co-ordinated from a single center, Medina, for a specific religious purpose, to extend the rule of God's believers over the unbelievers as commanded by God himself. This central leadership, direction, and religious purpose led to a result quite different from that of the Germanic invasions in the West. Instead of conquering, settling, and then ruling the new lands, the Arab conquerors stayed together as soldiers, living in garrison cities (*amsar*), military districts (*ajnad*), and even military monasteries (*ribat*), whose members remained celibate.[12] The Arab conquerors remained apart from the societies they conquered and showed little interest in governing the new lands, leaving the old systems, leaders, kings, and governmental officials in place to continue to administer the conquered lands. The military garrisons remained just that, fortresses that accommodated the Arab armies, which could be sent forth on further conquest or used to suppress revolts. This arrangement was possible because the Arab armies, although receiving religious direction from the center, were not really structured armies at all. They were tribal coalitions led by local chieftains, comprised of emigrants from Arabia who left their homes to serve as soldiers in a holy crusade. In Islam, all believers were soldiers. There was no Muslim army distinct from Muslim society. The Muslims were a holy army and society, so that living apart from the conquered infidels with their families at government expense until called to further holy war worked well.[13]

The Arabian population that gave rise to the early Arab armies was small and scattered, but routinely carried arms. The tribal leaders lived in houses in towns that were arsenals where the arms of the clan were stored. Tribal conflict over trade routes, personal rivalries, and blood feuds was endemic, and Arab tribes had a long history of fighting. In addition, the early wars between Medina and Mecca during Mohammed's time and the later civil war over his succession provided Arab soldiers and commanders with considerable combat experience. Some commanders and soldiers had gained additional experience serving in the armies of Byzantium and Persia.[14] These early Arab armies were equipped with locally made weapons, including swords, lances, shields, and felt armor. Armor seems to have been common although helmets were not. The sword and spear dominated the battlefield.[15] The horse was in short supply in Arabia, with the consequence that Arab armies did not develop cavalry until much later, when adequate supplies of cavalry mounts could be obtained by conquest. What few horses were found in these early Arab armies were so valuable that they were led to the battlefield and only mounted for combat itself. Armed with lances, Arab cavalrymen were too few to play an important tactical role. Usually the cavalry would hover on the flanks of the infantry waiting to exploit any flight or loss of cohesion of the enemy, at which time it would attack. The tactical role of cavalry as a weapon of shock used against infantry was unknown.

Under these circumstances it is not surprising that early Arab armies fought mostly as infantry, a tradition that persisted long after they had developed large corps of heavy cavalry. As Delbruck notes, tribal warfare lent itself to individual combats rather than battle by units, and he suggests that these early armies fought in precisely this manner.[16] Evidence suggests, however, that one of the reasons why Mohammed was so successful in the tribal wars against Medina may have been because he taught his soldiers to fight in disciplined formations of infantry. Such formations were, of course, common in the army of Byzantium, but were contrary to the general Arab method of fighting.[17] Thus it might be surmised that Mohammed or one of his officers who may have had experience in the imperial army may have adopted the infantry formation and introduced it to the Arab armies. The Arab armies that attacked Byzantium and Persia may have been infantry armies, but they did not move on foot. Instead, they made extensive use of the camel in transporting their armies to the strategic objective.[18] This provided them with superior strategic mobility, enabling them to bypass enemy strongpoints and offer battle at times and places of their choosing. The guiding tactical concept was to move quickly to a favorable position, establish the infantry on the ground, and then force the enemy to attack at its disadvantage. Once the horse became widely available, Arab armies continued their practice of using mounted infantry in a strategic manner. Eventually, the Arab armies produced the best war horse of the day, the Syrian-Arab crossbreed, which combined the small strong North African Barb with the heavier Iranian mount.[19]

As noted earlier, once established in their new lands, the Arabs attempted to remain an ethnically homogeneous, warlike, and religious society apart from the conquered infidels. But their numbers were very small. Crone suggests that the total size of the Arab armies that left Arabia could hardly have exceeded 5,000 men, whereas the population of the conquered lands probably exceeded 20 million souls![20] All Arab emigrants lived in garrison cities or military districts and were registered in the *diwan* or "register." The registered soldier was entitled to monthly rations for himself and his family, and received an annual cash stipend as did his wife and children. Quarters were also provided for the soldier and his family. In return these religious warriors were available for military service at a moment's notice. As the Arab occupation stabilized, military calls to active service became relatively infrequent. When called to service, the soldier had to supply his own mount—horse or camel— and military equipment, which included a lance, sword, shield, bow, quiver, and armor, usually some form of mail.

Once registered on the *diwan*, the soldier remained on the role for life. There was no word for veteran soldier and no special provisions were made for them. Soldiers too old for service probably provided substitutes or worked for the army administration. Disabled soldiers were registered as cripples and continued to draw some portion of their annual pay and allowance.[21] Arab soldiers were usually forbidden to engage in agriculture, although in rare instances it was permitted. Such limitations on "fraternization" and economic activity worked against the creation of an Arab "society" in the conquered lands, a task left to the conquered infidels who converted to Islam. In some respects the *diwan* may have been adopted from the military role of the Byzantines, but with a very important difference: the *diwan* was not seen by the Arabs as an institution for the maintenance of the army, but as a social institution for the maintenance of Muslims. Stipends were not mere military pay, but a right claimed by every Muslim emigrant and his descendants as a reward for participation in the conquest of Islam over the infidels. Islam was religion, society, and army all in one, and the *diwan* was the mechanism for sustaining all three.

The attempt to sustain a separate Arab identity apart from the infidels was bound to fail in the long run on the grounds of numbers and conversions. Even as military manpower demands increased, the Arabs made no effort to recruit the able-bodied men of the conquered lands into their armies. Captives were often resettled on conquered lands, and some even served as special units (often private guards) or urban police. Gradually, native peoples were permitted to lend military service, usually ethnic or racial units serving as separate battalions. But once these captives converted to Islam they could no longer be enslaved, and more and more converts came to serve in the Muslim armies even as the purely Arab elements remained isolated in their garrisons. Over time the Arab elements of the Muslim armies came to see the military *diwan* as a social stipend, and the Arab elements gradually became a smaller and less used segment of the armies as the Arabs were gradually submerged into the Muslim armies of disparate peoples who had converted to the new faith.[22]

With gradual assimilation and wide-spread conversion, the old citizen armies eventually gave way to professional armies manned largely by non-Arab Muslims, although their commanders remained Arabs for many years. The regional armies of the old tribal chiefs survived for centuries, but for the most part were confined to their garrisons, supported by the *diwan*, and were of little use. As the Arabs were submerged in a sea of Muslims, the old tribal consensual style of government became more difficult to operate and proved insufficient to constrain tribal and personal ambitions. The result was two civil wars. The second war (684–692 C.E.) forced the Umayyads to abandon the old ideal of consensual rule completely, and they ruled by force supported by their professional army, comprised mostly of Syrian troops. Even so, it was not until the last Umayyad caliph (750 C.E.) that the armies became professionalized, and during the Umayyad period the old Arab armies changed considerably.

Under the Umayyads heavy cavalry became increasingly important. Originally, Arab cavalry was divided into armored and unarmored horse, or heavy and light cavalry. The heavy cavalry still comprised only a small number of units and was used mostly as shock troops along Byzantine lines. Light cavalry, when not used as skirmishers and reconnaissance, was used only to complete the destruction of already disorganized or broken units. Surviving records of the period describe the full equipment of the seventh century Arab cavalryman as lance, sword, shield, hauberk, packing needles, five small needles, linen thread, awl, scissors, horses' nose bag, and feed basket.[23] During the Umayyad period the bulk of Arab cavalry became armored in a transition toward the Byzantine model in mounts, armor, and weapons. Unlike the Byzantines, the Arab armies retained their old infantry traditions. Byzantine cavalryman, for example, were trained for use as shock troops fighting from horseback only. Arab heavy cavalry was trained in the old tradition of fighting first from horseback (or camel back) and then being able to dismount and fight on foot. Heavy cavalry never became a true arm of decision in Arab armies until much later, and heavy infantry remained the central combat arm. The cavalry would deploy safely behind the infantry formations and sally forth again and again as opportunity permitted, to attack the enemy and then retreat quickly behind its own infantry for protection. The idea of cavalry against cavalry in open combat was unknown to Arab commanders. When the Arab armies encountered the Central Asian horse archer on the rim of the empire, they were unable to find a tactical solution to this novel way of fighting. The Arabs did what the Byzantines and Persians had done before them; they hired whole contingents of horse archers and used them against their countrymen. The new cavalry threat forced a change in Arab cavalry equipment, most notably in the adoption of light felt armor for man and horse to protect against arrows, and the introduction of the iron stirrup over the objections of Arab scholars who claimed the device would make soldiers effete by hindering their ability to dismount rapidly in battle.[24] But even with the introduction of the horse archer, infantry remained the queen of the battlefield in Arab tactical thinking.

The Umayyad period was brought to an end by yet another civil war, and the Abbasids were brought to the throne by rebel armies raised in Iran. These troops replaced the Syrian troops of the Umayyads in imperial garrisons, and the capital was moved to Baghdad. These Iranian troops or *Khurasiani* were mostly horse archers, and this type of cavalry now became dominant in Arab armies. Although cavalry was now the arm of decision, infantry still played an important role on the battlefield and close infantry and cavalry cooperation remained central to the new Arab tactical design. These new troops wore clothes similar to the eastern Christian monks and wore beards and long hair. Great reliance was placed upon the bow and lance. The attack was marked by a shower of arrows as the cavalry closed with the enemy at the gallop, firing as it went. Once in contact, the lance came into play along with other weapons of close combat like the curved sword, mace, battle axe, and short sword of single edge design.[25]

The Abbasids made no effort to broaden the base of their army or government, relying instead on those groups and tribes of mostly eastern origin that had brought them to power. The Arab armies were now mostly cavalry armies, and since horses were expensive and training took a long time, it was more efficient for the Abbasids to rely on the natural horsemen of the *Khurasiani* rather than to outfit and train the Arabs themselves. The heavy reliance upon foreign troops and the failure to extend governmental participation to the powerful regional chiefs resulted in the imperial army being run more like a mafia than a military institution. The caliphs and the army became increasingly isolated from the society, with the consequence that the Abbasids were forced to deal with frequent revolts.

During one of the civil wars that threatened to topple the Abbasids, one of the participants, al-Mutasim (833–842 C.E.), had outfitted his army with 4,000 Turkish troops whom he had purchased as slaves and then freed for military service under his command. Once al-Mutasim had become caliph, he expanded the practice of purchasing and training Turkish slaves for service in his armies, thereby bringing into existence what Muslims came to call "the Mameluke Institution."[26] The essence of this institution was the systematic reliance of the caliphate upon soldiers of servile and non-Islamic origin. The use of other foreign, non-Muslim, ethnic units in the army also increased greatly. The result was that the areas of the empire under direct imperial control were policed by these slave Turks. Over time, most of the major military commands and some important governorships were assigned to Turkish officials as well. Eventually, the Mamelukes executed a military coup against the Abbasids and took control of the caliphate. For the next two centuries the Abbasid caliphs continued to rule from Baghdad but mostly in name only, while genuine power was exercised by the Turkish military commanders, who continued to pay lip-service to the rule of the caliphs. In reaction to this state of affairs, the governors of various provinces, using their regional armies as leverage, broke into open revolt time and again, with one province after another seceding from the old empire by force of arms. By the middle of the ninth century, the old Arab empire had ceased to exist, and with it the Arab "army of God," which had swept over the ancient Mediterranean world wielding the sword of Allah, also disappeared.

NOTES

1. Patricia Cone, "The Early Islamic World," in Kurt Raaflaub and Nathan Rosenstein, eds., *War and Society in the Ancient and Medieval Worlds* (Cambridge, Mass.: Harvard University Press, 1999), 309.

2. Hans Delbruck, *History of the Art of Warfare: Medieval Warfare* (Lincoln: University of Nebraska Press, 1982), vol. 3, 205.

3. *The Shorter Cambridge Medieval History* (Cambridge: Cambridge University Press, 1952), vol. 1, 229. It is highly unlikely that the size of this army was as large as the source suggests.

4. Ibid., 231.

5. Ibid., 232.

6. Albert Hourani, *A History of the Arab Peoples* (New York: Warner Books, 1991), 15.

7. *Islam* means "surrender"; thus *Muslims*, "those who are surrendered."

8. Hourani, 18.

9. Ibid., 19.

10. Cone, 313.

11. See Delbruck, 203 and *Shorter Cambridge Medieval History*, 225.

12. Cone, 311.

13. Ibid.

14. Hourani, 13.

15. David Nicole and Angus McBride, *The Armies of Islam* (London: Osprey Publishing, 1982), 9.

16. Delbruck, 209.

17. Nicole and McBride, 10.

18. Hourani, 14.

19. Nicole and McBride, 11.

20. Cone, 314.

21. Ibid., 313.

22. Ibid., 314.

23. Nicole and McBride, 11–12.

24. Ibid.

25. Ibid., 14.

26. Cone, 319.

_____

The Japanese Way of War
200–1300 C.E.

While Chinese empires rose and fell on the continent of Asia, a distinctive culture and military tradition arose in the Japanese islands a hundred miles away across the Tsushima Strait. The Japanese islands were close enough to the Asian mainland to be influenced by Chinese and Korean culture, but sufficiently distant over treacherous waters to make the journey difficult and to discourage outright invasion and occupation by Chinese or Korean (and later Mongol) armies. The Japanese themselves may have no greater natural inclination toward mayhem than another group of human beings, but there is within Japanese culture, history, and tradition a very strong element of warrior imagery.

The origin myth of the Japanese, *Nihongi*, first written down in the eighth century C.E. although many hundreds of years older, relates the tale of two deities, Izanagi-no-Mikoto and Izanami-no-Mikoto, who dipped a jeweled spear into the ocean. When the spear was removed, tiny droplets fell from the tip of the spear and coalesced into the first of the Japanese islands.[1] *Jimmu*, the "Divine Warrior," the legendary first emperor of Japan, attained the throne only after a long campaign against human and demonic foes. Other mythic heroes were portrayed as lonely warriors who fought with guile, courage, and skill at arms against great odds, ultimately to be physically, but not morally defeated, often ending their lives through ritual suicide.[2] Weapons were the symbols of political authority in Japan from earliest times, and the sword remains one of the three elements of the imperial regalia.[3] Warrior governments ruled Japan from the twelfth through the nineteenth centuries and, until the defeat of the Japanese Empire by the Allied coalition in 1945, the Japanese took great pride in their military prowess and warrior heritage, symbolized by the nimble, lightly armored, sword-wielding mounted bowman: the *bushi*, or, as he is better known in the West, the *samurai*.[4]

The thirteenth-century *samurai* was the inheritor of centuries of Japanese military development, beginning in the prehistoric era when tribal hunters and warriors traveled on foot, fighting with bows, short swords, and javelins. The earliest historical reference to Japan appears in the *Annals* of the Chinese Han Empire (206 B.C.E.–8 C.E.), wherein it is recorded that a number of little lineage-based states (*kuni*) of the Land of Wa (Japan) sent tribute missions to China. Archaeological evidence and Chinese accounts of later centuries describe a warlike, Iron Age culture based on rice cultivation. The warriors of the *kuni* fought with iron and bronze weapons against other *kuni* and other less advanced peoples, the *emishi* or "toad barbarians," on their frontiers. The Chinese records report that the men of Wa fought with halberds, shields, and wooden bows shorter below than above the handgrip. Their arrows were made of bamboo with iron and bone tips.[5] *Kuni* leaders who, in at least some cases, were women, combined political and religious power in their persons. The tombs of these leaders are highly decorated with military images and carvings. By the middle of the fourth century C.E., one *kuni* lineage claiming descent from the sun goddess consolidated its control through military conquest and established a confederation of tribal states in the Yamato region. The leader of the ruling lineage took the title *tenno*, or emperor or, literally, "heavenly sovereign." The ruling house became the imperial family. Its ancestral deity, the sun goddess, became the chief deity of the Yamato state and the emperor became the chief priest of the native Japanese religion of *Shinto*.

The introduction of Buddhism in the sixth century C.E. from China was part of a centuries-long cultural interaction between the Yamato state and the Asian mainland. In addition to Buddhism, Japan received other religious and cultural ideas from the mainland including the Chinese system of writing, its administrative methods and institutions, and Chinese military techniques including the use of the horse as an instrument of war. Perhaps the most important contribution of the Asian mainland to Japan was the establishment in the seventh century of a new government order based closely on the Chinese model. The powerful Chinese

Tang Dynasty of that time provided both a model and an incentive for the Japanese court to tighten its central administrative control and strengthen its military forces. This new system is known to historians as the *ritsuryo* state after the legal and administrative codes on which it was based. The Japanese adapted the Chinese model to their own culture.

A key element of the new system was the establishment for the first time of an imperial army. Previously, the Yamato army had been a collection of local forces belonging to local strongmen and noble houses. But in the later years of the seventh century, the Emperor Temmu, literally, "Heavenly Warrior," implemented a system whereby those same soldiers and leaders were brought more directly under imperial control. Tummu himself had come to power through a violent civil war and understood the danger of condoning the existence of military capabilities not under imperial control. He directed that all weapons of war be confiscated and stockpiled at district armories. A system of militia regiments was established throughout Japan. Two sets of frontier garrisons were established in the areas of greatest danger.

The provincial militia regiments (*gundan*) were administrative organizations responsible for conscription, training, and supervision of *heishi*, or peasant soldiers who could be called at least once a year to perform guard duty in the home province, in the capital, or with a frontier garrison.[6] These soldiers were also subject to mobilization in the event of insurrection or invasion. Each soldier was required to provide his own weapons, usually bow, arrows, and sword, his own clothing, and his own equipment such as cooking pots, flints, tinder, and tools. Some of these items were often taken for use by the larger unit to which he belonged. The *gundan* were composed of five to ten 100-man training battalions or *ryo* which, like the *gundan*, appear to have been administrative, not tactical, units. Each *ryo* included two fifty-man companies or *tai*. The *tai* were also the basic tactical combat units, and could be either infantry (*hotai*) or cavalry (*kitai*). Each *tai* was divided administratively into five ten-man *ka* or "campfires," the group of men who shared one tent and campfire, and tactically into ten *go* or squads, each of five *heishi* soldiers who fought as a team around a single shield. When an expeditionary army was mobilized, it consisted of a number of armies or *gun* divided into *jin* or combat battalions. Each combat battalion included a number of tactical companies organized for battle into two lines each of five five-man squads. Each *tai* included at least one crew-served weapon called an *oyumi*, a large crossbow or ballista. Each five-man *ka* carried a large wooden shield into battle. When deployed, the five-man squad braced

Figure 18.1
Ritsuryō **Military Organization**

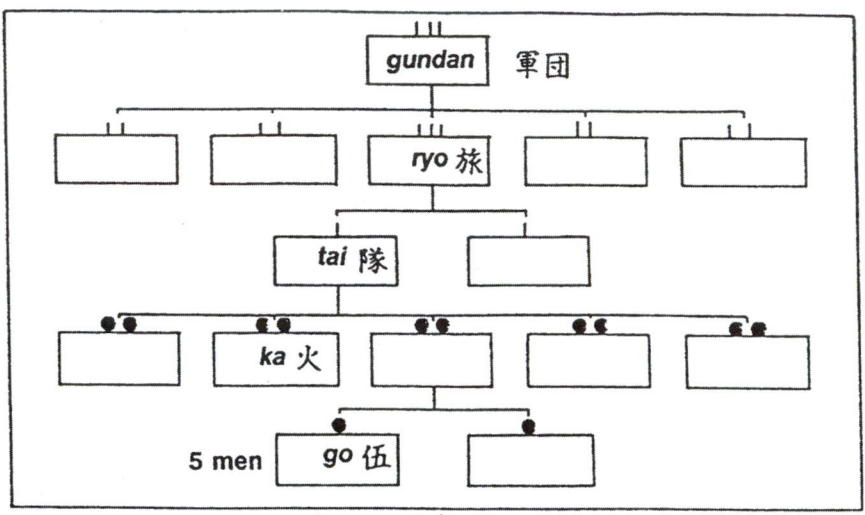

**Provincial Militia Regiment
(Administrative Organization)**

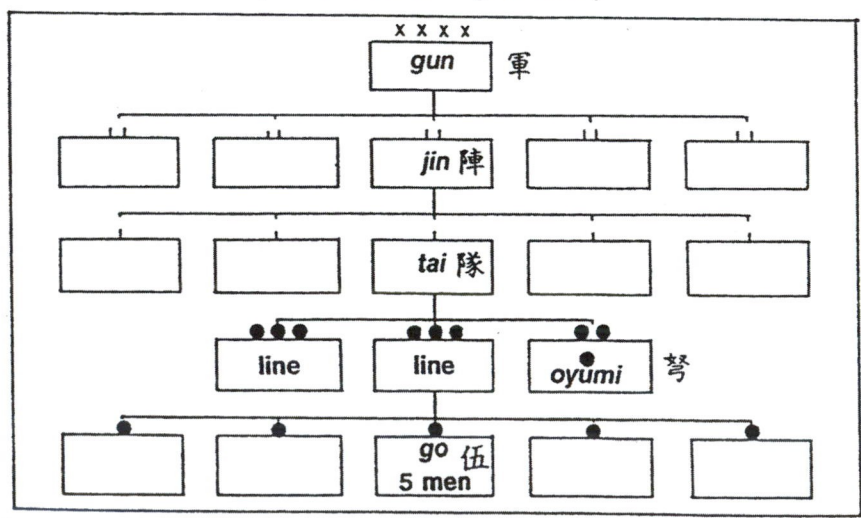

**Army
(Tactical Organization)**

the shield with a pole or strut and fought from behind it. A line of *heishi* with their shields formed a wooden wall. A notional provincial militia regiment and combat army are portrayed in Figure 18.1.

The provincial militia regiments did not last long. Within a century of their formation, they were discontinued except in the frontier regions. The decline of the provincial militia, a completely Japanese expression of military organization, was part of the overall trend as the Japanese assimilated and adapted the Chinese military model. The last battles fought by the imperial conscript army were in the closing decades of the eighth century as the army attempted to put an end to the barbarian threat in the north. Time and again armies of 100,000 men were sent to the northern provinces. Most were infantry-heavy forces who met with abysmal defeat. These costly campaigns were effective learning experiences for the Japanese military. The *emishi*, or toad barbarians, were skilled horsemen and mounted archers. Just as the Chinese had learned cavalry tactics from the barbarians of their northern areas, so, too, did the Japanese learn their military art from their barbarian foes.

By the end of the eighth century, the conscription system had been abandoned and the provincial militia regiments abolished. For a time district magistrates were authorized by the court to recruit relatives as *kondei* ("stalwart youth"), mounted fighters, to deal with lawlessness, insurrection, and piracy. As bands of mounted toughs ravaged the countryside, wealthy Buddhist monasteries organized private guard forces for security and to buttress their political influence. These bands of warrior monks or *yamabushi* were largely comprised of peasants who had left the land to avoid taxes and ruffians recruited by the clergy solely for their fighting skills. They became a disruptive part of the military scene, clashing with bands from other monasteries and terrorizing the land.

The imperial court responded by granting increased powers to the provincial governors to raise and maintain military units and by deputizing local strongmen and their bands of fighters to keep order in the manner of the late Roman emperors who, unable to keep order in the provinces, incorporated whole military units of barbarians to keep the peace. Court officials in Japan and other wealthy individuals soon turned to creating private military guards. Over time, the military skills of these units became associated with the families, giving rise to a hereditary military aristocracy. The warrior bands of the military families included relatives as well as fighters and other retainers who saw it to be in their interest to be a member of these warrior families. During this time Japan came to resemble the powerful Mafiosi families of latter-day Italy, with the difference that the Japanese family armies were openly armed to the teeth just as standing military forces were.

The power of the Japanese war bands was aided by the land reforms that removed ownership of the land from the emperor and transferred it to private hands. Deprived of tax revenue, the imperial court could no longer afford to maintain an army large enough to keep the military bands in check. The private land holdings, on the other hand, provided the economic base for the very war bands that the imperial court could no longer control. Over time, Japan fell into a system of warrior families based around landed estates, who fought each other over status and economic interests. Although the imperial court was dependent upon these warrior bands for protection and public order, in principle the *samurai* and the war band leaders remained subservient to the imperial court. Indeed, the word *samurai* means "one who serves." In practice, however, imperial authority depended upon sustaining a dominant coalition among rival military families. At the beginning of the twelfth century, two of these families, the Taira and Minamoto, fought the five-year Gempei war for political and military dominance of the country.

The Gempei War (1180–1185 C.E.) was a genuine civil war. At issue was which of the two families would dominate the imperial court and the country. The pattern of powerful warrior families struggling for power and the imperial throne begun with the Gempei War lasted almost 400 years until the Tokagawa Shogunate put an end to it around 1600 C.E. During this period Japan developed its warrior ethos and tradition to a fine edge, thoroughly weaving the warrior ethic into the practice of domestic and foreign policy. This tradition passed unbroken into the modern period and was on full display during Japan's conflict with the Allies during World War II.

At the time of the battle of Ichinotani (1184 C.E.), the weapons, armor, skills, and warrior ethos of the *samurai* warrior were at a technological and aesthetic peak. The warrior's primary weapon was a longbow carefully crafted of bamboo and wood. The *samurai*'s sword was a marvel of the metalworker's technology, an instrument of terrible beauty, and an object of religious veneration. The warrior's armor had been optimized for wear while mounted, designed to be as light and flexible as possible so he could easily draw the bowstring at full gallop. The lacquered strips of leather of which it was made and the colorful silk or leather thongs which held it together made a distinctive and colorful appearance.[7] There is no similar tradition of appreciation for the aesthetics of the implements of war found in the West, where such implements are regarded as mere tools.

The quintessential *bushi* was a mounted archer. The twelfth-century Japanese longbow (*yumi*) was seven feet long, with the grip placed about one third of the way up the bow, a design feature that made the weapon easier to fire from horseback or while kneeling. Originally made of boxwood, by the time of the Gempei War the bow was laminated with strips of bamboo and waxwood welded together with fish glue. The shaft was then bound with wisteria vines and lacquered. When unstrung, the tips of the bow curved forward. The curvature was reversed when the bow was strung. Bowstrings were made of grass fibers. The Japanese used a wide variety of arrows, including several for special purposes. One of these arrows had a v-shaped double-bladed tip to cut the lacings of an opponent's armor. Others were bulb-headed so that they whistled or hummed while in flight. The shafts of the arrows were about thirty inches long and had vanes made of feathers. Each *samurai* carefully chose the colors of his arrow feathers, once more reflecting the strong aesthetic dimension of war in the Japanese context.

While the *bushi* was primarily an archer, his sword was essential for close combat. The Japanese warrior's sword was both a highly functional weapon and an instrument of sacred and mystical significance. Swords were an inextricable element of Japanese mythology, exemplified by the sacred sword of the imperial regalia, which was believed to have been plucked by the younger brother of the sun goddess from the tail of a mighty serpent. The most widely used sword of the period was the *tachi*, a single-edged, elegantly curved weapon that was the consummate product of the swordsmith's art. The manufacture of the sword was to be undertaken only after ritual purification and prayer. In the forging process a bolt of steel was hammered paper-thin, folded over itself, and hammered again and again until scores of infinitesimally thin steel folded layers were cross-welded and laminated into a single blade. By coating the roughly formed blade with clay, scraping mud along the cutting edge and then tempering the sword with fire and water, the master swordsmith created a weapon with a flexible, nearly unbreakable body and a diamond-hard cutting edge that could be honed razor-sharp.[8] To this day Japanese swordsmiths who can fashion such weapons are regarded as "national treasures."

The common scabbard of the Heian period was made of wood covered in leather and heavily lacquered in a technique called *yakiurushi*, where the lacquer was burnt into the leather, producing a hard, black finish. A round wicker drum called the *tsuruwa*, literally, the "bow string wheel," was attached to the scabbard to hold an extra bowstring. The hilt was usually wound around with a thin lacquer strip and then coated with black lacquer like the scabbard. The *bushi* wore his sword in its scabbard suspended from his waist on the left side, cutting edge down so that the weapon could be drawn in one smooth movement.

Although the sword was the primary weapon of the Japanese warrior, he also carried others. Most *bushi*, for example, also carried a heavy

Figure 18.2
Japanese Warrior in Battle Dress

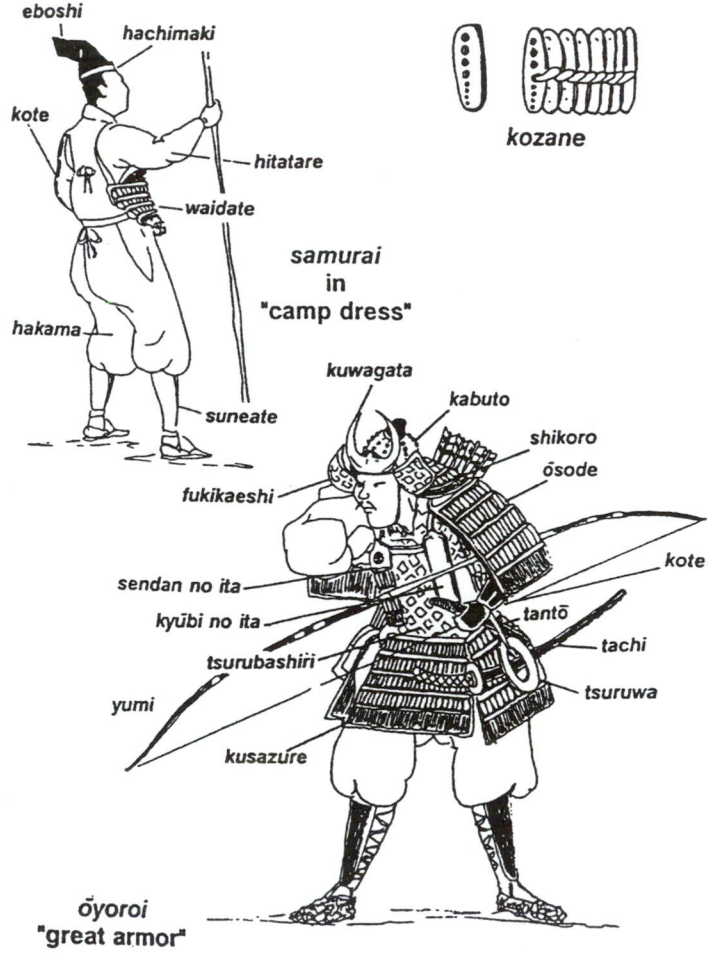

dagger or *tanto*, which was not used primarily as a combat weapon. Rather the *tanto* was used in a highly ritualistic manner to decapitate the *samurai*'s fallen enemy. The preferred technique was to plunge the dagger into the foe's neck and then rock it back and forth until the head was severed. Japanese texts were available to instruct the young warrior how to properly conduct a decapitation. Ancient Japanese warriors had made common use of spears, but this weapon seems to have fallen into disuse with the disbanding of the imperial infantry armies. The most common weapon of the footsoldier of this period, as distinct from the mounted *bushi*, was the *naginata*, also a favorite weapon of warrior monks. The *naginata* was a four-to-six-foot-long pole that mounted a double-edged sword blade at one end that could be used for both stabbing and slashing.

Japanese armor of this period bore a superficial resemblance to the lamellar armor common to the armies of the Asian mainland, particularly the Chinese and Korean. Early Japanese armor was fabricated of large metal iron or bronze plates and was far too heavy for use by the mounted warrior. By the ninth century, mainland influences and Japanese ingenuity had resulted in the distinctive *oyoroi* or "great armor" that became characteristic of the Japanese warrior for the next six centuries. The basic element of the *oyoroi* armor was a set of small, thin, perforated oblong scales called *kozane* comprised of hard leather and leather-covered metal. A number of these scales, laced together and lacquered, formed a hard rigid plate. These plates could, in turn, be placed together to form larger armor shapes. The aesthetics of armor fabrication in this manner was further evident in the use of colored silk or brightly colored leather lacings (*odoshi*) to give each set of armor a distinct appearance.[9] (See Figure 18.2.)

The dressing of the *samurai* in his armor was a highly ritualistic and even quasireligious ceremonial event. First the *bushi* put on a light gown with short, wide breeches. He bound his hair into a topknot and covered it with a tall, black cloth cap (*eboshi*) held on the head with the *hachimaki* or headband. The warrior next put on a brightly ornamented tunic or *hitatare* with matching baggy trousers (*hakama*), both of which were intricately embroidered and decorated with the warrior's family crests. Metal or leather greaves (*suneate*) protected the warrior's shins, and the *kote* or armored sleeve protected his left arm. Archer's gloves protected his hands while fur shoes were worn under his boots. When in camp or when fighting was not imminent, the warrior might wear a plate of armor called a *waidate* strapped to his right side. When preparing for battle, this complete set of undergarments was covered with a suit of *oyoroi* armor.[10]

The *oyoroi* battle-armor was ornate and complex in construction and resembled a four-sided box. It protected the torso like a cuirass along with a set of four skirt-like tassets or *kusazure* suspended from the torso box to protect the groin and thighs. Each side of the torso box and each tasset consisted of an armored sheet fabricated from plates of *kozane* leather laced together. Except for the right side armor, which was left loose to permit the warrior to use his bow or sword, the rest of the unit was permanently laced together. When preparing for battle, the warrior literally assembled the armored box and attached plates piece by piece in an elaborate ceremonial ritual that must have required considerable time to accomplish.[11]

The *bushi*'s helmet or *kabuto* was a bowl fashioned of iron plates held together by rivets. The top of the *eboshi* cap and the warrior's topknot within it thrust through a hole in the top of the helmet. The ears and neck of the soldier were protected by a half-skirt made of lacquered leather laced to the iron rim of the helmet, with great care always taken to ensure that the colored lacings of the helmet matched those of the rest of the armor. The distinctive look of the *samurai* helmet came from two side-plates (*fukikaeshi*) that curved back from either side of the face like wings. In many cases the helmet's appearance was further enhanced by a *kuwagata*, a large flat metal fabrication resembling a pair of horns that was attached to the front of the helmet.[12]

Not all *samurai* could afford expensive armor, nor did all *samurai* fight from atop an expensive mount. Poorer warriors made do with less and fought on foot. These warriors often wore a less extensive and less expensive version of armor called a *domaru*, comprised of the torso box and its side tassets. In place of the *kabuto* helmet, these less well-to-do warriors often wore a headgear made of curved iron plates to protect the sides of the head and neck. Other warriors of a lower order often fought without armor or helmet. Surviving scrolls of the period show some warriors fighting in bare feet and appearing naked under their armor. Another category of Japanese soldier of this period was the warrior monk. Armed usually with the *naginata*, the warrior monk might be outfitted almost identically to the secular *bushi* already described, even though he is most often portrayed in a less military manner, dressed in white or tan robes that covered his head, with the full suit of armor underneath.

The code of the Japanese warrior, *bushido*, or "the way of the mounted warrior," came to be widely known in the West after World War II, largely as a consequence of the poor treatment Allied prisoners suffered at the hands of the Japanese. At the time of the Gempei War, the code of *bushido* had not yet been written down. Yet, even then there was a sense that the warrior was a separate category of person, and a number of descriptive terms and phrases had already come into existence to set the practitioners of the profession of arms apart from others. There was, for example, the *kyuba no michi* or "the way of the horse and the bow"; the *yumiya toru mi no narai* or "the customs of those who draw the bow,"; and the *mononofu no michi* or "the way of the fighter."

As in other armies, the reputation of the Japanese warrior was confirmed by his courage and skill. One way in which a warrior's merit could be assessed was by witnesses, friend and foe alike, who could attest to his bravery. The surest proof of victory and valor in the Japanese tradition, however, was to return with the heads of his slain enemies. The *samurai* carried the *tanto* dagger precisely as a tool for decapitating his enemies. And since the enemy's head was the supreme prize, there was no incentive for the Japanese warrior to take prisoners. Japanese customs of war did not include surrender in the face of impossible odds nor did they instruct the gentle treatment of a foe who surrendered. The code of *bushido* stressed the transience of life and the requirement for an honorable death in combat. The worst fate of all, and the most dishonorable, was to be captured and executed by the enemy rather than fall in the act of combat itself. Ivan Morris has studied the "doomed warrior" tradition of the Japanese. He notes the humiliation of any *samurai* who permitted himself to be captured.

The soldier who allowed himself to be captured automatically lost his dignity as a warrior and could expect only the most brutal treatment: savage torture, a humiliating form of execution, mutilation of his corpse, and, worst of all, the epithet of *toriko* or 'prisoner.'[13]

The harsh treatment of Allied prisoners at the hands of Japanese soldiers during World War II becomes understandable in these terms. Prisoners were treated less than humanely by soldiers of a culture whose ancient military tradition affirmed that any soldier who surrendered lost any claim to moral and even human standing by the very act of surrendering. Too, the tradition of *bushido* explains why many Japanese soldiers fought to the death rather than surrender to Allied soldiers. In the Japanese view of things, death was morally preferable to the dishonor of surrender.

But what of soldiers who failed to die fighting and were in danger of being taken prisoner or who had failed in other respects? Not illogically, *bushido* offered the soldier an honorable death through suicide. Eventually, the preferred method of suicide for the *samurai* was *seppuku* or *harakiri*, the ripping open of one's belly. This particular method of self-destruction was still being practiced at the end of World War II. Its origins lie in the legends of the warriors of the Gempei War, who ended their lives in this manner.

The armies of this period were collections of war bands, raised, equipped, and led by their own commanders and bound together in temporary personal allegiance. As such, there was no standard Japanese military organization during this time. It was not until the Tokagawa

Shogunate of the fifteenth century that a formal military structure emerged in Japan. The ratio of mounted warriors to foot soldiers during the Gempei period was probably one to two, and the tendency of these armies to be organized along the lines of the old *ritsuryo* system, in units of five and ten, probably persisted. It is impossible to accurately judge the size of these armies, but it is likely that they numbered between 6,000 and 8,000 mounted archers and perhaps twice as many foot soldiers. The Japanese emphasis upon individual combat among warriors, as in the *Iliad*, made the development of any tactical system impossible, and the Gempei armies show little tactical sophistication. The influence of Chinese military philosophers, however, was much in evidence, so it is likely that at least some operational planning and strategic direction did occur. Still, when compared with other much older armies of the Near East and even the armies of China and the Mongols of the same period, the military organization of Japan falls short. It is difficult to resist the conclusion that the geographical isolation of the Japanese along with its almost, in military terms anyway, early Iron Age culture, worked against the development of even marginally sophisticated mechanisms and methods of war. And it would remain thus until the middle of the nineteenth century, when the modern military state finally came to replace the Tokagawa Shogunate and its traditional institutions, thus providing the cultural means to transform Japan from a feudal military power into one that made the world tremble.

NOTES

1. W.G. Aston, *Nihongi: Chronicles of Japan from the Earliest Times to A.D. 697* (Rutland, Vt.: Charles E. Tuttle, 1972), 9–12.

2. Ivan Morris, *The Nobility of Failure: Tragic Heroes in the History of Japan* (New York: Henry Holt, 1975), examines this phenomenon in Japanese myth, literature, and history.

3. Bruce L. Battne, "Foreign Threat and Domestic Reform: The Emergence of the *Ritsuryo* State," *Monumenta Nipponica* 41, no. 2 (1986): 201.

4. Technically, not all *samurai* were warriors and not all *bushi* were *samurai*, but the differences having to do with class, role, and court rank are beyond the scope of this discussion.

5. David John Lu, *Sources of Japanese History* (New York: McGraw Hill, 1974), vol. 1, 9.

6. Richard A. Gabriel and Donald W. Boose, Jr., *Great Battles of Antiquity* (Westport, Conn.: Greenwood Press, 1994), see "The Japanese War of War: The Battle of Ichinotani." I am grateful to my colleague, Donald Boose, for permis-

sion to use some of the material from this chapter, which he authored in our earlier work.

7. This description of Japanese weapons and armor is based on the following sources: Anthony J. Bryant, *Early Samurai: 200–1500 A.D.* (London: Osprey Publishers, 1991); Kanzan Sato, *The Japanese Sword* (Tokyo: Kodansha International, 1983); Leonard Tarassuk and Claude Blair, eds., *The Complete Encyclopedia of Arms and Weapons* (New York: Simon and Schuster, 1979); and Stephen R. Turnbull, *The Samurai: A Military History* (New York: Macmillan, 1977).

8. Gabriel and Boose, 583.

9. Ibid., 584.

10. Ibid., 585.

11. Ibid.

12. Ibid.

13. Morris, 15.

19

The Mongols
1206–1294 C.E.

The medieval European world of the thirteenth century knew the Mongols as the "Tartars," a corruption of the word *tartarus*, meaning Hades or hell in Latin. In the medieval mind, the Mongols became the Tartars, literally "the people from hell." To the military commanders of the West, the soldiers of the Mongol army seemed the devil's horsemen, capable of maneuvers and rates of movement never before seen by these Western commanders. The Mongol army of the time of the great Genghis Khan and his successor sons (1206–1294 C.E.) was the most efficient and effective military machine in the world. Under the guidance of a number of talented political and military leaders, the Mongol army destroyed every major military force between China and Central Europe that dared take the field against it. With few exceptions, each time the Mongol army engaged an enemy it did so at a significant numerical disadvantage. In almost every major battle the Mongols had the further disadvantage of having to conduct operations at the end of very long lines of supply, often conceding to their adversaries significant advantages in logistics and means of defense. In some ways even the military equipment of the Mongols was not up to the standards of its opponents, and few soldiers in the West would have easily submitted to the arduous way of life required of a soldier of the Great Khan. Despite all these factors, however, the armies of the Mongols were among the most successful in the history of warfare, surpassing in some respects the achievements of the armies of Alexander and Caesar. To the list of the great conquerors must be added the name of Genghis Khan.

Genghis Khan was born around 1167 C.E., the son of a Mongol clan chief named Yesugei. Yesugei named his son Temujin.[1] When the boy was in his early teens, Yesugei was assassinated, an event that touched off a twenty-year battle for control of the clan. During this time Temujin became an outlaw, and after many years of war with rival clans, he was able to establish his authority over the rest of his tribe. By 1206 C.E., as a result of war and diplomacy, Temujin had established his authority over the other clans of the steppes. In that year at a gathering of the clans, Temujin's authority over them was formally recognized with the bestowal of the title Genghis Khan, he who rules over "all who dwell in felt tents."[2]

Mongol society was organized along feudal lines in which each tribe was led by its own *khan*. Below the *khan* were the powerful barons called *noyans*, and below them were the *bahadurs*, the Mongol equivalent of knights. Each tribe was divided into patriarchal clans, each of which formed its own *ordu*. The term *ordu* simply meant camp. In the West, the camp of the Mongols was associated with their invading armies so that the word *ordu* became the word *horde*. Thus, "the Mongol horde." Traditionally, the clans within each Mongol tribe fought each other continuously over slaves, women, and horses. Temujin, along with Jebe and Subotai, were proficient horse thieves during Temujin's outlaw days. But once the clans were unified under Genghis Khan's authority, conflict among Mongols was outlawed and punished by death. The Mongol "nation" was really a coalition of various steppe tribes unified under the control of the Great Khan. Since Genghis' own tribe was called the Mongols, it became commonplace to refer to the various other tribes as Mongols as well. In reality there were scores of clans and tribes whose general identity gradually became submerged within the Mongol nation.[3]

Genghis Khan was a remarkable man who forged his people into a nation and bequeathed it a powerful military instrument with which to protect that nation and expand its power against all rivals. Despite his cruelty, much of it described as such by Western writers of the time, Genghis Khan seemed always to use it in a calculating manner for cold-blooded reasons of state. Feared by his enemies, the Great Khan was loved by his own people. He ruled his own people justly, gave them a new law and provided for its enforcement on an equitable basis, and tolerated all religions within the Mongol domain. This last facet of Mongol rule particularly surprised Western Christians and Muslims, who had come to accept religious wars as way of life. Mongol taxes, usually 10 percent of gross income, were moderate even by modern standards. Above all, Genghis Khan bequeathed peace to his people. It was said that a man could walk with a pocketful of gold from the Pacific Ocean to the Persian Gulf without fear of molestation. Genghis Khan gave the world an Asian version of the Roman peace, the *Pax Mongolica*.

The structure of the Mongol armies was initially the product of the organizational genius of one man, the great Genghis Khan himself. After uniting the steppe clans under his military and political leadership in 1206 C.E., Genghis formally organized a national army based on the decimal system. The decimal system of military organization was not Genghis' invention, but the traditional way tribal armies, including the armies of the Mongol tribe, had always organized themselves for war. It was Genghis' use of the decimal system to create a truly national army in which assignment to combat command was based on competence rather than tribal loyalties that was truly revolutionary. Figure 19.1 portrays the table of organization of the Mongol army.[4]

The smallest unit was a troop of ten soldiers called an *arban*, under the command of an officer called a *bagatur*. Ten *arbans* made up a squadron of 100 called a *djaghoun*, and ten *djaghouns* comprised a unit of 1,000 called a *mingan*. Ten *mingans* constituted the largest Mongol operational combat unit, the *touman*, consisting of 10,000 men.[5] A Mongol army would typically have two or three *toumans*, but could be tailored to any size. In the early days of the national army, officers were elected no doubt as a concession to tribal loyalty. But as the army became larger and more complex, election to command was retained only at the *arban* or lowest level, while command at the higher levels was appointed on the basis of demonstrated excellence in battle. Transfers between units were forbidden, and soldiers served their entire lives in a single unit. This practice, as it did with the Roman army, did much to enhance unit morale and combat cohesion.

The army was almost entirely comprised of cavalry, with 40 percent heavy cavalry and the remaining 60 percent light cavalry. There were some infantry units, of course, but these were mostly national units of conquered peoples pressed into military service for specific campaigns and regarded as completely expendable. Sometimes, these units were used as garrison soldiers or guards for the supply train. In sieges, they were often used in frontal assaults and suffered terrible casualties in order to spare Mongol casualties. For the most part infantry played only a small role in Mongol tactics. Most of what we know of the Mongol armies comes from the commentaries of their enemies. To explain their defeats at the hands of the Mongols, it became commonplace for Western

Figure 19.1
Table of Organization of the Mongol Army

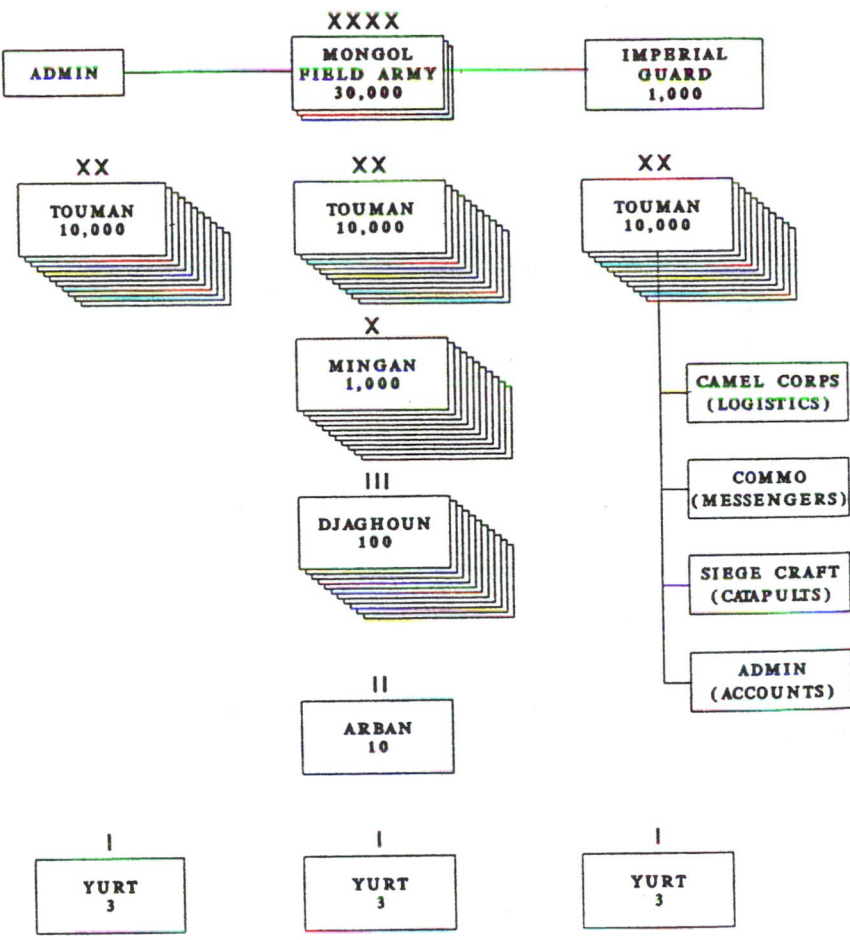

commentators to exaggerate the size of Mongol field armies. In fact, however, the Mongol armies were comparatively small for their time. During the *kuraltai* meeting of the clans in 1206 C.E., the size of the army recorded in the *Secret History of the Mongols* (the closest thing to an original Mongol source we have) was only 105,000 men. By 1227 C.E., according to Persian sources, the Mongol army had grown to only 129,000 men.[6] The Mongol practice of requiring each soldier to take along three horses as remounts in addition to his primary mount, and the habit before a campaign of spreading rumors that exaggerated the size of the Mongol army probably contributed to the propensity of Western sources to greatly overestimate the size of the army.

The raw material from which the Mongol soldier was forged made it possible to produce an excellent combat soldier. Mongols learned to ride at the age of three, taught not by their fathers but by their mothers. At age five the child was given a bow. From then on, the Mongol spent almost his entire life on horseback. The harsh environment of the Mongolian steppe with its extremes of temperature, strong winds, limited water, and scarce game accustomed the Mongolian horseman to hardship.[7] The Mongols were a naturally strong people with good eyesight and excellent visual memory. It was reported by travelers of the time that the Mongol could distinguish between man and animal across the Mongolian plain at a distance of four miles! The nomadic life equipped the soldier with a good knowledge of climatic conditions, water supply, and vegetation. Marco Polo reported that he had seen Mongol herdsmen go ten days without cooked food, subsisting on the blood drawn from their horses. The Mongol soldier routinely slept in the saddle and, with his remounts, was capable of movement over great distances without a rest. In 1221 C.E., for example, the army of Genghis Khan covered 130 miles in two days without stopping for food. In 1241 C.E., the great general, Subotai, moved his army toward Europe, covering 180 miles in three days in snow, again without stopping for nourishment. The nomadic way of life made the Mongol a natural soldier. When coupled with the discipline and training of their military system, it made the Mongols the most feared warriors in history—the devil's horsemen.

Tribal loyalties could be reduced somewhat by submerging the membership of the various tribes within the larger national military organization. But a true sense of national identity required a new code of Mongol behavior, and Genghis Khan devised just such a code, the *Yassak*. The Mongol tribes had fought one another for centuries. The practice of taking slaves and conducting cattle and horse raids against each other engendered fierce conflict. Moreover, Mongols were polygamous, but traditional values forbade marriage to a member of one's own clan. This forced males to kidnap wives from other tribes, creating more opportunity for internecine warfare. Genghis Khan forbade all of these practices among the united tribes, and enforced a new code with strict military discipline. The code provided a number of penalties for specific crimes, including execution for cowardice in battle.[8] A favorite Mongol saying in this regard was, "He who does not obey the *Yassak* loses his head." The *Yassak* worked to bind the Mongol tribes together because it had credibility in practice. In one case a general officer named Tuguchar, a son-in-law of Genghis Khan, failed to execute his orders properly during the Khwarizimian campaign. He was summarily removed from his command, reduced to the rank of common soldier, and lived the rest of his life as a soldier in the ranks until he died fighting in battle. The *Yassak* was a harsh military code, but it was applied equally across all social stations.

The senior leadership of the Mongol army were called *orloks* and were the most proven and experienced field commanders of the army. These senior commanders were selected strictly on the basis of experience and proven ability. In the early days these *orloks* had been selected from among Genghis Khan's most trusted comrades, and most of them had acquired battle experience alongside the Great Khan in his early tribal wars to form a Mongol nation. Two of these famous commanders, his "hounds of the Khan," were Jebe *Noyan* and Subotai *Bahadur*. Subotai, perhaps the most daring and successful of all field commanders anywhere in history, was said to be "of the Reindeer people," and may not have even been a Mongol. But he was Genghis' most trusted general. He fought over twenty major engagements in his career and never suffered a defeat. At the time when he commanded the Mongol invasion off Central Europe, Subotai was probably in his late sixties. The selection of combat leadership, especially at the senior levels, on the basis of proven military excellence provided the Mongol army with the best generals of its day, officers who rarely failed to defeat their Arab, Chinese, and Western counterparts.

The equipment of the Mongol soldier was simple, rugged, and, in the hands of the trained steppe cavalryman, deadly. The soldier wore either a brown or blue tunic, the *kalat*, made of cotton or, in the winter, of fur. Thick leather boots with felt liners for the winter were standard issue. Given the reliance of the Mongols upon the horse and stirrup, it is curious that these boots had no heels. On top of the *kalat* the heavy cavalry wore a coat of mail armor with a cuirass of ox-hide or iron scales covered in lacquered strips of leather. Light cavalry wore only the *kalat* and the lacquered armor, or a quilted *kalat* with no armor at all.[9] We know little about Mongol equipment prior to Genghis Khan. It is probable that when the various tribes were unified, those tribes that had served as mercenaries for the Chinese may have brought with them the superior weapons and armor of the Chinese. Certainly the Mongols learned the secret of tempering arrow and lance heads quite late, and it was only after Genghis' rise to power that the traditional materials of fire-hardened wood, bone, and horn were replaced by metal as military weapons stores.

After the first war with the Xixia (1207 C.E.), Genghis adopted the silk undershirt for his troops. This was an important innovation, somewhat comparable to the introduction of the flack jacket in modern armies. An arrow striking a soldier would not penetrate the silk undershirt. The twisting motion of the arrow wrapped the arrowhead around the silk and drove the material into the wound. Besides slowing the missile's penetration and reducing the severity of the wound, the silk made it much easier to extract the arrow from the body by pulling on the silk undershirt. Otherwise, pulling the arrow out by the shaft or pushing it through the body often produced horrible wounds and increased fatalities. Had the Mongols practiced even a rudimentary degree of personal hygiene, it is possible that the silk undershirt would have done much to reduce infection as well. As things were, however, the Mongols rarely washed, and it was not unusual for the undershirt to be replaced only after most of it had rotted away on the soldier's body!

On the march the Mongol soldier wore the traditional brimmed felt and leather hat with ear flaps for protection against the cold wind. In battle, however, the soldier wore a casque helmet of iron, although some were made of leather. Leather or cloth draped from the rear rim in Persian fashion provided some protection for the neck, and it is likely that some type of wool cap was worn underneath, and even a chin strap may have been used to hold the helmet in place at the gallop. Figure 19.2 depicts the headgear and equipment of the Mongol heavy cavalryman. Ribbons and fur trim around the brim denoted rank. Mongol heavy cavalry sometimes carried a small, round wicker shield covered with leather to use with the lance. Light cavalry was composed of horse-archers, and the shield was not regularly used since it interfered with the bow.

Heavy cavalry used the twelve-foot lance with a hook at the base of the blade for pulling adversaries off their horses. All Mongol cavalrymen carried two bows, one for short range and one for long range firing, with at least two quivers of thirty arrows for a basic combat load of sixty arrows. Arrows varied by length of shaft, weight as a determinant of range, and type of arrowhead. Some arrows had tempered iron tips for piercing iron. Fire arrows and whistling signal arrows were also used.[10] All Mongol soldiers carried the lasso and a small dagger. Heavy cavalry also carried the curved scimitar, probably adopted from the Muslim armies, and a battle-axe or mace. Mongol troopers carried spare clothes, fishing line, files for sharpening arrows, and a needle and thread. The saddlebag was somewhat waterproof, and was often tied to the tail of the horse when fording rivers.

The bow was the basic weapon of the light cavalry. It was a small reflex composite bow constructed of layers of horn and sinew laminated over a wooden frame. With a pull of 160 pounds, the Mongol bow had

Figure 19.2
Mongol Heavy Cavalryman

a maximum range of about 300 yards. This type of bow was rarely pulled to maximum power, however. The more common technique was to pull the bowstring rapidly back only a short distance and then release it in a snapping motion. The Mongols used a stone ring on the right thumb for grasping the bowstring that made this firing technique work acceptably well. The Mongol light cavalry were the best horse-archers in the world, and were trained to release their arrows when the hooves of the horse were all simultaneously off the ground. This prevented the shock of the hooves striking the ground from throwing off the cavalryman's aim.

The Mongols rode the Przevalsky breed of horse. This horse averaged thirteen to fourteen hands high, had thick legs, and was considerably shorter and less powerful than the warhorses of medieval Europe that carried the armored knight. This Mongol horse naturally used its hooves to scrape away snow from the tundra to reach grass or lichen underneath, and it even ate leaves from trees.[11] The ability of the animal to forage in snow made it possible for the Mongols to use their ponies in severe winter conditions. In one campaign, for example, Mongol armies crossed the Pamir Mountains in the dead of winter! The Mongol soldier always traveled with three horses besides his primary mount to use as remounts.

Mongol cavalry rode mostly mares, from which they could obtain milk and blood for food. The soldier trained his mounts to follow along behind him like dogs and even to respond to calls and whistles. This permitted large numbers of horses to move with the army without large numbers of attendants to herd and feed them. The horse came to occupy an almost mystical place in Mongol society, and Genghis Khan issued strict regulations governing the humane treatment of horses. A horse ridden in battle, for example, was never killed for food but, after his useful life, put out to grass.

The normal "iron rations" of the Mongol soldier consisted of ten pounds of dried, powdered milk curd, millet meal, and two liters of *kumis*, a powerful alcoholic drink made from fermented mare's milk and blood. Meat was carried under the saddle, where the sweat and movement of the horse cured and tenderized it. At the halt, Mongol soldiers would sometimes slice a piece of this jerky-like cured meat from under the saddle for a quick snack. Witnessing this, some foreign writers recorded that the Mongols actually ate meat cut from their live horses![12] The dried curd was mixed with water in one of the two canteens to yield a loose yogurt. Along with the army were herds of sheep, goats, yaks, and other domestic animals. Apart from what the army could plunder from the vanquished, the Mongol soldier ate almost anything, including rats, lice, and even the afterbirth of their foaled mares.

The individual soldier could be trained within his unit to sharpen his natural skills derived from nomadic life. Training the army to act in unison and to respond to command was another matter. The Mongols trained their armies in the *nerge*, the great animal hunt held at the beginning of each winter. The hunt lasted for three months and involved the entire army, assembled in full battle dress. The army was assembled along a line almost eighty miles long. At the command of the Great Khan, the army moved forward, driving before it all living things. The end point of the hunt was hundreds of miles away. As the army moved ahead day after day, the wings of the army gradually extended out to form a semicircle. Day after day the game was driven ahead and contained within the slowly closing circle. Eventually, the circle was closed and contracted tighter and tighter, driving the game toward the center. The soldiers acted in concert as units to prevent any game, even the smallest rabbit, from escaping the circle. If an animal slipped past a soldier, he and his officer were punished. As the circle tightened, the teeming game within it tried desperately to escape against the efforts of the soldiers to contain it. Then the killing began, and the soldiers dismounted and attacked the game with the object of killing everything within the circle! The bears, tigers, wolves, and other large animals struck out in terror, and hand-to-hand engagements between animal and man occurred. The killing ground or *gerka* ran red with blood until, at the request of the tribal elders, the Great Khan put a stop to the killing.[13] The hunt was excellent practice in that it trained the army to operate in concert, providing the leadership of the smaller combat units with an excellent opportunity to know and direct their troops in a difficult task.

The Mongol army attempted to institutionalize excellence in command and staff assignments by establishing the imperial guard or *keshig*. In the early days the guard had comprised only 1,000 men and consisted of the Khan's household, personal servants, and old trusted comrades from the tribal wars. The origins of the imperial guard in the personal bodyguard of the Khan were reflected in the names of the three guard units that comprised it. There were the *tunghaut* or day guard, the *kabtaut* or night guard, and the quiver bearers. By the middle of Genghis' reign, the *keshig* had expanded to almost 10,000 men and had become the Mongol equivalent of a staff and command college for combat commanders.[14]

The imperial guard was the home of the best, brightest, and most promising of the Mongol army's military commanders and staff officers. The candidates for membership in the *keshig* were identified early in their careers and selected on the basis of outstanding performance in lower level command and by an annual competition among all the outstanding men in the army. While some were granted membership because they were the sons of important nobility, those who failed to live up to standards were removed. Every officer in the *keshig* was trained in staff work and attended education and briefing sessions. Any officer of the imperial guard was presumed to be able to command a *touman* at a moment's notice if events required. The commands of a guardsman took precedence over those of the commander of any unit of *mingan* or below on the battlefield.

The imperial guard was regarded as the best fighting *touman* in the army and took its place next to the Great Khan in the center of the line, to be employed at his command. Each of the three *mingans* in the imperial *touman* had differently colored uniforms and horses for the day guard, night guard, and quiver bearers. The remaining seven *mingans* constituted the old elite life guards who fought with Genghis during the tribal wars and protected his person. The great general Subotai *Bahadur* had served with the life guards early in his career. The life guards wore black *kalats* and armor trimmed in red. Each guard rode a black horse with a red leather harness and saddle.

The exact structure of the Mongol staff organization is not certain, and it is not possible to reconstruct it in detail. However, it is noted in several sources that the Khan's military staff was composed of eleven senior staff officers, each one probably in charge of a specific staff section. It is certain that the army staff was located within the imperial guard, and it is likely that each *touman* had smaller, but similar, staff sections within its administrative staff structure. The general staff had sections dealing with medical transport, and it is well-known that the Mongol armies were equipped with units of Chinese, Indian, and Muslim medical practitioners. A mobile diplomatic corps was part of the staff and used to conduct negotiations. Units of interpreters were evident, as were scribes and record keepers, an interesting innovation for a people that were mostly illiterate. Most likely the habit was taken from the Chinese. An extensive intelligence apparatus, including sections that did nothing but assemble and analyze strategic intelligence, was part of the Mongol army, as were field agents, mapmakers, and surveyors. The Mongol intelligence officers counted and recorded everything, and an accurate body count was an essential part of any victory. To this end special squads roamed the battlefield after the fight, systematically cut off the right ear of every slain enemy soldier, and collected them in sacks for presentation to the commander![15]

The Mongols always pitched their camps facing south. Each wing of the army encamped in the same location relative to the center of the army, called the *khol*. The army of the left wing (*junghar*) always faced east, while the army of the right wing (*baraunghar*) always faced west. When encamped, the camp *yurtchis* (after *yurt*, meaning dwelling) served as the equivalent of modern quartermasters.[16] These officers chose the campsites, organized the flow of supplies, and established and operated communications. The highest-ranking *yurtchis* were responsible for conducting reconnaissance and intelligence gathering. Within the camp Chinese, Indian, and Persian physicians set up their dressing stations and treated the sick and wounded. Regular inspections of men and equipment were conducted, and the punishment for failing to keep equipment in good condition was severe. An extremely important function of the *yurtchis* was the care and operation of the army's camel corps, upon which it relied heavily for its supplies. While it is well-known that the Mongols were great horse breeders, it is often overlooked that they were also successful camel breeders. The Mongol armies were frequently supplied by large corps of camels shuffling between supply points and the army itself.

Among the more important staff officers and specialists were those in the imperial guard who dealt with siegecraft and artillery. During the first war against the Chinese, the Mongols quickly discovered that they were powerless to subdue cities. Accordingly, as they gained victory in China, they incorporated Chinese siege specialists and siege engines into their armies. Later, the Mongol army had a special corps of Persian engineers and siege experts within it. The army had a standing order to spare these experts in rival armies whenever a city was captured. From the use of siege engines the Mongols gradually developed field artillery.

Mongol siege engines included light and heavy catapults to launch all sorts of missiles against cities. Ballistae, like giant crossbows, were used, as was a variation of the European trebuchet in later years. These same machines were employed as artillery, shooting fireworks to confuse the enemy. Clay pots full of incendiary materials fire by timed wicks, naphtha pots, and something called a *duyao yanqiu* or a "poison-and-smoke ball" made of sulphur, nitre, aconite, oil charcoal, resin, and wax, were fired by these catapults.[17] The use of artillery was closely integrated into Mongol tactics, even against field armies deployed in the open and not behind defensive walls. At the battle of the Sajo River the Mongols opened the attack with an artillery bombardment.

Mechanical sophistication in siege operations never blinded the Mongols to the use of more primitive, but effective, means of assaulting cities. During the siege of Gurgandj, the capital of Kazrem, thousands of local citizens were herded together for the final assault on the walls and driven by the Mongols into the city's moat. The defenders slaughtered their own countrymen in the thousands until the moat was filled with corpses, upon which a ramp was constructed to assault the walls. The Mongols were capable of incredible cruelty, but their cruelty always served some military or political objective.

Mongol expertise in the military operational arts always functioned within the context of a larger political strategy, of which military operations were but a single part. This subordination of military to political objectives was clearly evident in the extensive preparations that preceded any Mongol military campaign. Sometimes these preparations required more than a year to complete. The imperial guard, for example, had a permanent and extensive intelligence section that dealt with political and strategic intelligence. They maintained up-to-date records on all major nations and provided written records and briefings to the military commanders. Political intelligence was regarded by the Mongols as the most important, and they were particularly interested in any personal rivalries among the enemy leadership that could be exploited during the campaign. The Mongol attack on Hungary, for example, was predicated on the assumption that the intense rivalry between the Germans and the Papacy would prevent any unified effort against the Mongol invasion. The Mongols correctly assessed that the petty rivalries of Russian and Polish princes would preclude any national effort against the Mongol forces. In both cases, they were correct. Mongol preparations for war always centered upon a strategic assessment of the enemy, including its ability to mount and sustain a successful coalition of forces and maintain the will to fight. Mongol intelligence officers were far more than "arrow counters."

Extensive psychological warfare efforts preceded a Mongol campaign, with different themes directed at diverse target audiences. Merchants and spies spread rumors, the wealthy were told that under the Mongols trade would prosper, while the poor were told that they would be liberated from their oppression and that a just law would govern their lives. Deliberate rumors exaggerating the size of the Mongol armies were sowed. Behind it all was the Mongol threat of cruelty and devastation, facts that needed little in the way of psychological explanation to make them credible. Preparation for war required that the campaigns be timed correctly so as to take maximum advantage of terrain, weather, and food supplies. Mongols always chose the season of the attack with great care. Iraq was invaded in the spring of 1258 C.E., a time when the heat was less severe and malaria not a danger. The Russian campaign of 1237–1238 C.E. was timed for the winter, when the rivers and marshes were frozen and the entire theater of operations resembled a vast snow-covered Mongolian plain.

The strength of the Mongol army lay in its ability to conduct combat operations with an efficiency and effectiveness that far surpassed the abilities of their enemies to resist. The Mongols seem to have been the first army to conceive of military command in a manner that stressed objectives, while leaving the choice of ways and means to the unit commander, a theory of tactical application and control that the Germans later called *Auftragstaktik*. Unit commanders were briefed on the general operational plan, and objectives were specified for each *touman*. Within these broad guidelines, the field commander was afforded the widest possible latitude in accomplishing the objectives. Stress was placed on initiative, innovation, and flexibility of execution.

The Mongol army advanced into enemy territory in large columns widely separated from each other. Command and control between the columns was maintained by units of courier riders moving constantly between the columns to maintain contact. The tactical communication system of couriers also used semaphore-like signals and even lanterns to send messages. This ability to communicate regularly, even daily, made it possible for the army commander to exercise command and control over the entire army even though it was widely dispersed. Each column was preceded by screens of cavalry scouts that acted as reconnaissance units, sometimes deployed as many as seventy miles to the front of the main column. Similar units were deployed on the flanks and to the rear of the army as it marched.[18] The operational principle was for the army to move divided while attempting to find the enemy. Once the enemy was located, light reconnaissance units could be used to fix him in place while the larger columns concentrated rapidly, striking the enemy at the decisive time and place or from a number of directions at once. The Mongol approach to contact represented a perfect application of the old dictum, "march divided, fight united."

Once contact was made and the decision to engage the main force taken, the *touman* advanced into battle in five single lines (*jaguns*). Each line was tightly packed to maximize the shock of impact, but the lines themselves were separated by a considerable distance, sometimes 200 yards. The first two *jaguns* were comprised of heavy cavalry, followed by three lines of light cavalry. As the lines closed with the enemy, the first line of light cavalry broke into a gallop and rode through the gaps in the lines of heavy cavalry to its front and engaged the enemy with volleys of arrow fire. At the same time, the rear ranks of light cavalry fired volleys over the heads of the heavy cavalry. As the first rank of light cavalry closed with the enemy, it rode obliquely across the front, firing as it went. If the timing was right—and it almost always was— just as the rate of arrow fire from the light cavalry reached its height, the light cavalry broke off and the heavy cavalry was upon the enemy in force, engaging him with maximum shock.[19]

If the light cavalry failed to open the enemy front, the Mongols might execute a maneuver called the *tulughama* or standard sweep (Figure 19.3). While the heavy cavalry engaged the enemy from the front, the light cavalry sent a wing around the entire formation to engage the enemy on the flank. Sometimes the light cavalry might ride entirely around the battlefield and strike the enemy from the rear. The idea was to strike the enemy from at least two directions, confuse him, break his ranks, and then drive home the attack with the last line of heavy cavalry.[20]

The charge of the heavy cavalry was always the main player in the endgame of a Mongol attack. All battlefield maneuvers prior to the actual charge were carried out in complete silence. The units were controlled by flags and signals. At the time of the attack, however, this silence was broken by the sound of the *naccara*, the great kettle drum that sounded

Figure 19.3
Mongol *Tulughama* Maneuver

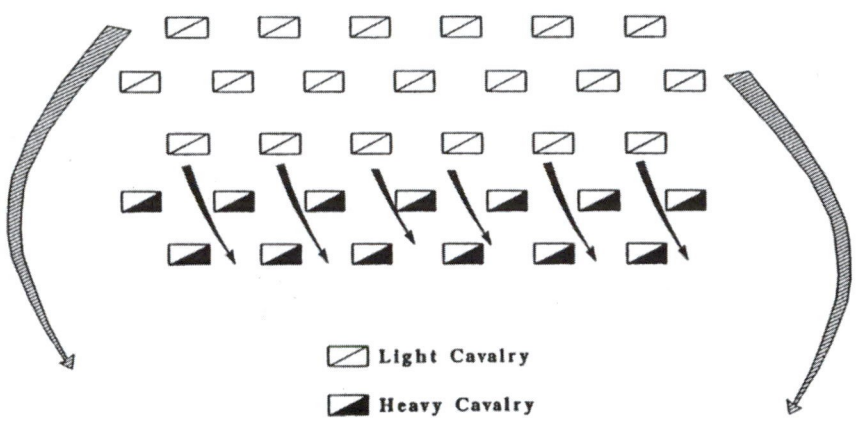

the beat and tempo of the attack. The silence was suddenly shattered by hideous yells and screams as the Mongols attempted to psychologically shatter the nerve of their enemy.

Another Mongol tactic was the *mangudai*, in which a unit of light cavalry rode directly at the enemy center, engaging in a hopeless attack. After some initial combat, and on signal, the horsemen would feign panic, break ranks, ride through their own formations, and turn and run in what seemed a disorganized manner. The idea was to entice the enemy to follow in force, something that European armies of mounted knights seeking individual glory seemed to find irresistible. During a chase of a mile or two sufficient to allow the pursuing enemy force to lose cohesion and scatter, the Mongols waited in ambush on the flank. Suddenly, from out of the concealment, came a hail of arrows followed rapidly by the charge of heavy cavalry on rested horses. Within minutes the enemy was surrounded. Mongol archers shot the horses out from underneath the enemy horsemen. On foot, the European or Muslim knights were easy prey to Mongol lancers or archers. Often, as at the battle of Liegnitz, the slaughter was horrendous. Mongol cavalry also fought in staggered formations or in open or closed files, depending upon the circumstances.

The Mongols were experts at pursuit. Their tactical doctrine defined victory as nothing less than the annihilation of the enemy army. Once the enemy had been driven from the field, the Mongols sometimes pursued for weeks until almost every enemy soldier was slain or captured. Operating as it almost always did at the end of long supply lines, no Mongol field army could risk leaving the remnants of an enemy army to reform and fight again, threatening their supply lines. Along with a ruthless pursuit, the Mongols would sometimes devastate the surrounding countryside. In 1299 C.E., for example, the Mongols defeated the Mamelukes at Salaamiyet. Mongol units were recorded as pursuing the remnants of the enemy army as far as Gaza, 300 miles from the battlefield!

Genghis Khan is supposed to have been told by a captured Chinese officer that while the Mongols had captured an empire on horseback, the empire could not be ruled from horseback. Genghis Khan bequeathed an empire to his son, Ogedai, who then had to govern it. Across such a far-flung realm as the Mongol empire, government was impossible without sound communications. In 1234 C.E. Ogedai Khan formalized the establishment of an imperial communication system called the *yam*. This was a system of horse-and-rider stations at fixed intervals of twenty-five miles (so Marco Polo tells us) across the entire length and breadth of the empire. Riders could be strapped in their saddles to ride throughout the night while the horse found its way to the next station as the rider slept. To reduce the time between changes of mounts, the messengers sometimes wore bells to warn the station attendants of their approach in time to prepare the fresh mount. The responsibility for staffing and operating the *yam* was given to the army, and communications stations were now routinely established in the wake of the army on the move. The *yam* also functioned as an efficient tactical and strategic communication system.[21]

NOTES

1. See David Morgan, *The Mongols* (Oxford, UK: Blackwell, 1986), 55–61 for a good account of Genghis Khan's early childhood. See also R.P. Lister, *Genghis Khan* (New York: Dorset Press, 1969), for more detail on the early years of the Great Khan.

2. Lister, 185.

3. Ibid.

4. Richard A. Gabriel and Donald Boose Jr., *Great Battles of Antiquity* (Westport, Conn.: Greenwood Press, 1994), 536.

5. Morgan, chap. 4; also, S.R. Turnbull and Angus McBride, *The Mongols* (London: Osprey Publishers, 1988), 22.

6. Morgan, 87.

7. Harold Lamb, *Genghis Khan* (New York: Doubleday, 1927), chaps. 1 and 2 for a good description of how difficult the life of the Mongols, especially Mongol children, was.

8. Ibid., 201–4 for a list of the laws of the *Yassak*.

9. For more on the armor, weapons, and equipment of the Mongol soldier see Michael Edwards and James L. Stanfield, "Lord of the Mongols: Genghis

Khan," *National Geographic* 190, no. 6 (December 1996): 14–16; Turnbull and McBride, 13–22; and Gabriel and Boose, 539–41.

10. Edwards and Stanfield, 13.

11. Gabriel and Boose, 541; also James Chambers, *The Devil's Horsemen: The Mongol Invasion of Europe* (New York: Atheneum, 1979), 56.

12. Turnbull and McBride, 17.

13. Morgan, 84.

14. Chambers, 59.

15. Edwards and Stanfield, 32–33.

16. Chambers, 55.

17. Turnbull and McBride, 30.

18. Chambers, 62. See also Edwards and Stanfield, 32 for a good graphic portrayal of the Mongol camp and army on the move.

19. Gabriel and Boose, 545–47.

20. Ibid.

21. Chambers, 60–61.

The Ottomans
1300–1453 C.E.

T he origins of the Ottoman army rest in the early military structures of the Turcoman nomads who founded the Ottoman state in the twelfth century. This army was basically composed of freebooting *ghazzi*, religious zealot volunteers spurred on by their faith in Islam who lived for raiding (*ghazzias*) and looting the lands of the infidel. The Turcoman army of these early days was strongly similar to the early Arabic armies, amounting to little more than horse-borne raiding parties incapable of sustained military action on any scale. The Turcoman army was essentially a military extension of the tribe, and had little organizational definition until 1300 C.E. or so, when Orkhan, the tribal emir, began to carve out a territorial base from the old Seljuk Turks in Anatolia. It was at this point that Orkhan began a formal reorganization of the army.

It would have been impossible to predict the rise of the Ottoman Empire from its lowly beginnings. The destruction of the Seljuk Turk holdings on the rim of Asia Minor by the Mongols under Halugu Khan in 1256–1260 C.E. shattered the Seljuk principalities and cast them adrift to seek their own fortunes. One of these small duchies was ruled by Osman or Othman, son of Ertughril, who had been given a fief by the last of the Seljuk Turk sultans as a reward for military services rendered. Othman ruled for thirty-seven years (1289–1326 C.E.), during which time he gradually tore from the Byzantines their last Asiatic province. In 1326

Othman took the important town of Brusa, the center of the fertile coastal Byzantine province of Bithynia. Three years later his son seized Nicaea (modern Iznik), and in 1337 C.E. he took Nocomedia (modern Ismid). From these humble beginnings the house of Othman—from which the name *Ottoman* is derived—produced seven consecutive generations of able male heirs who continued to expand the writ of the original fiefdom into a world empire.[1]

The social order created by Orkhan was a *ghazzi,* a religious state essentially tribal in organization. Although Islamic in form, the laws and customs of this early state were more reflections of Turcoman tribal customs, laws (the *yasa*), and animist beliefs than strict Islamic principles. Nonetheless, the state was military-religious in character and organized for war, in which the army was paid from booty obtained from raids against the Byzantines and other infidels living on the rim of Anatolia. From its inception in approximately the thirteenth century until the sixteenth century, the Ottoman army and society retained its *ghazzi* view of war, perceiving itself as religious raiders of the faith against the infidel, and treated the areas of the Balkans, around the Black Sea, and the Middle East as wild country in which adventurous soldiers could gain wealth and fame in the service of the faith.

Until the fourteenth century, the Ottoman army was essentially a feudal levy composed of Turcoman cavalry and a few infantry. This early army comprised several types of light cavalry contingents. The *akincis,* or religious volunteers, served in single campaigns and were paid with loot. If they served as an entire tribal contingent, they were called *yuruks.* They were typical steppe horse-archers and used the composite bow, leather lamellar armor, and the lasso. Some rough infantry, called *yaya,* were also used, as were contingents of heavy cavalry armed with the lance, saber, and mace. The army was recognized by its foes as fast, mobile, well-disciplined, and capable of inflicting ambush and surprise, but always fighting in *ghazzias* style. The army lacked any siege or engineering capability, and it became an Ottoman tactic to ravage the countryside, force the enemy into towns, and then blockade the towns and starve them into surrender.[2] By the middle of the fourteenth century, however, the army began to change and acquire more formal structure. It remained in a period of transition for the next two centuries, marked by increasing military sophistication and complexity, much of which it adopted from its Byzantine and European adversaries. By the 1600s C.E., the Ottoman army had emerged as one of the more complex and militarily capable armies of the period. Ottoman military power was sufficient to allow it to hold on to its large empire for another 300 years until it was dismantled by the Allied Powers after World War I.

The first attempt at formalizing the organizational structure of the Ottoman army was attempted by Orkhan Bey (1326–1359 C.E.), who instituted a permanent standing army cadre to serve alongside the traditional cavalry levy. The force was selected, trained, and paid for by the emir himself. These professionals were military adventurers from many lands and included significant numbers of Christians—ex-Byzantines and Christian Orthodox from the Balkans seeking to escape persecution at the hands of the Catholics. The original standing force was composed of cavalry and infantry. The horsemen, called *musellems* (tax-free men), were organized into units by the decimal system. The infantry soldiers, called *yaya*, were similarly organized. At first this new standing cadre was paid wages, but by the time of Murad I (1359 C.E.), a new system of vassalage and landholding was introduced that worked to provide the Ottomans with a social system similar to feudalism, from which they could draw an adequate amount of military manpower for national service.

As the basis for the military manpower system, the Ottoman feudal system is worth describing in some detail. Newly conquered land was divided up into small fiefs (*timars*) and distributed by the sultan to his soldiers and adventurers who fought well for him. In exchange for the fief, from which the holder could draw or earn a living, the holder had to provide the sultan with one fully equipped cavalryman whenever the sultan called for him. In practice, this meant that the fiefholder himself (the *timariot*) provided military service, although it was at least possible that in later periods this service could be rendered by providing the sultan with an equivalent amount of money. A particularly favored individual might be given several *timars*, similar to a small barony, in which case he still had to provide a cavalryman from each *timar* that he held. While in England and in Europe military service to the crown was limited in time from a single day to forty days duration, in the Ottoman system no such limits seem to have applied, and the soldier was usually called for the duration of the war or the campaign.[3] This eliminated the problem of army contingents returning home in the middle of the war, a common occurrence in feudal Europe.

In contrast to European feudalism, the genius of the Ottoman system was that the *timariot*'s tenure on the land was nonhereditary. When the fiefholder died, the land returned to the sultan and did not pass to the fiefholder's sons. Even if a son distinguished himself in military service and was awarded a *timar*, it was common practice not to award him lands held previously by his father or family but to give him an entirely new fief, often far from the old one. The idea behind these practices was to prevent the rise of local loyalties centered around powerful landed families who might be tempted to challenge the sultan's authority. Unable to obtain land through inheritance, the sons of the nobility could only obtain or retain their wealth by entering the service of the sultan and serving him loyally. In practice, this meant that there was always a large body of young men from the military classes eager for war and conquest as the way to obtain land and make their fortune. As long as there was plenty of land for the taking, as in the Balkans for example, the system worked well in providing an adequate supply of military manpower for the Ottoman armies.

The Ottoman system of feudalism required that military conquest of new lands be followed rapidly by large-scale settlement of the new lands with *timariots*. Settlement and vassalage followed the conquering armies, and the new conquerors settled down and stayed for centuries in these new lands. For the most part, the Ottomans did not persecute the infidel populations among whom they settled, and the common pattern of political rule was to establish legal treaty relationships with existing political authorities who recognized Ottoman suzerainty. After a while, the economic success of the new Ottoman order tempted many Christians to convert to Islam as a way of participating more fully in its economic and social benefits. As a result, a pattern developed, especially in East Europe, in which large populations of Muslims lived peacefully within Christian areas (themselves often split between Catholic and Orthodox) for centuries. One interesting aspect of this pattern is that Christian military contingents often fought with the Ottomans against other Christian armies. In Serbia, for example, the great Serbian folk hero, Kraljevic Marko, died fighting in the service of the sultan in 1395 C.E.

The *timariot* system provided the Ottomans with the manpower and political stability to build a regular army of some training and size. The greatest number of soldiers were the feudal cavalry, the *sipahi*, who were mounted men drawn from the *timar* fiefs. Added to these soldiers were infantry units drawn from a number of sources. There were the traditional religious volunteers who fought for booty, other infantry was composed of landholders who guarded passes and bridges, still others were mercenaries, and there were the *voyniks*—Christian infantry contingents drawn from the powerful families of the Balkan nobility. Infantry was not seen by the Ottomans as being as important as cavalry, and infantry was less professional in the mass than the cavalry. Nonetheless, within the standing army, there existed a corps of professional infantry that was probably the best in the world for its day. These so-called Janissaries, about whom more will be said later, were probably the best infantry professionals since the Roman legionnaires.

The size of the *sipahi* contingents in the Ottoman army at the time of the siege of Constantinople (1453 C.E.) is unknown, but may have exceeded 40,000 men. Most *sipahi* cavalry were lightly armed with lance, sword, and armor (chain, mail, or plate) of the cavalryman's own provision. Upon mobilization, one of every ten *sipahi* cavalrymen remained at home to maintain law and order and serve as a home guard. The rest collected themselves into regiments that reported to the provincial governors, who led large contingents to the sultan for command during the campaign. In addition to the mainline feudal cavalry, the Ottomans used various kinds of auxiliary cavalrymen for specific roles. The old *ghazzi* light horse raiders were often used as an advance cavalry screen. Their task was to move deep into enemy territory and disrupt communications and supply lines, seize important bridges and passes, and, of course, provide tactical intelligence. In other areas, the bedouin tribesmen of the Middle East also served as Ottoman auxiliary cavalry.[4] Christian contingents of cavalry provided by the nobility of the Balkans were common to Ottoman armies, and the sons of many Christian princes served in elite cavalry regiments in the capital, where, although they were technically hostages, they seemed to have served loyally and well and to have been accepted as military equals.

Although the Ottoman army was composed of the *sipahi* feudal cavalry, various infantry contingents, and contingents of Christian infantry and cavalry, the core of the Ottoman army was an elite military force of professional cavalry, infantry, and artillery units. This elite corps, called the *Kapikulu* Corps, provided the professional cadre for the Ottoman army in war. The Corps was the military elite of the Ottoman Empire, and its members were selected for military excellence, intelligence, and discipline. This spine of the Ottoman army was composed of heavy cavalry units, engineering and artillery units, and the famous Janissaary infantry regiments. Many of the *Kapikulu* officers, as well as most of the Ottoman political and administrative elite, began their careers as Janissaries, and since much of the training and education of the *Kapikulu* Corps closely paralleled the Janissary training, it is perhaps helpful to describe the Janissary system in some detail.[5]

Credit for forming the Janissary corps is, by tradition, given to Orkhan, the first sultan to attempt to create a professional army from the old Turcoman *ghazzi*. This may be because the early concept of the Janissaries may have been based around the older Islamic model of the military monastery, the *ribbat*. In fact, it is unlikely that the Janissaries were brought into existence until almost the middle of the fourteenth century. Evidence suggests that even at the end of this century, the Janissaries were little more than a personal slave guard of the sultan no more than 1,000 strong. By 1433 C.E., however, Murad II noted that the Janissary guard had grown to 3,000, and, by the time of the siege of Constantinople, the Janissaries seem to have numbered about 12,000 men. It was not until well after the end of the fifteenth century that the Janissaries became an even larger corps and became the praetorians that eventually came to rule the Ottoman state.

The term *Janissary* is a European corruption of the Turkish *yeni ceri*, literally "new troops." Originally a small slave bodyguard of the sultan, the Janissaries were recruited almost exclusively from Christian converts to Islam. In the early days, they were probably recruited from among Christians captured in the *ghazzi* raids. Since the Ottomans did not practice forced conversion in the conquered lands, much of the Ottoman Empire remained Christian, especially the European provinces. By the middle of the fifteenth century, the Ottomans were critically short of high-caliber military and administrative personnel of Islamic background to govern the empire. The Ottomans were quick to recognize the talents of the Christians and, in 1438 C.E., the *devsirme* was instituted. This regulation required that each Christian village within the empire provide the sultan with a quota of Christian boys between the ages of seven and ten on an annual basis. The numbers are uncertain, but in some years as many as 1,000 boys were taken from each province. Islamic law forbade the enslavement of other Muslims, so they were exempt from the levy. But in some provinces of Eastern Europe, Bosnia in particular, Muslim families bribed Ottoman officers to take their sons for the levy in order to provide them with a better station in life. Christian families also sometimes saw the levy as a way to provide opportunities for a son. It was from this raw material—the "tribute children"—that the Ottomans forged the military, political, and administrative elite of the empire through the Janissary system.[6]

The most intelligent boys quickly converted to Islam and were selected as pages to serve in the administrative offices of the capital, where they received further education and training before returning to the Janissary training. The rest of the tribute children were initially sent to farms to learn the Turkish language and the tenets of the Islamic faith. The new recruits were then sent to a series of "military monasteries," where they lived a celibate monastic life of discipline and education. The best were trained for seven years in elite schools that stressed character, leadership, military expertise, athletic prowess, languages, religion, science, and engineering. During their training, the young Janissaries were the private property of the sultan and had no legal rights at all. They were ruled by strong discipline and could be flogged or even strangled for disobedience. After a total of ten years of novitiate and formal training, if they passed examinations and were found fit, they were accepted into the Janissary corps. They were now permitted to marry, and many married girls who had been educated in special palace schools. While the Janissary was single, he lived a Spartan life of celibacy in the barracks unless appointed to high office.

Through the Janissary system, the Ottomans institutionalized excellence in the governmental and military spheres. The best often became officers in the *Kapikulu* cavalry, and others in military positions served as a general staff and training college for ensuring military excellence. Others were selected for governmental and administrative positions, and many rose to very high rank. It has been estimated, for example, that from the fourteenth through the sixteenth centuries, no fewer than two thirds of all the Ottoman grand viziers were graduates of the Janissary system.

By the time of Mahomet II (1451–1481 C.E.), the *Kapikulu* Corps had been in existence for sufficient time to prove its worth and loyalty, and had become a self-sustaining institution. Mahomet II increased the practice of giving *timar* fiefs to *Kapikulu* cavalrymen, thus balancing the power of the *sipahi*. Under Suleyman I, the *Kapikulu* Corps grew to 48,000 men and included 20,000 Janissaries. The two main military elements of the *Kapikulu* Corps were the heavy cavalry regiments and the Janissary infantry regiments. Special elite regiments of artillerymen and engineers also existed, but were not nearly as numerous or prestigious. The *Kapikulu* heavy cavalry were the most numerous military branch, and surpassed the Janissaries in numbers and social status.

The *Kapikulu* cavalry comprised six major units. Members of the Corps were generically known as "men of the regiments." Two regiments of *ulufeciyan* or "salaried men" were formed in the early fourteenth century and were organized into left and right regiments, denoting their place on the battlefield relative to the sultan. Two additional regiments, the *gureba* or "poor foreigners," were originally formed from the old *ghazzi* volunteers, and another regiment of the Corps, the "weapons bearers," probably had their origins in the early bodyguard of the sultan. Another special regiment, the "*sipahi* children," was created by Mahomet I, probably to cull the best of the feudal cavalry for his own elite guard.

Membership and especially officership in these elite units included the sons of regimental officers, ex-Janissaries who had distinguished themselves in military affairs, and a number of Arab, Persian, and Kurdish Muslims of proven military ability. The *Kapikulu* Corps was a true military meritocracy.[7]

The Janissaries constituted the elite infantry units of the corps and were formed into *ortas* or regiments. By the sixteenth century, there were 101 official Janissary infantry regiments ranging in size from 100 to 3,000 men. Later, more elite Janissary regiments were formed to act as the sultan's special bodyguard, and some of these new regiments served as the personal guard of high-ranking Janissary officers. For centuries the Janissaries were armed with the bow, javelin, and crossbow, but after the wars with the Hungarians (1440–1443 C.E.), the Janissaries gradually adopted the new firearms into their infantry formations.

The weapons of the *Kapikulu* cavalry and infantry units varied widely over time. The earliest Turkish sources on the subject date from the fourteenth century, and list the following weapons as pertaining to the early cavalry: the war hammer, various types of maces, arrow quivers, infantry crossbow, javelin, short sword, pike, saber, light spear, lance quiver, arrows, bow, bow case, war axe, and lasso. Clearly, no cavalryman carried all this equipment at the same time, and there was, as far as can be determined, no standard issue of weapons. The type and mix of weapons carried by the early Turkish armies depended on the wealth and preference of the cavalryman. By the time of the siege of Constantinople, the Ottoman heavy cavalryman carried a lance, saber, and mace, and was fully armored. Light cavalry carried the bow and the short javelin and other close-support weapons like the short sword or mace. The soldiers of the light infantry (nonelite) were usually armed with the bow if they were Turks and with the lance and sword if they were Christians of Balkan infantry contingents. The elite Janissary infantry carried the short composite bow and the curved short sword. Later, they were equipped with firearms.

As regards armor, the early Turkish light infantry wore leather lamellar armor, while the heavy elite cavalry was equipped with much of the armor kit common to the European knight of the period. Much of this armor was acquired as a consequence of Ottoman contacts with the Balkans and Byzantines. A list of cavalry equipment for the heavy cavalry includes the hauberk; lamellar, scale, mail, and plate armor; mail coif; and the *tugulka* or crested iron helmet. The famous "turban helmet" was made of iron and worn over a soft cap. It has a full-face aventail to protect the face and neck, a design that reflected an army in which arrow wounds were common.[8]

A third element of the *Kapikulu* Corps was the regiments of artillery-men and engineers, first formed as part of the corps by Murad II. These experts both manufactured and operated cannon. After the successful siege of Constantinople, a special transport regiment was created that manufactured and operated gun carriages, wagons, and even a special fleet of artillery barges on the Danube. Expert gunners were trained for the artillery regiments, and by 1575 C.E. the Ottoman army had more than 1,000 gun experts in its ranks. Of all the Muslims, the Ottomans were the most willing to adopt artillery and cannon, and, as with some other military technologies, the Balkans provided the Ottomans with much-needed expertise. The Turkish presence in the Balkans brought them into direct contact with the new cannon technology. The Serbs in particular had been importing Venetian guns since 1351. Within a few decades, the Serbs and others were manufacturing their own cannon. The Ottomans recruited these Balkan gun makers and gave them *timar* fiefs to ensure their loyalty. In the sixteenth century many Jews fleeing the persecution of the Inquisition landed in Ottoman lands, bringing with them expertise in gun manufacture.

The Ottomans quickly learned how to manufacture the new cannons, and often cast their cannon at the site of the siege rather than hauling them around the countryside. Once the siege was over, the cannon were presumably melted down again into ingots with handles and transported to the next siege site. The English did a lucrative business with the Ottomans by selling them broken bronze statues and bells looted from Catholic churches and monasteries. These statues were melted down and the bronze used again and again to cast and recast cannons. Ottoman gunpowder was more powerful than European black powder, an element that may also have contributed to the Ottoman preference for large-caliber guns. This circumstance seemed to have persisted until World War I, when Turkish armies were routinely equipped with .52 caliber rifles. Within fifty years of Constantinople, the Ottomans were experts at all the techniques of artillery, including crossfire, sequential firing from spaced batteries, curtain barrages to precede an assault, and the use of light, medium, and heavy cannon arrayed on target in sequence of destruction. Experts from the artillery and engineering regiments formed special units for mortars, grenadiers, bombardiers, mining, incendiary devices, and sappers. Ottoman artillery was excellent, and all of it was commanded by the elite regiments of the *Kapikulu* Corps.

Ottoman tactics gradually evolved to a level at which, by the sixteenth century, a sophisticated combined arms tactical system had been developed. The traditional *ghazzias* tactics of the horse-archer engaged in sporadic hit-and-run raids gave way to more sophisticated tactical applications as a result of experience gained in fighting the Byzantines and the Balkan states. The usual tribal incursions were replaced by well-planned and prepared campaigns in which food, transport, munitions, and intelligence were assembled in advance. Field discipline was harsh, as was training, and the Ottoman camps were kept clean by stern enforcement of sanitary regulations. At a time when European armies were routinely ravaged by disease, the Ottoman armies rarely suffered such outbreaks when on campaign.

The sultan himself commanded the army in the field on important campaigns, and his personal tent and retinue were protected by entrenchments, artillery gun wagons, and artillery and infantry fields of fire available upon command. Near the sultan stood his personal bodyguard and the Janissary infantry. On the flanks were the household heavy cavalry. Ahead of the heavy cavalry were the light cavalry, whose main tactical task was to engage the enemy and draw it toward the heavy cavalry. After absorbing the enemy attack, the heavy cavalry often withdrew, leaving the attackers exposed to artillery fire and expert small-arms fire from the Janissary infantry. While the attackers were engaged, the heavy cavalry reformed and attempted to strike the enemy from several directions and cut off their avenue of retreat. The Ottoman tactical system was sophisticated, highly dynamic, and depended ultimately upon training and discipline of the heavy cavalry to deliver the decisive blow at the proper time to shatter the enemy and pursue it to its death. Within a few decades of the fall of Constantinople, the Ottoman army had reached its peak of development.

NOTES

1. Richard A. Gabriel and Donald W. Boose, Jr., *The Great Battles of Antiquity* (Westport, Conn.: Greenwood Press, 1994), 646–47.

2. Ibid., 651.

3. Mark C. Bartusis, *The Late Byzantine Army: Arms and Society, 1204–1453* (Philadelphia: University of Pennsylvania Press, 1992), 184–85.

4. Hans Delbruck, *History of the Art of War: Medieval Warfare* (Lincoln: University of Nebraska Press, 1982), vol. 3, 473–80.

5. David Nicole and Angus McBride, *Armies of the Ottoman Turks, 1300–1774* (London: Osprey Publishing, 1983), 9–11.

6. Gabriel and Boose, 654.

7. Nicole and McBride, 9–11.

8. Ibid., 23.

21

The Evolution of Modern War
1453–2002 C.E.

Although this work deals with ancient armies and warfare, it seems fitting to include within it, in the form of an extended postscript, an analysis of the direction that warfare has taken since the last army of the ancient world met its end at Constantinople in 1453 C.E. If only to give the work a certain historical symmetry, a beginning and end as it were, the present chapter represents such an effort.

The Hundred Years War (1337–1457 C.E.) witnessed the beginning of modern national identification with and loyalty to the nation state as a series of dynastic wars served to crystalize national identities. The need for large military forces, including mercenary contingents, gave rise to the replacement of in-kind taxes with regular collections of specie. This, in turn, required the development of a centralized governmental mechanism as the embryonic states began to build a governmental infrastructure controlled by the king. Both during the war and for more than 100 years following it, Europe was plagued by bands of demobilized ex-soldiers who fought for pay and constantly switched sides. The problem was how to bring these military forces under the control of a national army. The solution was permanent pay, regular garrison locations, strict codes of military discipline, and the emergence of military rank and administrative structures. By the 1600s, for the first time since Rome, Europe once again began to develop stable, permanent armed forces directed by central national authorities and supported by taxation.

It was the emergence of a national authority that spurred the organizational, tactical, and technological development of armies during this period and set the pattern for the next four centuries. A permanent army of professionals could be disciplined and schooled in new battle tactics and trained to utilize the new firearms to great effect. This, in turn, helped stabilize the emergent role of infantry, whose musket and pike tactics now permitted thinner linear formations of infantry to be used on the battlefield. The invention and development of the firearm required a disciplined soldier, and this brought into existence a more permanent and articulated rank and administrative structure to train and lead the soldier. Permanent rank and military organization reappeared and, by the time of the Thirty Years War (1618–1648), all the major elements of the modern army had been set into place.

WEAPONRY

The most significant invention in weaponry of the period of the Hundred Years War was the introduction of gunpowder, which, when coupled with the introduction of new techniques for casting metal, produced the primitive cannon. The immediate impact of this new invention was the siege mortar, used to batter down castle walls. In 1453 C.E., the Ottoman armies used cannon fire to destroy the remnants of the Byzantine Empire at Constantinople. Mobile siege guns, although still cumbersome, played a leading role in several battles of the Hundred Years War.[1] This was the first effective use of field artillery in Europe. True field artillery appeared in the final decade of the fifteenth century, when the French mounted light cast bronze cannon on two-wheeled carriages pulled by horses. The introduction of the trunion at this time increased the ability to mount and aim these guns with greater accuracy. By the seventeenth century, gunmaking had progressed to the point where range, power, and major types of guns were to change little over the next two centuries.

By the fifteenth and sixteenth centuries, gunpowder was changing the battlefield. The appearance of the musketeer, the forerunner of the modern rifleman, and his firelock musket made it possible for tightly packed infantry formations to engage cavalry without having to engage directly in close combat. The slow rate of fire of these early short-range weapons, however, required that the musketeers be protected from the hostile advance, a problem that led to mixing musketeer formations with pikeman. Although the mix of pike to musket changed considerably over the next

300 years, the mixed infantry formation remained the basic infantry structure for the next three centuries.

The most immediate effect of portable firearms on the battlefield was, however, felt on cavalry. The invention of the wheel lock allowed the pistol to be aimed and fired with one hand. As the shock effect of cavalry was gradually reduced by the introduction of the pike and musket to the infantry, the cavalry armed itself with saber and pistol and began to rely more on mobility than shock.[2] At long last, after more than a 1,000-year interregnum, infantry was once more becoming the deciding force on the battlefield. Cavalry, no longer decisive, was used to pin the flanks of dense infantry formations in place so that they could be raked with artillery and musket fire. The siege mortar gave way to the smooth bore cannon, which could act as genuine field artillery. By the seventeenth century, horse-drawn artillery was replaced by genuine horse artillery in which all members of artillery units rode into battle, a development that greatly increased the flexibility and mobility of field artillery, making it a full partner in the newly emerging maneuver warfare.[3]

By the sixteenth century the feudal order was creaking toward its own demise, and in its place arose the nation state, controlled by the absolute monarch in command of a permanent standing army. The instrument of creating and protecting the nation state was the professional army. Whereas feudal armies had attempted to capture the enemy's castle strongpoints, the new armies engaged in wars of attrition in which the destruction of the enemy's armed forces was the primary goal. The stage was set for a new round of national conflicts propelled by the new ideology of nationalism and dynastic rivalry. These conflicts spawned yet another cycle of development in new and more destructive weapons.

Among the most destructive of these conflicts was the Thirty Years War (1618–1648), which began as a clash of feudal armies and ended by setting the stage for the development of modern war. During this period the musket revolutionized the role of infantry. The original musket was a firelock, itself a great improvement on the earlier matchlock. The matchlock required a forked stand to hold its long barrel. The rifleman had to ignite the powder in the touchhole with a hand-held burning wick, conditions that made the weapon very difficult to aim. The firelock used a trigger attached to a rod that moved a serpentine burning wick to the touchhole, thereby allowing the rifleman to hold the weapon with both hands and make an aimed shot. The lighter, more reliable, and more mobile firelock could fire a round every two to three minutes. For the first time the infantry had a relatively reliable and accurate firearm.

The firelock was later replaced by the wheel lock, in which a rotating geared wheel powered by a cocked spring caused the flint to ignite the powder in the flashpan. A century later the wheel lock was replaced by the flintlock, in which a spring-loaded hammer struck a flint, igniting the charge. By the 1800s this mechanism was replaced by the percussion cap, a truly reliable system, and with each development the rifle became more certain to fire on cue while the rate of fire increased.

Corned powder was a significant innovation of this period. Early gunpowder for rifles and cannon tended to separate into its component materials when the powder was stored for long periods or when moved in the logistics train. The separation made it unlikely that the powder would explode evenly in the barrel, thereby increasing misfires and propelling the bullet at much lower velocity. The trick was to shape the component materials in gunpowder like little nuggets. This reduced the problem of settling and made the powder more certain to fire evenly, thus maintaining the velocity of the projectile. The result was longer range and deadlier cannon and firearms.[4]

In the sixteenth century the rifleman carried his powder and ball, ranging from .44 to .51 caliber lead shot, in small leather bags. In rainy weather the weapons often would not fire because of damp powder. The introduction of the paper cartridge by the Swede Gustavus Adolphus in the Thirty Years War greatly improved the reliability of the rifle and increased its rate of fire. Riflemen could now fire two rounds a minute instead of a single round every two to three minutes. By the end of the U.S. Civil War the totally self-contained modern cartridge with powder and bullet in a single metal container made its appearance and, by the Franco-Prussian War of 1871, the breech-loading rifle had become standard issue for European armies. Two decades later the clip and magazine-fed rifle revolutionized infantry tactics. The breech-loading magazine-fed rifle made it unnecessary for the rifleman to stand or kneel to reload. This made possible the introduction of truly modern dispersed infantry tactics, which further increased the ability of infantry to fire and maneuver.[5]

Regardless of the type of firing mechanism, the musket remained an inaccurate weapon with limited range and slow rate of fire until the Civil War. The smoothbore musket was usually ineffective beyond 100 or so yards. By the early 1700s the British Brown Bess could hit a man at eighty yards with some regularity. But it was the Americans who truly revolutionized riflery by inventing the first reliable rifled barrel, the famed Kentucky Rifle. The invention and use of rifling made it possible to hit a target reliably at 180 yards and increased the range and accuracy by a factor of three.[6]

The rifle made a significant impact on the battlefield. In feudal armies infantry was packed into dense squares to maximize firepower and resistance to shock from cavalry attack. As the rifle became more reliable and firepower more deadly at long range, it became possible to thin out the packed masses of infantry into lines while still providing sufficient firepower and defense from cavalry attack. Gustavus Adolphus was the first to deploy his infantry in lines four men deep, alternating pikemen with musketeers. This was the birth of linear tactics, which remained unchanged in their essentials almost until the twentieth century. Linear tactics provided the infantry with yet more mobility without sacrificing firepower or defense, thereby opening the way for more sophisticated battlefield maneuvers and tactical deployments. No longer the primary striking force, the pikeman had the task of protecting the musketeers from cavalry attack. As muskets became more reliable, powerful, and accurate, thinner and thinner infantry formations could be used without sacrificing killing power until, finally, the pikeman disappeared from the field altogether.

The legacy of the pikeman remained in the form of the bayonet, still standard issue in modern armies. The first bayonets were plug bayonets inserted into the muzzle of the rifle. This, of course, made the firearm inoperable, and the musketeer still had to rely heavily upon the pikeman for protection. By the end of the seventeenth century the ring bayonet was introduced. This allowed the rifle to fire while the bayonet was in place, but the attachment arrangement was clumsy and unreliable. Shortly after the ring bayonet, the standard barrel bayonet attached to a permanent stud welded to the rifle barrel made its appearance and, within a decade, became standard issue in all European armies.[7] The musketeer had now become his own pikeman. Musket infantry was now expected to protect itself from cavalry attack and, when closing with the enemy, to fight hand-to-hand with the bayonet. By combining the functions of the musketeer with the pikeman, all infantry could now be armed with firearms. The result was that the killing power of infantry increased greatly. In 1746 the fluted bayonet made its appearance at the Battle of Culloden and has remained one of the basic close combat tools of the infantryman ever since.[8]

Still other advances increased the power of infantry. In the mid-1700s the Prussians introduced the standard size iron ramrod, replacing the nonstandard wooden model. The result, when coupled with good training of the soldier, was to double the rate of musket fire. At the same time infantry began to diversify its weapons capability as the primitive hand grenade made its appearance. The first hand grenades were little more than hollow iron balls packed with black powder and ignited by a burning wick. Within a decade, however, the infantry grenadier had become a standard feature of European infantry formations.

The most significant advances in firepower and range came in the area of artillery.[9] At the beginning of the Thirty Years War artillery was still handcast by individual craftsmen. The weight of these individualized artillery pieces was often too great to make them mobile enough for effective use against enemy formations, although they served well enough in sieges. Gustavus Adolphus standardized the size of cannon and shot, and produced the first lightweight artillery guns. He also standardized infantry rifle barrels and musket shot. This system of millimeter caliber measurement was adopted almost universally and is still used today in most modern armies.[10] Adolphus standardized artillery firing procedures as well so that his artillery gunners could fire eight rounds from a single gun in the time it took a musketeer with a firelock to fire a single round.[11]

Over the next century the French introduced a number of innovations in artillery including mounting the gun on wheeled carriages and the trunion to improve aiming. Until this time most artillery was drawn by horses, while the artillery crews walked. This arrangement considerably slowed the mobility of the artillery on the battlefield, and it was common practice never to move the guns once they had been deployed. Frederick the Great of Prussia introduced the idea of mounting the guns and crews on horseback and wagons, the invention of horse artillery. This innovation greatly increased the mobility of field artillery so that commanders could routinely move the guns around and change deployments for maximum effect.[12] At the same time, of course, guns were becoming lighter and the aiming mechanisms more accurate. The result was the introduction of a truly deadly combat arm that would, over time, be responsible for more casualties than any other weapon.

The range of smoothbore cannon gradually increased over the years until, by the Napoleonic era, light cannon could fire about 300 yards, or about the range of the Roman *ballistae*. Up until the Crimean War (1854), 70 percent of all cannon shot fired was solid ball shot. But as early as the 1740s artillery gunners had various types of artillery rounds at their disposal. Heavy rounds that exploded on contact were used primarily by howitzers while artillery guns, those with a flatter trajectory, commonly used canister, chain, and grapeshot against cavalry and infantry formations. Later, these rounds were coupled with exploding charges ignited by timed wicks, which made it possible to burst artillery rounds over the heads of the enemy, greatly increasing lethality and casualties.

It was in the Civil War that rifled cannon came into its own, with a corresponding increase in range and accuracy. Still later, advances in breech loading, gas canister sealing, and recoil mechanisms greatly increased rates of fire.

THE DAWN OF MODERN WAR

The period between the fifteenth and the seventeenth centuries witnessed the emergence and consolidation of the nation state as the primary form of sociopolitical organization and as the most dynamic actor in international affairs. With the collapse of feudalism the new dynastic social orders of the West had to develop new forms of social, economic, and military organization, all of which eventually influenced the course of weapons development and the conduct of war. At the beginning of the period the most common form of domestic political organization of the nation state was the monarchy. By the seventeenth century the monarchs had gradually subdued or destroyed all competing centers of political power and parochial loyalty within their national borders, and the Age of Absolutism began, a period where national monarchs wielded absolute power over their politicosocial orders. One consequence was almost 100 years of war declared at will by various monarchs upon one another, often over trivial and personal concerns.

Over the next century, however, the power of the national monarchs was gradually circumscribed by other sectors of society, some of them arising as a consequence of the changing economic structure. Expanding domestic and international economies brought into existence new classes of domestic political claimants who demanded a share in the power of the political establishment. By the nineteenth century this process of empowerment of new societal segments culminated in the rise of representative legislatures, which gave these new classes at least limited participation in public policy. Not surprisingly, the increased influence of these new domestic political actors was roughly proportional to the degree that they were valuable to the monarch in continuing his conduct of war and foreign policy.

As the social and economic structures of the nation states became more complex, they gave rise to merchant and financial classes that gradually began to challenge the monarchical order, usually based upon the support of the landed aristocracy as the primary source of wealth and power, and to demand a greater share in the political process. The emergence of new financial instruments (hard currencies, banking systems, letters of credit, international trade, crossnational financing and manufacturing) to cope with a developing international economy forced the national monarchs into an ever greater degree of dependence upon the new classes to raise armies and fight wars. By the eighteenth century, few national monarchs could afford to maintain armies or fight wars without the help of the merchant and financial classes.

Economic concerns began to drive military ambitions at least equally with political and military concerns. The internationalization of economic affairs made it impossible for any one state to secure solely by itself the resources for war. The result was that it was no longer possible for any single state to gain military dominance over all other states or even a coalition of states for very long. The military adventures of any one state could only hope to achieve marginal gains at the expense of others. Under these circumstances, the international order became characterized by a constantly shifting (and thus unstable) balance of power among many national entities.

The economic costs of weapons and warfare increased enormously, and wars of this period often produced near or actual financial collapse for the participants. Professional armies and weapons were extremely expensive to produce and maintain relative to the resource base needed to sustain a large military force, and a number of major states were forced into bankruptcy.[13] Moreover, the destruction and economic dislocation measured by the loss or transfer of manpower from agriculture and industry, the high costs of borrowing on domestic and international financial markets, the disruption of domestic and international trade, all served to make even a successful war a near financial disaster. These circumstances gradually forced the monarchs to share power with the new merchant classes, who controlled the financial sinews of war.

By the early 1800s the transition from the old feudal orders to the modern national era was complete insofar as weaponry, tactics, and military organization were concerned. The old monarchical political order hung on for yet another century, but more in form than in substance. Militarily, the pike had all but disappeared from the battlefield, and the new musket infantry had come of age fighting in disciplined linear combat formations. Mobile artillery had also come into its own and had become a major killing combat arm that could be used in coordination with cavalry and infantry. Most importantly, standing armies in a genuine modern sense had come into being, with organization, logistics trains, and hierarchical structures comparable to those found in modern-day armies.

It was Napoleon who introduced a new element into this equation and, in doing so, revolutionized the conduct of war. Until Napoleon, armies were essentially professional forces whose manpower was drawn from the least socially and economically useful elements of the population. Most common soldiers were drawn from the ranks of the urban poor who had no skills, or the excess rural population that had no land. Even the officer corps was drawn from the second and third sons of the nobility, the first son remaining behind to manage the family's estates or business interests. Loyalty of these forces was based largely upon regular pay and draconian discipline. Napoleon's revolution was to introduce the mass citizen army based on conscription, and to develop an officer corps selected for its talent (and ideological loyalty) rather than its social origins. While a number of industrial and agricultural innovations made it possible to extract ever larger numbers of manpower from the economic base without serious disruption, the size of Napoleonic armies was impossible to maintain unless the entire social and economic resources of the state were also mobilized for war. The age of modern war was beginning to dawn.

The old idea of loyalty to the king and regular pay were replaced in the Napoleonic armies with loyalty based upon national patriotism fired by the idea of social revolution. This made it possible for Napoleon to raise mass armies, which came to characterize the national armies of the next two centuries. The idea of a "nation in arms" based on national patriotic fervor and sacrifice to ideals meant that all segments of the population were expected to contribute to the war effort. National economies were now marshaled to support war and, in a sense, private control of the resources of war passed under the control of the state. The economic structures of the state were required to produce the sinews of war on command, its weapons and manpower, even to the detriment of other aspects of economic and social activity if necessary. The most significant contribution of the Napoleonic era, then, was the production of a new national model for war.

Historians often call the American Civil War (1860–1865) the first truly modern war, for it was the first conflict to take maximum advantage of the new efficiencies of production brought into being by the Industrial Revolution. For the first time a war involved the entire populations of each combatant. Large conscript armies, larger than the world had ever seen, required a large industrial and agricultural base to feed, clothe, and supply them for combat. The Industrial Revolution, most particularly the factory system and machine mass production, along with technological innovations in metallurgy, chemistry, and machine tools, provided for an explosion in military technology. New means of economic organization and impressive increases in productivity made it possible to free large numbers of men for military service without bringing with it serious economic dislocation in the national wartime economy. The newly developed railroad system allowed the transport of men and supplies to support military operations on an unprecedented scale. The result was a war in which the civilian population that manned the productive base of the war machine became at least as important as the war machine itself. It was, as well, the first time that the production base and the civilian industrial manpower pool became legitimate and necessary military targets.

The Crimean War (1853–1856) witnessed the first use of rifled and breech-loading cannon by the British army. Both of these improvements had been used as early as the sixteenth century, but only as prototypes. Technical problems in barrel casting and breech sealing had prevented their development on a wide basis. By the end of the Civil War no fewer than half the Union artillery was comprised of rifled and breech-loading guns. Rifled cannon had longer ranges, more penetrating power, and greater accuracy than the old smoothbore, and had a much greater rate of fire. Improved black powder also added to the shell's velocity and range. Near the end of the war the first primitive recoil mechanisms further increased the rate of fire and accuracy of the rifled field artillery cannon.[14]

The musket, of course, had acquired rifling long before the Crimean War. The most important innovation to Civil War musketry came with the introduction of the canoidal bullet. Shaped like a small egg, it had a hollow "basket" behind the penetrating head. Cast in one piece of soft lead, the new bullet expanded the "basket" as the hot combustion gases filled the rear of the bullet upon firing. The soft lead expanded outward to force the raised spirals on the bullet into the rifled grooves in the barrel. The result was greater sealing of the propulsive gases in the barrel and a tighter grasp of the rifling by the bullet. Both range and accuracy increased greatly. During the Civil War a rifled musket could easily kill at 1,000 yards and was deadly accurate at 600 yards.[15]

Near the end of the war the Spencer repeating carbine appeared. This rifle was a .56 caliber repeating firearm with a seven-shot capacity. In the hands of a competent rifleman, this weapon could expend all seven rounds in the time it took a musket rifleman to load and fire a single round. Advances were also made in handguns, long the mainstay of the cavalry, that could fire six shots of .44 caliber ball before requiring reloading. Infantry firepower continued to increase with the introduction of the first primitive machine gun, the Gattling gun. This mechanized contraption was a multibarreled gun that rotated each barrel in succession into firing positions by means of a cast gear as the firing handle was turned. The Gattling gun was capable of a sustained rate of fire of 100 rounds a minute, almost equal to the rate of fire from forty infantrymen. By 1900, Hiram Maxim, an American, invented a truly modern machine gun capable of a sustained rate of fire of 600 rounds a minute.

A number of other technologies of the Industrial Revolution were turned to military use during this time. Probably most important for its impact on military operations was the railroad. Industrial nations lived by rail transport, and modern armies soon discovered that it was possible to move very large quantities of men and material over great distances very rapidly by using the rails.[16] Mobility of deployment increased dramatically, as did the means of sustaining large forces in the field over vast distances by supplying them by rail. It is important to remember that until the introduction of the railway to war, no army could move any faster than foot or horse could carry them. A limitation on tactical mobility that was six millennia old disappeared in less than half a decade.

Tinned food, although first used in small amounts by Napoleon, now became common and contributed to logistical capability, as did the first use of condensed food.[17] The telegraph made it possible for the first time for corps and army level commanders to exercise relative tactical control over their subordinate units. When the telegraph was used in conjunction with the railway, it became possible for units to achieve both tactical and strategic surprise at force levels never witnessed before. The iron-clad steam-powered ship signalled the end of the era of wood and sail, and the regular use of the balloon for military purposes presaged the use to which the early airplane would be put in the next century.

Behind these military applications lay a multitude of innovations brought into being by the Industrial Revolution. Among the most important of these were the factory system, mass production, and the use of machines to make any number of military weapons and products from canteens to boots to jackets. The factory system represented an entirely new form of socioeconomic organization for work in that it made possible the gathering into one large workplace of larger numbers of workers directed at a specific task than had ever been possible before. Mass production, especially Eli Whitney's concept of interchangeability of parts, made possible levels of weapons production never before imagined. Making things by machines meant that rates of production rose to unprecedented levels as energy and mechanical power was applied to the work task. Implements of all types could be manufactured at a faster unit production rate, and since machines do not require rest, production schedules could be extended around the clock.

The lesson that European powers learned from watching the Civil War from afar was that military might now required a sufficient industrial base and supply of manpower that had, except for the brief period under Napoleon, never before been placed under arms. Unfortunately, none of the European military establishments seem to have appreciated the fact that the Industrial Revolution had brought into being a qualitative change in the nature of combat killing power. As European armies adopted each new weapon, they foolishly retained the traditional and familiar unit formations and battlefield tactics, both of which had already been made fatally obsolete by the range and firepower of the new infantry and artillery weapons. Thus, when the British finally adopted the machine gun to their infantry formations, they assigned only one gun per battalion, relying upon the traditional rifleman to provide the firepower for the defense. Not a single European power recognized that the qualitative change in killing power had made offensive operations a deadly practice. The battlefield advantage had swung almost entirely to the defense.

The lessons regarding manpower and industrial production, however, were not lost on the European general staffs, and the armies of Europe began to expand to record size. These armies created even larger reserve forces that could be mobilized on short notice and moved along military rail nets to augment the standing forces in one large-scale, and almost irreversible, deployment maneuver. The railway officer who could plan and implement deployment schedules became the most valuable officer on the newly created professionalized general staffs. In Germany, almost the entire civilian railway service was staffed by retired professional sergeants still under military obligation as reserve forces. As the Industrial Revolution developed one innovation after another, more and more military applications were found. The result was that the armies of the early twentieth century had at their disposal a killing and destructive capacity greater than anything the world had ever seen. The fatal flaw was that they did not know it.

In the half-century between the end of the Civil War and the start of World War I there were no fewer than six military conflicts involving one or more of the major powers as combatants. Almost a score of smaller colonial wars were fought in the same period. These conflicts provided the impetus to apply the inventions and technologies of the Industrial Revolution to new weapons. These frequent, if short, wars provided laboratories to test the new implements of destruction.

Among the more important developments of this period was the total replacement of muzzle-loading smoothbore cannon with rifled breach loaders. By 1890, every major military force in the West was equipped with this type of cannon. Time fuses were developed in France around 1877 and served to make overhead burst artillery more lethal than ever. The first smokeless powder, more stable and potent than black powder, was developed in 1884, and in 1891, the British synthesized a new shell explosive, cordite, that became the standard artillery explosive by 1914. In 1888, modern long-recoil hydraulic cylinders were introduced to stabilize artillery pieces, an improvement that almost tripled the rate of fire and accuracy of field artillery guns. The rifled breech loading artillery gun now operated with "fixed ammunition," brass and steel shells in which powder, fuse, and projectile were one piece. The introduction of shrapnel shells added even more to the destructive power of artillery. In 1896, wire-wound heavy guns were constructed, making gun barrels much stronger and less brittle than cast barrels. A short time later, frettage, a method of manufacture in which hot steel tubes were shrunk one into another to make gun barrels, allowed the introduction of more durable and much higher caliber guns. Improved breeches and gas sealing systems completed the development of artillery in this period. In 1897, the French 75-millimeter field gun was introduced, which incorporated all of the improvements mentioned above. The maximum rate of fire of this gun was twenty-five rounds per minute. In the 1880s, massive siege cannon, often mounted on railway cars, began to make their appearance as the antidote for huge concrete and steel fixed fortifications. The Krupp siege cannon, "Big Bertha," could raise an 1,800 pound shell three miles into the air and hit a target at very high velocity 10,000 yards away.[18]

In 1870, the French had deployed the *mitrailleuse*, a highly reliable, if somewhat cumbersome, 25-barrel machine gun capable of firing 125 rounds a minute while accurate at 2,000 yards. By 1900 Hiram Maxim had invented a truly modern and portable machine gun with a rate of fire of 600 rounds a minute. At this rate of fire a single machine gun could produce as much fire as 100 riflemen. In 1870, the Prussian Dreyse "needlegun" introduced the modern firing pin system for the rifle, once again increasing rates of fire. The introduction of the magazine (Lee-Enfield) and clip-fed (Mauser, Springfield) bolt-action rifles by the time of the Boer War increased the firepower and mobility of the infantry yet again.

The Russo-Turkish War of 1877–1878 was the first war in which the infantry was uniformly equipped with modern repeating rifles and the artillery with breech-loading rifled cannon. By the outbreak of the Russo-Japanese War (1904–1905) the use of indirect heavy artillery fire was standard military practice. The invention of improved panoramic sights, goniometers for measuring angles, the use of the balloon for directing fire, and the field telephone allowed forward artillery observers to direct artillery fire on targets the gunners could not see. Advances in fire control made it possible for the first time to mass the fire of an entire artillery corps upon a single target.[19]

NAVAL AND AIR WEAPONRY

Between the fifteenth and eighteenth centuries the development of naval weapons was hardly perceptible. Ships remained platforms for carrying infantry and, later, became gun platforms. Sail and wood construction limited the role of ships and greatly reduced the number and caliber of guns that could be placed upon them. In the 1800s a new form of propulsion, the steam engine, began to change the role of the ship. The first steam-powered naval ships were produced in the 1820s, but the need for side paddlewheels and huge engines still limited the ship's role as a gun platform. By 1850, the first screw propeller made the side-wheeler obsolete, and freed deckspace necessary to carry more guns. The modern artillery shell, however, had already made the wooden-hulled vessel obsolete, and in 1855 the French introduced iron plating along the wooden hull for increased protection. Even so, the need for heavy modern guns and large steam engines placed too much strain on wooden-hulled ships, and in 1860 the British launched H.M.S. *Warrior*, the world's first iron-hulled warship.

The armored turret was first used on ships in 1868, and gradually the advances in artillery weapons—quick firing, fixed ammunition, breech-loading, rifled guns—were seriously applied to naval guns. Ships began to mount multiple turrets, first with one gun per turret and, finally, by 1900, a standard four guns per turret. The caliber of guns grew from twelve-inch guns (1908) to fifteen-inch guns as standard by 1914. The last decade of the nineteenth century saw the introduction of steel construction for naval vessels. By 1913, naval vessels were powered by oil instead of coal boilers, greatly increasing propulsive power while reducing engine space. All of these advances culminated in the production of the dreadnought-class warship, the first modern battleship. In less than 100 years, naval ships of the line had gone from the first simple iron-clads to modern battleships. H.M.S. *Dreadnought* was launched in 1906 and displaced 17,900 tons, was 527 feet long, and 82 feet at the beam. She carried ten 12-inch guns, twenty-seven 12 pounders, and five 18-inch torpedo tubes. Powered by 23,000 horsepower engines, she could make 21 knots. But in less than a decade she had become obsolete.

The invention and improvements in mines and, later, the guided torpedo, made even the largest warships vulnerable. The controlled mine was developed by the United States in 1843, and was detonated by electric current from wires leading to shore. Chemically triggered contact mines were in use as early as 1862. By World War I, the mine had become a potent defensive weapon capable of sinking the largest ships. The torpedo—called the "locomotive torpedo" because it proceeded under its own power and did not have to be towed like earlier models— made its appearance in 1866. The first models, developed by the Austrians, had a range of 370 yards at six knots, and packed an eighteen-pound explosive warhead. By 1877, the contrarotating propeller was fitted to a torpedo, an innovation that kept the torpedo steady on course. Soon the torpedo was fitted with a horizontal rudder to keep it at constant depth as it ran to its target. By 1895, the invention of the gyroscope improved the torpedo's accuracy, and by the turn of the century a torpedo could carry a 300-pound warhead to 1,000-yard range at thirty knots.[20] This weapon called into existence a new class of cheap, fast, and destructive naval vessel, the torpedo boat.

The most revolutionary naval advance of this period was the submarine. By 1900, the gyroscope, the gyrocompass, the use of steel hulls, a safe method of propulsion in the internal combustion engine, and the accumulator battery combined to make the submarine possible. The development of the reliable torpedo provided the submarine with an excellent weapon of attack. In 1900, the six major navies of the world had only ten submarines among them.

In 1905, an American submarine, the USS *Holland*, became the prototype for other navies with submarine forces. Displacing 105 tons, the *Holland* had three separate water-tight compartments housing her engine, control, and torpedo rooms. Her second lower deck housed the tanks and battery engines. The *Holland* could make almost nine knots while submerged. A few years later the British introduced the conning tower and periscope, while the Germans in 1906 contributed the development of double-hulls and twin screws for propulsion and stability. By 1914, the six major naval powers of the world put 249 submarines to sea.

In 1903, Orville Wright made the first sustained powered flight, twelve seconds, in a heavier-than-air flying machine powered by the new internal combustion engine. In just two years the Wright Flyer had improved to the point where it could stay airborne for forty minutes at a speed of forty-five miles per hour. In 1907 the pusher biplane was flown and, by 1908, the Wright airplane was staying in the air for 2.5 hours. The invention of ailerons to control the aircraft around its roll axis greatly increased the maneuverability of the machine.[21] For the most part, how-

ever, military men saw the airplane as performing the limited functions of the old balloon, observation and reconnaissance.

In 1910, the American Eugene Eli took off in an airplane from a platform erected on the deck of a naval cruiser and, a year later, it was proven possible to land the aircraft back on the flight deck. In 1911 another American, Glen Curtis, became the first man to carry out a practice bombing run against a naval ship, touching off a fierce debate about the vulnerability of ships to air attack. In the same year two-way radio communication from an airplane to the ground was accomplished, an invention that made possible aerial artillery observation and fire direction. Also in 1911, Glen Curtis manufactured the first seaplane and foresaw its use as a weapon against the submarine. In that same year the U.S. Army dropped the first live bombs from an airplane, and the first machine gun was mounted on an aircraft, the French Nieuport fighter. A year later monocoque construction was introduced, a method of arranging stress points in aircraft construction that made possible greater loads on aircraft structures. In that same year airplane flying speed increased to over 100 miles per hour. In April 1912, the establishment of the Royal Flying Corps in England gave birth to the first official air force.

In 1913, speed (127 mph), distance (635 miles), and altitude (20,079 feet) records were set as the airplane began to improve its capability as a weapon of war. The Russians introduced the world's first heavy bomber, the *Sikorsky Bolshoi*, with a wingspan of over ninety feet. During the Turko-Italian War (1911–1912) in Libya, the world witnessed the first military use of the airplane in war. The Italians first employed the airplane for artillery observation and were the first to introduce aerial photography. Italian pilots were the first to drop bombs against an enemy force in combat. The age of the modern strike and bomber airplane as major implements of modern war was underway.

WORLD WAR I

The social, political, and economic context in which armies were raised and wars were fought had changed considerably in the seventy-five years since the Civil War. The political structures of the national states of Europe were under attack from new ideologies of the Left and Center that greatly weakened the power of the executive while increasing the influence of the legislatures. Traditional ruling elites now had to share power or were replaced by elected leaders. The monarchies, while retained in form, lost most of their substantive power. The need for polit-

ical leaders to sustain their electoral bases required that conflicts be cast in highly moral and ideological terms. Wars now became moral crusades, a fact that made them easier to start and more difficult to resolve short of total victory.

The search for economic self-sufficiency led each major power to engage in the quest for colonial empire that could provide stable sources of raw materials and secure markets for manufactured goods.[22] Inevitably, conflicts in peripheral colonial areas brought the major powers into collision on the rim of Europe until, in 1914, these conflicts engulfed the heartland of Europe itself. The rapid development of military technology led to a continuous arms race. This state of affairs, in turn, provoked a spate of alliances and counter-alliances among the major powers and the fragmented smaller states of eastern Europe. The stage was set to draw the larger states into direct conflict whenever the smaller states collided with one another.

The size of the standing armies of the day grew in response to the need to take advantage of the new military technologies. The destructiveness of modern weapons required that large numbers of fighting men be readily available. Propelled by the strategic doctrine of the day that held that the side that mobilized quickest would have the advantage of striking a lethal blow, nations established large reserve forces that could be mobilized and deployed within days. Once mobilization plans were set in motion, however, they could not be easily stopped without conceding a significant military advantage to one's opponent. Once war broke out, the entire economy and productive capacity of the nation was to be marshaled for war. If Napoleon had created the new reality of a nation in arms, it was World War I that gave birth to the idea of a nation at war.

On the eve of World War I, Europe was a tinderbox waiting to explode. National economies were prepositioned for war, large standing armies faced one another across unclear and disputed territorial boundaries, civilian populations were capable of being put into uniform within days of mobilization, the major powers were caught in a series of entangling alliances with small unstable states whose local conflicts could quickly escalate into war, an arms race fed a growing fear, and the strategic doctrine of the day required one to strike first. Superimposed upon it all was a political process that produced unstable political leadership, which had to sustain itself by appearing strong and uncompromising on national security issues. Those, in turn, were driven by ideological and moral perspectives that made compromise almost im-

possible. When a stray shot was fired in the narrow streets of Sarejevo, it produced a genuine world war. And the lights went out all over Europe.

World War I became known as the "machine gun war," and it is estimated that fully 80 percent of all British ground casualties were caused by the machine gun.[23] In a war of fixed positions, artillery guns grew larger, firing ever larger shells in concentrated barrages for days at a time. The siege mortar reached almost 42 inches in diameter, and railway guns fired 210 millimeter rounds 82 miles. Trench mortars reached 170mm caliber and could fire poison gas shells, mustard, and chlorine, as well. Poison gas released from canisters made its appearance in 1915, and the age of chemical warfare was born. The gas mask became standard military equipment, and the pack howitzer for use by mountain infantry made its battlefield debut, as did the first antiaircraft guns.

A truly revolutionary development was the first operational battle tank. The early tanks were very unreliable as temperatures in the crew compartments often exceeded 100 degrees fahrenheit from the heat of the engine. By 1917, however, a much improved tank, the Mark IV, was introduced at the Battle of Cambrai, and history's first massed tank attack, involving over 476 tanks, took place. In the spring of 1918 the French introduced the lighter and faster Renault FT, the first tank to use a revolving turret. By the end of the war over 6,000 battle tanks had been built and deployed by Allied armies. The age of armor had begun.

The war at sea remained deadlocked. The British countered the German submarine threat by inventing the ship convoy. Of the 16,070 ships that sailed in British convoys, only ninety-six were lost to submarine attack. In 1915 the first use of the hydrophone made it possible to detect submarines by sound. A year later the first submarine was destroyed by yet another deadly invention, the depth-charge. By that time naval forces routinely used the seaplane, and in 1917 HMS *Furious* added the world's first operational flight deck to her forward superstructure. In the same year HMS *Argus* became the first naval vessel to be built with both a take-off and landing deck. With the incorporation of the American deck catapult and arresting gear, the prototype of the modern aircraft carrier was born.

The war quickened the development of the first aircraft designed for military use. The interrrupter gear made possible the mounting of machine guns on aircraft by allowing the guns to fire through a turning propeller. Improvements in design, materials, and structure of aircraft manufacture made it possible for aircraft to fly at 140 miles an hour at altitudes of 22,000 feet. The first bombers capable of 2,000-pound bomb loads appeared. The devastating capability of the strike aircraft was only a decade away.

WORLD WAR II

Europe emerged from World War I almost bankrupt. While research and development into new weapons continued during the interwar period, it did so on a much smaller scale than before the war. Overall expenditures on military equipment and manpower declined as the nations of Europe tried to find the money to repair their devastated domestic infrastructures. The political and social institutions of the European powers were badly shaken by the lingering effects of the war. The war had produced revolution in Russia, leading to the establishment of a Soviet state. In Italy, Benito Mussolini deposed the Italian monarchy and produced the first Fascist state. Germany's monarchy was replaced with a weak republican government that proved unable to deal with the increasing social instability, succumbing in the end to Nazism. France's republican institutions were attacked from within by both Left and Right, so sapping the political will of the citizenry that, in the spring of 1940, the French surrendered to the German army almost without firing a shot. In England the hold of the traditional ruling classes was weakened considerably by an assault mounted from the Left. Only America, whose losses in the war had been very light, seemed immune from the destabilizing aftershocks of the Great War.

Most of the European powers could no longer sustain large military establishments. In 1918, German military forces were reduced by the dictate of the victorious powers, and spent almost nothing on military development until 1932. England reduced her air and ground forces significantly. By 1939 her navy was a shell of its former self. France reduced her expenditures as well, choosing to concentrate on ground forces, leaving her naval, air, and armor forces too small to counter the German threat. The United States rescinded military conscription and reduced military expenditures across the board. American ground forces shrunk to under 200,000 men, armor was nonexistent, and the air force could deploy only a handful of obsolete machines. Soviet attempts at military growth were crippled by famine, political terror, and civil war. By the early 1930s, however, the new Red Army had the largest artillery and tank forces in the world. But as a result of Stalin's purges, these formations were broken up and the officer corps killed or imprisoned. When the Soviets finally came to blows with tiny Finland, they were barely able to achieve a victory.

Only in Japan and, to a lesser extent, in Italy did military expenditures and weapons development increase significantly. After 1932, Germany embarked upon a major rearmament program under the Nazis. In Japan the need to build an industrial base sufficient to maintain a modern military establishment led to the creation of a military society whose every effort went toward increasing the military prowess of the state. The Japanese reliance on overseas sources for critical raw materials forced it to engage in wars of conquest in Asia to gain control of oil fields, steel deposits, and other raw materials needed as sinews of war. Mussolini's attempt to make Italy a great power foundered on the insufficient resource base of Italy. Italy never obtained sufficient coal, steel, and oil supplies, required by a first-rate military machine. By 1939 when Italian military prestige was at its highest and Italian airplanes, ships, and small arms were among the best in the world, the fact remained that Italy's industrial base was never adequate to sustain a large modern military machine for very long.

Yet, it would be incorrect to assume that the development of weaponry came to a halt during the interwar years. The tank, for example, continued to improve markedly with the appearance of the low profile hull, the revolving turret, better gunsights, and improved tracks and suspension. By the 1930s the Russians had developed the famed T-34, the best tank of its day. Tank cannon grew larger to 90-millimeter guns, and new propellants and shot, the sabot round, made these cannon even more deadly. The tank called into existence the first antitank guns. The German *Gerlich* gun, for example, fired a 28-millimeter round of tungsten carbide at 4,000 feet per second, and was capable of penetrating any known tank armor. A later German invention, the "eighty-eight," was originally developed as an antitank weapon but doubled as both an antiaircraft and direct fire gun. It is generally adjudged the best weapon of its kind in World War II.

Developments in aircraft design—the stressed metal skin and the monoplane—made the introduction of fighter aircraft possible. Engines over 1,000 horsepower made speeds of over 350 miles per hour commonplace. The long-range bomber capable of flying at altitudes over 40,000 feet at ranges of 5,000 miles was developed. At sea the light and fast destroyer was built to protect the larger battleships. More sophisticated submarines could remain at sea for 60 days at a time. A new torpedo, the Type 33 Lance, driven by oxygen and leaving no track appeared, with a range of 25 miles at 36 knots. Torpedoes now typically carried warheads of 400 pounds of high explosives. The aircraft carrier came into its own. The Japanese carrier, *Kaga*, carried 60 aircraft and displaced 39,000 tons.

The American carrier, *Lexington*, displaced 36,000 tons and carried 90 aircraft. The integration of naval and air forces within a single combined combat arm was almost complete.

The destructive power of the combat arms—infantry, armor, and artillery—greatly increased in World War II. Infantry, armed in large numbers with the new all-metal submachine gun, delivered firepower at rates five times greater than the infantryman of World War I. Infantry carried its own antitank weapons in the form of the American 3.5 inch Bazooka (named because of the sound it made when fired) rocket launcher or the German *Panzerfaust*. Dependable motorized transport, the Jeep, the "deuce and a half" truck, and the armored personnel carrier—fully tracked, half-tracked, or pneumatic tire vehicles—increased infantry mobility twentyfold and enabled it to keep pace with the rapid armor advance.

The tank saw a remarkable increase in its combat capability and, for the first time in almost 700 years, cavalry again played an important role on the battlefield. The Russian T-34, originally produced in 1935, was possibly the best battle tank of the war. Mounting an 85-millimeter gun with a new muzzle-brake to reduce recoil, the T-34 made 32 miles an hour with a range of 180 miles. It introduced the sloped armored glacis in front to deflect antitank rounds, and had a ground pressure of 10 pounds per square inch which, on its American-designed Christie suspension, allowed it to traverse terrain that most Allied or Axis tanks could not. The American Sherman tank introduced cast armor to replace the old welded armor, the volute-spring bogie suspension, and rubber block treads that increased track life by 500 percent. The Sherman used a revolutionary hydroelectric gun-stabilizing system and improved triangle sights. Tank engines grew more powerful and more reliable, and the tank quickly became the centerpiece of the striking forces for all armies except the Japanese.

Artillery developments came in response to the need to defend against armor and air attack. The result was the self-propelled artillery gun. These guns, often reaching 8-inch or 122-millimeter caliber, were mobile artillery mounted on tank chassis. Self-propelled artillery came in two forms: the assault gun and the light assault gun. The arrival of the ground attack fighter required improvements in antiaircraft guns. The Bofors 40-millimeter cannon was capable of firing two rounds per second over a slant range of 4 miles. The American M-2, 90 millimeter gun fired 25 rounds per minute to a height of 9 miles. The introduction of reliable electronic fire control systems with radar detectors and trackers linked to primitive computers provided great advances in the lethality of anti-aircraft guns.

Unguided rocket artillery, first used by the Chinese 1,000 years earlier, reappeared in the form of the German 15-centimeter *Nebelwerfer*, which could fire six 70–pound rockets in less than 3 seconds. The Soviet *Katusha*, first at 90 millimeter and then 122 millimeter, fired over 40 rockets at once. The American entry, the Calliope, fired 60 rockets at a time. Used as area saturation weapons, these rockets caused large numbers of psychiatric as well as physical casualties.[24] The variable timed fuse introduced by the Americans increased the lethality of artillery fire by a significant degree. Each shell contained a tiny radio transceiver within it that could be set so that the round exploded at a precise distance above the ground. This innovation increased the killing power of artillery by ten times over shells fitted with conventional fuses.

The war at sea saw the demise of the battleship as it became increasingly vulnerable to air and undersea attack. The aircraft carrier became the major naval weapon. Carriers like the *Essex* and *Midway* class carried over 100 strike aircraft, were 820 feet long with beams of 147 feet, and could move at 32 knots. Carrier-based aircraft were remarkable machines. These aircraft carried 2,000 pounds of bombs, flew at 350 miles per hour, attacked with rockets, torpedoes, and machine guns, and ranged over 300 miles. Although submarines operated with new electrical motors to make them increasingly difficult to detect, antisubmarine technology improved markedly. Radar and radio sets allowed antisubmarine aircraft to detect submarines at night. New depth charges provided surface vessels with new means of submarine destruction. By 1944, the submarine was no longer a significant threat to surface combatants.

The air war saw the emergence of greatly improved strike aircraft. The British *Spitfire* and other aircraft on both sides could range outward for hundreds of miles at speeds over 400 miles per hour. Ground support tactics developed rapidly as strike aircraft made heavy firepower at close ranges available to advancing infantry and armor. The heavy strategic bomber appeared capable of bomb loads of 20,000 pounds. The B-29 *Superfortress* carried 20,000 pounds of bombs 3,250 miles at an altitude of 31,850 feet. By war's end the Germans (ME-262), the British (Vampire), and the Americans (P-59 Aircomet) had all produced prototypes of jet powered aircraft. In August 1945 the United States unveiled the most awesome weapon of war yet invented by man, the atomic bomb, and devastated the civilian population centers of Hiroshima and Nagasaki. Warfare had undergone yet another revolutionary change.

POST–WORLD WAR II

The debut of nuclear weapons makes it necessary in modern times to clearly distinguish between nuclear and conventional weapons. Only eight years after Hiroshima, nuclear artillery shells were invented, and three years later these shells were small enough to be fired from a 155-millimeter howitzer. By 1970, U.S. and Soviet navies had deployed nuclear torpedoes capable of sinking the largest aircraft carriers with a single shot. Nuclear bombs that in the 1950s weighed many tons became smaller so that they could be placed under the wings of fighter aircraft. In the 1950s nuclear reactors were used for the first time to power a strike carrier. Within ten years nuclear powered missile frigates and cruisers appeared. Nuclear missiles mounted on nuclear powered submarines capable of staying submerged for months were developed and deployed by the 1960s. These missiles grew in range until it was possible to place several Multiple Independent Reentry Vehicles (MIRVs)—(warheads) on a single missile. By 1985 the *Trident* II submarine carried 24 missiles, each mounting 10 separate warheads of almost half a megaton each. Firing submerged, the *Trident*'s missiles have a range of over 8,000 miles. Land-based strategic missiles are capable of destroying cities from 10,000 miles away in a single blow.

There is a sense, as Napoleon is supposed to have remarked, that quantity conveys a quality all its own. The increase in destructive capacities of conventional weapons has also been enormous, so much so that in any other age these quantitative changes in destructive power would have been regarded as qualitative revolutions in the nature of war. In the modern age, it is nuclear weapons that provide the baseline from which weapons effects are measured. Thus, it does not seem so horrendous, for example, that whole battalions can be exterminated by a single barrage from new artillery weapons when it is possible to exterminate whole cities in the time it takes a flash bulb to burn out. Like most things in modern life, even the destructive effects of war have become relative.

In 1980 the U.S. Army estimated that modern nonnuclear conventional war had become 400 to 700 percent more lethal and intense than it had been in World War II, depending, of course, on the battle scenario.[25] The increases in conventional killing power have been enormous, and far greater and more rapid than in any other period in man's history. The artillery firepower of a maneuver battalion, for example, has doubled since World War II, while the "casualty effect" of modern artillery guns has increased 400 percent. Range has increased, on average, by 60 percent, and the "zone of destruction" of battalion artillery by 350 percent.[26]

Advances in metallurgy and the use of new chemical explosives has increased the explosive power of basic caliber artillery by many times. A single round from an eight-inch gun has the same explosive power as a World War II 250-pound bomb. Modern artillery is lighter, stronger, and more mobile than ever before. Computerized fire direction centers can range guns on target in only fifteen seconds compared to the six minutes required in World War II. The rates of fire of these guns are three times what they used to be. So durable are the new artillery guns that they can fire 500 rounds over a 4-hour period without incurring damage to the barrel. Range has increased to the point where the M-110 gun can fire a 203-millimeter shell 25 miles. The self-propelled gun has a travel range of 220 miles at a speed of 35 miles per hour. Area saturation artillery, in its infancy in World War II, has become very lethal. A single Soviet artillery battalion firing 18 BM-21 rocket launchers can place 35 tons of explosive rockets on a target 17 miles away in just 30 seconds. The American Multiple Rocket Launching System (MRLS) is a totally mobile self-contained artillery system that can place 8,000 M-77 explosive rounds on a target the size of six football fields in less than 45 seconds. Air defense guns have developed to where a single M-163 Vulcan cannon can fire 3,000 rounds of explosive 20-millimeter shot per minute with almost 100 percent accuracy within 2 miles of the gun position. Modern antiaircraft guns command 36 times the airspace around their position as they did in World War II.[27]

Tanks have improved in speed, reliability, and firepower. Modern tanks can make forty miles per hour over a 300-mile range, or three times that of earlier tanks. A tank equipped with modern gunsights and cannon stabilization system has a probability of scoring a first round hit of 98 percent, thirteen times greater than World War II tanks. Modern battletanks, unlike any earlier variety, can also fire while on the move. Their probability of hitting the target while moving is almost ten times greater than that of a World War II tank firing from a stabilized position. New propellants and ammunition design have increased the lethality of the modern tank. During the Iraqi–United States war in 1991, Armor Piercing Discarding Sabot (APDS) rounds moving at 5,467 feet per second pierced four feet of sand in bunkered berms and still destroyed enemy tanks. Tank gunsights, lasers connected to computers, can locate a target in the dark, smoke, rain, or snow at 2,000 yards.[28]

The armed combat helicopter has produced a revolution in tank and armor killing power available to the combat commander. These weapons can be configured to kill either troops or tanks and are truly awesome weapons. The *Apache* gunship carries sixteen *Hellfire* antitank missiles that need only minimal further direction after they are fired to home in on the target. New sights allow the helicopter to acquire its target from more than five miles away. The helicopter has added new mobility and stealth to the battlefield permitting a division commander to strike with troops or antitank weapons sixty miles to his front, four times the range in World War II. The infantry, too, has increased its range, mobility, and firepower with new armored personnel carriers and infantry fighting vehicles. Infantry can also bring to bear shoulder-fired antiaircraft missiles and Jeep and Hummer mounted TOW antitank missiles with devastating results.[29]

The modern battlefield is a lethal place indeed. To place the increased intensity of the modern nonnuclear conventional battlefield in perspective, one need only remember that in World War II heavy combat was defined as two to four combat pulses a day. Modern combat divisions are configured to routinely deliver twelve to fourteen combat pulses a day and to fight around the clock by night operations. A modern U.S. or Soviet motorized division can deliver three times as much firepower at ten times the rate as each could in World War II.[30] By these and any other historical (or human) standard, even conventional weapons have in a very real sense become quite unconventional.

The concentration of sheer destructive power in the hands of modern armies is, in itself, a truly significant change in the nature of warfare. However, perhaps more important than the exponential change in the *tools* of war is the *manner* in which modern wars are fought. In this regard two characteristics of modern war are so significantly different from the nature of past wars as to be regarded as substantial *qualitative* revolutions.

The first qualitative revolution in modern war is the ability of the technology of target acquisition to literally destroy any target that ventures upon the battlefield. Modern military forces are equipped with a wide range of electronic, laser, infrared, satellite, and optical devices that can turn the nighttime battlefield into day. Modern tank sights can easily locate a target in complete darkness at 3,500 yards. Even when the target cannot be seen by optical enhancing devices, its silhouette can be discerned by infrared and laser sights. Further, modern armies are now in their third generation of "smart munitions," which make it possible to virtually guarantee that if a target can be located it can be hit with alarming certainty and rapidity. One major result of these technological developments has been the disruption of the historical nexus between the size of combatants and their lethality. Now, for the first time in history, the size of an army is far less important to its ability to achieve victory than the degree of killing technology that it can bring to the battlefield. If the 1991 Gulf War proved anything, it was the demonstration of this proposition.

A second qualitative revolution in the conduct of war is the manner in which it is fought. Modern war is a war of speed, mobility, penetration, encirclement, envelopment, and, ultimately, of force annihilation. World War II was a linear war in which combat occurred along a generally well-defined front line with usually safe rear areas. World War II was also a tactical war in which most of the fighting was accomplished by units of division strength or less. The conventional war of the future presents a far different set of circumstances.

In modern conventional war, linear tactics are replaced by "swirling tactics." The combat reach of modern armies is so long and the mobility of combat vehicles—both air and ground vehicles—so great that armies must now plan to fight three battles at once. Combat doctrines require that units be able to fight the "direct" battle—that is, to engage units directly to their front. But doctrine also requires that armies be able to simultaneously fight the "deep" battle, to reach out and strike deeply behind the enemy's lines with large combat forces to disrupt timetables, supplies, and reinforcements. Of course, one sides' deep battle is the other side's "rear" battle so that armies must plan to deal with sizeable enemy forces engaged in attacking the rear. Some idea of the ferocity of these "rear" battles can be gained from the fact that the units attacking the enemy's rear are of division size or larger. Simultaneously, attack aircraft and helicopters roam hundreds of miles behind the lines wreaking havoc with their weapons.

Accordingly, the entire battlefield is highly unstable, a war not of fixed lines, but of swirling combat in which units will be expected to fight isolated from parent units. Units will be trapped, decimated, bypassed, isolated, and often expected to fight until they can no longer do so. In short, modern war is not a war of offense and defense as in World War II, but a war of meeting engagements in which all units are expected to conduct a continuous offensive.

Modern conventional war is no longer a tactical war in which most of the fighting is done by relatively small units of division size or less. Instead, modern war is an operational level war in which the scope of command and control moves back from the line divisions to the corps and theater commands. Larger units are simultaneously committed for objectives of greater scope. The operational level of war produces far more intense and destructive battles ranging over greater areas often, paradoxically, over shorter periods of time. These battles require the total integration of all combat resources within the theatre of operations to maximize the application of force. Modern battles are fought around the clock until objectives are achieved. The fall of night, historically the respite of the combat soldier, will come no more.

Taken together, then, it is fair to say that the qualitative revolutions in the technology of target acquisition and destruction, when coupled with the qualitative revolution in the manner in which wars must be fought on the modern battlefield, combine to produce a style of warfare that is itself qualitatively different from almost all war that has gone before. The challenging task for the modern officer is how to master these new circumstances.

LETHALITY AND CASUALTIES

Beginning in 1860 the pace of weapons development increased enormously as the Industrial Revolution produced one technological advance upon another. Among the most important consequences of the factory system, mass production, and machine manufacture was the great reduction in time required between new ideas and the manufacture of production prototypes. New concepts were quickly reduced to drawings, then to models, then prototypes, and finally to full-scale implementation within very short periods of time. The wide-spread introduction of technical journals quickened the time it took for innovations in one discipline to have an impact on another related field. The result was a rapid increase in information transfer. The overall consequence of these circumstances was the rapid application of new weapons and other technologies of war to the battlefield at a pace never seen before in history, with the corresponding result that weapons became more lethal than ever.

Lethality in war is always, however, the sum total of a number of factors that go quite beyond the inherent death-dealing capabilities of a military technology. For example, before a new weapon can reach its killing potential, military commanders have to discover new methods of fighting to bring the new weapon to bear in a manner that maximizes its killing potential. Once the killing power is exposed for all to see, however, one's opponent adopts passive and active means for limiting the most deadly effects of the weapon. This, in turn, requires new changes in tactics and combat formations in an attempt to preserve the killing power of the new technology. Inevitably, the result is a dynamic balance of behavior and technology that usually results in a state of affairs where the killing power of the new weapon remains somewhat higher than the weapon it replaced, but often not greatly so. It cannot be stressed too strongly in calculating the killing power of weaponry that any failure to adapt either weapons or tactics to new circumstances can be catastrophic. Thus, the failure of the World War I armies to alter their battle tactics in light of the machine gun's enormous rates of fire resulted in horrendous casualties in the early days of the war. The similar refusal of British commanders at the Somme to change their practice of massed infantry attacks against entrenched positions resulted in 54,000 men being killed or wounded in less than ten hours. Similarly, Saddam Hussein's insistence in the Gulf War of meeting American firepower with the same defensive tactics he had employed in the Iran-Iraq war resulted in the destruction of large numbers of soldiers in less than 100 hours of fighting.

T.N. Dupuy has calculated the effects of weapons as their killing power is affected by changes in a number of objective factors such as rates of fire, number of potential targets per strike, relative incapacitating effect, effective range, muzzle velocity, reliability, battlefield mobility, radius of action, and vulnerability in order to arrive at what he calls a Theoretical Lethality Index for each weapon that specifies its lethality power. But such objective factors, when weighed against the single variable of dispersion, do not reliably predict the ability to produce casualties under actual battlefield conditions. The result is that, when measured over time, the measurable casualty effects of modern weapons paradoxically result in far fewer casualties when measured against the weapons of the past.

Dupuy notes that when measured against the nongunpowder weapons of antiquity and the Middle Ages, modern weapons, excluding nuclear weapons of course, have increased in lethality by a factor of 2,000. But while lethality has increased by a factor of 2,000, the dispersion of forces on the battlefield made possible by mechanization and the ability of fewer soldiers to deliver exponentially more firepower has increased by a factor of 4,000![31] The result has been that wars since 1865 have killed fewer soldiers as a percentage of the deployed combat force than was the case in previous wars. Except for the Napoleonic wars, which utilized the tactical field formation of the packed marching column, every war since 1600 has resulted in fewer and fewer casualties as a percentage of the committed forces for both the victor and defeated. It is clear that as weapons became more and more destructive, armies reacted by adjusting their tactics to increase their dispersion of forces so as to minimize the targets provided to the new weapons. Again, the overall result has been a decline in battle casualties even as the lethality of weapons increased.

Some historical examples help clarify the point. Until the Napoleonic wars the proportion of casualties, killed and wounded, to total effective forces under the system of linear tactics had steadily declined from 15 percent for the victors to 30 percent for the losers in battle during the Thirty Years War to about 9 and 16 percent respectively during the wars of the French Revolution.[32] Napoleon's use of column tactics forced him to reduce the dispersion of forces in the face of increased killing power of musketry and artillery.[33] The result was an increase in Napoleon's casualty rates to 15 and 20 percent. By 1848, dispersion had once again become the basis of tactics and increased with each war over the next 100 years. The result was a decline in the number of soldiers killed per 1,000 per year. In the Mexican War, U.S. forces lost 9.9 soldiers per 1,000 per annum. For the Spanish-American War the corresponding figure was 1.9, for the Philippine Insurrection it was 2.2, for World War I it was 12.0, and for World War II it was 9.0. Only during the Civil War, which saw many battles in which massed formations were thrown against strong defensive positions (the opposite of dispersion) did the rates of the North, 21.3, and the South, 23.0, again begin to approach those of the Napoleonic period.[34] Thus, barring incredible tactical stupidity, as lethal as modern weaponry is and as intense as modern nonnuclear conventional wars are, they generally produce fewer casualties per day of exposure than the weapons and wars of the past.[35] Even in the Gulf War of 1991, which saw a force of almost 400,000 hammered by unlimited conventional airpower for a month and attacked by a large modern mobile armor force with an enormous technological advantage in weaponry, the estimated casualty figure for Iraqi forces equals only approximately 7.1 percent.

Adamson's study of casualty rates from antiquity to Korea reaches the same conclusion with respect to mortality rates. Given that weapons changed little from the times of antiquity through the period of the Middle Ages, it might be somewhat safely assumed that the data provided for the Greek and Roman periods were roughly similar to that of the later periods of antiquity prior to the advent of gunpowder weapons. Adamson presents the mortality data for various wars at different periods of history, with the lethality of weapons factored in along the time dimension. The results demonstrate that although weapons became more and more lethal with each war, the mortality rates for each war tended to decline, with the highest found during wars of antiquity and the lowest reflected in modern wars. Once again the conclusion is that adjustments in tactics, mobility, and dispersion have by and large off-set the increased killing power of modern weaponry.[36]

It has been only 350 years since the early prototypes of the modern gunpowder armies of the present day first emerged on the battlefields of the Thirty Years War. In that time the destructive power of weapons and the organizational sophistication of military forces have proceeded at a developmental pace that has no historical precedent. Both of these elements, in turn, are the products of larger social and technological forces that have truly revolutionized the manner in which man lives out his life. For more than 5,500 years of man's existence in organized human societies, since early Sumer, the means and methods by which men destroyed each other in war changed only little. In the last 350 years they have changed so drastically as to be quite literally beyond the imagination of the soldiers and commanders who have gone before us. In this sense the advent of modern weapons can only be seen being among man's most ingenious innovations.

What has not changed, of course, is the death and the pain. Regardless of weaponry, the wounded soldier still bleeds, still suffers pain, and still fears that he will not survive his wounds. The psyche that rests at the core of man's very humanity still must endure terrifying fear, and the fear of death and maiming that drove the ancient soldier to psychiatric collapse seem not to have been abated at all by modernity, nor driven from man's consciousness once shot and shell begin to fly. And for most men in combat the risk of being killed or driven mad by those fears remains as real as it was for those who stood at Marathon, Arbela, or Cannae.

NOTES

1. T.N. Dupuy, *The Evolution of Weapons and Warfare* (New York: Bobbs-Merrill, 1980), 101.

2. Seigneur de Tavannes, writing in the sixteenth century, noted the impact of the pistol on warfare when he wrote, "A cavalry battle which, in the past, would have lasted three or four hours and not killed ten men out of five hundred, has now become a murderous affair and the outcome of the battle is now decided in less than an hour." Quoted in Robert Laffont, *The Ancient Art of Warfare* (London: Cressent Press, 1966), vol. 1, 443.

3. The innovation of horse-drawn cavalry for artillery is generally attributed to the Prussian king, Frederick the Great.

4. Dupuy, 295.

5. Richard A. Gabriel, "The History of Armaments," in *The Italian Encyclopedia of Social Sciences* (Rome: Marchese Graphiche Editoriali, 1990), 9–10.

6. Ibid.

7. Vauban is generally credited with the invention of the ring bayonet. See Dupuy on this point, 131.

8. The fluted bayonet had a channel depression running down the side, the "gutrunner" as it was commonly called, which supposedly made the bayonet easier to extract from the victim's body. The English seem to have been the first army to use this new device in battle, although its origins remain obscure.

9. A short but complete account of the development of artillery through the ages is found in Albert Manucy, *Artillery through the Ages* (Washington, D.C.: U.S. Government Printing Office, 1985).

10. Gabriel, 8.

11. Ibid.

12. Before the increased mobility provided by horse artillery, it was commonplace for one side to overrun the gun positions of the other. Since during battle forces ebbed and flowed over the same position several times, a way was found to render artillery useless once it had been overrun. Armies utilized special squads of "spikers" whose task it was to drive a large iron spike into the touch-hole of the enemy cannon, making the weapon unuseable.

13. The best work on the relationship of national economies to modern war in this period is still Paul Kennedy, *The Rise and Fall of the Great Powers* (New York: Random House, 1987).

14. Gabriel, 8.

15. Dupuy, 191.

16. The world's armies were quick to realize the military potential of the railway. In the Italian War of 1859, the French moved 604,000 men and 129,000 horses by rail in three months. Dupuy, 202.

17. Borden developed condensed milk partly as a military ration that would not spoil. It was also widely used by travelers crossing the American continent by horse and wagon.

18. Gabriel, 12.

19. The technique of massing artillery guns on target is called sheaving, after the agricultural process of bunching individual stalks of wheat or wood together in a single bundle. It is an American invention. As late as World War II, Soviet forces still massed guns hub to hub in the old manner and had considerable difficulty in sheaving artillery fire.

20. Gabriel, 13.

21. The aileron was not, however, an immediate success. The famous German ace, Max Immelman, flew a Foker Eindecker that had no ailerons. Immelman shot down many Allied aircraft and invented the complex maneuver that bears his name to this day, the Immelman turn.

22. Germany was the single exception among the great powers and did not pursue colonial ambitions with any vigor. German policy in this respect had been set thirty years before by Chancellor von Bismarck, who remarked that the colonies "were not worth the bones of a single Pomeranian grenadier."

23. Gabriel, 15.

24. These various area saturation weapons inflicted mostly pyschiatric casu-alties, as is the norm when troops in the defense are barraged with indirect fire. The Russian and German models both had holes in the stabilizing fins of the rocket so that the round made an eerie, high-pitched sound as it flew toward its target.

25. Richard A. Gabriel, *No More Heroes: Madness and Psychiatry in War* (New York: Hill and Wang, 1987), 42.

26. Ibid., 22.

27. Ibid., 35.

28. Ibid., 27–29.

29. Ibid.

30. Ibid., 42.

31. T.N. Dupuy, 309–12. See also by Dupuy, *Numbers, Predictions, and War* (New York: Bobbs-Merrill, 1979).

32. Ibid., 310.

33. Ibid., 170.

34. Ibid.

35. The exception to this trend is the rate of psychological casualties, which have increased enormously as the tempo and lethality of war have increased.

36. P.B. Adamson, "A Comparison of Ancient and Modern Weapons in the Effectiveness of Producing Battle Casualties," *Journal of the Royal Army Medical Corps* 123 (1977): 93–103.

Selected Bibliography

Adams, W. Lindsay. "In the Wake of Alexander the Great: The Impact of Conquest on the Aegean World." *Ancient World* 27 (1996): 29–37.

Adamson, P.B. "A Comparison of Ancient and Modern Weapons in the Effectiveness of Producing Battle Casualties." *Journal of the Royal Army Medical Corps* 123 (1977): 93–103.

Adcock, F.E. *The Greek and Macedonian Art of War*. Berkeley: University of California Press, 1957.

Adcock, F.E. *The Roman Art of War under the Republic*. Cambridge: Harvard University Press, 1940.

Aldea, Peter A., and William Shaw. "The Evolution of Surgical Management of Severe Lower Extremity Trauma." *Clinics in Plastic Surgery* 13, no. 4 (October 1986): 554–62.

Alexander, Bevin. *How Great Generals Win*. New York: W.W. Norton, 1993.

Alexander, Franz G., and Sheldon T. Selesnick. *The History of Psychiatry*. New York: Mentor Books, 1966.

Ames, Roger. *Sun-Tzu: The Art of War*. New York: Ballantine Books, 1993.

Ammianus Marcellinus. *Roman History of Ammianus Marcellinnus*. Berlin: Rolfe translation, 1939.

Anderson, J.K. *Ancient Greek Horsemanship*. Berkeley: University of California Press, 1957.

Anderson, J.K. *Military Theory and Practice in the Age of Xenophon*. Berkeley: University of California Press, 1970.

Anderson, J.K. "Wars and Military Science: In *Civilization of the Ancient Med-*

iterranean, edited by Michael Grant and Rachael Kitzinger, 679–89. New York: Charles Scribner, 1988.

Angold, M. *Byzantium 1025–1204: A Political History*. London: Longman, 1984.

Animal Management. London: British Army Veterinary Department, 1908.

Appian. *The Civil War*. New York: Loelo, 1964.

Arnold, T. *The Second Punic War*. London: Macmillan, 1886.

Aston, W.G. *Nihongi: Chronicles of Japan from the Earliest Times to A.D. 697*. Rutland, Vt.: Charles E. Tuttle, 1972.

Austin, M. "Hellenistic Kings, War, and the Economy." *Classical Quarterly* 36 (1986): 450–466.

Balmforth, Edmund. "A Chinese Military Strategist of the Warring States: Sun Pin." (Ph.D. diss., Rutgers University, 1979).

Balsdon, J.V.P. *Julius Caesar and Rome*. Harmondsworth, UK: Penguin, 1971.

Barbieri-Low, J. Anthony Jerome. "Wheeled Vehicles in the Chinese Bronze Age, 2000–771 B.C.E." (Master's thesis, Harvard University, 1997).

Bar-Kochva, B. *The Seleucid Army: Organization and Tactics in the Great Campaigns*. Cambridge: Cambridge University Press, 1976.

Baronowski, D. "Roman Military Forces in 225 B.C.E." *Historia* 42 (1993): 181–202.

Bartusis, Mark C. *The Late Byzantine Army: Arms and Society, 1204–1453*. Philadelphia: University of Philadelphia Press, 1992.

Basham, A.L. *The Wonder That Was India*. New York: Grove Press, 1954.

Bath, Tony. *Hannibal's Campaigns*. New York: Barnes and Noble, 1992.

"Battle of the Teutoburg Forest." *Archaeology* (September–October 1992): 26–32.

Battne, Bruce L. "Foreign Threat and Domestic Reform: The Emergence of the *Ritsuryo* State." *Monumenta Nipponica* 41, no. 2 (1986): 199–219.

Berthold, Richard M. "The Army and Alexander the Great's Successors." *Strategy and Tactics* 152 (June 1992): 45–47.

Bishop, M.C., and J.C.N. Coulston. *Roman Military Equipment from the Punic Wars to the Fall of Rome*. London: Batsford, 1993.

Blankenship, K.Y. *The End of the Jihad State*. Albany: State University of New York Press, 1994.

Boak, Arthur. *Manpower Shortage and the Fall of the Roman Empire in the West*. Ann Arbor: University of Michigan Press, 1955.

Bosworth, A.B. *Conquest and Empire: The Reign of Alexander the Great*. Oxford: Oxford University Press, 1988.

Bradford, Alfred S. *With Arrow, Sword, and Spear*. Westport, Conn.: Greenwood Press, 2001.

Breasted, James Henry. *Ancient Records of Egypt*. Chicago: University of Chicago Press, 1906.

Breasted, James Henry. *The Battle of Kadesh: A Study in the Earliest Known Military Strategy*. Chicago: University of Chicago Press, 1903.

Breeze, D.J. "The Organization of the Legion: The First Cohort and *Equites Legionis.*" *Journal of Roman Studies* 59 (1969): 50–55.

Brunt, P.A. "Alexander's Macedonian Cavalry." *Journal of Hellenic Studies* 83 (1963): 27–46.

Bryant, Anthony. *Early Samurai: 200–1500 A.D.* London: Osprey, 1991.

Burn, A.R. *Persia and the Greeks.* London: Arnold Press, 1962.

Burne, Alfred. *The Battle of Kadesh.* Harrisburg, Pa.: Military Service Press, 1947.

Burne, Alfred. "Some Notes on the Battle of Kadesh." *Journal of Egyptian Archaeology* (1921): 191–95.

Burns, Thomas S. "The Battle of Adrianople: A Reconsideration." *Historia* 22 (1973): 336–45.

Caesar, Julius. *The Civil War.* New York: Penguin, 1988.

Caesar, Julius. *Commentaries on the Gallic War.* New York: Penguin, 1982.

Cambridge Ancient History, "The Augustan Empire, 44 B.C.–70 A.D.," vol. 10. Cambridge: Cambridge University Press, 1966.

Cambridge Ancient History, vol. 7. Cambridge: Cambridge University Press, 1953.

Cambridge History of India. Delhi: 1968.

Campbell, J.B. *The Emperor and the Roman Army.* Oxford: Blackwell, 1984.

Caven, Brian. *The Punic Wars.* New York: Barnes and Noble, 1992.

Cawkwell, G.L. *Philip of Macedon.* London: Farber, 1978.

Chadwick, John. *The Macedonian World.* Cambridge: Cambridge University Press, 1976.

Chambers, James. *The Devil's Horsemen: The Mongol Invasion of Europe.* New York: Atheneum, 1979.

Chang, Kwang-chih. *The Archaeology of Ancient China.* New Haven: Yale University Press, 1977.

Chang, Kwang-chih. *Shang Civilization.* New Haven: Yale University Press, 1980.

Childe, Gordon V. "Horses, Chariots, and Battle-Axes." *Antiquity* 15 (1941): 196–99.

Childe, Gordon V. "War in Prehistoric Societies." *Sociological Review* 23 (1942): 126–38.

Clay, A.T. *The Empire of the Amorites.* New Haven: Yale University Press, 1919.

Cleaves, F.W., trans. *The Secret History of the Mongols.* Cambridge, Mass.: Harvard University Press, 1982.

Connolly, Peter. *Greece and Rome at War.* Englewood Cliffs, N.J.: Prentice-Hall, 1981.

Connolly, Peter. *The Roman Army.* London: Macdonald Educational Press, 1975.

Conteneau, Georges. *Everyday Life in Babylon and Assyria.* London: Edward Arnold, 1954.

Cook, J.M. *The Persian Empire*. London: Schocken, 1983.

Cornell, Timothy. *The Beginnings of Rome: Italy and Rome from the Bronze Age to the Punic Wars*. London: Routledge, 1995.

Cottrell, Leonard. *Hannibal: Enemy of Rome*. New York: Holt, Rinehart, Winston, 1960.

Cottrell, Leonard. *The Warrior Pharaohs*. New York: Putnam, 1969.

Creasy, Edward S. *Fifteen Decisive Battles of the World*. New York: Dorsett, 1987.

Creel, Herrlee G. "The Horse in Chinese History." In *What Is Taoism? And Other Studies in Chinese Cultural History*. Chicago: University of Chicago Press, 1970.

Creel, Herrlee G. *The Origins of Statecraft in China*. Chicago: University of Chicago Press, 1970.

Crone, Patricia. "The Early Islamic World." In *War and Society in the Ancient and Medieval Worlds*, edited by Kurt Raaflaub and Nathan Rosenstein, 309–32. Cambridge, Mass.: Harvard University Press, 1999.

Crone, Patricia. *Slaves on Horses: The Evolution of the Islamic Polity*. Cambridge: Cambridge University Press, 1980.

Davies, Roy. *Service in the Roman Army*. New York: Columbia University Press, 1989.

Dayal, Raghubir. *An Outline of Indian History and Culture*. 2nd ed. New Delhi: The India Press, 1984.

DeBeer, Gavin. *Hannibal: Challenging Rome's Supremacy*. New York: Viking, 1970.

Delbruck, Hans. *History of the Art of War Within the Framework of Political History*. Vol. 1: *Antiquity*. Westport, Conn.: Greenwood Press, 1975.

Dennis, George T. *Three Byzantine Military Treatises*. Washington, D.C.: Dunbarton Oaks, 1985.

Dien, Albert E. "The Stirrup and Its Effect on Chinese History." *Ars Orientalis* 16 (1986): 33–56.

Dikshitar, V.R. Ramachandra. *War in Ancient India*. New Delhi: The India Press. 1948.

Dio Cassius. *Roman History*, books 18–25. New York: Penguin, 1972.

Diodorus, Siculus. *Universal History*, books 17, 18.

Dixon, K.R., and P. Southern. *The Roman Cavalry from the First to the Third Century A.D.* London: Batsford, 1992.

Dodge, Theodore A. *Hannibal: A History of the Art of War Among the Carthaginians and the Romans Down to the Battle of Pydna, 168 B.C.* 2 vols. Boston: Houghton, 1891.

Drews, Robert. *The End of the Bronze Age: Changes in Warfare and the Catastrophe ca. 1200 B.C.E.* Princeton, N.J.: Princeton University Press, 1993.

Duffy, Christopher. *The Military Experience in the Age of Reason*. New York: Atheneum, 1988.

Dupuy, T.N. *The Evolution of Weapons and Warfare*. New York: Bobbs-Merrill, 1980.

Dupuy, T.N. *Numbers, Predictions, and War*. New York: Bobbs-Merrill, 1979.

Dupuy, T.N., and R. Ernest Dupuy. *The Encylopedia of Military History*. New York: Harper and Row, 1986.

Duus, Peter. *Feudalism in Japan*. New York: Knopf, 1969.

Dywer, Gwynne. *War*. New York: Crown, 1985.

Eadie, J.W. "The Development of Roman Mailed Cavalry." *Journal of Roman Studies* 57 (1967): 161–73.

Edgerton, Robert. *Like Lions They Fought*. New York: Free Press, 1988.

Edwards, Michael, and James L. Stanfield. "Lord of the Mongols: Genghis Khan." *National Geographic* 6, no. 190 (December 1966): 11–16.

Encyclopedia Britannica, 15th ed., s.v. "Bronze Age."

Encyclopedia Britannica, s.v. "History of Egyptian Civilization."

Encyclopedia Britannica. 15th ed., s.v. "Metallurgy."

Encyclopedia Britannica, 15th ed., s.v. "Sumerian Civilization."

Engels, Donald. *Alexander the Great and the Logistics of the Macedonian Army*. Berkeley: University of California Press, 1978.

Erman, Adolf. *Life in Ancient Egypt*. New York: Dover Publications, 1971.

Erman, Adolf, and C. Blackman. *The Literature of Ancient Egypt*. Metheun, Mass.: Little Brown, 1927.

Fabricus, E. "Some Notes on Polibius' Description of Roman Camps." *Journal of Roman Studies* 22 (1932): 78–87.

Fairbank, John King. *China: A New History*. Cambridge, Mass.: Harvard University Press, 1992.

Fairbank, John King. "The Varieties of Chinese Military Experience." In Frank Kierman and John K. Fairbank, *Chinese Ways of Warfare*. Cambridge, Mass.: Harvard University Press, 1974, 1–24.

Farris, William Wayne. *Heavenly Warriors: The Evolution of Japan's Military, 500–1300*. Cambridge, Mass.: Harvard University Press, 1992.

Faulkner, R.O. "The Battle of Megiddo." *Journal of Egyptian Archaeology* 28 (1942): 43–49.

Faulkner, R.O. "Egyptian Military Organization." *Journal of Egyptian Archaeology* 39 (1953): 36–48.

Ferrill, Arthur. "Herodotus and the Strategy and Tactics of the Invasion of Xerxes." *American Historical Review* 72 (1966): 102–15.

Ferrill, Arthur. *The Origins of War*. London: Thames and Hudson, 1985.

Finley, M.I. *The Ancient Enemy*. Berkeley: University of California Press, 1973.

Friday, Karl. *Hired Swords: The Rise of Private Warrior Power in Early Japan*. Palo Alto, Calif.: Stanford University Press, 1992.

Frolich, H. *Die Militarmedicin Homers*. Stuttgart, 1879.

Frost, H.M. *Orthopaedic Biomechanics*. Springfield, Ill.: Charles C. Thomas, 1973.

Frye, Richard N. *The Heritage of Persia*. Cleveland: World, 1963.

Fuller, J.F.C. *The Generalship of Alexander the Great*. New Brunswick, N.J.: Rutgers University Press, 1960.

Fuller, J.F.C. *Julius Caesar: Man, Soldier, Tyrant*. New York: DaCapo, 1965.

Fuller, J.F.C. *A Military History of the Western World*. 3 vols. New York: DaCapo, 1954.

Gabriel, Richard A. "Armaments." *Italian Encyclopedia of Social Sciences*. Rome: University of Rome, 1990: 1234–37.

Gabriel, Richard A. "The Battle of Kadesh." In *U.S. Army War College Ancient Battle Series*. Carlisle, PA.: 1991.

Gabriel, Richard A. *The Culture of War*. Westport, Conn.: Greenwood Press, 1990.

Gabriel, Richard A. *Great Captains of Antiquity*. Westport, Conn.: Greenwood Press, 2000.

Gabriel, Richard A. *No More Heroes: Madness and Psychiatry in War*. New York: Hill and Wang, 1987.

Gabriel, Richard A., and Donald W. Boose, Jr. *The Great Battles of Antiquity: A Strategic and Tactical Guide to the Great Battles That Shaped the Development of War*. Westport, Conn.: Greenwood Press, 1994.

Gabriel, Richard A., and Karen S. Metz. *From Sumer to Rome: The Military Capabilities of Ancient Armies*. Westport, Conn.: Greewood Press, 1991.

Gardiner, Sir Alan. *Egypt of the Pharaohs*. London: Oxford University Press, 1961.

Goedicke, Hans. "Considerations on the Battle of Kadesh." *Journal of Egyptian Archaeology* 52 (1966): 71–80.

Goedicke, Hans. "Egyptian Military Actions in Asia in the Middle Kingdom." *Revue d'Egyptologie* 42 (1991): 89–94.

Goetz, A. "Warfare in Asia Minor." *Iraq* 25 (1963): 125–30.

Goffart, William. *Barbarians and Romans: The Techniques of Accomodation*. Princeton, N.J.: Princeton University Press, 1980.

Goldsworthy, Adrian. *The Roman Army at War, 100 B.C.E.–200 C.E.* Cambridge: Cambridge University Press, 1996.

Gordon, D.H. "Fire and Sword: Techniques of Destruction." *Antiquity* 27 (1953): 159–62.

Graham, Philip. *Metal Weapons of the Early and Middle Bronze Age in Syria and Palestine*. 2 vols. Oxford: B.A.R. International Series, 1989.

Grant, Michael. *The Army of the Caesars*. New York: Charles Scribner, 1974.

Grant, Michael. *The History of Ancient Israel*. New York: Charles Scribner, 1984.

Grant, Michael. *History of Rome*. New York: Charles Scribner, 1978.

Green, Peter. *Alexander of Macedon: A Historical Biography*. Berkeley: University of California Press, 1991.

Greenhalgh, P. *Early Greek Warfare: Horsemen and Chariots in the Homeric and Archaic Ages*. Cambridge: Cambridge University Press, 1973.

Griffith, Guy. *Mercenaries of the Hellenistic World*. Cambridge: Cambridge University Press, 1935.

Griffith, Samuel B. *Sun-Tzu: The Art of War*. London: Oxford University Press, 1971.

Grimal, Nicolas. *A History of Ancient Egypt*. London: Blackwell, 1988.

Grousset, Rene. *The Empire of the Steppes: A History of Central Asia*, translated by Naomi Wolford. New Brunswick, N.J.: Rutgers University Press, 1970.

Gruen, Erich. *The Hellenistic World and the Coming of Rome*. Berkeley: University of California Press, 1984.

Gruen, Peter. *Alexander of Macedon*. Garden City, N.Y.: Doubleday, 1950.

Grundy, G.B. *The Great Persian War*. London: J. Murray, 1990.

Gurdjian, E. Stephen. "The Treatment of Penetrating Wounds of the Brain Sustained in Warfare: A Historical Review." *Journal of Neurosurgery* 39 (February 1974): 161–69.

Gurney, O.R. *The Hittites*. Baltimore: Penguin, 1962.

Hackett, Sir John. *Great Battlefields of the World*. New York: Macmillan, 1984.

Hackett, Sir John. *Warfare in the Ancient World*. New York: Sidgwick and Jackson, 1989.

Halden, John. "The Byzantine World." In Kurt Raaflaub and Nathan Rosenstein, *War and Society in the Ancient and Medieval Worlds*. Cambridge, Mass.: Harvard University Press, 1999.

Hammond, N. "Training in the Use of the Sarissa and Its Effect in Battle." *Antichthon* 14 (1980): 53–63.

Hammond, N., and G.T. Griffith. *A History of Macedonia*. 2 vols. Oxford: Oxford University Press, 1979.

Hammond, N.G.L. "The Two Battles of Chaeronea." *Klio* 33 (1938): 186–218.

Hanson, Victor David. *The Western Way of War: Infantry Battle in Classical Greece*. New York: Knopf, 1989.

Hardy, E.G. "Augustus and His Legionnaires." *Classical Quarterly* 14 (1921): 187–94.

Harrison, Mark. *Viking Warrior*. London: Osprey, 1993.

Hawkins, J.D. "Assyrians and Hittites." *Iraq* 36 (1974): 67–83.

Head, D. *The Achaemenid Persian Army*. Stockport, Ill.: Montvert Publications, 1992.

Healy, Mark. *Qadesh: Clash of the Warrior Kings*. London: Osprey, 1993.

Heath, E.G. *Archery: A Military History*. London: Osprey, 1980.

Herzog, Chaim, and Mordechai Gichon. *Battles of the Bible*. Jerusalem: Steimatzky, 1978.

Hignet, C. *Xerxes' Invasion of Greece*. New York: Oxford University Press, 1963.

Hill, D.R. "The Role of the Camel and the Horse in Early Arab Conquests." In *War, Technology and Society in the Middle East*, edited by V.J. Parry and M.E. Yapp. London: Oxford University Press, 1975.

Hoffman, Michael A. *Egypt Before the Pharaohs*. New York: Knopf, 1979.

Hogg, O.F.G. *Clubs to Cannon*. London: Duckworth and Co., 1968.

Holladay, A.J. "Hoplites and Heresies." *Journal of Hellenic Studies* 102 (1982): 97–103.

Hourani, Albert. *A History of the Arab Peoples*. New York: Warner Books, 1991.

Howarth, Anthony. "Zama: Triumph of the Roman Way of War." *Strategy and Tactics* (August 1992): 5–14.

Huber, Karen C. "Triumphant Over All People: Constantine the Great." *Military History* (October 1991): 9–13.

Hudson, Harris Gary. "The Shield Signal at Marathon." *American Historical Review* 42 (1936–37): 359–443.

Inalcik, H. *The Ottoman Empire: The Classical Age*. New York: Praeger, 1973.

Jackson, A.V. *Persia: Past and Present*. New York: Macmillan, 1966.

Jackson, A.V. Williams. *History of India*. London: The Grolier Society, 1906.

Jarcho, S. "A Roman Experience with Heat Stroke in 24 B.C.E." *Bulletin of the New York Academy of Medicine* 43, no. 8 (August 1967): 767–68.

Jimenez, Ramon L. *Caesar Against Rome: The Great Roman Civil War*. Westport, Conn.: Greenwood Press, 2000.

Jones, Archer. *The Art of War in the Western World*. Urbana: University of Illinois Press, 1987.

Jones, Gwyn. *The Vikings*. London: Oxford University Press, 1968.

Jordanes, T. *Gothic History of Jordanes*. Translated by Charles C. Mierow. London: 1915.

Kaegi, W.E. *Byzantium and the Early Islamic Conquests*. Cambridge: Cambridge University Press, 1992.

Kagan, Donald. *The Archimedian War*. Ithaca, N.Y.: Cornell University Press, 1994.

Kar, H.C., Lt. Col. *Military History of India*. Calcutta: Firma KLM, 1980.

Kelly, Thomas. "Thucydidies and the Spartan Strategy in the Archidamian War." *American Historical Review* 87 (1982): 399–427.

Kennedy, Paul. *The Rise and Fall of the Great Powers*. New York: Random House, 1987.

Keppie, L. *The Making of the Roman Army from Republic to Empire*. London: B.T. Batsford, 1984.

Kerstein, Morris, and Roger Hubbard. "Heat Related Problems in the Desert: The Environment Can Be the Enemy." *Military Medicine* 149 (December 1984): 650–56.

Kiernan, Frank A. "Phases and Modes of Combat in Early China." In *Chinese Ways in Warfare*, edited by Frank A. Kiernan and John K. Fairbank. Cambridge, Mass.: Harvard University Press, 1974, 27–66.

Kiernan, Frank A., and John K. Fairbank, eds. *Chinese Ways in Warfare*. Cambridge, Mass.: Harvard University Press, 1974.

Kiss, Peter A. "Horsemen of Cruel Cunning." *Military History* (December 1986): 34–41.

Korfmann, Manfred. "The Sling as a Weapon." *Scientific American* 229 (1973): 34–42.

Kramer, Samuel N. *The Cradle of Civilization*. New York: Time Inc., 1969.

Kramer, Samuel N. The *Sumerians*. Chicago: University of Chicago Press, 1963.

Krige, E.J. "The Military Organization of the Zulus." In *Peoples and Cultures of Africa*, edited by E. Skinner. Garden City, N.Y.: Natural History Press, 1973.

Laffont, Robert. *The Ancient Art of Warfare*. New York: Time-Life Books, 1969.

Lamb, Harold. *Genghis Khan*. New York: Doubleday, 1927.

Lamb, Harold. *Hannibal: One Man Against Rome*. Garden City, N.Y.: Doubleday, 1968.

Lawrence, A.W. "Ancient Fortifications." *Journal of Egyptian Archaeology* 51 (1965): 69–94.

Lawrence, A.W. *Greek Aims in Fortification*. Oxford: Oxford University Press, 1979.

Lazenby, J.F. *The Spartan Army*. Wiltshire: Aris and Philips, 1985.

Lewis, Mark Edward. *Sanctioned Violence in Early China*. Albany: State University of New York Press, 1990.

Liddell-Hart, B.H. *A Greater Than Napoleon: Scipio Africanus*. London: Blackwell and Sons, 1926.

Lister, R.P. *Genghis Khan*. New York: Dorsett Press, 1969.

Littauer, M.A., and J. Crouwel. *Wheeled Vehicles and Ridden Animals in the Ancient Near East*. Leiden: E.J. Brill, 1979.

Lloyd, Alan, ed. *Battle in Antiquity*. London: Duckworth and Swansea, 1996.

Lloyd, Seton. *The Archaeology of Mesopotamia*. London: Thames and Hudson, 1978.

Lu, David John. *Sources of Japanese History*. New York: McGraw Hill, 1974.

Luckenbill, D.D. *Ancient Records of Assyria and Babylon*. 2 vols. Chicago: University of Chicago Press, 1926.

Luttwak, Edward N. *The Grand Strategy of the Roman Empire*. Baltimore: Johns Hopkins University Press, 1976.

Macqueen, J.G. *The Hittites and Their Contemporaries in Asia Minor*. London: Thames and Hudson, 1986.

Majno, Guido. *The Healing Hand*. Cambridge, Mass.: Harvard University Press, 1975.

Majurmdar. R.C. *Ancient India*. Delhi, 1977.

Malinowski, Bronislaw. "An Anthropological Analysis of War." In *War: The Analysis of Armed Conflict and Aggresssion* edited by Fred Harris and R. Murphy, 245–68. Garden City, N.Y.: Natural History Press, 1968.

Manitius, W. "The Army and Military Organization of the Assyrian Kings." *Zeitschrift fur Assyriologie* 24 (1910): 90–107.

Manti, Peter A. "The Cavalry Sarissa." *Ancient World* 8 (1983): 75–83.

Manucy, Albert. *Artillery Through the Ages*. Washington, D.C.: U.S. Government Printing Office, 1985.

Markle, M. "The Macedonian Sarissa, Spear, and Related Arms." *American Journal of Archaeology* 82 (1978): 483–97.

Markowitz, Michael C. "The Thousand-Year Garrison State: The Evolution of the Byzantine Army." *Command* 7 (November-December 1990): 42–61.

Marsden, E.W. *Greek and Roman Artillery*. Oxford: Clarendon Press, 1971.

Marshall, S.L.A. *The Soldier's Load and the Mobility of a Nation*. Quantico, Va.: Marine Corps Association, 1950.

Martin, H.D. "The Mongol Army." *Journal of the Royal Asiatic Society* 1 (1943): 46–85.

Maspero, Henri. *China in Antiquity*. Boston: University of Massachusetts Press, 1978.

Mass, Jeffrey. *Warrior Government in Early Medieval Japan*. Palo Alto, Calif.: Stanford University Press, 1974.

McGeer, E. *Sowing the Dragon's Teeth: Byzantine Warfare in the Tenth Century*. Dumbarton Oaks Studies 33. Washington, D.C.: Dumbarton Oaks, 1955.

McGrew, Robert E. *Encyclopedia of Medical History*. New York: McGraw-Hill, 1985.

Mellaart, James. *The Neolithic of the Near East*. New York: Scribner, 1975.

Mertz, Barbara. *Red Land, Black Land: Daily Life in Ancient Egypt*. New York: Peter Bedrick Books, 1990.

Milius, R.D. "Alexander's Pursuit of Darius through Iran." *Historia* 15 (1966): 249–57.

Moorey, P.R.S. "The Emergence of the Light, Horse-Drawn Chariot in the Near East, 2000–1500 B.C." *World Archaeology* 18 (1986): 196–215.

Morgan, David. *The Mongols*. Oxford: Blackwell, 1986.

Morris, Ivan. *The Nobility of Failure: Tragic Heroes in the History of Japan*. New York: Henry Holt, 1975.

Needham, Joseph. *Science and Civilization in China*. Cambridge: Cambridge University Press, 1954.

Nelson, Harold Hayden. *The Battle of Megiddo*. Chicago: University of Chicago Press, 1913.

Nesbit, J. "The Rate of March of Crusading Armies in Europe: A Study and Computation." *Traditio* 19 (1963): 176–81.

Newark, Timothy. *The Barbarians*. London: Blandford Press, 1985.

Nicole, David, and Angus McBride. *Armies of the Ottoman Turks, 1300–1774*. London: Osprey, 1983.

Nicole, David, and Angus McBride. *The Armies of Islam*. London: Osprey, 1982.

Nissen, Hans. J. *The Early History of the Ancient Near East*. Chicago: University of Chicago Press, 1983.

Oakeshott, Ewart R. *The Archaeology of Weapons*. New York: Praeger, 1963.

Oates, D. "Fort Shalamaneser: An Interim Report." *Iraq* 21 (1959): 98–129.

O'Connell, Robert L. *Of Arms and Men.* New York: Oxford University Press, 1989.

O'Connell, Robert L. "The Roman Killing Machine." *Quarterly Journal of Military History* 1 (Autumn 1988): 30–41.

Olmstead, A.T. *The History of Assyria.* Chicago: University of Chicago Press, 1951.

Olmstead, A.T. *History of the Persian Empire.* Chicago: University of Chicago Press, 1948.

Oman, Sir Charles. *The Art of War in the Middle Ages.* Ithaca, N.Y.: Cornell University Press, 1953.

Oppenheim, A. Leo. *Ancient Mesopotamia.* Chicago: University of Chicago Press, 1977.

Oxford History Of India. Oxford: Clarendon Press, 1958.

Park, Robert. "The Social Function of War." *American Journal of Sociology* 46 (1941): 551–70.

Parker, H.M.D. "The Legions of Diocletian and Constantine." *Journal of Roman Studies* 23 (1933): 175–89.

Parker, H.M.D. *The Roman Legions.* Cambridge: Heffer, 1958.

Parry, V.J. and M.E. Yapp, eds. *War, Technology and Society in the Middle East.* London: Oxford University Press, 1975.

Patrick, Stephen B. "Byzantium: The Forgotten Empire." *Strategy and Tactics* 138 (October 1990): 16–19, 50–56.

Patrick, Stephen B. "The Dark Ages: A Military Systems Profile, 500–1200." *Strategy and Tactics* (March 1993): 7–26.

Peers, C.J., and Angus McBride. *Ancient Chinese Armies, 1500–200 B.C.E.* London: Osprey, 1990.

Piotrovsky, R. *The Ancient Civilization of the Urartu.* London: Cresset Press, 1969.

Plutarch's Lives, vol. 2. New York: Random House, 1992.

Polibius. *The History of Rome.* London: William Heinemann, 1922.

Postgate, J.N. *Taxation and Conscription in the Assyrian Empire.* Rome: Biblical Institute Press, 1974.

Pritchard, James B. *Ancient Near Eastern Texts.* Princeton, N.J.: Princeton University Press, 1955.

Pritchett, W.K. *The Greek State of War.* Berkeley: University of California Press, 1971.

Raaflaub, Kurt, and Nathan Rosenstein, eds. *War and Society in the Ancient and Medieval Worlds.* Cambridge, Mass.: Harvard University Press, 1999.

Reades, J. "The Neo-Assyrian Court and the Army: Evidence from the Sculptures." *Iraq* 34 (1972): 87–112.

Redford, Donald. *Akhenaten: The Heretic King.* Princeton, N.J.: Princeton University Press, 1984.

Redford, Donald. *Egypt, Canaan, and Israel in Ancient Times*. Princeton, N.J.:
    Princeton University Press, 1992.

Rice, Tamara Talbot. *Everyday Life in Byzantium*. New York: Dorset House
    Publishing Press, 1967.

Riches, David. *The Anthropology of Violence*. Oxford: Basil Blackwell, 1986.

Robinson, H. Russell. *The Armor of Imperial Rome*. London: Arms and Armor
    Press, 1975.

Rossabi, Morris. *Khubilai Khan: His Life and Times*. Berkeley: University of
    California Press, 1988.

Roux, Georges. *Ancient Iraq*. New York: Penguin, 1964.

Roy, P.C. *The Mahabharata*. 2nd ed. Calcutta, 1919.

Saggs, H.W.F. "Assyrian Warfare in the Sargonid Period." *Iraq* 25, part 2 (Au-
    tumn 1963): 141–49.

Saggs, H.W.F. *The Greatness That Was Babylon*. New York: Praeger, 1962.

Saggs, H.W.F. *The Might That Was Assyria*. London: Sidwick and Jackson,
    1984.

Salmon, E.T. "The Roman Army and the Disintegration of the Roman Empire."
    Proceedings of the Royal Society of Canada 52 (1958): 43–60.

Sandars, Nancy K. *The Sea Peoples: Warriors of the Ancient Mediterranean,
    1250–1150 B.C.E.* London: Thames and Hudson, 1985.

Sato, Kanzan. *The Japanese Sword*. Tokyo: Kodansha International, 1983.

Sawyer, Ralph D. *The Seven Military Classics of Ancient China*. Boulder, Colo.:
    Westview Press, 1993.

Schonberger, H. "The Roman Frontier Army in Germany." *Journal of Roman
    Studies* 59 (1969): 144–97.

Schulman, Alan R. "Chariots, Chariotry, and the Hyksos." *Journal of the Society
    for the Study of Egyptian Antiquities* 10 (1980): 105–53.

Schulman, Alan R. "Military Organization in Pharaonic Egypt." In *Civilizations
    of the Ancient Near East*, edited by Jack M. Sasson, vol. 1, 289–301.
    New York: Scribner's, 1995.

Schulman, Alan R. *Military Rank, Title, and Military Organization in the Egyp-
    tian New Kingdom*. Berlin: Bruno Hessling Verlag, 1964.

Schneider, Joseph. "On The Beginnings of Warfare." *Social Forces* 31 (1952):
    68–74.

Scullard, Howard H. *Scipio Africanus: Soldier and Politician*. Reprint. Ithaca,
    N.Y.: Cornell University Press, 1970.

Scullard, Howard H. *Scipio Africanus in the Second Punic War*. Cambridge:
    Cambridge University Press, 1929.

Sekunda, N. *The Persian Army, 560–330 B.C.D.* London: Osprey, 1988.

Shaughnessy, Edward L. "Historical Perspectives on the Introduction of the Char-
    iot into China." *Harvard Journal of Asiatic Studies* 48, no. 1 (1988): 189–
    237.

Shaw, Ian. *Egyptian Warfare and Weapons*. Buckinghamshire: Shire Pub-
    lications, 1991.

Shinoda, Minoru. *The Founding of the Kamakura Shogunate, 1180–1185*. New York: Columbia University Press, 1960.

Shuckburgh, E.S. *Augustus Caesar*. New York: Barnes and Noble, 1997.

Sinor, D. "The Inner Asian Warriors." *Journal of the American Oriental Society* 101/102 (1981): 133–44.

Snodgrass, A. *Arms and Armor of the Greeks*. Ithaca, N.Y.: Cornell University Press, 1967.

Snodgrass, A. *Early Greek Armor and Weapons*. Edinburgh: Edinburgh University Press, 1964.

Snodgrass, A. "The Hoplite Reform and History." *Journal of Hellenic Studies* 86 (1965): 110–22.

Smith, R.E. *Service in the Post-Marian Roman Army*. Manchester: Manchester University Press, 1958.

Spalinger, Anthony. *Aspects of the Military Documents of the Ancient Egyptians*. New Haven: Yale University Press, 1982.

Starr, Chester G. *The Roman Imperial Navy*. Cambridge: Heffer, 1960.

Statistical Abstract of the United States. Washington, D.C.: U.S. Government Printing Office, 1988.

Steinman, Alan. "Adverse Effects of Heat and Cold on Military Operations." *Military Medicine* 152 (August 1987): 387–91.

Stillman, Nigel, and Nigel Tallis. *Armies of the Ancient Near East*. Sussex: Flexiprint Ltd., 1984.

Strabo. *The Geography of Strabo*. Translated by Horace Leonard Jones. 8 vols. London: Loeb Classical Library, 1922.

Suetonius, Gaius Tranquillus. *The Twelve Caesars*. London: Penguin, 1957.

Sykes, Gen. Sir Percy. *A History of Persia*. 2 vols. London: Macmillan, 1958.

Syme, R. "Some Notes on the Legions under Augustus." *Journal of Roman Studies* 23 (1933): 14–33.

Tacitus. *The Annals*. New York: Penguin, 1972.

Tacitus. *Germania*. New York: Penguin, 1972.

Tacitus. *The Histories*. New York: Penguin, 1972.

Tadmor, H. "The Campaigns of Sargon II of Assur." *Journal of Cuneiform Studies* 12 (1958): 22–46.

Tarn, William W. *Hellenistic Military and Naval Developments*. London: Ares Publishers, 1975.

Thapar, Romila. *A History of India*. Middlesex: Penguin Books, 1966.

Threadgold, Warren. *Byzantium and Its Army*. Palo Alto, Calif.: Stanford University Press, 1995.

"The Roman Empire and Military Airlift." *Wall Street Journal*, 9 December 1988, A7.

Titus Livius (Livy). *The History of Rome*. London: G. Bell and Sons, 1919.

Titus Livius (Livy). *The War With Hannibal*. New York: Penguin, 1965.

Toy, Sidney. *A History of Fortifications from 3000 B.C. to 1700 A.D.* London: Heinemann, 1955.

Tripathi, Ramashankar. *History of Ancient India*. Delhi, 1999.

Turnbull, Stephen R. *Battles of the Samurai*. London: Arms and Armour Press, 1987.

Turnbull, Stephen R. *The Mongols*. London: Osprey, 1980.

Turnbull, Stephen R. *The Samurai: A Military History*. New York: Macmillan, 1977.

Turney-High, H.H. *Primitive War: Its Practice and Concepts*. Columbia: University of South Carolina Press, 1971.

Twitchett, Denis, and Michael Loewe. "The Ch'in and Han Empires, 221 B.C.E.– 220 C.E." In *The Cambridge History of China*, vol. 1, 52–72. Cambridge: Cambridge University Press, 1986.

Varley, H. Paul. *Warriors of Japan as Portrayed in War Tales*. Honolulu: University of Hawaii Press, 1994.

Vaughn, P. Byron. "Local Cold Injury: Menace to Military Operations." *Military Medicine* 145 (May 1980): 304–7.

Vegetius, Renatus Flavius. *The Military Institutions of the Romans*. Harrisburg, Pa.: Stackpole Press, 1960.

Venel, S. "War and Warfare in Archaeology." *Journal of Anthropology and Archaeology* 3 (1984): 116–32.

Vickers, Ralph. "The Mongols and Their Impact on the Medieval West." *Strategy and Tactics* (March/April 1979): 23–28.

Vickers, Ralph. "The Siege of Constantinople: The End of the Middle Ages, 1453 A.D." *Strategy and Tactics* 66 (January–February 1978): 4–17.

Wagner, Donald B. *Iron and Steel in Ancient China*. Leiden: E.J. Brill, 1993.

Waldron, Arthur. *The Great Wall of China: From History to Myth*. Cambridge: Cambridge University Press, 1990.

Walker, Richard. *The Multi-State System of Ancient China*. Hamden, Conn.: The Shoestring Press, 1953.

Warmington, B.H. *Carthage: A History*. New York: Praeger, 1960.

Warry, John G. *Warfare in the Classical World*. New York: St. Martin's, 1980.

Watson, G.R. "The Pay of the Roman Army: The Auxiliary Forces." *Historia* 8 (1959): 372–78.

Watson, G.R. "The Pay of the Roman Army: The Republic." *Historia* 7 (1958): 113–20.

Watson, G.R. *The Roman Soldier: Aspects of Greek and Roman Military Life*. Ithaca, N.Y.: Cornell University Press, 1969.

Webster, Graham. *The Roman Army*. Chester: Grosvenor Museum, 1956.

Webster, Graham. *The Roman Imperial Army*. New York: Barnes and Noble, 1969.

Wenke, Robert J. *Patterns of Prehistory: Man's First Three Million Years*. New York: Oxford University Press, 1980.

Werner, E.T.C. *Chinese Weapons*. Singapore: Graham Bush, 1989.

Whatley, N. "On Reconstructing Marathon and Other Ancient Battles." *Journal of Hellenic Studies* 84 (1964): 119–39.

Wilcox, Peter, and Rafael Trevino. *Barbarians Against Rome*. London: Osprey, 2000.

Wilson, David M. *The Vikings and Their Origins*. London: Thames and Hudson, 1989.

Winter, F.E. *Greek Fortifications*. Toronto: University of Toronto Press, 1971.

Wise, Terrence. *The Armies of the Carthaginian Wars*, 265–146 B.C.E. London: Osprey Series, 1988.

Wiseman, D.J. "The Assyrians." In *Warfare in the Ancient World*, edited by Sir John Hackett. London: Sedgwick and Jackson, 1989.

Wood, W.J. *Leaders and Battles: The Art of Military Leadership*. San Francisco, Calif.: Presidio Press, 1984.

Wright, Quincy. *A Study of War*. Chicago: University of Chicago Press, 1965.

Xenophon. *Anabasis*. Translated by Carleton I. Brownson. 2 vols. Cambridge: Loeb Classical Library, 1922.

Xenophon. *Cyropaedia*. Translated by Carleton I. Brownson. Cambridge: Loeb Classic Library, 1922.

Yadin, Yigael. *The Art of Warfare in Biblical Lands in Light of Archaeology*. New York: McGraw-Hill, 1963.

Yadin, Yigael. "Hyksos Fortifications and the Battering Ram." *Bulletin of the American School of Oriental Research* 137 (1955): 23–32.

Yamada, Nakaba. *Ghenko: The Mongol Invasion of Japan*. New York: E.P. Dutton, 1916.

Yeivan, S. "Canaanite and Hitite Strategy in the Second Half of the Second Millennium, B.C.E." *Journal of Near Eastern Studies* 9 (1950): 101–7.

Zoka, Yaha. *The Imperial Iranian Army from Cyrus to Pahlavi*. Teheran: Ministry of Culture and Arts Press, 1971.

Zun, Ofer. "The Psychology of Warfare: The Evolution of Culture, Psyche, and the Enemy." *Journal of Peace Research* 24 (1987): 125–34.

Index

About the Author

RICHARD A. GABRIEL is a military historian and Adjunct Professor of Humanities and Ethics at Daniel Webster College. His most recent books are *Great Captains of Antiquity* (Greenwood, 2000) and *Gods of Our Fathers* (Greenwood, 2001).